W9-BJE-864

LEVI BRANCH LIBRARY
3676 S. THIRD ST.
MEMPHIS, TN 38109
789-3000

AUG 25 1994

DISCARDED BY
MEMPHIS PUBLIC LIBRARY

GANGS

SUNY Series in Urban Public Policy
James Bohland and Patricia Edwards, editors

GANGS

The Origins and Impact of
Contemporary Youth Gangs
in the United States

EDITED BY

SCOTT CUMMINGS

AND

DANIEL J. MONTI

STATE UNIVERSITY OF NEW YORK PRESS

Published by
State University of New York Press, Albany

© 1993 State University of New York

All rights reserved

Printed in the United States of America

No part of this book may be used or reproduced
in any manner whatsoever without written permission
except in the case of brief quotations embodied in
critical articles and reviews.

For information, address State University of New York Press,
State University Plaza, Albany, N.Y., 12246

Production by Marilyn P. Semerad
Marketing by Theresa A. Swierzowski

Library of Congress Cataloging-in-Publication Data

Gangs : the origins and impact of contemporary youth gangs in the
    United States / edited by Scott Cummings and Daniel J. Monti.
        p.   cm. — (SUNY series in urban public policy)
    Includes bibliographical references and index.
    ISBN 0-7914-1325-X. — ISBN 0-7914-1326-8 (pbk.)
    1. Gangs—United States. I. Cummings, Scott, 1944-
II. Monti, Daniel J. III. Series: SUNY series in urban public
policy.
HV6439.U5G37 1993
364.1'06'60973—dc20   92-2533
                                                                        CIP

10 9 8 7 6 5 4 3 2

Contents

v

Preface

The subject of this book is gangs and the types of behavior frequently associated with gangs. Each author has studied these phenomena or considered how the conventional world reacts to gangs and gang-like activity. Each chapter contributes pieces to the puzzle of how gangs are to be addressed as a social phenomenon. None of the authors, however, firmly and convincingly fits together all the pieces to that puzzle.

There is no shame in this admission. No one ever has advanced a definition of gangs or an explanation for gang activity that most, much less all, serious observers would embrace. At times, there even has been some question as to whether a gang could be conceived of as a "group." None of the present authors stakes out such an extreme position. All would view gangs as groups exhibiting certain traits that simultaneously mimic and mock the conventional adult world. Precisely what those "traits" are is likely to vary from place to place, over time, and among different observers. The range of groups that reveal gang-like traits is so great as to make cautious researchers leery of simple taxonomies and definitions. It is no less difficult to define and categorize gang behavior.

Among the traits commonly associated with gangs are the following: age- and sex-segregated cliques of young persons, sharing a certain group identity and occupying particular geographic territory, often in opposition to real or imagined "enemies," and who frequently behave in a destructive, disruptive, or illegal manner. None of us would have much trouble imagining "gangs" of minority youths, dressed out in certain colors or clothing, and striking menacing poses at "outsiders." We would have more difficulty conceiving of gangs as young men strutting through high school corridors while dressed out in identical team jackets or a set of college students being formally initiated with secret rituals into a group dedicated to a "brotherhood," carousing, and intermittent outbursts of vandalism. Fraternities and football teams are not "gangs" in the commonly accepted sense of that term; but they do exhibit certain traits that frequently are associated with gangs. What a gang is and is not, then, may be more difficult to define today. Or, we simply may be more attuned to the subtle shadings in what passes for conventional and gang behavior.

There also are variations among gangs. They are more or less integrated into the conventional adult world and "legitimate" institutions. They are more or less likely to engage in "deviant acts," including violence. They are more or less protective of their "territory" and group traditions. The individual participants are more or less self-conscience about their identity as a gang member. "Gang behavior" sometimes is observed in groups of young persons that might not be viewed as gangs by some observers. For instance, a "wilding" group like the one studied by Cummings might have become a better organized "gang" had its career not been interrupted by the police. The group of young men examined by Pinderhughes shares many similarities with gangs, even if the boys do not call themselves gang members. There are times when groups who have given themselves names still resist being called a gang.

The purpose of the authors in the present volume is to describe in rich detail the various ways in which young persons organize themselves and behave as gangs. It is not our intention to show where gangs fall on a continuum of voluntary associations formed by young persons. Nor is it our hope to make gangs look less threatening by arguing that they are not much worse that other types of groups. We try instead to show how gangs and ganglike activity fit in different community or institutional settings.

It is important to take the information presented in this book and see how much closer it takes us to a clear definition and understanding of gang behavior. When we do this it becomes obvious that our conventional understanding of gangs must change because the phenomenon itself has changed. Gangs in the late twentieth century are different in some important ways from gangs of the early twentieth century. Gangs are not found, as many persons once believed, only in city "slums." They can be found in fairly attractive and stable working- and middle-class city and suburban communities as well. Most gangs today may be composed of young persons from racial or ethnic minorities. However, there still are predominantly white gangs, and racially mixed gangs have become more common. There also are growing numbers of gangs composed exclusively of young women. More persons are likely to remain active gang members as they grow older than was once the case. More gangs today also appear to be involved in serious and profitable criminal enterprises, to be murderously combative, mobile, and openly antagonistic to community institutions and the people living around them.

It is not terribly hard to account for the changes. When gangs were studied systematically for the first time, cities still were fairly compact and the focus of much industrial activity. The "minorities" clamoring for attention were from Europe by and large, and most could claim a nominal attachment to the customs and history of the Europeans who preceded them. Today, urban America looks a great deal different. Cities no longer are centers for industrial employment and their populations have spread throughout the surrounding counties. A greater portion of the people living in cities is less well-to-do and traces its ancestry to non-European countries. The social infrastructure of cities has been worn thin by decades of urban redevelopment efforts and population movements. It is harder today to find a basis for vigorous and sustained community efforts in many city neighborhoods. A combination of factors that could and could not have been foreseen has conspired to make our cities and many suburbs less viable and secure places to live. The changes we have observed in gangs can be tied to the changes that have occurred in communities where gangs are found.

It is harder to suggest what should be done to address the problems created and laid bare by gangs. Information presented in this book and elsewhere reveals two important facts about the way gangs are approached by the conventional adult world. First, gangs most often are viewed as a law enforcement problem. Second, law enforcement strategies are not particularly helpful in treating either the immediate symptoms or the basic causes of illegal gang activity. If we have learned anything about gangs, it is that they acquire a great deal of satisfaction and support for their battles with real and perceived enemies. Policies whose basic thrust is to jail gang members and eradicate gangs are more likely to help promote gang activity than to discourage it.

There is some evidence to suggest that employment and community development projects can reduce or at least contain gang activities. It also appears that neighborhood groups can seduce gang members or push them out of an area when the community is mobilized against gangs. Once conventional adult institutions behave competently, gang members find themselves under greater surveillance and are restrained. The gang itself may continue and again serve as an effective bridge between the world of youth and the world of adults, but it will not be nearly so pernicious. To accomplish this, public and private leaders and neighborhood groups need to show more interest in investing time and resources in communities where gangs are found and in the gang members themselves.

It is not at all certain that such a commitment is forthcoming. In the meantime, it is the responsibility of persons such as the contributors to this book to present clearly and consistently what gangs are and what they are not. Absent such information, the public dialogue over what to do about gangs will continue to be swayed more by our prejudices than by hard and unattractive facts.

PART I

WHAT WE KNOW AND DO NOT KNOW ABOUT GANGS

1

Origins and Problems of Gang Research in the United States

DANIEL J. MONTI

A dramatic increase in gang activity during the past decade caught most everyone by surprise and all of us unprepared to speak in an informed way to the challenges it posed. That some portion of this activity was tied to a robust and violent trade in illegal narcotics was especially worrisome. Law makers and law enforcement officials in several states and Washington, D.C., hurriedly fashioned programs to address problems created by gangs, but they spoke less convincingly about the conditions that might have created gangs. All the while, a frightened and sometimes outraged American public watched as young people took their own lives and the lives of innocent bystanders with cool detachment and growing regularity.

Social scientists were particularly hard pressed to say anything useful or insightful about the upsurge in gang activity. Researchers found themselves studying gangs in earnest for the first time since the 1960s, using information and "theories" that seemed woefully outdated. Their work was hampered by several factors. Notable among them were the fad-like character of much social science research, methodological arguments over the best way to study gangs, and the near absence of any serious study of gangs as a historical phenomenon. Social scientists tried to

3

sound convincing, but much of the time they literally did not know what it was they were talking about.

In this chapter we will explore how social science research came to such a sorry state. Particular attention will be paid to those problems that have most hampered research into gangs. Research that preceded the work presented in this volume will be reviewed and tied to a tradition of social activism and efforts to shape social policy.[1] This review will be fairly general, because Joan Moore will examine more closely in the next chapter how previous research came to shape current thinking about such groups.

One question dealt with by Moore and raised implicitly in the work of several contributors to this book revolves around the ways gangs are studied. Persons have strong opinions on this subject and believe that the validity of some research may be doubted because of the manner in which it was carried out. It seemed appropriate to raise this issue at the outset so that the reader might appreciate the various methods used to study gangs and render some judgement as to which approach, if any, they considered more valid.

THE LEGACY OF FREDERIC THRASHER

What we think about contemporary gangs and the best ways to respond to them still is influenced by the work of Frederic M. Thrasher, whose study of 1,313 gangs in Chicago during the 1920s remains a classic.[2] The world Thrasher knew has changed, and so, too, have gangs. He wrote about gangs in an industrial city that was still growing, still employing full-time residents in blue-collar jobs, and still predominantly white. He could not have known that the first industrial revolution already was coming to a close, and that soon the economy of Chicago and many established cities would change in unexpected and uncongenial ways. He had no reason to imagine that suburban development, already an accomplished fact, would become an overwhelming factor in the decline of central cities after a second world war. Nor could he have guessed at the impact of these changes on a poor minority population stuck in an urban economy that no longer manufactured many things.

The urban world familiar to Thrasher was unsettled, to be sure, but it was not hopeless or unmanageable. Most of the problems and problematic people in the city, experts thought, could be found in an area sandwiched between the vibrant downtown business district and neighborhoods filled with stable working-class families. That sandwiched area, referred to somewhat ominously as the "zone in transition," was where Thrasher's "gangland" could be found. The "zone in transition" was unattractive, dirty, and filled with industry, railroad yards, ghettos, and the city's most recent immigrants. It was, in Thrasher's words, an "economic, moral, and cultural frontier" where the civilizing influences of American society had yet to be felt." Rowdy, rambunctious, and altogether "foreign" in its style and smell, the "zone in transition" was a place where the "demoralizing" and "disorganized" life of poor people could be viewed and possibly adjusted.

Frederic M. Thrasher was one of those "better" persons who, as scientists and reformers, believed that good science could help the poor adjust to a more conventional world. He was aware of Chicago's shortcomings and wanted to do something that might improve the situation faced by many of its residents. Thrasher was not alone. Many well-placed Chicagoans and social service agencies were committed to addressing the same problems. They assisted Thrasher and his colleagues, and they took seriously the findings presented in the social scientist's reports.

Looking back, it is not easy to see what difference all of the studying and reforming made in the lives of those being studied and reformed. This is not surprising, or at least it should not be surprising. Thrasher, his cohorts, and the two dozen or more social service agencies that contributed to the "exploratory survey" of 1,313 gangs in Chicago were good soldiers in a moral reform crusade to clean up American cities and city residents that had begun in the early nineteenth century.[4] More often than not, the good works of such reformers had little impact on the daily lives of most persons targeted for assistance. These good works certainly did not change the basic economic and social conditions affecting the inner-city poor; nor were they intended to. The idea behind most reform crusades was to help the poor and the immigrant become more like regular Americans or at least a bit more comfortable with their situations.

The various social service agencies that supported Thrasher's research had outposts in the "economic, moral, and cultural frontier" where "gangland" was found. Services of one or another kind were offered from the outposts, but that may not have been their most important accomplishment. What mattered more was their institutional presence and the link they represented to a larger, more cosmopolitan world.

"The broad expanse of gangland with its intricate tribal and inter-tribal relationships," wrote Thrasher, "is medieval and feudal in its organization rather than modern and urban."[5] The social service agencies, schools, and police department represented the modern and urban world in gangland and served as a buffer between the local residents and the larger community. These organizations may not have succeeded in their mission to serve and make better the people of gangland, but they did succeed in presenting something of gangland to the larger community. This is what made Thrasher's research so important. It provided "a general picture of life in an area little understood by the average citizen."[6]

The picture presented by Thrasher was at once revealing and maddeningly superficial. Subsequent writers took Thrasher to task for many shortcomings in his work. Data were collected in an unsystematic way, and his analysis of those data was not terribly thorough. Important variables such as the age of gang members or the organizational features of the gangs were not related in a straightforward way to differences in the behavior of gangs. There were gaps in the information collected for Thrasher, and the author acknowledged those holes. At the same time, however, Thrasher probably did as much as he could have with the information that was available. He presented many parts of a grand mosaic and challenged others to pursue specific questions in a more systematic way. It was as if Thrasher had been dropped in the middle of a fabulously rich deposit of old bones and had only begun to wade through them and assemble a picture of the beasts to which they might have belonged. His major contribution was to lay out the broad outline of all the groups he found and to describe, often quite vividly, the various ways they organized, behaved, and related to the community. Thrasher's explicit intention was to develop hypotheses for others to examine; it was not to build a theory about gangs.

Thrasher's work was not devoid of theory, however. Indeed, his descriptions and analysis of gangs were rooted in contemporary theories about collective behavior. *The Gang* also was laced with conventional assumptions about life in poorer innercity neighborhoods. Both strains of thought were brought together in Thrasher's basic argument about gangland and "ganging." Gangs were viewed as primitive and destructive groups that emerged "spontaneously" from the "disorganized" neighborhoods in the "zone in transition." This theme runs throughout the book, despite evidence of sophisticated planning and organizational skills on the part of gang members, and the author's frequent allusions to linkages between gangs and more conventional institutions.

One who has done field work usually is not ambivalent about the group or custom being investigated. More often the observer carries on something closely resembling a love-hate relationship with the subject. This is particularly true in the case of someone who studies groups or customs different from his own. He can be attracted to them even as he waxes on about their atavistic quality. So it was with Frederic M. Thrasher and gangs. In *The Gang*, Thrasher alternated between statements about the "demoralizing" effect of gangs on boys and the community and allusions to the "romantic" life of gang members and their frequent displays of devotion to each other.

Thrasher never resolved the tension between these two ways of viewing gangs, and that probably was a good thing. Had he been wedded to the idea that gangs were nothing more than a perverse aberration of childrens' play groups, *The Gang* would never have shown the many subtle shadings of gang behavior or revealed the complex relation between gangs and more conventional groups. Had Thrasher "gone native" and completely romanticized the gang boy's world, he might have ignored some of the really troubling consequences of "ganging" for the participants and the community. Thrasher was not in any danger of going that far, of course. By training and inclination, he saw a close relation between the way groups or activities were arranged in different geographic areas and the kind of moral order or culture exhibited in those areas. It was logical for him to connect the emergence of gangs with the "disorganized" slums filled with people on the margins of an "American" culture. Given this theoretical orientation, one can be pleased that Thrasher described gangs and their behavior in sufficient detail to allow us to point out the gap between prevailing stereotypes about gangs and gangs as their members knew them.

What follows is a brief description of the major questions about gangs articulated by Thrasher and the answers that he and subsequent researchers have offered in response.[7]

WHAT IS A GANG AND WHO IS IN IT?

Thrasher and others generally found gangs to be a phenomenon of adolescence. Few gangs were composed exclusively of young children or adults. The membership of some gangs was drawn from a fairly broad spectrum of ages, and the size and age profile of gangs could change over time.

Early researchers found no gangs composed exclusively of girls. This was attributed to the greater control imposed by parents on their daughters. Occasionally, a girl was extended membership in a gang because of sexual favors she granted to the boys. Groups of girls sometimes attached themselves to specific boy gangs.

Gangs were formed out of "play groups" found in a particular neighborhood. The identity of the group was fixed by defending that territory against "outsiders," a term reserved for a long list of persons and groups against whom the gang had a real or imagined grudge. Routine confrontations with "outsiders" helped the gang to sustain its group identity. Most young men "grew out" of the gang habit as they matured and assumed more adult responsibilities.

The parochial quality of gangs was reinforced by their segregated membership. Most gangs were composed of persons of the same race or nationality. Gangs that drew members from different nationalities were common; gangs that drew members from different races were rare. Virtually all gangs were composed of persons who came from the ranks of the poor or less well-to-do.

More recent studies reveal that some things about gangs and their membership have changed. The majority of gang members still are adolescents, but more members today may be drawn from younger children and young men no longer in their teenage years. It seems that fewer young men are "maturing out" of gangs than was once the case. Their reasons for remaining active gang members probably are related to their inability to assume more conventional adult roles and acquire jobs in the regular economy.

The phenomenon of age-graded sets in gangs has persisted, at least in larger and better established gangs. Most gangs still consist of persons drawn from the same race, though examples of integrated gangs have been noted. Nationality distinctions among persons with some kind of European ancestry no longer seem relevant in gangs composed of "white" youngsters. Gangs still draw most of their members from less well-to-do households, and the identity of gangs remains most permanently fixed through their combat with real or imagined outsiders.[8]

The single greatest change in gangs and gang membership has involved young women. Once satisfied to be part of a girl's auxiliary to a boy's gang, more young women have come to develop their own independent gangs. Even less is known of female gangs than is known of their male counterparts, but the increasing prevalence of female gangs probably is tied to the loosening of constraints on young women generally and the much heralded erosion of minority families in urban areas.[9]

WHERE ARE GANGS FOUND?

Thrasher and his colleagues thought that only certain kinds of neighborhoods—poor, predominantly foreign-born or minority, industrialized, overcrowded and rundown—were likely to have gangs. Early research focused on slums as disorganized places, particularly when one racial or ethnic group was "invading" an area inhabited by a different population. Clashes between gangs from the two populations were common and provided evidence, at least to outsiders, of the disorganized character of slum life.

Subsequent researchers identified gangs in areas that were poor but not at all disorganized. These so-called "stable slums" had been occupied by the same racial or ethnic group for a long time. Hispanic gangs found in barrios of southwestern cities often were cited as examples of this phenomenon. Such gangs, it was speculated, probably were different from the gangs in disorganized slums.[10]

Researchers generally have not found gangs, or have not looked for them, in places other than slums. Where gangs are found, or thought to be found, implies much about the organization, behavior, and thinking of the gangs and the community of which they are part. The geography and morality of gangland have not changed. Gangs are still thought to be a phenomenon of slums, and gangs can be ascribed traits (e.g., rudeness, aggressiveness, criminality, parochialness, and disorganization) that outsiders typically attribute to the communities where gangs were found. Gangs remain a metaphor for all that is seductive and dangerous about ethnic groups and the slums they inhabit.[11]

HOW ARE GANGS ORGANIZED?

There always has been a contradiction between what persons thought gangs were like and how gangs actually appeared upon close inspection. This tension has been seen most consistently in descriptions about gang organization. On the one hand, researchers make allusions to the informal, spontaneous, and evanescent quality of gang organization. Thrasher's allusion to gangs as a form of "collective behavior," Yablonsky's assessment of gangs as "near groups," or Cohen's recent allusion to gangs as a "collectivity" speak to the tendency of persons to deny gangs intellectual credibility and practical significance.[12] It is difficult to accept gangs as a legitimate, viable group. On the other hand, firsthand observations of how gangs actually behave frequently belie the impression that gangs are incapable of carrying on relatively sophisticated and long-term activities.

Thrasher found that gangs might have begun as simple play groups, but they could develop relatively sophisticated structures and "traditions" that lasted beyond the tenure of individual members. When the gang acted as an economic unit its members often had distinct roles and responsibilities. On most other occasions, the status of individual members was essentially equal and decisions were reached by consensus.

Given the communal origins of such groups, there was a limit to how large and complex they could become. Larger groups divided themselves into sets based upon the age of the members. There sometimes was friction among members, and there were recognized ways to reduce the friction. When those procedures failed, it was not uncommon for the gang to split and become two distinct gangs.

Gangs sometimes formed alliances and assisted each other in a variety of ways. The alliances were brittle, however. Allies were known to have disagreements that ruptured their confederation.

Thrasher wrote about four types of gangs: diffuse, solidified, conventional, and criminal. Yet it was evident from the case histories of gangs that characteristics of more than one type of gang were observed in different groups. There was no clear line distinguishing diffuse from solidified gangs or conventional from criminal gangs in the 1920s, and that remains true today.[13]

A number of subsequent researchers have tried to develop ways to classify the organization and structure of gangs. The only thing these classification schemes have succeeded in doing, Irving Spergel indicates, is to

> suggest a bewildering array, complexity and variability of [gang] structures. Gangs may not be simply solidary, loosely knit, or bureaucratic so much as variable small networks . . . more or less cohesive or clearly structured at various periods of their development.[14]

The fundamental building block of gangs remains the age-graded set or clique of local youngsters. However, these cliques can combine, dissolve, and be reassembled in a variety of ways. Gangs may not be as large as a corporation or as tightly regimented as an army unit, but they manage to survive and even thrive in an inhospitable environment every bit as well as other groups do in a more conventional environment. Indeed, as many observers have noted, gangs often serve effectively as surrogates for families that do not work especially well for some gang members.

IN WHAT KINDS OF ACTIVITIES DO GANGS ENGAGE?

The commission of delinquent acts is so well tied to gangs that it usually appears in the definition of gangs. Thrasher discovered that gang members engaged in many activities together, only a portion of which could be classified as delinquent. Much of the time gang members played, explored, "hung" around the neighborhood, or "loafed" in their "hiding places" just as other boys did. They supported each other during difficult times and simply enjoyed each other's company on most occasions. Friends sometimes fight, however, and Thrasher's gang boys were no exception.

Thrasher found that gangs created special names for their groups and peculiar ways of speech to better distinguish themselves from outsiders and to reinforce their identity in a particular group. Thrasher recognized that this enabled gang members to keep secrets from those not privileged to be members. It also was apparent that gangs were borrowing such practices from more conventional groups.

The delinquent acts engaged in by gang members often did not require all members to participate. Some delinquent activities required the collaboration of numerous boys, however. The only activity that demanded the attention of nearly all members was fighting; fighting was taken quite seriously because it involved the protection of their territory against other gangs. Resources acquired through one or another illicit means were shared by all members, just as the honor or dishonor attached to winning or losing a fight was shared by all members .

"The struggle" against outsiders, Thrasher observed, played a significant part in the gang's routine affairs and folklore. Members of other gangs would have appreciated this, even as they ridiculed their enemies. However, Thrasher also noted the tendency of other persons to dismiss as trivial the ongoing fight between gangs and their real or imagined enemies. One supposes that the persons Thrasher had in mind were adults who did not know how important the struggle was to the creation and maintenance of every gang.

Thrasher understood that the struggle became an even more vital part of a gang's existence as the group slipped or jumped into more routine and profitable criminal enterprises. The amount and severity of violence associated with the struggle certainly increased with the seriousness of those enterprises, a fact that probably accounts for the sharp decline in the number of gangs composed of older adolescents and/or adults.

Some researchers such as Whyte, Suttles, Moore, and Vigil tried to show how gangs fit into the daily routine of a community. Life in most neighborhoods did not revolve around fighting and delinquent or criminal acts, and most gangs were not preoccupied with such activities. Important as delinquency and fighting may have been to individual gang members or the group as a whole, there were many conventional activities that also served to solidify bonds among gang members and to establish an identity with outsiders.

This point has been lost in many studies of gangs and delinquency that followed Thrasher's work. It became ignored nearly altogether during the past decade as many street gangs began to distribute and sell illegal narcotics and engage in running gun battles with each other. Given changes in the economies of urban areas over the last few decades, it may be that more gangs and gang members have begun to slip into routine and serious criminal activities earlier, and remain more firmly fixed to such behavior longer, than was once the case.

It is not that earlier gangs were immune to the attractions of criminal enterprises. The gangs studied by Thrasher appeared to be an important part of their neighborhoods' economy, however unconventional parts of that economy might have been. They used some of what they stole and sold the remaining stock to area residents, no doubt at prices that enabled people to buy things they otherwise could not have afforded. These activities were condoned by area residents.

Thrasher described a variety of other ways in which gang members acquired money and goods that were used by individuals or shared by the whole group. Some of these activities were more profitable and better organized than others. He provided no good estimate of how much time gang members spent planning or executing such schemes, but he conveyed the impression that these were routine activities.

The gang as a whole probably was not involved in any single criminal incident, though varying numbers of its members were. A "group factor" or influence was apparent, and still is apparent, in the illegal activities of those members.[15] Thrasher argued that the rules and ethics of gangs encouraged such enterprises and carried the promise of protection for individuals being sought by the authorities. Gangs did not cause crime in the sense that they brought lawlessness to an otherwise law-abiding community. Gangs made more efficient and extensive those activities that were an accepted part of the area's unconventional or hidden economy. In this sense gangs did make crime a more serious or pronounced part of the community's routines and its residents' habits. The "organized and continuous" criminal activities of youth gangs also blurred the distinction between adolescent and adult gangs; and they made it easier and more natural for young persons to adopt a criminal career or at least become involved in more serious crimes.

Insofar as Thrasher's findings have any validity today, it would seem that more or less organized and profitable criminal activities continue to play an important part in the existence of most gangs. Involvement in criminal activities is nothing new to gangs. It is not, however, the only or most important thing that gangs do for their members or in the community.

WHAT IS THE GANG'S RELATION TO THE COMMUNITY?

Thrasher found the gang to be a natural part of the local community. Its members and general activities were known to area residents. Gang members identified closely with their neighborhood and defended it as well as themselves against the encroachment of outsiders.

The reactionary or defensive quality of many gang activities did not escape Thrasher's attention. Gangs fought representatives from other neighborhoods or groups of a different race and nationality. Their alliances with other groups were based on their mutual dissatisfaction with gangs from more distant parts of town. Their antagonism toward organizations or agencies sent into the neighborhood to save its residents from themselves was similarly motivated. The "general soreness at the world" which Thrasher attributed to gang members was not directed at everything or everyone. It was directed at those persons and things that interfered with the customs and routines of the gang and, more generally, of the community.

Adult organizations that made space in their world for gangs were assisted by the boys. Adult organizations that tried to dissuade boys from becoming gang members or tried to disband gangs altogether fared less well at the hands of the boys. To be sure, much of what gangs did to assist the local politician was of dubious legality; but the politicians who employed them and the local residents who bought stolen goods from them accepted the boys as they were. The settlement houses, police, and schools harassed the boys and tried to make them give up a group and style of life that they wanted or needed.

Thrasher bemoaned the gang boy's detachment from the larger community and its civic affairs. He also worried about the boy's lack of preparation for the "conventional world." At the same time, Thrasher showed just how well connected the gang boy was to the workings of his local community's political and economic routines. What Thrasher really objected to were the gang boy's unwillingness to become more "American" and the "corrupting" influences of local adults who "used" the boys for their own selfish ends. When he allowed himself to see it, Thrasher conveyed a strong sense of the gang boys as primitive rebels who resisted the intrusion into their neighborhood of "American" standards and customs that Thrasher and the agencies that collaborated with his work would have preferred the gang boy to adopt.

Subsequent researchers did not pay much attention to the different ways in which gangs fit into their home neighborhoods. There were several notable exceptions to this, but social scientists generally analyzed gangs outside the social context in which they were found. Much more attention was paid to aspects of gang structure and behavior or to theories and typologies about gangs and juvenile delinquency.

This is unfortunate, because it appears that the relation between at least some gangs and their community might have changed in important ways during the last few decades. Some gangs might have become less connected to the conventional institutions in their neighborhood and, perhaps, as a result are more likely to attack local citizens and exploit those organizations that remain in the community. This certainly would help to account for the rapacious profiteering some gangs enjoy by virtue of selling drugs to local residents and the violence and fear they introduce to their neighborhood in the course of such transactions. In the absence of long-term studies of how gangs fit into their local community, we are forced to guess how that relation may have changed or to suppose that such a relation never existed. Were it not for Thrasher's work, we might easily suppose today that gangs always had been isolated in their local community.

WHAT IS TO BE DONE ABOUT GANGS?

Thrasher was well aware of efforts by conventional institutions to address "the gang problem." There was ample evidence even in his day to suggest that making the individual boy the target of intervention strategies had not worked. Nor had police suppression been particularly helpful. Even when gangs were successfully disbanded there were few, if any, alternative things for boys to do.

Thrasher was impressed with the way politicians and saloon owners had coopted gangs and noted that some legitimate institutions also had tried to do this. Some modest successes had been achieved by encouraging gangs to carry out their feuds with other gangs through athletic contests. Thrasher also noted, however, that sometimes the effort backfired. Established gangs were known to have disrupted larger organizations that tried to adopt and change them. Apparently, it also happened that boys who were not members of a gang had formed one as a result of having been brought together by a conventional organization. Efforts to address "the gang problem" by changing the gang itself, therefore, had only limited success and had some potential drawbacks.

The possibility of dealing with gangs as part of a bigger effort to reorganize the whole community was considered by Thrasher. It was raised, however, only in the context of preventing crime. It was not tied to a broader campaign to improve the economic conditions that persons faced in gangland and which provided much of the impetus for gangs to acquire money through illegal activities. This idea did not occur to Thrasher, who thought that the local public school would be the best spot to mount a community-wide campaign to prevent crime.

Little has changed since Thrasher chronicled what was being done to address the gang problem in Chicago during the 1920s. More is known today about gangs, but this additional experience and information have had no discernible impact on the way outsiders from the conventional world treat gangs. Gangs continue to be addressed as a residual by-product of a still diseased community.[16]

Remedies for the gang problem continue to take two different, but complementary, tacks. One set of treatments leaves the gang in the community and exposes it to the civilizing influences of a more conventional world. Stiff doses of "good" socialization provided by street workers or youth outreach specialists are intended to save youngsters and whole groups from themselves. The idea is to redirect gangs and make them the vehicle of their own transformation. A related strategy has conventional agencies setting up programs for the entire community. The gang itself is not necessarily the target of these programs. It may only be the indirect beneficiary of an improved and better organized community. The harsh conditions that spawn gangs would not be overcome. Instead, conventional institutions would try to smooth the community's rough edges and introduce a degree of order into an otherwise mean and disorganized social world.

A second and more aggressive set of treatments removes the gang or many of its members from the community or tries to mobilize the community against the gang. The idea behind these strategies is that local institutions have grown flabby and too tolerant of gangs. Bigger agencies from outside the gang's territory work in such a way as to better control or supervise gangs with the assistance of institutions from the gang's neighborhood.

The distinction between smoothing a community's rough edges and pushing its institutional residents around to the point that they better control local gangs probably was clearer in theory than in practice. Nevertheless, more recent thinking about the gang problem clearly indicates that the most popular way to handle gangs is to remove them from the community or, barring that, to supervise and control their activities much more closely.[17] Particular emphasis is being placed on the police and schools as agencies well positioned to monitor and manage gang activities. Prevention and detention are the key words in the current debate about how best to handle the gang problem.

It is hard not to find this approach attractive when young men in many cities are turning streets into drug bazaars and shooting galleries. Appealing as such an approach may be, it ignores several important things that we have learned or forgotten about gangs. First, only a few strategies to curb gang activities have had any success over the years, and these successes have not been widely replicated. Many efforts to control gangs failed, and some things that were tried actually made gang-related problems worse.

Second, one thing that worsened the current gang situation has been the tendency of public officials to take no action when gangs first appear and then to overreact when gangs finally become too obvious to ignore.[18] Both reactions have the unintended effect of promoting gang activity by initially ignoring it and then challenging the gangs once they are well established. It must be recalled that conflict with outsiders reinforces the bonds among gang members and prompts them to take more aggressive actions against their real and supposed enemies.

Third, there is a great discrepancy between the public hue and cry over gang activity and the rather modest steps actually taken to address the gang problem. The unstated policy of government toward gang activities is to tolerate them. If there is a point beyond which such activities will not be tolerated, it is clear that point has not yet been passed. The moral outrage expressed about gangs may be little more than an acceptable way for us to scream at the darkness even as we throw up our hands in resignation. Were the conditions that create gangs more widely experienced and the violent things gangs do routinely felt outside minority communities, our outcry might be more closely matched by concerted action.

Fourth, the outline of an argument by Thrasher in which gangs are described as primitive rebels has been all but lost in the current uproar over gang violence and drug dealing. Thrasher noted how gangs resisted the encroachment of outsiders and carried out nearly continuous skirmishes with businesses or institutions popularly viewed as exploitative. The reactionary quality of much gang activity was subsequently identified by other researchers as well; but it has been largely overlooked in recent years because many gangs seem to have turned against everyone and everything.

Yet the posture of many contemporary gangs that it is "us against the world" can be tied to that longer tradition of constructing artificial barriers between themselves and hostile outsiders.[19] If the perimeter of their fortress has shrunk over the years, it is a measure of the desperate situation faced by young persons in their own community. It also helps to account for the willingness of gang members to turn against adults in their neighborhood and to extend their fights into places like schools which once were islands of relative calm inside an otherwise "disorganized" community.

Fifth, the control of gangs always has been a high priority for persons who wanted to do something about the gang problem. Legislation to treat gang members more harshly than other persons who commit crimes, the creation of military-like boot camps for juvenile offenders, and the banning of gang colors and clothing from schools all speak to a tradition of dealing with gangs through detention and repression. Observers over the years have spoken of gangs as a symptom of more serious and deeply rooted problems in the communities where gangs were found. With the exception of broad-based efforts to mobilize communities for the prevention of crime and the anti-poverty programs of the 1960s, however, there has been little attention paid to restructuring local communities in order to address the gang problem or to providing young persons with economic and social alternatives to gang activity.[20]

This is unfortunate inasmuch as the absence of jobs in the conventional economy is widely viewed as responsible for pushing young persons into drug dealing; economic incentives have been suggested as a means of coopting gang members.[21] It will be recalled that Thrasher was impressed by the ability of local persons such as saloon owners and politicians to coopt gangs by offering them intermittent financial support. Had he and other reformers at the time been more creative in their use of material incentives and less concerned with wrestling gang boys away from wicked characters in the neighborhood, they might have discovered things that could have been put into use today. In the absence of such information, contemporary observers must develop such programs in a politically inhospitable environment or fall back on the more conventional techniques of several generations of well-intentioned reformers who were at least as interested in maintaining their own privileged positions as they were in saving gang members from themselves.

THE RESEARCHER AS ACTIVIST AND SCIENTIST

It is not easy to see the world through the eyes of someone else, particularly when the other person is different from us in important ways. That should not deter us, because a big part of the reason for studying people different from ourselves is to learn more about them and, if we are fortunate and sensitive, to learn a bit more about ourselves as well. This is what Thrasher tried to do, and why he succeeded as much as he did. Thrasher was not afraid to look hard at something most persons of his day, and our own, would rather ignore.

Thrasher was more than a dispassionate observer of gangs and the world in which they lived. He also was an activist, a person committed to putting what he learned into practice so that the lives of others might be improved. One can and should question what Thrasher hoped to accomplish and the adequacy of the information upon which he intended to act. One cannot doubt, however, that he was engaged in matters of importance or that he tried to make a difference.

Thrasher did not trip or back into his study of gangs. Given the assistance he received from organizations in Chicago, it is clear that he had a pretty good idea of what he was trying to do and that some notable Chicagoans agreed with him. The legitimacy conferred upon him and his study from the outset could only have sustained him during the tough moments that must have arisen, as they do in any research project, much less one dealing with a sensitive social problem.

Social scientists are accustomed to courting public and private leaders in order to do or publicize their research. Most of us are aware that our work can be used or abused by persons with a social or political agenda to promote. Thrasher had no difficulty reconciling his roles as scientist and activist, though his work revealed the tension between those competing responsibilities. Today we are more self-conscious about this tension and argue about it among ourselves. There are a variety of ways in which the argument could unfold, but it emerges most clearly in discussions over the most effective and legitimate ways to study gangs. The means employed to study gangs and the data yielded by each are treated as windows into the researcher's soul, or at least his politics.

A curious and somewhat arbitrary distinction often is made between socalled "etic" and "emic" methods of studying gangs. The former, it is suggested, allow the researcher to stand far removed from the groups and behavior being discussed. Information about gangs is filtered through official reports (e.g. crime statistics) or acquired with the assistance of officials (e.g. conversations with jailed gang members). Critics of studies based on such data believe that barriers separating the researcher from his subjects need to be removed, if one is to acquire a more accurate picture of gangs. In a more "emic" approach, firsthand observation replaces predigested government reports. Interviews are conducted free of any hint of official coercion or oversight.[22]

It certainly is legitimate and useful to assess the advantages and disadvantages of different research strategies. Too often, however, certain social or political goals are ascribed to persons employing one or another method and data. One critic of so-called "etic" techniques, John Hagedorn, decries what he calls "courthouse criminology" and "surrogate sociology."[23] Interviews with a few officials charged with the responsibility of "handling the gang problem" or with reformed and jailed gang members, Hagedorn maintains, are highly suspect. The interviewed parties are assumed to be hiding something or advocating something that is in their interest. Cooperation with the scientist might be a means to achieve one's personal goals or to defend one's organization. In either case, argues Hagedorn, the scientist is likely to acquire information that reinforces the outlook of bureaucrats and law enforcement officials who want to dramatize or downplay the behavior of gangs and reinforce what they typically do when such problems arise.[24]

Critics of research based on "etic" methods prefer to do field studies that break down the barriers between the researcher and the object of his study. If at all possible, the study should be conducted in collaboration with the gangs. Joan Moore is a great advocate and pioneer of such research, and she describes her approach in the next essay. There are practical problems associated with this kind of research. It is expensive and time consuming, and it can be dangerous. Advocates of an "emic" approach to studying gangs, however, believe that it is the best way to acquire accurate and revealing information about gangs. One supposes that the information would be more sympathetic to gangs, but only in the sense that members' views of the world would be given an honest and thorough portrayal. The researcher would not extend approval, or condemnation, to gang members for their actions. The politics of such researchers are assumed to be more liberal, if only because the researchers appear willing to challenge prevailing assumptions about gangs and policies intended to deal with problems associated with gangs.

There is validity in the criticisms raised against "courtroom criminology" and "surrogate sociology."[25] My experience studying gangs in St. Louis and in hearings of the Missouri State Advisory Committee to the U.S. Commission on Civil Rights suggests that some law enforcement and school officials have only the faintest of ideas about what is happening in the community or they misrepresent what they know in order to convey an impression that their institutions are dealing effectively with gangs. Academic researchers may be no better. One set studied police reports on homicides in an attempt to identify patterns in the causes of murders in St. Louis. In testimony before a subcommittee of the Missouri State Advisory Committee, a representative of this group claimed that there were few gang-related killings in St. Louis. He was certain that police records would be accurate because everyone was sensitive to the gang situation. Unknown perhaps to the researcher, homicide detectives were not knowledgeable about gangs and the police department was making a concerted effort to downplay gang activities in the city. The "data" provided to the subcommittee were highly suspect, but the researchers' project went forward with support from city hall.

It is easy to identify studies that contain such suspect data.[26] Several presented in this book would be among them. Scott Cummings studied a "wilding gang" from Fort Worth, Texas and interviewed its jailed members. Jerome Skolnick and his colleagues interviewed California gang members who were in prison at the time of the study. My own study of St. Louis gangs was based largely on interviews of youngsters that were conducted in police stations and schools. I also used crime statistics provided by the city police department. Pat Jackson consulted newspaper stories and transcripts from legislative hearings in order to describe the response to gangs in California.

None of the authors, to my knowledge, would claim that his study was perfect or that he was satisfied completely with the amount and quality of the data in his possession. I also suspect, however, that each would take exception to the idea that his data were invalid and findings suspect. The data each acquired were relevant to the question posed in the research project and collected fairly.

Given the fluid and violent character of the group Cummings studied, for example, it would have been all but impossible to find and interview individuals outside of a controlled setting. It also would have been dangerous. The young men involved expressed no reluctance about being interviewed; and their comments about the group to which they belonged and life in general were consistent with statements made by youngsters interviewed by other researchers in less confined settings. Skolnick and his co-workers were not interested in the daily routine of gang members in or out of prison but in the way gangs were organized in different parts of the state and how they carried out drug sales. The information they acquired went beyond that presented in earlier work but was consistent with insights gleaned from studies of gangs in California and elsewhere. My project also was designed to gather relatively basic information about gang conduct and organization. No one was asked to compromise himself or his gang by revealing things that could make them legally vulnerable. In fact, they were instructed not to do so. All interviews were confidential and subjects anonymous. Persons were given opportunities to terminate their interview. Few did. The information I acquired differed substantially from what police had told me in many instances, but it was consistent with what some officers knew and it did not change dramatically from one gang to the next.

Gangs can be studied in a variety of ways, with varying distances kept between the researcher and subjects, and with different goals in mind. What one can and cannot do in a particular study depends a great deal on the access one has to the subjects or sites under investigation. On the other hand, the questions one seeks to answer may make firsthand observations more or less imperative. There simply is not one best way to study gangs.

It is my experience that all but the most calloused and bruised young person will be willing to teach an adult many things about gangs, as long as the adult is willing to be taught and allows the young person not to implicate himself or any specific person as having committed a particular offense. Where one interviews these persons is less important than the subjects' knowledge that they control what is said and know how the information will be used. Informed consent is crucial in such matters.

Conversations with other gang researchers about this issue and reviews of their research suggest to me that we all get remarkably similar stories. Some are less detailed and far reaching, perhaps, but certain ideas, feelings, and recollections consistently turn up in our interviews. I think some researchers are too quick to reject data acquired in institutional settings, and too ready to overlook or dismiss the problematic nature of data gathered out in the field. Ultimately, the information one acquires about gangs is filtered by someone or something. Even the most committed field worker knows that there are some places gang members go and some things gang members do that cannot be observed firsthand.[27] Moreover, familiarity with the groups under study does not guarantee that interesting data will be collected at all or well and that revealing analyses will be made of gang organization and conduct.[28]

John Hagedorn and other gang researchers favoring more "emic" study methods probably would disagree. In fact, he has gone so far as to argue that "minority social scientists are best suited" to study contemporary gangs and that white researchers must show they are "on the community's side," if they are to get valid information.[29] An important corollary to this position is that the benefits of the research somehow should be shared with the community.

Hagedorn is a thoughtful person, and his position warrants serious attention. Field workers know that their race, sex, age, and a host of other personal attributes affect the types of sites and groups to which they might have access. Informants also must trust the researcher, if valid data are to be acquired. Finally, the idea that the researcher's knowledge, contacts, and work might be used to help the group being studied certainly has much to recommend it. Few persons would argue against the position that researchers should give back something for all they have received.

Hagedorn's position is somewhat more extreme, however. It is indefensible to argue, for instance, that minority researchers necessarily will get more or better information and have less to prove to their subjects than would white researchers. In the present book Howard Pinderhughes presents some interesting preliminary findings from his dissertation on racially motivated attacks in Brooklyn, New York. His subjects are working- and lower-class white ethnics. Mr. Pinderhughes is of African American descent. The present author, clearly showing the effects of what anthropologists call hybrid vigor, has interviewed many black youths who were gang members. While it is unlikely that either of us could have conducted a long-term ethnographic study of gangs in our respective study sites, it was possible to acquire much detailed information about these groups and their members. A degree of trust was needed and achieved between the researcher and his subjects, trust enough to acquire the information needed to answer the questions posed by the researcher.

The idea that white researchers must show solidarity with the community being studied is equally flawed. It presumes, inaccurately, that community members have a single view of gangs. Even gang members do not have a single view of their group or of their involvement with it. Any attempt to display an uninformed sympathy for a given view of gangs is likely to make potential informants suspicious and raise serious doubts about the researcher's objectivity. Experienced field workers understand that the risks of "going native" are every bit as serious as those entailed in accepting uncritically the opinions of agency officials, politicians, repairmen, and car dealers. As Anne Campbell has said so well with regard to studies of female gangs, "some writers . . . accepted the more romantic presentations given by girl(s) . . . uncritically. . . . [S]uch gang rhetoric is not designed solely to fool researchers, but also to fool the gang members using it."[30] Whatever good might come of social scientific research would be jeopardized by the researcher's naivety.

One needs to be sensitive to the strengths and shortcomings of different methods, deal with them as best one can, and acknowledge the possible impact they might have on the work in question. In general, it is possible to blend different methods for the same project, and probably a good idea to do so. One cannot afford to ignore what the "official" portrayal of gangs is. Pat Jackson's discussion of responses to gangs in California would be useless without such information; and I would have been unable to identify differences between gang and nongang areas had I not consulted crime reports routinely assembled by police officials. However, it is terribly important to have as close to a firsthand view of gangs as one can. Absent such information it is not possible to balance or complete the picture of gangs drawn by agencies and officials who have pet policies to defend or promote. One can protect the anonymity of individual gang members or whole groups and check out the information they provide without violating their trust. One need not hide behind information sanitized by government representatives or indulge the willful hyperbolist who poses as an informant.

Disagreements over the appropriate or most effective way to study gangs mask a far more important difference among gang researchers: The extent to which gangs are viewed as an integral part of a community that has little value in the eyes of outsiders. It will be recalled that Thrasher held contradictory views about the relation between gangs and the communities where they were found. On the one hand, he thought of "gangland" as a disrupted community and gangs as a manifestation of the disorder bred there. On the other hand, he observed how gangs fit in neighborhoods and contributed to their economic and political routines.

Subsequent researchers have been unable or unwilling to determine which view is more accurate or whether some combination of the two would be useful in framing analyses and explanations of gang behavior. Joan Moore, in the next chapter, says that gangs are treated as symbols of the community or social class from which they emerge. Our reaction to gangs gives expression to broader and deeper concerns about the social class and communities from which most gangs come. Moore's point is well taken, but her contribution has been to articulate clearly that which Thrasher left unstated over seventy years ago. Today we are most concerned about gangs composed of black youth stuck in something called the "underclass." In 1920, persons were concerned about white ethnic gangs found in industrial slums. The population at risk may have changed, but the fears and symbols of those fears have not.

Persons who study gangs can be divided into two categories. The first category consists of persons who view gangs as poor excuses for groups. Gangs may be "near groups," collectivities, packs, mobs, or any number of other foul-sounding things; but they cannot be accorded the same intellectual credibility as more "normal" forms of human association. The neighborhoods that spawn gangs are similarly tainted. They are viewed as desperate places where most forms of social control have broken down. The second category of gang researchers includes persons who accept gangs as a valid form of human association, similar in some ways to other groups but also revealing important differences. These researchers are not necessarily fond of gangs. They recognize that gang members can do awful things to themselves and other persons. However, they are not prepared to dismiss as aberrations either gangs or the communities where gangs are found. Gang neighborhoods may have great problems, but they also are resilient. Gangs are an expression of that resiliency. Until such time as more researchers and policy makers appreciate this fact, we are unlikely to deal effectively with gangs and the problems they create.

NOTES

1. Daniel J. Monti, "The Practice of Gang Research," *Sociological Practice Review* (1) (January 1991): 29-39.

2. Frederic M. Thrasher, *The Gang* (Chicago: University of Chicago Press, 1927).

3. Ibid., p. 21.

4. Paul Boyer, *Urban Masses and Moral Order in America: 1820-1920* (Cambridge: Harvard University Press, 1978).

5. Frederic Thrasher, *The Gang*, p. 5.

6. Ibid., p. xi.

7. See for example: Herbert Bloch and Arthur Niederhoffer, *The Gang: A Study in Adolescent Behavior* (New York: Philosophical Library, 1958); Richard Cloward and Lloyd Ohlin, *Delinquency and Opportunity: A Theory of Delinquent Gangs* (Glencoe, Ill.: Free Press, 1960); Albert Cohen, *Delinquent Boys: The Culture of the Gang* (Glencoe, Ill.: Free Press, 1955); David Curry and Irving Spergel, "Gang Homicide, Delinquency and Community," *Criminology* 26 (1988): 381-405; Edward F. Dolan and S. Finney, *Youth Gangs* (New York: Julian Messner, 1984); Howard Erlander, "Estrangement, Machismo and Gang Violence," *Social Science Quarterly* 60 (2) (1979): 235-48; John Hagedorn, *People and Folks: Gangs, Crime and the Underclass in a Rust Belt City* (Chicago: Lake View Press, 1988); Ruth Horowitz, *Honor and the American Dream* (New Brunswick, N.J.: Rutgers University Press, 1983); Malcolm Klein, *Street Gangs and Street Workers* (Englewood Cliffs, N.J.: Prentice Hall, 1971); Walter Miller, *Violence by Youth Gangs and Youth Groups as a Crime Problem in Major American Cities*, National Institute for Juvenile Justice and Delinquency Pre-

vention, Office of Juvenile Justice and Delinquency Prevention, U.S. Justice Department (Washington, D.C.: U.S. Government Printing Office, 1975); Joan Moore, *Homeboys* (Philadelphia: Temple University Press, 1978); Irving Spergel, *Youth Gangs: Problems and Response* (Chicago: University of Chicago, School of Social Service Administration, 1989); Gerald D. Suttles, *The Social Order of the Slum* (Chicago: University of Chicago Press, 1971); James D. Vigil, *Barrio Gangs* (Austin: University of Texas Press, 1988); William F. Whyte, *Street Corner Society* (Chicago: University of Chicago Press, 1943); Lewis Yablonsky, *The Violence Gang* (New York: Macmillan, 1962).

8. James D. Vigil, "Cholos and Gangs: Culture Change and Street Youth in Los Angeles," in *Gangs in America*, ed. C. Ronald Huff (Newbury Park: Sage Publications, 1990), pp. 116-28.

9. Anne Campbell, *The Girls in the Gang* (New York: Basil Blackwell, 1984).

10. Vigil, "Cholos and Gangs."

11. C. Ronald Huff, "Introduction: Two Generations of Gang Research," in *Gangs in America*, ed. Huff, pp. 24-36.

12. Albert Cohen, "Foreword and Overview," in *Gangs in America*, ed. Huff, pp. 7-21.

13. Ko-Lin Chin, "Chinese Gangs and Extortion," in *Gangs in America*, ed. Huff, pp. 129-45.

14. Spergel, *Youth Gangs*, pp. 61-62.

15. Campbell, *Girls in the Gang*; Jeffrey Fagan, "Social Processes of Delinquency and Drug Use Among Urban Gangs," in *Gangs in America*, ed. Huff, pp. 183-222.

16. C. Ronald Huff, "Denial, Overreaction, and Misidentification: A Postscript on Public Policy," in *Gangs in America*, ed. Huff, pp. 310-17.

17. Walter B. Miller, "Why the United States Has Failed to Solver Its Youth Gang Problem," in *Gangs in America*, ed. Huff, pp. 263-87.

18. Hagedorn, *People and Folks*.

19. Jack Katz, *Seductions of Crime* (New York: Basic Books, 1989), p. 119.

20. Irving Spergel and G. David Curry, "Strategies and Perceived Agency Effectiveness in Dealing with the Youth Gang Problem," in *Gangs in America*, ed. Huff, pp. 288-309.

21. Hagedorn, *People and Folks*.

22. Ruth Horowitz, "Sociological Perspectives on Gangs: Conflicting Definitions and Concepts," in *Gangs in America*, ed. Huff, pp. 37-54; James D. Vigil and John M. Long, "Emic and Etic Perspectives on Gang Culture: The Chicano Case," in ibid., pp. 55-70.

23. John Hagedorn, "Back in the Field Again: Gang Research in the Nineties," in ibid., pp. 240-62.

24. Ibid., p. 250.

25. Ibid., pp. 250-56.

26. Cheryl Maxson and Malcom Klein, "Street Gang Violence: Twice as Great, or Half as Great," in ibid., pp. 71-100; Jeffrey Fagan, "Social Processes of Delinquency and Drug Use Among Urban Gangs," in ibid., pp. 183-219; Irving Spergel and G. David Curry, "Strategies and Perceived Agency Effectiveness."

27. Vigil and Long, "Emic and Etic Perspectives," pp. 58-59.

28. Carl Taylor, *Dangerous Society* (East Lansing: Michigan State University Press, 1990).

29. Miller, pp. 263-64.

30. Anne Campbell, "Female Participation in Gangs," in *Gangs in America*, ed. Huff, p. 174.

2

Gangs, Drugs, and Violence

JOAN MOORE

F_{ew} phenomena studied by social scientists are as easily stereo-typed as gang violence. This is doubly unfortunate in that the real problems of gangs are often lost in a kettle of stereotypes. Some of these stereotypes are harmless; many, however, are dangerously wrong. My first task is to identify some of these mistaken ideas and to investigate a few possible social sources.

My second task is to look at research. Usually research is a cure for popular stereotypes, but gang research is different. Much of it does not seem to cure any of the mistaken notions. Often the typical methods and theories applied to the study of gangs simply buttress the stereotypes. We will see why this is true for a couple of the major stereotypes. Finally, from this investigation some conclusions will be offered.

STEREOTYPES

There have been young male groups called "gangs" throughout American history, and they have always generated considerable public concern about violence.[1] But when historians try to reconstruct what actually happened with those early city gangs, they usually find that facts are few. The truth is, nobody knew much about those groups, and most of what historians tell us comes from the newspapers of the day. This is also true now. What we know is distorted. One venerable researcher summed it up by saying "It is possible that we know less about the current problem than we knew about gangs and gang violence in the 1960s."[2]

What are the major stereotypes about gangs? Most typically, it is that gangs are composed of late-adolescent males, who are violent, drug- and alcohol-soaked, sexually hyperactive, unpredictable, confrontational, drug-dealing criminals. Nowadays gang members are stereotyped as black or Hispanic; gangs thrive in inner-city neighborhoods, which they intimidate, dominate, and prey upon. Really, gang members are the quintessential "folk devils," as one author described similar youthful villains in England.[3] They are demonic, and all the worse for being in a group.

It is an important part of the stereotype that there is no variation in gang structure or behavior. A gang is a gang is a gang. Thus when the media discover a gang that indulges in a new horror (satanism, for instance, or crack dealing), all gangs are assumed to indulge in the same behavior. They are all bad, and bad in the same kinds of ways. If it were proven beyond a doubt that one particular gang did not deal crack today, it would be expected to sell crack tomorrow. All gangs are thought to have a high potential for developing the worst behavior displayed by any one of them. There is no variation among them and it is assumed that gangs will inevitably become even more menacing.

Underlying this stereotype is yet another unexamined idea. Not only is every gang like every other gang, but there is no good in gangs. This aspect of the stereotype focuses on criminal behavior and ignores behavior that links gangs in more conventional ways with other youth groups and with the community.[4] A related problem is the tendency to confound individual and group criminality. The old-fashioned popular association for the term "gang" was the *West Side Story* image of a group of kids whose members were aggressive and rebellious—but appealing. That idea has been replaced largely by the "gangster" image of a highly disciplined criminal organization with elaborate networks of "soldiers" under strict control from the top. Recently, a confusing blend of the two images has been purveyed in the media where the gang is seen as an organized drug enterprise staffed by unpredictably aggressive and rebellious young people. In either case, the members *share* criminality.

The validity of these stereotypes will be considered later. First, however, we need to explore why gangs should be so subject to stereotyping.

WHY STEREOTYPES?

It is not difficult to come up with a sociological explanation. Let us look first at how stereotypes operate. What we see is that pre-existing popular views about gangs are mobilized and amplified in periodic waves of fear and outrage about particularly visible, usually criminal behavior by young people acting in groups. Sometimes—as with the crack scare of the late 1980s—this behavior is framed as a "crime wave."

A good name for the intersection of stereotype and crime wave is "moral panic."[5] Moral panics build on existing cleavages in the society—cleavages of race and class. In the case of gangs, they build on fear and ignorance of what is happening in the inner city. And they reinforce the convictions of conventional Americans that their moral universe is superior and their fear that this moral universe is under assault. The mechanism for developing a moral panic is hard to describe and is really not well understood. However, it is obvious that moral panics are especially likely to focus on young people precisely because young people—the adults of the future—pose the most serious challenge to the continuity of their elders' core values. If their socialization goes awry, then the future of the community may be in jeopardy.

This perspective also helps explain why a moral panic about gangs should peak in the late 1980s. The anxiety about minorities—and minority youth in particular—is responsive to the increasingly serious economic situation for minority young people in inner-city communities. There have been real changes in the economy of the country. New jobs have been created, but manufacturing jobs are disappearing. Poorly educated people are taking lower-level service jobs.

Wilson's work on the underclass argues that at least for blacks all of these changes are related.[6] Deindustrialization has eliminated many good entry-level jobs. Middle- and working-class blacks have abandoned the inner city, leaving the city to ever-increasing proportions of "underclass" residents. This is the environment in which new youth gangs have emerged within this decade, even in cities that had not seen gangs for more than a generation.[7] The real problems of minority youth and a possible underclass are effectively symbolized to a general public by the moral panic about minority youth gangs.

Why do stereotypes persist? They hang on partly because of real problems in doing research and real problems in social theory. First we will look at the research; then we will look at theories about gangs.

STEREOTYPES AND RESEARCH

There is very little contemporary empirical research on gangs, and what there is often reinforces stereotypes. This does not mean that the stereotypes are true. It does mean that it is difficult to conduct empirical research on gangs without falling victim to a variety of distorting traps.

Most researchers, indeed, never even try to do direct research with gangs: they utilize existing official data sources—usually from the criminal justice system—and have no direct contact with gang members. Hagedorn calls this "courthouse criminology."[8] Obviously, police are concerned with crimes, and their definitions of gangs, like the following one from Los Angeles County, concentrates on criminality. This definition also establishes the criminal conspiracy concept of gangs, thereby abolishing the distinction between individual and collective criminal behavior:

> A gang is a group of people who form an allegiance for a common purpose and engage in acts injurious to public health and public morals, who pervert or obstruct justice or the due administration of laws, or engage in (or have engaged in) criminal activity, either individually or collectively, and who create an atmosphere of fear and intimidation within the community.[9]

Police are not sociologists, and their definition contrasts sharply with the more community-oriented definitions of some sociologists. Short, for example, defines a "gang" as follows:

> . . . a group whose members meet together with some regularity, over time, on the basis of group-defined criteria of membership and group-determined organizational structure, usually with some sense of territoriality.[10]

Short goes on to comment that his definition "includes neither delinquent nor conventional behaviors, since these usually are what we wish to explain." Those courthouse criminologists who use police records must live both with the police definition of gang and their sometimes erroneous identification of individuals as gang members. In some jurisdictions, like Los Angeles, they must deal with the fact that police records confound individual and gang criminal activity, labeling as "gang" activity some acts that members consider individually motivated.[11]

Few people study gangs in their natural settings. Though the study of gangs originated in the empiricist days of the 1920s Chicago school, street ethnography did not become a strong tradition, as it did with research on illicit drugs.[12] Of course it is difficult to do street ethnography with any youth group, let alone a quasi-illicit one. Gang field research on the streets, while often rather boring, can also be dangerous.[13]

When researchers do make an effort to talk with gang members, the most obvious trap is that much of that research is conducted in more or less coercive institutional settings, and the nature of the setting may easily help distort the findings. Incarceration facilities are the most obvious example. First, of course, there is a sampling problem: gang members who go to jail are not necessarily representative of the gang. Then, too, research inside institutional settings is constrained by the fact that the status of the respondent revolves around his/her inmate role—present, past, or future. The gang member is removed from the everyday realities of the gang-home-community web. He or she is so focused on the immediate personal situation and on the gang in prison that distortions are bound to occur, even if the respondent were not consciously lying. Furthermore, unless the respondent has good reason to trust the interviewer, there is no particular incentive to be truthful. There may be many incentives to lie or distort the truth.

Researchers who find their samples in community agencies—e.g. gang intervention programs—may face similar problems unless they spend considerable time with their respondents and use the community agency as a beginning point, rather than as the sole source of access to gang members. For example, gang members who come to an agency may present a sampling problem similar to that of gang members in jail, even when researchers make strenuous efforts to avoid bias.[14] A potential motivational distortion is that repentant or "redeemed" gang members in a program may overemphasize the evils of the gang they have just left, and program staff—usually embattled in any local government—may have even stronger selective and interpretive biases, trying to justify their own program. In addition, active young gang members are often so caught up in their own fantasies and mythologies that a researcher may find it difficult to extricate self-aggrandizing myths from the often grubby realities.

It takes time to study gangs, and the most convincing researchers have developed enough rapport, often over several years, to be able to convey something approximating an emic point of view—a term that anthropologists use to refer to the gang as viewed by its members.[15] The entry points vary considerably. Taylor, for example, was a long-time resident of the community he studied, and put his insight—and his security firm—to the study of the gangs that were disrupting the local community.[16] Vigil, another example, also grew up in neighborhoods with gangs and was peripherally involved himself.[17] He provides an important cultural context for his generalizations about gangs, and his life histories of young gang members take on particular significance in that context. Hagedorn directed a gang-serving agency for a period of time, and collaborated with one of his former clients in his study of Milwaukee gangs.[18]

I have used a research strategy that has concentrated on retrospective studies of gang life—what we have called a "collaborative model."[19] This is somewhat similar to the street ethnography approach; the important exceptions are that research contact points are men and women who have been members of the gangs, and that the research design and instruments are developed in collaboration with these same people. In the research we have done following this model, we have relied on lengthy semi-structured interviews. A collaborative approach forces academic researchers, with all of their frequent misperceptions, false questions, and facile misinterpretations, to actually interact throughout the research process with men and women who have been immersed in the gang subculture, and to test out ideas before they become incorporated into instruments and findings. In my own experience, the continued confrontation with an insider perspective has been one of the most important benefits of the collaborative approach. It is a vital corrective.

The collaborative approach also helps overcome the typical sampling problem in that it provides an effective means to develop probability samples of gang members. Thus in one study we asked staff to compile a roster of original members, verify and correct the roster in the course of subsequent interviews,[20] and actually locate a high proportion of a sample of members through their networks.[21] The research we have done has been retrospective, but that is not inherent in the collaborative approach; Hagedorn used the collaborative approach with active young-adult gang members, asking about current status,[22] and his findings did not reflect the limitations of retrospective studies.

CONCEPTUAL FRAMEWORKS AND THEORIES ABOUT GANGS

The paucity of research on gangs would not be such a problem if gangs were like most things studied by sociologists—that is if they were part of everybody's experiences. But to most researchers they are esoteric. Hence the researcher must derive most of his or her conceptual framework either from theoretical sources (which are thin at best) or from some other source, usually one that is rooted in a current public issue, widely discussed on television and in the newspapers.

This poses problems, because the sporadic panics about gangs and drugs usually are so intense and so moralistic that police and media actually define the phenomena. Both police and media have powerful motives of self-interest. Police tend to limit the focus of their concern to law enforcement issues and the need for more police power. The media sensationalize their coverage in order to attract an audience. What is known about gangs and crack, for example, comes almost entirely from the media and police, and it is sensationalized.

Theories about gangs are thin at best but can provide a richer conceptual framework. Most social scientists who study gang violence have made some effort to describe the characteristics of the gangs beyond simple stereotypes. The most ambitious of these studies date back to the 1950s and 1960s, when the theoretical perspectives on gangs were reexamined for the first time since Thrasher's seminal work on the hundreds of Chicago ethnic youth gangs in the 1920s.[23]

Like the police and media, some of those theorists also focussed on some hypothetical and quintessential features of "the gang." They had no interest in variations among gangs. For example, Yablonsky argued that youth gangs are casual and rather fragile groupings.[24] He generalized that the violent gang is a "near group," with little cohesion, shifting membership, and pathological leadership. Gang violence was seen as a manifestation of collective behavior, with little to do either with drugs or with any community characteristic. Another theorist searching for the essence of gangs was the most notable subcultural theorist of the same era, Walter B. Miller. He argued that the gang and its violence simply reflected "the focal concerns of lower-class culture" thus allowing for little variation either in violence or in other behaviors.[25] As recently as 1974 Miller reaffirmed this basic thesis, arguing that "variations in gangs are only 'elaborations of existing forms, rather than genuinely original additions to or changes in traditional features.'"[26]

The most important typology was that of Cloward and Ohlin. By contrast, it *did* allow for variation and, quite explicitly, for drugs and for violence.[27] Their basic concern with community variation was an important breakthrough. They distinguished three types of gangs—criminal, violent, and retreatist—each in a special kind of lower-class community. All three types of gang arise from disparities between aspirations of young persons and the opportunities they have in poor communities. Therefore, the local opportunity structure came to be a prime determinant in creating one of these three subcultures.

Even though it is a fruitful conceptual framework, the details of their taxonomy are simply not convincing. The portrait of "criminal" gangs was drawn almost entirely from images of Al Capone's Chicago. Such gangs were to be found in "stable" slums which had an organized criminal enterprise. Youth gangs served as recruiting grounds for those adult criminal organizations. (Ironically, Cloward and Ohlin did not even draw on Thrasher's classic study of more than one thousand youth gangs of the 1920s to amplify their view of youth gangs.) The second type, the "violent" gangs, were to be found in slums that were unorganized, unstable, and transient. Cloward and Ohlin took as examples the massive housing projects of large Eastern cities. Such disorganized communities, they said, did not offer the structured criminal opportunities of the older criminal slums. The third type, the "retreatist" gang, had a drug-using, kicks-oriented subculture, and emerged among those individuals or gangs that "failed to find a place for themselves in criminal or conflict subcultures."[28] The empirical grounding for this category was also very slight.

Some social scientists still completely ignore community character-istics (e.g. Miller, who emphasizes gang motivation[29]), but Cloward and Ohlin have followers among contemporary researchers. Some actually use their typology quite uncritically,[30] and others adapt pieces of it.[31]

However, Cloward and Ohlin's original evidence is rather skimpy, and their taxonomy is of questionable applicability in today's poor minor-ity communities. Today's housing projects in Chicago, for example, are the territory of gangs that are both violent and criminal.[32] Chicano gangs in East Los Angeles housing projects, on the other hand, are both drug using and violent—not in the least bit retreatist!

Nonetheless, Cloward and Ohlin's focus on how variations in com-munity opportunity structures affect variations in gang behavior remains extremely important. Given the changing circumstances of inner-city communities, gang researchers should be particularly sensitive to the need to develop a community-oriented approach. Some are transcend-ing the specifics of Cloward and Ohlin's typology and looking at new variables—both with regard to community and with regard to gang behavior. Sullivan's comparative study of white, black, and Puerto Rican neighborhoods offers important leads because he concentrates on varia-tions in job-getting networks as direct evidence of the chances that young people have for leaving any delinquent youthful ties.[33] MacLeod's work points to the importance of family definitions of the local opportunity structure.[34] Short reflects on the neighborhoods he studied in the 1960s as well as on recent changes.[35] He notes the importance of relations between older role models and younger boys in the creation (or destruction) of what he calls "social capital," and suggests that neighborhood stability may be an element. Elsewhere I have suggested that some of the differ-ences between Chicano gangs in Los Angeles and black gangs in Mil-waukee may be attributable to differences in the socioeconomic position of the minorities in the two cities.

Underclass problems in the inner city are increasingly visible. Researchers of inner-city gangs almost by necessity are examining com-munity variations. The basic theme—opportunity structures—may be the same as Cloward and Ohlin's, but the theme is being specified in different ways by various researchers.

In the remainder of this chapter I will focus on two features of the stereotype about gang violence. The stereotype that there are "no varia-tions" among gangs will be examined in relation to variations in violence from time to time and place to place. Then, the confusion between indi-vidual and gang-related violence will be explored. In tracing both of these stereotypes I will draw on studies that I have been associated with, pri-marily of Chicano gangs in East Los Angeles and of black gangs in Mil-waukee.

CHANGE AND VARIATION

Before discussing variations in violence between the two cities, it is important to look at the differences between gangs in the two cities. All gangs are *not* alike, and these cases illustrate the point.

The Nature of Gangs in Los Angeles and Milwaukee

The Chicano gangs we have studied in East Los Angeles generally started out in the 1930s and 1940s as adolescent friendship groups.[36] There was a more or less clearly defined territory, in which most of the members lived, and fights between neighborhood gangs were frequent and bloody. Members' families tended to live conventionally. Although some families may have been troubled, this was by no means true for all of them.

As the members of the original clique aged, the clique began to splinter. Some of the members married and settled down. Others remained involved in a street lifestyle, often mired in heroin use (which became serious in the 1950s) and finding only marginal—if any—employment in between periodic spells in prison. In a few years, another clique of the gang came into being. The gangs developed an age-graded system. Each clique was fairly self-contained, with not much association between older and younger cliques (although this may be changing).

As time passed, the gangs became quasi-institutionalized, and street socialization became more important. Normal adolescent interests in partying and dating combined with street socialization and the gang value of defiance of authority. This led the gang to accept or encourage drug use by most members and property offenses by some members.[37] Most serious drug users in these neighborhoods had their start with gang homeboys. The gangs were—intentionally—highly visible. They fought other gangs and they sprayed their graffiti all over the place. Police harassed them and some members went into juvenile facilities for longer or shorter periods of time.

The East Los Angeles gangs are the rowdiest of all the adolescent peer groups in the community. They have the reputation of being—and usually are—the roughest, the most drug-using, and the most sexually active group around. There is violence inherent in some of the gang processes, but the gang's major reference group is other adolescent groups. While adolescent members look upwards in the age system to older men who have been in prison, the adolescent gang is not a unit in a massively organized crime syndicate. Apart from gang fighting, graffiti, and occasional forays into vandalism (which *are* gang activities), delinquency, including drug dealing, is a matter of individual or pair activity, and not an activity of the gang as a whole.

Gang ties are very important into adulthood for those members who become seriously involved in drugs and/or prison. Violence is different and has different roots in the adolescent period as compared with the violence associated with adult ex-gang member activities. Violence among adult ex-gang members is intense in prison, with prisoners replicating the gang affiliations and gang battles of adolescence, though typically on a broader scale.[38] Gang members also kill and are killed during adulthood in the course of individual criminal activity that is often drug related, but such violence is clearly not gang related.

Milwaukee gangs started in the 1980s in black communities that were being seriously affected by economic restructuring. Good factory jobs were disappearing and were being replaced by service jobs and welfare (with an estimated 43 percent of the black population receiving Aid to Families with Dependent Children [AFDC] payments in 1987).[39] Hagedorn argues that the situation had all the characteristics of a developing underclass, in the sense that Wilson used the term.[40] The gangs crystallized in the midst of a break-dance fad, with considerable fighting. They borrowed the Chicago gang imagery of two nations—Vice Lords and Black Gangster Disciples. The gangs were *not* territorial, because city-wide school desegregation provided a nonneighborhood basis for affiliation. Unlike the Los Angeles gangs, Milwaukee gangs prized strong leadership and a ritualized hierarchical organization. Unlike the gangs of East Los Angeles, some of the gangs did indulge in gang-as-a-whole delinquencies, in addition to the minor vandalism and individual delinquencies that paralleled those of East Los Angeles.

The local job situation meant that few of the original Milwaukee gang members matured out of their gang involvement. As time passed, some of the gangs dissolved as their leaders went to prison—largely on property offenses. Other gangs began to develop age-graded structures, with "graduation" from one clique to another. The gangs became more neighborhood oriented, and more territorial. Cocaine use and marketing became increasingly important in the Milwaukee gangs during the late 1980s. Small groups of young men who had been together in the gang began to go seriously into drug marketing: some made it big, but most went in and out of drug dealing, preferring legitimate jobs when they could get them because of the dangers of drug marketing. Things were made more violent when an entirely new criminal organization began to participate in the drug marketing.

Changes in the Gangs and Changes in Violence

The gangs in both cities changed over time. Some of these changes were particularly relevant to the kind of violence that is uniquely and distinctively gang related: that violence which stems from fights between rival gangs during adolescence.

In East Los Angeles, gang warfare became increasingly lethal during the 1970s. Gang homicide was a leading cause of death for Chicano adolescents.[41] This escalating gang violence was primarily related to gang processes during adolescence. Each clique wanted to match or outdo its predecessor clique in standing up for the gang name. For many cliques this meant increasing the rate and the intensity of violence. It meant more guns and more impersonal violence directed at bystanders in, for example, drive-by shootings in rival gangs' neighborhoods. The general escalation of violence may also have been related psychopharmacologically to drug use within the gang. There was increased polydrug use and more use of drugs like barbiturates and PCP, which have been found to be associated with violence. More recent (and generally more violent cliques—those active in the 1970s) were using significantly more drugs during their late teens—the more violent years.

It is important to note that within this general escalation of violence, there was substantial interclique variation. Most of this variation was related to elements of the gang subculture, like the clique's emphasis on and definition of *locura* or wildness. In some cliques *locura* was defined in violent terms. In others, even in gangs with a long history of violence, *locura* came to be defined more in terms of drug experimentation than of violence. These cliques were quite peaceful. However, Cloward and Ohlin's notion that crime for profit cannot tolerate the chaos of violence in gangs was not corroborated. There was no statistically significant relationship between the number of members in the clique dealing drugs and the number of deaths in gang warfare.[42]

It is also important to note that after a decade or more of escalation, the level of lethal intergang violence in East Los Angeles began to decline sharply in the 1980s.[43] There are several possible reasons for this to have happened. The simplest may be that intergang violence has its own dynamics. It stands to reason that a gang whose members are regularly killed will ultimately have some difficulty in recruiting—even from the most ambitiously rowdy youngsters. Thus, escalating violence may carry the seeds of its own destruction.

But there are other possible answers, too. One is that during the decade when gang violence was peaking, East Los Angeles saw one gang program after another disappear. The gangs were increasingly left to themselves—and the police. This actually may have enhanced the sense in the gangs that they were "outlaws" who were not acceptable in community programs. Yet in the 1980s, a program began to hire gang members in East Los Angeles to mediate and reduce the violence, on a gang-by-gang basis. A number of respondents felt that this program really had an impact.

In Milwaukee's short gang history, violence began to accelerate dramatically with the increased importance of cocaine and the entry of organized crime into drug dealing. The level of drug-related homicides reached unprecedented heights, but whether these can be called gang homicides is another question. Certainly gang members were killed, and yet some gangs were scared away from drug dealing altogether.[44]

In summary, then, gangs change. In East Los Angeles each successive clique showed different kinds of behavior and values. These gangs became quasi-institutionalized, as did some of the Milwaukee gangs, but it is difficult to predict exactly how any gang will evolve.[45]

Moreover, it is also obvious that gangs differ from one place to another and from one ethnic group to another. Gangs appear in distinct "culture areas," and these culture areas differ from one ethnic group to another even within the same city. For example, during the 1970s, deaths from gang violence were very high among Hispanics in both Los Angeles and Chicago, but were low among blacks in both cities. Presently the reverse is true in Los Angeles, and Chicago seems to be going through a similar transformation.[46] Whatever is happening to "gangs" in these two cities, it is happening differently in black and Hispanic communities.

GANG VIOLENCE AND INDIVIDUAL VIOLENCE

Now let me turn to the second major stereotype, the tendency to attribute all behavior performed by gang members to the gang as a whole. This becomes important in untangling many of today's confusions about so-called gang violence. One of the most common interpretations of today's gang violence, for example, is that it stems from gang involvement in increasingly violent drug marketing.

This stereotype is apparently valid for some gangs and some offenses in Milwaukee, as indicated earlier, but it has not been valid in East Los Angeles. In the peak adolescent years in those gangs, some members commit property offenses—usually small scale—and sometimes these involve violence. Occasionally the member does this on his or her own, but more often with another homeboy or homegirl.

Is this gang-related violence? Gang members would fiercely contest such an interpretation. They would argue that this is not a *gang* activity, but an individual activity.

The same pattern continues into young adulthood, but the line becomes blurred. By this age, a good portion of the gang—usually the more stable members—are involved in their jobs and their families, and their priorities have changed. Most of the members that are still hanging around are also involved in a drug-related street lifestyle, with continuous "ripping and running." Some of the drug users market drugs—and so do some of the nonusers: it is a lucrative business until you are caught. Almost inevitably, dealers turn to their homeboys and homegirls when they do go into business. Some of the drug deals go sour and there is violence.

Is *this* gang-related violence? Again, gang members would contest such an interpretation. The gang itself is not acting as a unit to deal drugs. Individual members of the gang are dealing drugs and drawing on one another as their partners, completely outside the context of the gang as a whole.

Does it make any difference? I think it does. Many of the people hanging around with the East Los Angeles gangs in young adulthood are people at loose ends with their lives, still preoccupied with adolescent loyalties. They do *not*, however, consciously participate in a violence-prone criminal activity. They may be aware of such activities, and they may occasionally dabble in illegal income-generating activities, but they have not, in their minds, joined a criminal group. This self-concept makes a difference to their future lives.

It is particularly important to sort out the drug factor, because it has generally been assumed that the recent increase in gang-related violence in a number of cities is related to the increase in gang involvement in the sales of cocaine and crack. It was assumed that gangs were a ready-made crack marketing unit, since they were already "organized." It was further assumed that gangs were highly prone to violence. Police believed this interpretation and so did the media.

However, when these assumptions were actually tested with Los Angeles Police Department data for 1983 to 1985, they proved to be wrong.[47] Cocaine drug sales did increase markedly during the period, as expected. Involvement of individuals identified as gang members in drug sales did increase slightly, but the overwhelming majority of individuals arrested by police from these five South Central Los Angeles stations (75 percent) were not gang members. In cases where more than one person was involved in the sale, the number of members from the same gang actually declined. Most important, perhaps, when gang members were involved in cocaine sales, the transactions were not more likely to involve violence or the presence of guns.

Most of these arrests were for small-scale dealing, and the authors reasoned that such low-level activities are less likely to provoke much violence. Thus, the researchers thought that they might get some answers by looking at homicides. The answers point in the same direction. Drug motives did not increase in homicides involving gang members, whereas they did in homicides that did not involve gang members. Cocaine, then, had a big impact in generating violence, but it was not because of gang-member involvement.

These are surprising findings only if one has in mind the image of "gang" as a tightly organized violence-prone criminal conspiracy, ready to move into drug dealing effectively and efficiently when a new drug comes along. The findings are also surprising if one believes that whatever a gang *member* does necessarily involves the gang as a whole. Some of the gangs involved in these arrests in South Central Los Angeles may well be like this, and, since 1985, more gangs may have become like this. There are such gangs in other cities. Padilla, for example, finds that the Chicago Puerto Rican gangs he studies are such "ethnic enterprises." It may be that some of the more loosely organized gangs will evolve to become organized criminal groups.[48] Nevertheless we do not know that from the arrest data, and we don't know it from what the police or the media tell us. In fact, Klein et al. took their hypotheses from what the police believed was happening at the time, and one of the most interesting implications of their research is that the police were wrong.[49]

Just to confound the matter further, in at least two cities—Detroit and New York—researchers studying crack-dealing organizations report that although these organizations *call* themselves gangs, they did not grow out of youth gangs and they have none of the characteristics discussed earlier.[50] They are criminal organizations that happen to call themselves gangs. And Williams also describes youthful criminal organizations that deal cocaine in New York, but they are not the same as youth gangs: they were a localized group of friends who got together to make money dealing drugs.[51]

The crack economy has vastly increased the number of drug dealers in several inner-city communities: the technology and availability of cocaine have coincided with a shriveling of decent job opportunities in many of these communities. And, according to recent evidence, crack dealing almost invariably involves violence; dealers threaten both each other and the community.[52] Yet the role of gangs in this expanding crack economy is still open to question and poorly understood.

IMPLICATIONS

To recapitulate what has been said so far, there is one kind of gang-related violence that is exhibited by all gangs—intergang conflict. Gang members and innocent bystanders alike are hurt and killed in this kind of violence. Sometimes it seems that this kind of violence does nothing but escalate, without abatement. Still, as the East Los Angeles case illustrates, intergang conflict can also decline, and the decline may happen on its own or with the help of programs that intervene. Such declines may have little or nothing to do with drugs.

There is another kind of violence that appears to be related to gangs, but the connection is even fainter. That is the kind related to illegal activity—particularly drug marketing. It is not safe to assume that drug-related violence is inherent in gangs. Some youth gangs develop into criminal organizations, but this is not the norm. Some violent criminal organizations may be composed of men and women who were once associated with gangs, but there is little evidence that *this* is the norm, either. However, there certainly is evidence that violent drug-dealing organizations have grown and flourished with no gang connections whatsoever.

In many cities throughout the country, gangs have been cropping up for the first time since the 1950s.[53] Gangs have proliferated at the same time as crack cocaine dealing has proliferated, in many of the same neighborhoods. Police and media have been quick to jump to the conclusion that the two are connected, and that we are facing a national—or at least a regional—conspiracy. But in at least two cities, Milwaukee and Columbus, where such claims were made, we have research evidence to the contrary.[54] The gangs grew up out of local circumstances: they were not branches of a criminal organization.

The truth seems to be that there are good explanations for gangs to be starting up now and for there to be an upsurge in illegal drug marketing—gang and nongang—in these communities. If a community's economy is not based solidly on wages and salaries, other economies will begin to develop. This is the essence of Wilson's argument about an emergent underclass. Welfare, bartering, informal economic arrangements, and illegal economies become substitutes—simply because people must find a way to live. Young people growing up in such communities have little good to anticipate.

It is obvious that research on gangs should take these factors into account. It is indeed time to transcend both the limitations of earlier community-oriented taxonomies of gangs as well as the naive empiricism of many studies. Any new taxonomy of gang violence as related to drugs must take into account the variations in local underclass development and in local underground economies, especially the extent to which these underground economies are based in drug dealing.[55] In addition, ethnicity and other subcultural variations among gangs should be recognized. Finally, variations in gang social structure and in gang values regarding violence or the gang's role in the neighborhood should be taken seriously as variables affecting the extent to which gangs may become involved in violent drug dealing. Even the scanty data now available point to these variables as critical in explaining variations in gang violence; and even though I cannot present a developed taxonomy to rival that offered by Cloward and Ohlin, I can argue with some vehemence that such a taxonomy should be a goal.

NOTES

1. D. Johnson, *Policing the Urban Underworld* (Philadelphia: Temple University Press, 1979).

2. I. Spergel, "Violent Gangs in Chicago: In Search of Social Policy," *Social Service Review* 58 (1984): 199-225, p. 199.

3. S. Cohen, *Folk Devils and Moral Panics* (Oxford: Martin Robinson, 1980).

4. Cf. R. Horowitz, "The End of the Youth Gang," *Criminology* 21 (1983): 585-600.

5. Cohen, *Folk Devils*. See also M. Zatz, "Chicano Youth Gangs and Crime: The Creation of a Moral Panic," *Contemporary Crises* 11 (1987): 129-58, for a specific instance of a moral panic about Chicano gangs in Phoenix.

6. W. J. Wilson, *The Truly Disadvantaged* (Chicago: University of Chicago Press, 1987).

7. J. Needle and W. Stapleton, *Police Handling of Youth Gangs* (Washington, D.C.: U.S. Dept. of Justice, Office of Juvenile Justice and Delinquency Prevention, National Institute for Juvenile Justice and Delinquency Prevention, 1983).

8. J. Hagedorn, "Back in the Field Again: Gang Research in the Nineties," in *Gangs in America* ed. R. Huff (Newberry Park: Sage Publications, 1990).

9. Provided courtesy of Wesley McBride of the Los Angeles Sheriffs. The definition was arrived at in 1989, after substantial in-house discussion. The deliberate phrasing, "either individually or collectively," relates to an effort to hold the gang legally responsible for criminal acts of individual members.

10. James Short, "New Wine in Old Bottles? Change and Continuity in American Gangs," in *Gangs in America*, ed. Huff.

11. Los Angeles Police and Sheriffs departments both count as "gang homicides" all homicides in which somebody they identify as a gang member is involved either as perpetrator or as victim. Other jurisdictions, e.g. Chicago, only count as "gang homicides" those homicides in which there is a documented gang motivation. See Moore, 1988. Klein and Maxson, 1985, used the broad Los Angeles definition of gang homicide in their efforts to distinguish gang from nongang homicides, and this poses some problems for their analysis.

12. C. Akins and G. Beschner, eds., *Ethnography: A Research Tool for Policymakers in the Drug and Alcohol Fields*. DHHS Pub. No. (ADM) 80-946 (Washington, D.C.: U.S. Government Printing Office, 1980).

13. Cf. Discussion in Hagedorn, "Back in the Field Again."

14. J. Fagan, "The Social Organization of Drug Use and Drug Dealing Among Urban Gangs," *Criminology* 27 (1989), pp. 633-69.

15. Diego Vigil and John Long, "Emic and Etic Perspectives of Gang Culture: The Chicano Case," in Huff, *Gangs in America.*

16. Carl Taylor, *Dangerous Society* (East Lansing: Michigan State University Press, 1990).

17. Diego Vigil, *Barrio Gangs* (Austin: University of Texas Press, 1988).

18. J. Hagedorn and Perry Macon, *People and Folks* (Chicago: Lake View Press, 1988).

19. See J. Moore, "The Chicano Pinto Research Project: A Case Study in Collaboration," *Journal of Social Issues* 33 (1977): 144-58; and J. Moore, R. Garcia, and R. Salcido, "Research in Minority Communities: Collaborative and Street Ethnography Models Compared," in *Ethnography: A Research Tool*, pp. 46-63, ed. Akins and Beschner.

20. Joan Moore and John Long, *Final Report: Youth Culture vs. Individual Factors in Adult Drug Use* (Los Angeles: Community Systems Research, Inc., 1987).

21. Short also tried to follow up on members of the gangs he had studied over a three-year period of field work (James Short and Fred Strodtbeck, *Group Process and Gang Delinquency* [Chicago: University of Chicago Press, 1965]). In his comment on his follow up, he notes that he was able to locate almost all members of the more persistent gang, the Vice Lords, whereas he had far less success in locating members of the more transient gang, the Nobles (Short, "New Wine in Old Bottles?"). Our success in locating members may have stemmed from the institutionalized status of the Chicano gangs we studied.

22. Hagedorn, *People and Folks.*

23. F. Thrasher, *The Gang* (Chicago: University of Chicago Press, 1927).

24. L. Yablonsky, *The Violent Gang* (Baltimore: Penguin, 1970).

25. W. B. Miller, "Lower Class Culture as a Generating Milieu of Gang Delinquency," *Journal of Social Issues* 14 (1958): 5-19.

26. W. B. Miller, "American Youth Gangs: Past and Present," in *Current Perspectives in Criminal Behavior*, ed. A. Blumberg (New York: Alfred A. Knopf, 1974), pp. 291-320.

27. R. Cloward and L. Ohlin, *Delinquency and Opportunity* (New York: The Free Press, 1960).

28. Ibid., p. 183.

29. W. B. Miller, *Violence by Youth Gangs and Youth Groups as a Crime Problem in Major American Cities* (Washington, D.C.: U.S. Dept. of Justice, Office of Juvenile Justice and Delinquency Prevention, National Institute for Juvenile Justice and Delinquency Prevention, 1976).

30. W. Kornblum, "Ganging Together: Helping Gangs Go Straight," *Social Issues and Health Review* 2 (1987): 99-104.

31. Recently, Curry and Spergel applied the typology to an understanding of variations in gang homicides in Chicago (D. Curry and I. Spergel, "Gang Homicide, Delinquency, and Community," *Criminology* 26 [1988]: 381-405).
Lacking an ethnographic basis to characterize local neighborhoods, the authors used ethnicity instead. With no ethnographic justification, their measure of ". . . social disorganization was simply and grossly the concentration of Hispanics in a community" (p. 387). Their concern was with "the classic social disorganization model of areas inhabited by residents who are marginally integrated into the city's organizational and political life" (p. 386). Such communities may well be highly integrated in ethnic terms, a factor which the authors overlook. In any event, this ungrounded imputation of "disorganization" to Hispanic communities in Chicago is a far cry from the disorganization originally discussed by Cloward and Ohlin. Hispanic communities in Chicago had very high rates of gang homicide, but Curry and Spergel's argument that this is because they were disorganized is simply not convincing.

32. U. E. Perkins, *Explosion of Chicago's Black Street Gangs, 1900 to Present* (Chicago: Third World Press, 1987).

33. M. Sullivan, *"Getting Paid": Youth Crime and Work in the Inner City* (Ithaca, N.Y.: Cornell University Press, 1990).

34. Jay MacLeod, *Ain't No Makin' It* (Boulder, Colo.: Westview Press, 1987).

35. Short, "New Wine in Old Bottles?"

36. Data for this section are derived largely from data gathered under grant number DAO 3114 from the National Institute on Drug Abuse. Points of view and opinions stated in this document do not necessarily represent the official position or policy of the National Institute on Drug Abuse. For details on sampling, etc., see Joan Moore, *Going Down to the Barrio* (Philadelphia: Temple University Press, 1991).
In the study discussed here, we interviewed 25 percent probability samples of 8 male and affiliated female cliques in two long-standing gangs, for a total of 157 respondents. Half of the cliques had been active in the 1940s-1950s, and half in the 1960s-1970s.

37. J. Moore and D. Vigil, "Chicano Gangs: Group Norms and Individual Factors Related to Adult Criminality," *Aztlan* 18 (1987): 27-44.

38. J. Moore, with R. Garcia, C. Garcia, L. Cerda, and F. Valencia, *Homeboys: Gangs, Drugs, and Prison in the Barrios of Los Angeles* (Philadelphia: Temple University Press, 1978).

39. Unpublished data provided by John Hagedorn of the Milwaukee Department of Social Services, 1990. Data on Milwaukee gangs are derived from Hagedorn, *People and Folks*, and, for recent developments, personal communication with Hagedorn.

40. Hagedorn, *People and Folks.*

41. F. Loya, P. Garcia, P. Sullivan, L. Vargas, N. Allen, and J. Mercy, "Conditional Risks of Homicide Among Anglo, Hispanic, Black and Asian Victims in Los Angeles, 1970-1979," in *U.S. Department of Health and Human Services, Report of the Secretary's Task Force on Black and Minority Health, Vol. 5: Homicide, Suicide, and Unintentional Injuries* (Washington, D.C.: U.S. Government Printing Office, 1986).

42. Gang reminiscences, however, suggest that gang warfare did decline during the first years after the introduction of heroin use in the 1950s, when users went from one neighborhood to another to get high.

43. B. Baker, "Chicano Gangs: A History of Violence," *Los Angeles Times,* December 11, 1988, p. 1.

44. Hagedorn, 1990, personal communication.

45. J. Moore, "Introduction: Gangs and the Underclass: A Comparative Perspective," in *People and Folks,* J. Hagedorn, pp. 3-17.

46. Curry and Spergel, "Gang Homicide, Delinquency, and Community."

47. M. Klein, C. Maxson, and L. Cunningham, *Gang Involvement in Cocaine "Rock" Trafficking.* Final Report for the National Institute of Justice (Los Angeles: University of Southern California, 1988).

48. Moore, "The Chicano Pinto Research Project."

49. Inciardi reported that in Miami a similar media connection was made between gang activity and crack dealing. But grand juries empaneled in 1985 and again in 1988 (after a substantial increase in the number of gangs) found that youth gangs were not involved in crack dealing. James Inciardi, "The Crack/Violence Connection Within a Population of Hard-core Adolescent Offenders" (paper presented at Drugs and Violence Technical Review, National Institute on Drug Abuse, September 1989).

50. Personal communication, Jeffrey Fagan, 1989; T. Mieczkowski, 1989; Taylor, *Dangerous Society,* 1989.

51. Williams, T., *The Cocaine Kids* (New York: Addison-Wesley, 1989).

52. B. Johnson, T. Williams, K. Dei, and H. Sanabria, "Drug Abuse in the Inner City: Impact on Hard Drug Users and the Community," in *Drugs and the Criminal Justice System,* ed. M. Tonry and J. Q. Wilson (Chicago: University of Chicago Press, 1989).

53. Needle and Stapleton, *Police Handling of Youth Gangs.*

54. Hagedorn, *People and Folks;* R. Huff, "Youth Gangs and Public Policy in Ohio: Findings and Recommendations" (paper presented at the Ohio Conference on Youth Gangs and the Urban Underclass, May 25, 1988).

55. And by no means all of them are. In the early 1980s, the numbers business was the biggest illicit employer in one Brooklyn neighborhood (C. Silberman, *Criminal Violence, Criminal Justice* [New York: Vintage], cited in R. McGahey, "Economic Conditions, Neighborhood Organization and Urban Crime," in A. J. Reiss and M. Tonry, eds., *op. cit.*, 1986); in another Hispanic community in Brooklyn, organized auto theft was the principal illicit employer (McGahey, ibid.).

PART II

THE BEHAVIOR AND ORGANIZATION OF GANGS IN DIFFERENT SETTINGS

3

Anatomy of a
Wilding Gang

SCOTT CUMMINGS

INTRODUCTION

Public concern over teenage violence in cities has sharply increased over the past ten years. According to many criminologists and public officials, some acts of youthful violence have instrumental purposes. Intergroup conflict over urban turf can be viewed as an effort to control public space and limited community resources.[1] Violence over drug trafficking is often produced by efforts to secure and monopolize a market.[2] Creating what Moore calls "moral panic," however, some forms of youthful violence have assaulted the ethical and humanistic sensibilities of conventional Americans.[3] Perhaps no other form of gang violence has produced more public outrage than what the popular press has labeled "wilding."

"Wilding" is a street term signifying new dimensions in public concern over teenage violence. Seemingly without instrumental purpose, wilding is described by journalists as "running amok" in the community, as the senseless perpetuation of violence for fun and amusement.[4] Wilding violence rudely penetrated the moral consciousness of the American public with the brutal attack and rape of a female jogger in Central Park in the spring of 1989. Despite the sensational nature of the Central Park case and the continuing publicity surrounding it, students of gang violence know relatively little about wilding behavior or how frequently it occurs. It is not known, for example, if those who participate in wilding violence are actually members of established gangs. Further, it is not clear if wilding groups represent a special type of violent gang. Drawing upon conventional definitions of gangs, it seems apparent that neither social scientists nor law enforcement officials know if wilding youth meet with any degree of regularity, exhibit forms of group identity and cohesion, are organized, or show any sense of territoriality.[5]

Some of the existing research dealing with gang violence is partially relevant to wilding behavior. Lewis Yablonsky studied violent gangs and concluded they are "near groups," showing little of the highly organized structure of established street gangs.[6] Generalizing from his research findings, he maintains that violent gangs show a low level of group cohesion, and that membership is often unstable and shifting. According to Yablonsky, leadership in a violent gang is pathological, and acts of violence are best viewed as forms of collective behavior rather than rational disputes over drug traffic or territory. Yablonsky, however, did not systematically study acts of violence similar to those found in the Central Park case.

Cloward and Ohlin also observed that violent gangs typically do not exhibit the instrumental behavior found in criminal subcultures.[7] Unlike criminal or retreatist patterns, violent gangs are found in unorganized and transient communities where opportunities for criminal activity are not as abundant. Violent behavior, therefore, may not serve any immediate or apparent social purpose, and may be unrelated to economic gain or material acquisition.

While conventional theories of gang behavior may help illuminate selected aspects of wilding violence, social scientists actually know very little about this increasingly important subject. The theoretical and methodological barriers preventing acquisition of more knowledge about wilding behavior are increased when the violence is interracial. The criminal victimization of whites by blacks is a controversial area of study. While data indicate that most violent crimes such as murder and rape occur within a racial category, interracial assault still elicits intense reactions among members of the dominant group.[8] Widespread support of white retaliation against alleged black criminals in American history, and more recent support of subway vigilante Bernard Goetz, stand as testimonials to the emotional intensity accompanying minority victimization of majority group members.[9]

This chapter reports the results of an ongoing, ten-year case history of an urban neighborhood characterized by high rates of interracial violence and crime. During the early 1980s, the community experienced a wave of wilding violence. The victims of the wilding attacks were elderly whites; the victimizers were black teenagers. Through a case history approach, tentative conclusions are reached about the factors explaining wilding violence in the study community. Wilding behavior is defined as a special form of gang violence. Generalizations about wilding attacks are forwarded, and their relationship to established theories about gangs are discussed. In order to ensure anonymity, I will refer to the study community as Rosedale Heights and have assigned fictitious names to all subjects.

The Research Site

Rosedale Heights, a community of about ten thousand people, is located in the Greater Fort Worth, Texas, metropolitan area, one of the largest and most rapidly growing urban regions in the nation. Once considered one of the more fashionable residential areas in the city, ghettoization has permanently altered the nature of community life and culture. Racial steering among real estate brokers, informal agreements among home owners, and overt discrimination initially kept many black families out of Rosedale. Busing and court-ordered school integration cracked through some of the resistance. Eventually, a residential trickle broke through the walls of racial exclusion. By the late sixties, major weaknesses in the walls of segregation were evident. By the late 1970s, resistance had collapsed, and Rosedale became a predominantly black neighborhood. White flight and the movement of the black middle class to the more prosperous suburbs sealed the fate of Rosedale as an unstable, decaying neighborhood.

In 1950, the three census tracts which comprised the geographic center of Rosedale were close to 100 percent white in racial composition. Even in 1960, racial patterns of residential settlement showed remarkable stability in the three tracts. The 1960 census showed that about 98 percent of the households in the community were occupied by white families. In 1970, however, the transition was beginning to surface in official statistics. The two tracts which comprised the residential and commercial core of Rosedale revealed that approximately 30 percent and 40 percent of the residents, respectively, were black. By 1980, these two areas had shifted to 63 percent and 82 percent black.

Census tracts often do not correspond to the actual boundaries of urban neighborhoods. The natural geographic boundaries which have historically defined the community of Rosedale show an even greater concentration of black families in the area. When driving or walking through the streets and blocks of Rosedale, one occasionally encounters isolated clusters of Chicano families. Their houses tend to be grouped along specific streets in selected blocks. One also encounters some young, white, working-class families. They moved to Rosedale in response to the drop in housing prices or rental fees that accompanied racial transition. The bulk of those living in Rosedale, however, are black.

Sprinkled throughout the area, one finds about 250 elderly whites.

They are the original occupants of Rosedale. In 1980, about 75 percent of them were females. The average age was about seventy-five years old. Most were living on fixed incomes, many below poverty levels. Due to a combination of age, income, and personal choice, they had been left behind in Rosedale. Over the past decade, they have been systematically victimized by teenagers. The crimes ranged from street thefts and muggings to rape and murder. This chapter will focus upon only one facet of the myriad of adolescent criminal activity occurring in the neighborhood since the mid-1970s: a small group of teenagers who terrorized the elderly between 1981 and 1982. The acts of violence perpetrated by these individuals correspond to what the popular press now calls episodes of "wilding." To locate the acts of violence in a wider milieu of neighborhood life and culture, a brief overview describing the criminal victimization of the elderly is necessary.

The Interracial Context of Crime

Between April and August, 1977, over forty rapes occurred in Rosedale. While the age of the victims ranged between thirty-three and eighty-five, the attacks directed toward the elderly were especially violent. Two teenagers were eventually apprehended and convicted. Over 80 percent of the rapes were cleared with these two convictions, all the victims being elderly whites. About fifteen cases remain unsolved. All the unsolved cases are comprised of violent sexual assaults, some resulting in murder.

Survey data established that rates of criminal victimization among the elderly of Rosedale were two and three times higher than the city average, as were rates of unreported crime. Official police records confirm what residents of the metropolitan area already know about Rosedale. There are four "bad areas" in the city: Northside, Southside, Rosedale, and Freetown. Southside and Freetown bound Rosedale geographically. The three areas are merging racially, socioeconomically, and spatially. At the same time, they have historically existed as separate urban neighborhoods. Northside is a predominately Chicano community, with small clusterings of black and working-class white enclaves. In the spring of 1983, the city released official crime statistics. The data were reported by city council districts. While the formal council districts do not exactly correspond to the natural boundaries of Rosedale, they nonetheless revealed the magnitude of the crime problem in the community at the time of the wilding episodes.

In 1982, the council district corresponding roughly to the Rosedale area reported eighteen murders, a figure that placed it third highest in the city. The Northside district reported twenty-three murders, and in Southside twenty-two people lost their lives. Rosedale ranked second in rapes, with 79 sexual attacks being committed there in 1982. In the Southside district, 112 rapes were reported, and in Northside 56 women were raped. Overall, the Rosedale council district accounted for 12 percent of all crimes reported in the city. Freetown reported the highest proportion of crime with 15 percent of the total, followed closely by the Northside and Southside districts, each accounting for about 14 percent of all reported crimes in the city. Over 55 percent of all reported crimes in 1982 were committed in these four districts.

Between June 1 and September 30, 1982, four homicides occurred in Rosedale, along with three rapes, fourteen street robberies, and sixty-three residential burglaries. The chief of police in the city was quoted as saying that the young people who perpetrated the crimes have the "morals of wild animals." For the most part, the victims were elderly whites. Of the rape victims, all were elderly white women. The sixty homes that were burglarized were all occupied by white retirees. And fourteen of those who experienced household robberies were also violently assaulted. The average age of the victims was between seventy and eighty-five. The chief of police also said it appeared that members of a gang were terrorizing the elderly of Rosedale. He added that if they were caught during the act of robbery, "they didn't hesitate to kill."

As a result of the summer crime wave, by September 1982, the elderly of Rosedale comprised an armed camp. Appearing on the front page of the city's largest newspaper, Saturday, September 11, 1982, was the following in bold print: "Thugs Victimize Aged in Rosedale." The latest victim of the violence was a seventy-four-year-old woman. She had lived in Rosedale for more than fifty years. As a result of the attack, she was confined to one of the local hospitals hovering near death. Her face was severely battered from a beating suffered at the hands of two or more adolescents. They broke into her home earlier in the week, waking her from a nap by jamming a pencil-like object up her nose and demanding money. When the woman did not respond immediately, she was beaten and kicked. She was discovered several hours later when her husband returned home from an errand. He found her on the floor, unconscious in a pool of blood. The only items missing from the house were forty dollars, and an old wrist watch that no longer worked. She eventually died in the hospital.

The woman was the forty-sixth elderly victim attacked between June and September 1982. The first serious assault leveled against the elderly was perpetrated in March. The number of incidents grew steadily after that time. Ten violent crimes were perpetrated in July, twenty-two in August, and eight during the first nine days of September. As a result, the police were pressed to devote more units, time, and special patrols to the Rosedale area. A police spokesperson said that most of the crimes were directed against older white women living alone. Young males—

ranging in numbers between one and five and between fourteen and twenty years old—were forcibly entering the homes of elderly women. They were robbing and violently beating their victims. The police suspected that a gang was systematically terrorizing the elderly of Rosedale. The deputy chief told the press:

> In my opinion, it's not two or three. It's more like 15 or 20. I'm taking this very personally because I have an elderly mother who lives alone. And I'm very much offended by people who victimize old people, and we're going to stop it.

Three violent murders during the summer pushed the city and its officials to a crisis situation. On June 10, Mrs. Ethel Marlow was found dead. She was a retired bookkeeper, eighty-eight years old, who had lived in Rosedale for most of her adult life. Three or more individuals had broken into her house, and dragged her from room to room. The attackers eventually killed her by jamming a broom handle down her throat, stabbing her more than thirty times, and crushing her skull by repeated blows with their feet. The house was ransacked.

On July 25, another violent murder occurred. Mr. Clyde Robinson, a fifty-seven-year-old resident of Rosedale, pulled alongside a car wash. Four youths jumped in front of his moving car, opened the door on the driver's side, and pulled Robinson to the street. The four boys kicked the man, eventually beating him to death with his own cane, which was lying beside him in the car. The four teens took his wallet and disappeared into the evening. And on September 30, two or more teens broke into the home of Mr. and Mrs. Ralph Johnson. About 9 o'clock, they broke down the door of the eighty-seven-year-old man's home. They ransacked the house and stabbed Johnson to death. His seventy-nine-year-old wife, Marie, was severely beaten. The assailants escaped in the couple's 1978 Pontiac, later found about five blocks from the murder.

By the first of October, a one thousand dollar reward had been posted for any information leading to the arrest and apprehension of those responsible for the summer crimes. More than forty city fire fighters volunteered to walk the Rosedale area, door to door, and distribute reward information and posters. Numerous community leaders and local officials publicly pleaded with those responsible to end the terror. Residents were exhorted to step forward with any information useful to the police. Frustrated and impatient, a police spokesperson told the press:

> The roots of the problem are deeper than the police department can attack. We have no control over social problems or social change.

By the second week of October, the violence ended as quickly as it began. An informant told police that several youths she knew might be involved in the attacks. The lead proved accurate, and eventually led to the arrest and indictment of six young residents of Rosedale. Two of the boys were sixteen, two were fifteen, one was seventeen, and the other was twenty. The press described the adolescents as a "loose-knit gang" that had terrorized the neighborhood for over a year. Two of the boys were brothers, two were uncle and nephew. They were charged with burglary and the beating deaths of Mrs. Ethel Marlow, Mr. Clyde Robinson, and Mr. Ralph Johnson.

The adolescents were certified to stand trial as adults. In April 1983, the first youth was prosecuted and found guilty of capital murder. The youth was found guilty on three counts of murder, and sentenced to life in prison. By December 1983, the remaining adolescents were prosecuted and sentenced. Because of plea bargaining, lesser charges were leveled against the other members of the "gang." Two other adolescents were eventually arrested and charged. One was tried as a juvenile; the other was eventually released because of insufficient evidence. The latter suspect was not prosecuted even though he was linked to the crimes by gang members.

CASE HISTORIES

The Social and Psychological Roots of Wilding

In this volume, both Moore and Monti discuss the relationship between the social organization of gangs and the communities in which they are found. Hagedorn also describes the connection between the evolution of gangs and the local environment.[10] Case histories reveal the intersection of societal forces and individual biographies. Each of the case histories presented in this chapter illustrate the social and psychological factors that nurtured and sustained the violent behavior of Rosedale's wildings. While the case histories are limited to those apprehended and convicted of criminal behavior, they undoubtedly reveal common experiences in the lives of many other black youngsters caught in the hopeless maze of poverty and street crime. The purpose of the case histories is to focus attention on the social and psychological factors that influence wilding violence.

Billy Hardin was twenty years old when he turned himself in for the murder of Clyde Robinson. He had lived in Rosedale for four years, having resided in other parts of the city before moving there. He was employed at the time of his arrest, making about four dollars an hour. His longest tenure in a job situation spanned only two months. He had one child, nearly three years old, who lived with her mother in Kansas. He never married, and paid no child support to the mother of the child. He had a prior arrest record for burglary, and a history of heavy drinking. He was described to me by a paralegal assistant as a prototypical "loser," as someone who is just "nowhere." Billy ". . . is just lost; there's no way to get through to him." Hardin's verbal skills were limited and his official psychological profile portrayed him as having a low level of intelligence.

There are six siblings in his immediate family, three older brothers and two sisters. Both of his parents are absent from his household, and have been for some time. He was living with his sister at the time of his arrest. She was the head of the family unit. His sister and her husband work, and were seldom present in the home. He has never met his father, and knows him by name only. Some of his brothers and sisters were fathered by different men. Hardin dropped out of school in the seventh grade, and worked at various, short-term jobs. He pumped gas, washed dishes, peeled vegetables, and worked briefly in a battery shop. He had a marginal attachment to the economy four years prior to his arrest, and "earned" money primarily through short-term work, petty theft, and burglary. He boasted about having a strong attraction to white and Oriental women, and told me: "I don't much like being around my own color."

Before moving in with his sister, he lived with an older brother. His brother tried to serve as the head of the household since both parents were absent from the home. Hardin first started to lose interest in school in the fifth grade:

> The first time I missed school was about the fifth or sixth grade. Me and this girl just went off [to have sex] and I just got used to it. I just started doing it all the time. Then I started getting expelled. I used to get two whippings a day from my oldest brother for missing school. In the seventh grade I missed, and I knew I was gonna get a whipping. I ran away then and left for about three years. I went to live with my sister.

Billy said that he "just skipped school and growed up." He was raised on the streets with little or no guidance from established social institutions. His older brother tried unsuccessfully to discipline him. Caught up in his own struggle to make a living and support a family, the brother failed in his attempt to be a surrogate parent. His sister tried to provide support and a place to stay; she too, however, had her own burdens to shoulder.

Hardin appeared alienated from religious institutions in the black community. He attended church occasionally, but was unimpressed by what he encountered. He last participated in a church service four years prior to his arrest:

> I always believed in God. I used to go to church off and on with my girlfriend. She really talked to me. Preachers don't have much to say

to kids. Every time I got to church I see lots of kids get put out of church. They be playing, and running around and yelling.

Most of the money he received from stolen goods was spent on drugs and alcohol. Goods were pawned at local shops:

You can sell it in a pawn shop. They usually have an older person that deals in stuff. They also give you grass for stuff. They sell dope—marijuana—all over school. The teachers, they be knowing about it, but they don't do nothing.

Items that are easily pawned include televisions, stereos, guns, radios, and jewelry. He was also involved in car theft. The actual theft of the car only garnered twenty dollars; he knew, however, that the adults got paid "a grand" for the car. Most of the kids who steal cars spend the money on drugs. Explaining the nature of street life in Rosedale, he said, "The kids I know, they'd rob me if they had a chance; if they know that I got something." Hardin verbalized no explanations about why he participated in theft and ultimately murder. Other than immediate gratification, he had no vocabulary to describe his actions. Unlike some of his associates, he had little comprehension of the institutional forces that compelled him to drift in and out of crime.

Lawrence and Earl Coleman were raised in a similar family situation. The father was not present in the home, and the mother of the two brothers tried her best to raise a family of six children by working as a domestic, or short-order cook, or in any other type of employment she could secure. The Coleman brothers were involved in church activities as preteens, and achieved a reputation as potentially good athletes in grade school.

Despite a more stable socioeconomic environment within the family than that encountered by Billy Hardin, the Coleman brothers were exposed to a history of violence within the household. They were known by neighbors and peers as tough, "wise guys." A next-door neighbor remarked that:

They were some of the most roguish fellows around. You can't tell them nothing. They thought they owned this world. When you see them one at a time, they were nice as you would want them to be. But when you got two or three of them together, there is no telling what they would do.

The next-door neighbor was beaten by the two Coleman brothers, with the assistance of four other teenagers, when he went to their home to complain about bottles and rocks being thrown at his house. The neighbor and his brother suffered head cuts and multiple bruises as a result of a beating administered with sticks and rocks. The mother of the Coleman brothers did not intervene in the confrontation.

Ralph Coleman, the older brother of Earl and Lawrence, plea bargained on a murder charge in connection with a 1979 death of a Carswell Air Force Base serviceman. Then age fifteen, the older brother pleaded guilty to robbery with bodily injury. He served time in the state penitentiary from November 1979 until he was paroled three years later. Members of the Coleman family have a sustained history of being out of work, out of school, and in trouble. Their reputation in the community as violent, aggressive kids was widespread.

Several students from Rosedale High School told me they feared the Coleman brothers, and did not want "to cross them" in any way. A twelve-year-old boy who lived near the Coleman household said the Coleman kids terrorized the neighborhood with unprovoked attacks. On many occasions, he said, the Coleman brothers had tried to beat him and other kids on the street. Neighbors maintained that during the day, the Coleman brothers and other teenagers would drink beer in the alley between their house and other residences. During the night, the boys would burglarize houses and try to sell stolen radios, televisions, and stereos. Neighbors reported to the police that the Coleman brothers had offered to sell them guns, jewelry, small appliances, and other items. They assumed the items were stolen because neither of the two brothers was employed.

Both Earl and Lawrence Coleman had a history of periodic trips to juvenile detention centers. Their school attendance was uneven to nonexistent. The younger brother was known as a very aggressive and "dirty" player by the coach of a grade school soccer team. The vice principal of Rosedale Middle School commented about the Coleman brothers:

> I've never been able to get them to attend school. They may have been on the rolls, but they did not attend school. I can't say nothing good about them.

The youngest Coleman brother enrolled in Rosedale High School in September of 1982, and withdrew in October. The other brother, at the time of his arrest, was not enrolled in school at all. Before dropping out of school, both were chronically absent or tardy.

The two Coleman brothers, in association with two to four other teenagers, systematically prowled the streets of Rosedale. Their criminal activities were always perpetrated in a group; seldom was the act of theft carried out alone. Lawrence Coleman told me:

> It was mostly just when we'd get together. Sometimes we'd plan it out. We'd check a house out to see if no car was there. Sometimes, you know, you can go up to the door and see if the screen is hooked and stuff. See if there are lights on and stuff like that.

In addition to petty theft and household robbery, the Coleman brothers also sold fake drugs:

> There are a whole bunch of ways to get money. Like, one guy, you know, he make some of that fake—ah, hash—, you know. Cook it up and sell it. Five dollars a block. Some people sell fake pills and stuff. They make money that way.

Charles Raymond Roosevelt was the most articulate member of the wilding group. Because of his marginal association with the Coleman brothers and other members of the group that terrorized Rosedale, he was able to plea bargain a five-year sentence. His socioeconomic and family profile was consistent with his partners in crime. Eighteen at the time of his arrest, he had lived in Rosedale for less than four years. In addition to himself, there are eight members of his immediate family, including two brothers and five sisters. According to him, "Three of us got the same daddy; three more of us got a different daddy." Both his biological father and stepfather live in Dallas, about forty miles away. They see him infrequently. His mother, the head of the household, works as a maid and household worker in the white suburbs. She takes the bus to her various places of work. Charles dropped out of school in the eleventh grade, a pattern similar to other members of his family.

Since dropping out of school, he spent most of his time on the streets of Rosedale:

> Rosedale is like a club, you know, nothing but a disco club. You go there to get drunk, to look for girls. You know, to mess with the girls, to look for a date, to carry on, you know. Just a day's vacation. That's all it is.

Rosedale is a good place to get high, and spend the day on the streets:

> They got a certain person, you know, like someone who is running a drug house. You know, he goes to school and puts it out from there.

Because drugs are costly, theft and sale of merchandise are the only ways to stay high:

> There's different ways, you know, like most people get a car and get them a couple of batteries. You know, go sell it to a filling station or something. Steal some tools. Most people I know be smoking grass here and there. But if they want some stiffer drugs, like some cocaine or heroin, they go try to hold up something.

The drug traffic in Rosedale is extensive. One major source of drugs, according to Roosevelt, is a place called The Texas Nigger, a club located about two miles from the center of Rosedale. Most of the kids in Rosedale know where the "drug houses" are located. "It's just a little old area, you know, where they have houses selling weed and stuff."

Roosevelt's drift in and out of crime is directly related to his marginal attachment to the local labor market. He has never held a full-time job. His employment history resembles that described by Elliot Liebow in *Tally's Corner*:[11]

> You know, they got these little old centers, recreation centers, that they be hiring for little old, part-time jobs out of school, summer jobs. They got grocery stores that hire people. If a person really wants a job, he can get it. There ain't no doubt about it. I was working at this Paris Coffee Shop. I was working downtown at the Hilton Inn. Then I was working at Terry's Grill, downtown. I had a little old job on weekends, helping this dude set up fruits and stuff.

He got most of these jobs by simply being on the street at the right time, or by inquiring directly. Most of the jobs, however, were part time or short term. Because work was uneven and unreliable, crime became more lucrative than the "straight" labor market.

Roosevelt provided a fairly detailed description of how kids obtain money through theft, burglary, and street confrontation:

> I guess they kind of have fun; it's easy money, you know, without getting a job. Most likely, they'll find somebody to deal with, you know, like a drug house. Trade this off for some weed or some money or something. You know, like a diamond ring, trade it for $15 or $20. He can probably make $200 in two or three hours. It depends on what he gets. You know, how he gets it and what he do with it.

The money earned from theft is spent on things that give the thief pleasure and promote a comfortable lifestyle:

> The average person, you know, he liable to go buy him a pair of pants, shirts, some shoes. Go out to a little old dance. Just enjoy it, you know. Really, you know, just enjoy it.

Roosevelt, more so than any of the other adolescents interviewed, seemed to understand clearly the forces that pulled him into crime. Not only did he seem to understand them, but he was also able to articulate quite accurately the sociological factors which generated and sustained criminal behavior. Explaining that he tried to avoid groups of young people because trouble would soon follow, he said he preferred to be alone. "A crowd draws attention, so I just lay my way out of it really." Many acts of theft and violence flow from the challenges and dares issued in a group situation:

It starts out just drinking and messing around. He's liable to do something. Go break in a store or something. His partner see that he stole something. "I ought to go rob something to make myself look good," you know, all of them try to race to be the leader. It just keeps going and going just like a chain. I guess they figure out who's the toughest. It don't never stop, you know. Kids don't get in trouble by themselves. It mostly happens in a crowd. Like one being encouraged by the other. Just to be top, like, you know, "you're a punk if you don't do that." Just little old names that they use to encourage it.

According to Roosevelt, the primary difference between kids who are in trouble and those who are not is the simple absence of money. Explaining the intersection between poverty and strain within the black family, he shared his own thinking about why certain kids were always involved in crime:

The average black dude, he wants to be standing out there, just pitching hisself. Mostly all black dudes I know want that.

But the kids who don't get into trouble are the ones with

. . . money. They have better clothes. It's a family matter. You know, like they ain't got no brothers and sisters, so they can ask for telephones and clothes and stuff. For them, it [the money] just goes further, you know; it's just two people when they ask for clothes. There may be five or six brothers and sisters in another family, and there be two in this other family, and they got to take it from the others. Two parents, you know, for two kids, but one parent trying to supply for five needs [makes things difficult].

Perceiving the advantages accrued to a small family with two working parents, he explained:

The father, he lets them drive and takes them places, and give them money. If a lady is trying to supply for five boys, she's having a hard time. It's just that she can't. The other kids complain if one gets something better. Two parents, they both be working and he's got a good job. The kid [in the bad situation], the dude just starts running with the crowd. He starts helping the mother, trying to take pressure off her. They get out there and try to make a fast dollar. You know, when kids ask mother for something, she can't give it to them because there's too many kids.

But many kids think that theft will help the family. Within some situations, theft is interpreted as the child's contribution to family welfare:

The average kid sees his mother struggling and [trying to] provide needs for him. He kind of thinks he's helping if he just leaves and goes about his business, stealing and stuff. He thinks he's helping but he ain't doing nothing but hurting 'cause she's got to worry about him, about him stealing to take pressure from her. The brother does it, and his brother is liable to see him, and he goes out to do the same thing. In the other house, you know, they got three bedrooms, just living the average life. The other kids have two or three in one room and he get tired and says, "I'm going out on my own." And he starts selling drugs, you know.

When asked to explain why kids in Rosedale steal from the old whites, he candidly observed that racial and class antagonism played a part in the street crimes with which he was so familiar:

The blacks figure, you know, that the world owes them something. They just take what they want. You know, the whites, they have a history and a background. They have their banks, and their doctors and lawyers and stuff, you know. Blacks come over to Rosedale and figure if they [the whites] done that, I'll just break into their house, and try to rule and take over. They figure that the whites that are there [in Rosedale] have something better that they want. But they don't know that the people who stayed in Rosedale are all older. They be of the same class. There ain't no color out there. They [the teenagers] didn't know that, but there ain't no color in Rosedale. Just everybody struggling, trying to do good. But most black people think that white people got more in their house. They try to see what they can take. But they ain't realizing that they be struggling just like they be doing.

Violence dominated the family and neighborhood environment of Johnny Lee Brown, considered by most to be the leader of the gang. He and his two brothers compiled a history of violent and aggressive confrontation with neighbors, peers, and teachers. His mother has had numerous confrontations with the police, school officials, and various other representatives of established institutions. She has a reputation of reaching quick conclusions about the racial motives of white school officials, police officers, juvenile case workers, and social welfare administrators. Police officers dispatched to investigate frequent complaints of neighborhood violence have been called "honky," "racist," and "white mother fuckers" by Johnny's mother, or accused of treating her children poorly because they are "black." She does not hesitate to call whites "prejudiced" or "white bigot." It is apparent from police reports and interviews with social workers and neighbors that the mother of Johnny Lee harbors intensely negative feelings toward whites. While antiwhite sentiments and suspicions exist in some degree among many blacks, it is reasonable to surmise that high levels of racial animosity exhibited by Johnny Lee's mother probably encouraged and nurtured intensely negative and hostile feelings toward whites among her children. Sustained exposure to poverty and to their mother's attitudes towards whites, especially whites in positions of authority or who exercised some institutional influence over their lives, undoubtedly legitimized hostile feelings in the minds of her children toward the white world.

At the time of his arrest, Johnny Lee Brown was sixteen years old. His socioeconomic profile and family background was similar to those of other members of the group involved in the summer murders of 1982. There are seven members of his family including his mother. His father is absent from the home. He has two brothers and three sisters, his older siblings being the product of an earlier union. He seldom has contact, and has not established any lasting relationship, with either his biological father or the man who fathered his stepsiblings. His mother worked for a while at a Volkswagen supply plant, but got laid off. She was employed as a clerk at Burger King at the time of his arrest. Her employment record reflects that of a woman who tried the best she could to earn a living through whatever opportunities might be available.

Johnny Lee never held a steady job and seldom worked part time. He attended a neighborhood school until moving to Rosedale. He grew up in another part of the city and moved to Rosedale during his sixth year of school. During the first two years of high school, he was bused to another part of the city. He seldom attended classes in high school, and was constantly in trouble with teachers and administrators.

He told me:

> When we get together, before we come to school, we get full of that drink and smoking them weeds. When we get to school, we don't do nothing. They like to show off. They like to mellow people and mellow the teachers and things. Like say something smart to the teachers and everybody will laugh at that teacher. And they send you to the office. Kids are always beating teachers at Rosedale too. They get together and they outdo the other. I know that if I was at Rosedale, I'd get in trouble.

He was not involved in any school activities, although he briefly developed an interest in track during the seventh and eighth grade. He said he liked track and wanted to be a runner. He could beat people and it made him feel good to run fast and win. He wanted to be a car mechanic and have a family. He had a girl friend at the time of his arrest. She was also sixteen. Johnny Lee told me, "She's gonna' have a baby in June; I talk to her every time I get out of my cell."

Extensively involved in theft, burglary, and street crime, he developed an official record in juvenile detention centers and in formal police reports. He was known by social workers, teachers, and juvenile detention officers as an extremely violent and fearless kid. A police officer told me: "The kid will fight anything." During interview sessions in the county jail, I was warned by guards to be extremely careful. Both black and white guards said they can "see it in his eyes." They claimed to possess an ability to recognize certain traits associated with pathologically violent inmates. He was confined to special facilities because of his violent nature, and was always given special treatment by juvenile case workers for fear that he might attack other adolescents. In the county jail, he was also isolated because other inmates often attack or violently molest those accused of assaulting children and the elderly.

Despite a reputation for extreme violence, Johnny Lee was not an imposing or intimidating figure. Only about five-feet, five-inches tall, his small but muscular physique was somewhat inconsistent with his widespread reputation as a violent criminal. His face and arms, however, revealed clues about the anger lurking behind the improbable exterior. His face was chipped and knotted with small scars sustained from street fights. His knuckles, hands, and arms were etched with white and pink lines where the healing process could not conceal prior confrontations. Despite a diminutive stature, his face radiated anger. A scowl was permanently embossed on his forehead, and his nostrils flared when he spoke.

His involvement in and knowledge about street crime in Rosedale was extensive. Like his associates, he said that car theft garnered only about twenty dollars for each vehicle. To avoid "getting busted," he only sold the keys to stolen automobiles. The car key would be purchased and the buyer told where the stolen vehicle was located. Stolen televisions could be sold to a pawn shop for about forty dollars, or to someone in the neighborhood for about the same price. Stereos, radios, guns, and rings were also easy to turn over in Rosedale. Drugs were easy to sell, but it was difficult to enter the substance market. Drugs were too expensive for most kids to buy in volume; consequently, it was not possible to make much money selling them. Individual "joints" could be purchased for one or two dollars, and "pills" cost about four or five dollars.

All of those arrested and convicted of the Rosedale summer murders viewed Johnny Lee as a tough kid. He was admired by other members of the gang, and most spoke reverently about his violent exploits and praised his reputation as someone "you don't mess with." When about thirteen years old, he bashed another kid's face to a pulp with a brick and fists, and threw him out of a second-story window of a neighbor's house:

> So, I pick up a brick, and he goes off in the house. And I say, "Hey man, tough man, get you out of that house." His friends say to me,

"Get out of that house." And I say, "I'm going in there to get him." So, the dude that stayed there, he go around to the back of the house and I follow him. And my friends, they stay around front. I go to the back and go in. I see him running and I go upstairs and I catch him. I still have the brick in my hand and I beat him up with the brick [crushed the kid's face]. I'm beating him with my brick, then he ran and dived out the second story window. He landed on the roof, right through the glass. So, they told him, "Don't mess with him if he's gonna mess with you like this." We don't have no trouble no more.

The police came and took pictures and interrogated those involved in the brick fight. Johnny Lee said that every time he passed the kid's house the boy's father would come out with a shotgun and say not to mess with his son.

Similar incidents were laced throughout his childhood and adolescent years, but the story of the second-story brick fight established the reputation of Johnny Lee in both police records and within the adolescent street culture of Rosedale. Other confrontations, however, were equally important in securing his family's reputation as aggressive and violent. A black woman who had lived across the street from his household said that she was forced to move after neighborhood violence, primarily initiated by Johnny and his brothers, became intolerable.

Another neighbor, a twenty-five-year-old white woman, Mrs. Sutton, lived two houses down from Johnny Lee. A working-class family that moved to Rosedale in response to the drop in housing prices, the Suttons lived in the area for five months before leaving. Mrs. Sutton said that she carried a shotgun around the house for fear that she and her five-year-old son would be attacked when her husband was at work. She claimed that she and her husband worked in shifts to maintain a twenty-four-hour vigil over their life and property. They kept written logs documenting the violence and rowdy activity initiated by Johnny Lee, and eventually turned them over to police detectives in the hope of spurring arrests.

City police actually filed reports on two assaults during July and August of 1982 in which Johnny Lee and his brothers were suspects. In a July 30 confrontation, Johnny Lee's mother called the police and reported that a man had fought with her boys and threw a brick through her window. Police records reveal that about forty minutes after the call, police were dispatched to the Sutton home to discover that James Sutton and a friend, Michael Jeter, were beaten by youths armed with sticks and pipes. Sutton told police that a band of teenagers had ringed his car and beat him and his friend with iron pipes and two-by-fours. A confrontation ensued between Johnny Lee's mother and the police, as she verbally directed racial abuse at the police and victims. No arrests were made.

About three weeks later, another incident occurred between the Suttons and Johnny Lee's mother. Mrs. Sutton was beaten by three teenagers who allegedly harassed her while she played with a puppy in her yard. Police records indicate that when she crossed the street to tell the boys to stop throwing rocks at her dog, she was attacked and beaten. One of the boys was charged with delinquent conduct in the attack. Johnny Lee and his stepbrother were listed as accomplices in the assault, but not arrested and formally charged.

Wilding Gang Violence: A Theoretical Synthesis

It is difficult to derive generalizations from case studies. Events and personalities may be unique. The social milieu in which the cases are found may not represent the circumstances most frequently present when comparable events occur. With these caveats fully acknowledged, I am nonetheless inclined to draw several conclusions from the Rosedale case study. These tentative conclusions can at least serve as informed hypotheses for the reader, shaping further research about wilding behavior.

First, wilding groups are a type of violent gang. While not as organized as the "near group" or the prototypical violent gang examined by Yablonsky, wilding behavior is collective and partially planned. Unlike the gangs studied by Yablonsky, however, the sole purpose of wilding is not always violence. He maintains that ". . . the violent gang is primarily organized for emotional gratification, and violence is the theme around which all activities center."[12] The Rosedale case clearly shows that violence is typically combined with theft and other forms of criminal enterprise. At the same time, violence plays a central role in creating group cohesion, and appears to provide a source of interpersonal bonding and emotional gratification. The violence appears less spontaneous than that portrayed in journalistic accounts of wilding. In some cases, wilding violence is preconceived, anticipated, and deliberate.

Second, and consistent with Yablonsky's findings, violent behavior is collective and its direction is prompted by dares and challenges within the wilding group. He argues that: "The group pattern of violent expression appears to be a more acceptable and legitimate form for acting out pathology than is individual violent behavior."[13] In all of the wilding episodes in Rosedale, the beatings and murders were administered by a group. Typically, the leader initiated the first blow, and established the tone of the attacks. Violence escalated as each member of the group competed with the other to raise the level of violence to a more vicious and brutal plateau.

One member of the gang described to me the escalation accompanying the murder of Ethel Marlow. After being pulled from her bathtub, slaps in the face led to dragging her from room to room to identify where money or other valuables were hidden. She was then pushed to the floor, and kicked and stomped in the head. The violence then escalated to multiple stabbings, the insertion of a broom handle down her throat, and further desecration of the unconscious body through spray painting the genitals and other body parts. The wilding participants were high on drugs, the brutality being accompanied by laughter and surrealistic amusement.

The other two murders revealed similar patterns of collective involvement. Clyde Robinson was initially pulled from his car by the gang leader. One participant told me they had encountered the victim in the Kroger store, where they decided to harass him as he shopped. Because of his angry response to them in the store, they followed him outside and jumped in front of his car as he left the lot. The group took his wallet before beating him to death on the sidewalk. The third murder was committed with considerable resistance on the part of the victim. Again, however, the violence was collective, brutal, and moved through various stages of competitive escalation. After murdering the husband, the group beat the elderly wife who was confined to a wheelchair.

Third, wilding participants are not typically members of established or more highly organized gangs. Wilding groups appear to be comprised of marginal and pathological individuals who operate on the fringes of social groups and other adolescent subcultures. At the time of the wilding episodes in Fort Worth, there was considerable evidence of organized gang activity in both the black and Chicano communities. To the best of my knowledge, however, none of the wilding participants were affiliated with established gangs. Because of the spectacular nature of wilding crimes, the full weight of law enforcement and community pressure is usually directed toward the apprehension of group members. It is not likely, therefore, that wilding groups will evolve into more fully developed violent gangs, or that members will be absorbed into established gang structures.[14] In comparison to other types of gang violence discussed in this volume, wilding is not always compatible with the protection of turf, the maintenance of group honor and reputation, or the monopolization of the drug marketplace.

Fourth, there is often an interracial dimension to wilding violence. The interracial dynamics are partly fueled by the press. Black victimization of whites has always produced intense and hostile reactions on the part of the dominant group and its institutions. At the same time, wilding crimes usually display elements of sadistic and wanton violence that mobilize the collective wrath of all elements of society. Despite the moral outrage and sensational journalism accompanying wilding violence, our case suggests that racial hatred and antagonism are clearly present. We know that racial hatred and extreme prejudice produced flagrant acts of brutality on the part of whites throughout American history. It is surely not surprising to find, therefore, that the pathology of racism generates equally abnormal forms of human cruelty on the part of socially marginal and personally unstable blacks.

Similar to the violence reported in the recent Central Park case, one of the Rosedale wildings confessed that it was "fun" to be loose on the streets. After murdering Ethel Marlow, the wildings split approximately forty dollars and spent the rest of the evening playing video games at a local video store. Consistent with classic forms of racism, the victim's human qualities were obscured by strong interpersonal biases and hostilities. Of special significance in wilding violence are the racial attitudes and behaviors of the group leader. In the Rosedale case, the wilding leader revealed an established history of interracial antagonism and conflict.

Fifth, the wilding leader exerts a strong influence on the behavior of group members. Yablonsky maintains that the leader of a violent gang is pathological and socially marginal:

> Combined with the needs of other disturbed gang members, the result is mob action at a rumble. Such gang-war episodes, provoked by leaders, produce a pattern of hysteria and group contagion characteristic of the leaders' personality. This "disturbed leader" pattern, interaction with other susceptible youths, and an opportune situation provide the active ingredients for a "senseless" violent-gang killing.[15]

The findings of the Rosedale case are partially consistent with Yablonsky's observations. While gang rumbles are clearly not the focus of attention in this chapter, it is apparent that the wilding leader played a pivotal role in all three murders. I am not arguing that Johnny Lee Brown was a Charles Manson type of figure. Wilding violence is different from the ritual killings occurring in this latter case, and is distinct from the intergang violence studied by Yablonsky. Wilding episodes are not part of cult activities and have no religious or satanic dimensions. At the same time, they do appear to be strongly influenced by a pathological leader whose reputation for violence has been idealized by members of the group. As explained by Yablonsky,

> Cast in his violent role, he is a shining example for core gang followers. The leader, in their view, has "heart," and will pull a trigger, swing a bat, or wield a knife without any expression of fear or, most important, regret.[16]

Sixth, drug and alcohol abuse usually accompany wilding violence. During all three murders, and during other break-ins, members of the wilding group were high on marijuana, hashish, or cocaine. They had usually consumed some alcohol as well, typically beer or wine. I could not determine from interviews if the altered state of consciousness facilitated the brutality or enhanced the experience of violence. Heavy drug and alcohol consumption, however, were present during the wilding attacks.

Seventh, economic self-interest is also manifested in wilding attacks. While violence is not always essential to the accomplishment of burglary or street theft, wilding behavior contains elements of simple material gain. Crime against property is a direct response to the cycle of poverty and despair shaping the lives of many young blacks in cities. For numerous minority teenagers in Rosedale, the combined impact of poverty and racial oppression has produced systematic patterns of petty theft, household robbery, and wanton violence. These patterns are nurtured by feelings of racial antagonism toward whites, and sustained by the disintegration of neighborhood institutions. They steal because they want things they cannot afford. They steal in order to supplement the family income, and help provide the simple necessities of family life. In some cases, family norms actually support and encourage criminal behavior.

A public defender with a high minority case load observed that most of the clients he represented committed crimes in response to drugs, alcohol, and simple economic deprivation. Among teenagers and younger clients, the problems were mostly economic in nature. He reported that at Christmas time, it was not unusual for members to steal a tree, decorations, and presents for the entire family. The alternative was no Christmas at all:

> If you can steal a package of baloney, that's one thing Mama won't have to buy. It works real good, you know. One kid steals some baloney; one steals a loaf of bread; one steals some cookies. They all come home that night and have supper together. It's fun. I don't think it's all malicious. A lot of it is fun, but most of it is just plain old economics.

Based upon interviews with social workers and attorneys, the profile of delinquent youth in Rosedale follows a consistent pattern. The family lives in poverty conditions. Parents are employed in bad jobs within marginal industries. Parents tend to be either AFDC recipients, or are receiving some form of state assistance. The father is not educated and does not have the skills needed to secure a stable job. The kids have inadequate clothing and no spending money. They are not equipped for the job market and often drop out of school before graduation. Most of the kids have tried various kinds of drugs, and drink more than other adolescents in their age group. They work odd jobs, mostly of short duration. If they do get part-time jobs in a place like McDonalds or Burger King, they have to travel to the suburbs, and most don't have bus fare. As a result, they lose the job, or fall further behind in school. They are trapped. With no prospects for the future, crime becomes a rational response to the absence of tangible opportunities.

Legitimate opportunities for success and upward social mobility are not present in Rosedale. While the youth of Rosedale covet the material goods and rewards held out to them by the larger society, they do not have access to the traditional means to acquire them.[17] As a result, they find it easier to take what they want. Cloward and Ohlin maintain the breakdown between socially approved goals and the means to obtain them push many lower-class youths to create delinquent subcultures.[18] The alternative values found within these subcultures reinforce delinquent modes of obtaining status, material rewards, and the resources necessary to maintain a deviant lifestyle. Clearly, wilding gangs are aberrant and antisocial adaptations to the cycle of poverty and racism prevalent within urban ghettos like Rosedale.

Eighth, wilding gangs will most likely emerge in low income communities experiencing rapid social change. Consistent with the observations of Cloward and Ohlin and Yablonsky, violent gangs are nurtured in unstable neighborhoods where formal social controls are absent, and traditional codes of behavior are in a state of flux.[19] During periods of rapid social change, community institutions are radically transformed. Not only are traditional social arrangements altered during periods of change, but the individual's relationship to those institutions undergoes significant modification. In unstable communities, the agencies of social control and socialization cease to operate in a smooth and effective manner. Durkheim contended that when the institutions and groups to which people belong become drastically disorganized, they exert less and less influence over individual behavior.[20] In a situation where traditional institutional arrangements are in a state of chaos and chronic breakdown and economic deprivation is present, individuals often recognize no established rules of conduct other than those rooted in immediate self-interest. Durkheim calls such a situation "anomic," or normless.

Some criminologists contend that juvenile delinquency occurs when traditional mechanisms of social control are either weakened or break down altogether. Drawing from his analysis of urban delinquents, Travis Hirschi observed that criminal behavior becomes more probable when the individual's bond to society weakens.[21] He posits that an individual's relationship to a social group is at its lowest point when that person ceases: (1) to care about the opinions and evaluations of the larger collectivity; (2) to invest time and emotional energy in conventional behavior; (3) to become involved in established institutions and practices; and (4) to believe in the legitimacy of community traditions.

Yablonsky maintains that:

One of the circumstances which negatively affects the proper socialization of youth in the disorganized urban condition is the breakdown of old social controls without any adequate replacement for
those forces that would tend to curb deviance.[22]

The process of invasion and succession not only eroded traditional
mechanisms of social control in Rosedale, but also transformed the institutions responsible for bonding the individual to society: schools,
churches, neighborhood, and family. Moreover, newly arriving immigrants to the city typically bring with them values and behavioral patterns that are inconsistent with established practices and expectations.
Yablonsky contends that children, more so than adults, often experience
the most intense forms of conflict over appropriate forms of behavior in
rapidly changing situations: "Conflicts may arise between the different
norms supported by parents, the school, and those operative in the neighborhood."[23]

During the course of neighborhood transition, Rosedale's traditional
institutions were demolished. In the face of accelerated community
change, it is not realistic to assume that stable black institutions can be
created rapidly enough to replace those in the process of decline and
decay. The ghettoization of Rosedale occurred too quickly to be mediated
by liberal social policies, civil rights legislation, or by local initiatives to
build community institutions. Levels of socioeconomic status dropped too
fast to convince merchants to stay in the area, or to compel financial establishments to continue the extension of credit to residents. Churches were
abandoned too soon to ask ministers to consider an integrated congregation. The black middle class passed through Rosedale too hastily to make
any lasting contributions to sustain or modify existing institutions. White
flight and block busting drove real estate prices to bargain-basement levels
too precipitously for rational investors to continue buying in Rosedale.
The numerical base of the area's black population expanded too swiftly for
the police and city government to keep up with demands for amplified services. The racial transition of Rosedale was poorly managed by public
officials, community leaders, and citizens.

The cultural and socioeconomic differences between Rosedale's new
and older residents made it very difficult to develop any sense of collective
identification with community traditions. Bonds of neighboring within
the newly emerging black community searched for new form and structure. New black merchants scrambled to secure a stable market. New black
preachers competed for parishioners and set their sights on acquiring
abandoned white churches. The ties between parents and neighborhood
schools lay dormant, shattered in the wake of court-ordered busing. The

relationship of merchant to community, teacher to parent, and family to neighbor weakened. The linkage of clergy to congregation, police to community, and neighbor to neighbor was split and fragmented. The moral bond nurturing a sense of community in Rosedale vanished in the path of racial transition and white flight.

These tentative conclusions suggest a complex system of social forces giving rise to wilding violence. While all appear to play an important role in the emergence of wildings, the research findings do not clarify what factors are most important in the production of this serious social problem. Many black youngsters encounter comparable levels of economic deprivation, discrimination, and chronic exposure to family and community breakdown. Yet, they do not exhibit the pathological behaviors characteristic of wilding gangs. Clearly, psychological as well as social factors are operative in the creation of wilding gang behavior.

Further, the case histories provide incomplete information about the magnitude and frequency of wilding violence. While some cases have received widespread national publicity, others have remained matters of local concern. Whatever limitations are present in the Rosedale case study, however, it is clear that we need more research on wilding violence in order to formulate public policies capable of alleviating the problem. It is in the spirit of this latter objective that our generalizations about wildings are offered to the social science community.

NOTES

1. Elijah Anderson, *Streetwise: Race, Class, and Change in an Urban Community* (Chicago: University of Chicago Press, 1991); Gerald Suttles, *The Social Order of the Slum* (Chicago: University of Chicago Press, 1968).

2. Carl S. Taylor, *Dangerous Society* (East Lansing: Michigan State University Press, 1990); Ralph Weisheit, ed., *Drugs, Crime and the Criminal Justice System* (Cincinnati: Anderson Publishing Co., 1990).

3. See Joan Moore, "Gangs, Drugs, and Violence," chapter 2 this volume.

4. Susan Baker and Tipper Gore, "Some Reasons for Wilding," *Newsweek*, May 29, 1989, pp. 6-7; James S. Kunen, "Madness in the Heart of the City," *People*, May 22, 1989, pp. 107-111; David Gelman and others, "The Mind of the Rapist," *Newsweek*, July 23, 1990, pp. 46-52; George Will, "America's Slide into the Sewers," *Newsweek*, July 30, 1990, p. 64.

5. Richard Cloward and Lloyd Ohlin, *Delinquency and Opportunity: A Theory of Delinquent Gangs* (New York: The Free Press, 1960); Lewis Yablonsky, *The Violent Gang* (Baltimore: Penguin Books, 1967).

6. Yablonsky, ibid.

7. Cloward and Ohlin, *Delinquency and Opportunity*.

8. David Gelman and others, "Mind of the Rapist"; Robert O'Brien, "The Interracial Nature of Violent Crimes: A Reexamination," *American Journal of Sociology* 92 (January 1987): 817-35.

9. Lillian Rubin, *Quiet Rage* (Berkeley: University of California Press, 1986).

10. John Hagedorn and Perry Macon, *People and Folks* (Chicago: Lake View Press, 1988).

11. Elliot Liebow, *Tally's Corner* (Boston: Little, Brown, 1967).

12. Yablonsky, *Violent Gang*, p. 146.

13. Ibid., p. 150.

14. Hagedorn, *People and Folks*, notes that some gangs in Milwaukee evolved from relatively small social groupings. Wilding groups do not seem to have the potential to develop into larger, more established gangs.

15. Yablonsky, *Violent Gang*, p. 215.

16. Ibid., p. 214.

17. Robert Merton, *Social Theory and Social Structure* (New York: The Free Press, 1968).

18. Cloward and Ohlin, *Delinquency and Opportunity*.

19. Ibid.; Yablonsky, *Violent Gang*.

20. Emil Durkheim, *The Division of Labor in Society* (New York: The Free Press of Glencoe, 1933).

21. Travis Hirschi, *Causes of Delinquency* (Berkeley: University of California Press, 1969).

22. Yablonsky, *Violent Gang*, p. 169.

23. Ibid.

4

"Down With the Program": Racial Attitudes and Group Violence Among Youth in Bensonhurst and Gravesend

HOWARD PINDERHUGHES

INTRODUCTION

A young African American male is walking through a white neighborhood, some might say he's in the "wrong part of town" when he's attacked by a group of white kids from the neighborhood. The kids, all male and between the ages of fifteen and twenty-one, are not members of an organized group; it is just a gathering of neighborhood teens who regularly hang out together getting high and partying. The youth were pretty high and drunk when they heard that an African American man was walking through their neighborhood. Somebody in the group vociferously suggested that the group "take care" of the intruder. The weapons of choice are baseball bats or heavy sticks which have been brought in anticipation of the night's activities. The group found the African American man easily and attacked him with the bats and sticks, while yelling racial epithets and warning him to stay out of their neighborhood.

The scenario fits many bias-related crimes—certainly the most vicious and infamous cases. It describes the murder of Michael Griffith whose car broke down in a white neighborhood in New York City. On December 20, 1986, a group of over twenty white youths attacked Griffith and two other African American men in the Howard Beach section of Queens. In the wake of Griffith's death, the eyes of the entire nation became focused on race relations in New York City. The incident shocked New York and the rest of the country. Racial murders were supposed to be a thing of the past—from the dark days of segregation in the South, perpetrated by small-town whites in anonymous sheets. Yet this happened in the North, in the nation's largest city—in the lap of liberalism.

The scenario also characterizes the racially motivated murder of Yusuf Hawkins which took place in Bensonhurst, Brooklyn, one of the neighborhoods which this chapter examines. On August 23, 1989, Hawkins and two companions were in Bensonhurst to look at a used car when they were attacked by a mob of over twenty white youth. In the trial of the young white youths involved in the mob which attacked Hawkins and his two companions, the incident was presented in the courtroom and through the media as a tragic one-night occurrence which happened almost accidentally; the result of a confluence of factors which included Hawkins and his companions being "in the wrong place at the wrong time"—walking down a street in Bensonhurst where the mob of young whites mistook them for another group of African Americans whom they thought were coming into their neighborhood to cause trouble. Deeper reasons for why the tragic incident happened were never analyzed.[1]

The Howard Beach incident was only one of 235 racially motivated crimes investigated by the New York City Human Rights Commission in 1986.[2] In 1987, the number of racially motivated crimes shot up to 463, and it reached 550 in 1988. Both victims and assailants came from many different backgrounds. The one common feature of the assailants was their age. Over 70 percent of those arrested for perpetrating bias crimes in 1987 and 1988 were under the age of twenty. Attacks occurred in many different neighborhoods and in all five boroughs of the city.

One distinguishing characteristic of bias-motivated crimes committed in the last five years, as contrasted with the three previous years, is the identity of the victim and the types of attacks. In 1982, 50 percent of the confirmed bias-motivated crimes were characterized as anti-Semitic and the vast majority of these crimes were directed against property. This trend continued until 1985, when African Americans became the number one target of bias-related crimes and the percentage of physical assaults increased significantly. Of the 463 reported bias-motivated attacks in 1987, 173 victims were black, 108 were Jewish, 105 were white, 30 were Latinos, and 24 were homosexuals. The present pattern reveals a rise in physical bias-related attacks, with people of color and gays and lesbians as the primary targets of these attacks.

The rise in the number of bias-related incidents indicates an ominous trend—a trend that reverses the gradual liberalization of American ethnic and racial attitudes and indicates rising levels of intolerance among youth. There is virtual consensus among social scientists doing research on intergenerational differences in racial attitudes that there has been a steady and gradual increase in the level of tolerance of each successive generation since the 1940s. Scholars who have studied racial attitudes in the last thirty years have reported a strong and steady change in white American attitudes toward the principle of racial equality.[3] The positive trends in attitudes of whites toward African Americans has largely been the result of intergenerational differences rather than individual attitude change.[4] In contrast, the rise in hate violence has been primarily initiated by young people under the age of twenty-one.

This chapter is part of a larger study of ethnic and racial attitudes among youth and the rise in racial conflict in New York City. In that study, the attitudes of youth from thirty-seven different neighborhoods were examined. The sample included youth, between the ages of fourteen and twenty-one, who reside in New York City. The young people surveyed and interviewed come from a wide range of ethnic and racial backgrounds, with large numbers of Italians, African Americans, Puerto Ricans, Jews, Albanians, and Irish.

The focus of this chapter is on youth from two predominantly white neighborhoods in Brooklyn—Gravesend and Bensonhurst. It summarizes an analysis of data from focus group interviews held in these neighborhoods with white youth who are residents of Gravesend and Bensonhurst. Field work in both neighborhoods revealed a consistent pattern of racially motivated violence. This chapter examines the relationship between socioeconomic factors, the role of peer group participation and identity formation, and the ethnic and racial attitudes of youth from Bensonhurst and Gravesend by examining the factors which combine to produce three outcomes: (a) a climate conducive to racially motivated violence, (b) the attitudes necessary to perpetrate this violence, (c) the mechanisms which facilitate the perpetration of this violence.

THE COMMUNITIES

Bensonhurst and Gravesend are adjacent communities in southern Brooklyn. Both neighborhoods are part of a strip of white ethnic neighborhoods, primarily working class, predominantly Italian American and Jewish, which stretch across the southern section of Brooklyn. The communities are composed of residents who used to live in central Brooklyn and Queens. Many of these families moved out of their previous neighborhoods thirty or forty years ago when African Americans, Puerto Ricans, Asians, and West Indians began to move in. This historical experience affected the attitudes and sentiments of the white residents towards these groups. All minority groups, but African Americans and Puerto Ricans particularly, became perceived as a direct threat to the quality of neighborhood life; as intruders who had the potential to ruin the stable, close-knit, safe, ethnic niche the white community had taken years to establish.

These attitudes are well documented by Jonathan Rieder in his book *Canarsie: The Jews and Italians of Brooklyn Against Liberalism*, which focuses on a community with a similar history and demographic composition to Gravesend and Bensonhurst.[5] Rieder found that Italian and Jewish residents in Canarsie viewed maintenance of the ethnic and racial composition of their neighborhood as the most important factor for community harmony. Canarsie residents viewed African Americans and Puerto Ricans with mistrust, fear, and loathing, and as the harbingers of neighborhood deterioration, crime, decay, and chaos.

THE YOUTH

The young people interviewed in Bensonhurst and Gravesend are products of a legacy of racial tension and neighborhood defense. They have grown up in close-knit, exclusively white communities which distrust strangers and fear African Americans. This distrust is heightened by years of accumulated negative perceptions and stereotypes of outsiders, particularly African Americans and Puerto Ricans. As importantly, many of these youth are outcasts in their own community. These are the youngsters who are viewed as hoodlums by most of community residents; many are alienated from their families.[6]

White youth interviewed in Gravesend and Bensonhurst were surprisingly open in describing their attitudes about racial tension in New York City. All of the young people had strong opinions about race relations, particularly the young men. All agreed that race relations among young people in New York City were extremely poor. They explained racial tensions were the result of six factors: (1) deteriorating economic conditions, (2) blacks starting trouble, (3) a media which favored blacks, (4) racial prejudice, (5) black political and economic power in the city, and (6) the actions of Al Sharpton.[7] The most significant finding of the study is that youth in Bensonhurst and Gravesend felt that they were victims of favoritism toward blacks, reverse discrimination, double standards, and increasing black power in New York City.

Their sense of victimization was heightened by their fear that blacks were taking over the city." The election of an African American mayor in 1989 was viewed as strengthening the political and economic power of blacks in New York City. These youth saw the mayor as working only to help black people. They felt that the city government was being run by black people, for black people. The mayor's victory fueled pre-existing prejudices and fears that blacks were gaining control of New York City; a fact which would make it more difficult for working-class whites to maintain the ethnic composition of their neighborhoods and their job security.

My father told me that (as a result of the new black Mayor) they are going to fire all the white construction workers in the city and hire all black guys.

Dinkins, he's all for the blacks, 100 percent. Not like Ed Koch who used to care about people in white neighborhoods.

Koch, he was for everybody. He went out into the neighborhoods and talked to people one on one.

When Dinkins was elected I wanted to move out of the city.

The black people will get more attention than they already receive—they get power.

That' right, the black people really think they got it now.

The young men and women who live in these communities are primarily from working-class families. Many face uncertain futures. In the last fifteen to twenty years, industrial jobs, which were traditionally available for white youth from these communities, have been disappearing from the city's economy at an alarming rate. Between 1969 and 1981, New York City lost 650,000 jobs, most of them in the manufacturing sector.[8] As a result, after a decade of expansion in the sixties, employment decreased steadily from 1970 to 1980. Although the actual number of workers increased from 1978 to 1984, the increase was almost exclusively in the service sector where many of the employees are female. The highest percentage increase in new jobs was in business and related professional services. Jobs in business, professional social and religious services, education, media, and health care accounted for 76 percent of the total increase. While some of these were clerical, janitorial, and support jobs, the prospects for employment for working-class youth, particularly males, were definitely constricted.

Competition for employment in the city has been accompanied by an increase in the drop-out rate for youth in New York City from 13.5 percent in 1983 to 25 percent in 1987. Although the situation is considerably worse for African American and Puerto Rican youth, with official drop-out rates of 24.3 and 31.3 percent respectively, the drop-out rate also increased for Italian American students.[9] Italian Americans are now the third most likely group to drop out of high school. In addition, the percentage of white students in the New York City public schools has steadily decreased from 62.7 percent in 1960 to 23.7 percent in 1980.[10] Whereas whites were the majority in 1960 and remained the single largest group in 1970, they are now a distinct minority in the city's public schools.

White youth from Bensonhurst and Gravesend consistently referred to economic constraints and economic problems as the primary reasons for racial problems in the city. Although they lacked a developed analysis or ideology, these teens felt and thought that they are in unfair competition with other groups, particularly blacks whom they saw as benefiting from "special" treatment. Many of the ideas and feelings expressed by white youth, and their resultant sense of victimization, were based on three primary perceptions: (1) that blacks are taking jobs away from whites; (2) that blacks are responsible for crime in the city; and (3) that blacks are not sufficiently punished for their criminal activity. These themes came up over and over again in discussions with white youth.

> The situation is more racial because the economy has changed. By sticking together they [blacks] get a job before a white person because they have to hire so many minorities. This frustrates white people. White people don't get together.

> The situation is much worse for white people than it used to be. There is more competition. They are going to give blacks more jobs because people will be afraid of calling it racial.

> Companies have to give certain jobs to blacks even though they don't qualify as much as the whites, and I don't think that's fair.

> Why is it that Black people think we owe them something?

> How come when somebody white gets shot, we don't make a big deal about it?
> We don't do nothing, we all sit on our asses.
> We should be fighting for our rights.
> That's right, fight back.
> Instead of fighting among ourselves, we need to get together and fight back.

These youths consistently referred to the media as presenting a distorted view of white youth and white ethnic communities. They felt that the media unfairly portrayed young whites and did not tell the truth about young black males. They had a strong perception that the media only showed the bad things that happened in their (white) neighborhoods and reported on events which were not racially motivated as if they were. They stated that there should be more equal media coverage.

The media is more worried about what white people are doing to blacks than what black people are doing to whites.

If a white person attacks a black person, they throw the book at him. Meanwhile black kids are getting away with murder and nobody says anything about it, not the media, not the police, nobody.

There's a double standard in the media. If a black kid gets jumped by a bunch of white kids, they say it's racial. Friends of mine get jumped by black kids all the time and nothing ever happens.

The media is pushing the black people's case and it's pissing off white people.

Many of the youth felt that the media contributed to racial tensions by sensationalizing racial incidents—by exaggerating reports of racial violence in the city, the media made young people feel like they had to defend themselves against other groups. The youth's perception of the media's treatment of them and their communities reinforced their perception of themselves as victims of a system which favors blacks.

The media makes a little issue into a big racial shit.
It's the media that does it all.
Yea, it's the media that puts everything in our head that makes us want to be bad.
That's right, they hype it all up.

When something happens to a black guy, its like wham—everything's all hyped up. They don't put nothing about like when old white people get jumped in these neighborhoods.
Or like in Central Park. If that was a black girl who got raped, forget it, they would have castrated those kids.

In particular, Al Sharpton was seen as an instigator of racial tensions. These youth believed that Sharpton fueled racial hysteria about incidents that were not racially motivated. In every interview session with youth from Bensonhurst and Gravesend at least one youth stated that Sharpton needed to be killed.[11] The youth also felt that black people saw everything as racial. African Americans who marched through Bensonhurst to protest Hawkins's murder were criticized for disrupting their community.

The problem in Bensonhurst is the blacks marching down 20th Avenue.

Sharpton is the problem. If he'd tell his people to forget about it, everything would be okay.

He's an instigator, he should be shot.

Sharpton started all the problems. You don't see him marching in Bensonhurst without a million police.
I'd like to see him walk there by himself.
I can't wait til watermelon season starts.

Many of the young people focused on stories and accounts of crimes committed by blacks and saw these as the source of the racial tension in the city. There was widespread feeling among the youth that blacks were violent troublemakers who were especially dangerous and bold in large groups. They agreed that blacks who ventured into their neighborhoods were looking for trouble. These youths were sure that there could be no other reason for blacks to come into the neighborhoods. Consequently, these white youth felt they had the right to defend their territory against blacks; that it was up to them to "stop the blacks"; and that if they attacked these outsiders, they'd be sending a message to blacks outside the neighborhood to stay out.

Blacks just keep stealing everybody's sneakers. They will kill you for your sneakers. They start a lot of trouble. If they want trouble, they're going to get trouble.

A group of black kids come into your neighborhood—they are looking for trouble. Why else are they there?

The police know the blacks don't belong in our neighborhoods—everybody knows if they are here they must be looking for trouble.

What is a 16 year old kid without a driver's license [Yusuf Hawkins] doing walking into an all white neighborhood at 9:30 at night looking for a used car? He was out looking for trouble and he found it. Those guys did what they had to do.

If they are stupid enough to walk, one person, at night—they're not looking for a fight but they are stupid and crazy.

THE ROLE OF THE PEER GROUP

Negative attitudes toward blacks serve as "merit badges" for these white youth on the street, and, as the kids say, provide "proof positive that they are down with the program." The relationship of prejudice to individual and group identity is strong. These young whites are in a difficult economic situation. They are aware that they are viewed as hoodlums by the entire community. The only place where they receive positive reinforcement is on the street with their neighborhood crew. The result is that these youth are constantly trying to prove themselves worthy to their peers. In the context of the street, the proof lies in their ability to express the collective ideology and willingness to back up those ideas with brute force ranging from harassment to mayhem, sometimes tragically crossing the line to murder. That was the function and purpose of "going on missions."

All of the youth interviewed talked openly and excitedly about going on "missions." The entire ambience of the interview would change when they began to describe going on missions (a late night search to find individuals who did not belong in the neighborhood). The youth seemed to get a sense of self-worth and individual power, which was otherwise lacking in their lives, from going on "missions." Their sense of group cohesion and group solidarity was heightened if the victim was from another racial or ethnic group, high on the list of desirable targets. Their feeling of powerlessness because of their economic position and prospects and their social position in their community contributed to the visceral nature of the attitudes they had toward other races and ethnicities. They felt economically powerless and expressed frustrations that their community was politically powerless.

Oddly enough, youth in Bensonhurst and Gravesend steadfastly proclaimed that there was nothing "racial" about their actions. According to them, the media were responsible for making things "look" racial. They claimed that they were simply defending their neighborhood—that they would attack whites as well. They claimed that their main object was to take care of outsiders. However, their perceptions were belied by their own description of their nightly activities, which included regular searches for targets of racially motivated attacks.

The youth insisted that these missions were not racially motivated—that they went after whites as well as blacks, as long as they were from outside the neighborhood. However, during the course of the interviews, the youth described a hierarchy of groups that were desirable targets. Blacks were the primary target. If they could not find a black person, then a Dominican, a Pakistani, or an Indian would do. The list varied in its order of preference except for the position of blacks, who were always at the top of the list. The youth would attack other whites as well, but only if they were from a rival neighborhood that had started trouble in their neighborhood.

> If we fight against Bay Parkway, that's because we don't like each other. When we fight the blacks, it's because we don't like their color. All of Bensonhurst unites against them.

> You hang out and drink something or smoke something and you begin to feel hyped and you go looking for somebody. The best

is if you can find some blacks to fuck up. If you can't find blacks, then Pakistanis or Indians will do. If you can't find a Pakistani, then you look for a Puerto Rican.

Blacks, Pakistanis, everybody gets a little bit, racial slurs—like that. And if you're really hyped, you fuck them up good. Especially Dominicans.

The problem is mostly with blacks. There is not as much problem between whites and Asians or whites and Hispanics.
We don't have no problem with Asians.

Every weekend, me and him and a group of others would go out and get racial with—against Mexicans.
It wasn't really racial . . .
Oh, yea, we were racial. Alright, would you call this racial. Every Mexican we see, no matter what they were doing, if they weren't doing nothing, we'd still beat 'em up.

Alcohol is an important part of the street activity of these youth. Most youth agreed that alcohol and drugs were major reasons for racial violence and conflict. The drugs most often used were marijuana and cocaine. Though many youth admitted that they used drugs, they maintained that alcohol was the biggest contributor to the violence. The youth saw alcohol as helping them get primed for an evening of mayhem. They stated that it was alcohol which helped to make them feel strong and violent. They said it not only lowered inhibitions toward actions which they might not commit while sober, it also increased their bravado, their confidence, and their level of excitement.

Alcohol makes you violent—it makes you go on missions. After drinking a couple of 40's, all of a sudden you feel invincible.

You get a few in you, you smoke, do what you got to do—you start to feel hyped.
You start to feel nice and bold, like superman, like you can do anything.

When you get drunk you are a different person. Your attitudes changes, you get more courage, you don't feel nothing.

It [alcohol] makes you feel nuts. You walk around—you see a few blacks or somebody who don't belong around and boom, you start throwin' on them. You walk away, now you're really feeling nice. Your blood is pumpin' because you know you took care of business, did what you had to do.

You get drunk and go up to someone you don't like and beat the shit out of him. Someone of a different race, like an Indian guy.

The youth claimed they were fighting for "unity in their community." They translated their delinquent behavior into a defense of their neighborhood. The language used by the youth reflects their attitude that they have a responsibility and a duty to protect their neighborhood, defend their turf, and keep undesirable outsiders out of the neighborhood. Numerous statements by the youth that they "did what they had to do" confirmed their beliefs.

I did what I had to do. I have a reputation as a tough guy who defends the neighborhood and I want to keep it. People know when you've taken care of people who don't belong in the neighborhood. You get respect. Especially if it is some of the blacks from Marlboro projects.

When you're hanging out with your partners and you see somebody who don't belong on your block, like a black guy or a Dominican, and you do him [beat him up], you feel real together. Everybody's together doing what we have to do.

Everybody in the neighborhood knows what the deal is. The police don't care about it unless somebody gets killed. Everybody else figures we're just doing them a favor. As long as we don't bother neighborhood folks, it's no problem.

CONCLUSION

The Friday and Saturday night scenarios which these youth described were always similar. A group of neighborhood youth, mostly male, congregate at a regular hang-out spot. The composition of the group is very fluid. The groups do not have official names like many of the "posses," "crews," and gangs that exist throughout New York City. They are not organized gangs in the traditional sense. There is no official membership, no specific initiation rites, no street names, and no official leaders. These youth get together because they live in the same neighborhood. The participants on any particular night vary.

The missions they describe have three distinct purposes: (1) To give the youth a sense of power. Very simply, they aim to beat somebody up. Well primed with alcohol and drugs, they are itching to feel the elation of the power, control, and status they receive from administering a beating to a neighborhood intruder. (2) To defend their turf. The youth attack individuals or groups of persons whom they believe do not belong in the neighborhood. In this way they feel positive about their actions, justifying them as helpful to the community. (3) To prove themselves worthy in the eyes of their peers by demonstrating their toughness and hatred of certain groups.

Their activities are different from group muggings or wilding attacks, which have a more random nature. The youth stated clearly that they did not attack members of their community while on these missions. They are not involved in indiscriminate sprees of violence against the most vulnerable targets. Rather, they choose specific targets based on a well-established fear and hatred within their community of certain groups.

What emerges is a picture of the relationship, for these young people, between their individual identity, their developing ethnic identity, their perception of themselves in the world and in their community, and their negative attitudes and actions towards other groups. Racism, and in this instance racial violence, is essentially a group activity—rarely perpetrated by a single person working alone. For these young people, a part of establishing their identity and gaining a sense of self-worth is showing the rest of the group that they are "down with the program." In this case the program includes concrete proof of being tough, hating the appropriate enemies, and a readiness to take those enemies on to defend your principles and your turf.

> You go on missions to impress your friends. You get a name as a tough guy who is down with the neighborhood and down with his people.

> You prove you're a real Bensonhurst Italian who don't take no shit, who don't let the wrong kind of people into the neighborhood.

> You do it to feel powerful, to feel like you're somebody. So people will respect you.

> You do it cause you want to be cool.
> To get out their frustrations.
> Because there is nothing else to do.

> I grew up in an all black neighborhood and all my friends used to be black. Now I live in Bensonhurst and I can't tell my white friends what I really think because they'll kick my ass and I won't have any friends. The worst part is when I'm hanging out with my friends and a black person walks by and they want to do him—I have to do him too.

The Bensonhurst and Gravesend youth interviewed for this study provide important insights into the anatomy of a racially motivated attack and some of the reasons for the present increase in bias-related violence.

There are three major contributing factors in the youths' involvement in racially motivated attacks. First, structural conditions are obviously important. These young people face extremely uncertain futures. The jobs that existed for their parents and older brothers or sisters are no longer available to them as a result of the changing structure of the labor market. For a number of reasons, these youth believe that jobs are scarce for whites because of special treatment towards blacks. The overall context within which they view race relations is one where affirmative action functions as reverse discrimination and Third World immigrants are taking away additional jobs and invading their neighborhoods.

The perception of these white youth is that it is they who are disadvantaged, while people of color are gaining political power and getting special treatment. The attitudes of these youth reflect ideas and principles which have achieved prominence on a national level in debates over civil rights, affirmative action, and racial inequality. In the last ten years, neoconservative ideology has emerged as a strong current in public policy, academia, and politics.[13] The public positions taken by the Reagan and Bush administrations on these issues, the emergence of the theories of neoconservative scholars such as Thomas Sowell, Charles Murray, and Nathan Glazer,[14] and the imagery and language of the 1988 Bush campaign—as well as of politicians such as Jesse Helms and David Duke—all lend credence to the white youth's sense of victimization and provide a focus for their anger, frustration, and economic anxieties.

While the youth are not well informed about the specificities of neoconservative analysis, they relate to the images and symbols: A black person getting a job that a white person was more qualified for; blacks getting preferential treatment; young black males as criminals; blacks and Puerto Ricans as coming from welfare-dependent, single-parent families with a violent culture and unclean habits. A couple of the youth even cited Professor Michael Levin in their discussion of the violent, criminal danger blacks posed to their neighborhood.[15] Bernard Goetz was something of a folk hero for some of the youth who related to the fear of black violence and the need to strike back.[16] Within this context, their attacks on people of color are interpreted as fighting back, as a defense of their communities. For the white youth, blacks in their neighborhood after dark represent a clear and present danger to physical health and property through crime and violence. The white youth feel a sense of powerlessness in their lives which is projected onto African Americans and other groups. Though these white youth have a perception of African Americans as having power and perceive the violent actions they take against these groups as fighting back, in reality it is precisely because African Americans lack the power to deter the attacks that they are vulnerable targets.

Second, these white youth live in close-knit ethnic communities with a history of flight from neighborhoods where African Americans and other minorities have moved in. Though members of their community frown on their delinquent activities, there is some community support for the role these youth play in keeping unwanted minorities out of the neighborhood. The youth certainly have the impression that neighborhood residents at least look the other way in terms of their attacks on "unwanted" outsiders.

Much of the community rallied to the defense of the youths involved in the attack on Yusuf Hawkins, staunchly proclaiming that the incident was not racially motivated. A cloak of silence was placed over the events of August 23, 1989, resulting in an understanding that the participants were not to be criticized. In one focus group interview, a young woman inadvertently broke the code of silence and was immediately rebuked by angry stares and reminded of the code.

> Why do all the blacks want to put Keith [Mondello] in prison. He didn't pull the trigger, Joey did it.
> SHHHHHHHH
> At least that's what the police are saying but we don't even know if that's true.

Other evidence of tacit support of the youth's activities can be drawn from previous incidents in the neighborhood. The area has a history of racial tensions, marked in the 1970s by frequent racial violence at the high schools located in these neighborhoods.[17] In 1982, an African American transit worker was attacked and killed by a mob of whites. In 1988, on three separate occasions, flyers asserting that "orientals" were trying to take over the neighborhood were distributed throughout the neighborhood encouraging neighborhood residents to boycott Asian businesses and refuse to sell their homes to Asians.[18] There has been little coordinated neighborhood response to these incidents. In the absence of community control of racial violence, the youth of Bensonhurst and Gravesend find encouragement and support for their actions.

There has been significant outrage expressed by residents of Bensonhurst who have resented their community being labeled as racist. The difficulty in discussing community collusion with the violent activities is that the neighborhood becomes an exception—it appears to be more racist than other neighborhoods in south Brooklyn or in other parts of New York City. The labeling of Bensonhurst as a "racist community" diverts an analysis from factors which produce the present reality of racially motivated violence to an analysis of the people of Bensonhurst—from a more systemic and generalizable examination of the problem to a more microscopic, individual analysis. What sets Bensonhurst apart from other communities with similar demographics in south Brooklyn is simply that

Yusuf Hawkins died there. The statements of youth from other white neighborhoods in south Brooklyn in this study indicate that racially motivated attacks occur regularly in other white ethnic communities.

Third, and most important, the peer groups of which these youth are members reinforce negative attitudes toward other ethnic and racial groups and facilitate violence motivated by these attitudes by encouraging particular (violent) group behaviors. The youth gain a positive sense of themselves, a more cohesive group solidarity, and a heightened sense of identity from participation in group attacks against individuals or groups from different ethnic and racial backgrounds.

The most salient issues for them were turf defense, personal power, and self-worth, as well as a need to belong to a group. Their ethnic and racial attitudes were linked to these issues in a very pointed way. They were exposed to the attitudes through teaching by family, friends, the community, and outside societal messages, and they had internalized them through their actions in the group. The importance of having these attitudes was clearly linked to the development of their self-identity and their idea of their ethnic identity. As part of the identification process—the process of figuring out who they are and who they are not—these youth internalize and exhibit attitudes which will project the image of the tough, important, powerful member of the neighborhood who defends the community.

The process of affiliation is often linked to the process of differentiation.[19] The process of differentiation from African Americans and other groups by these white youth is linked to the process of affiliation with the neighborhood and the ethnic group. Thus, young Italian and Jewish working-class youth from Gravesend and Bensonhurst believe that disliking blacks is part of what it means to be a good Italian or Jew within the context of their place and role in their communities.

The development of self-identity is an extremely important process during adolescence.[20] The context in which this process takes place is critical to the development of attitudes towards self and toward others.[21] The youth in this study are all either high school dropouts or students in a high school program of last resort. They are youth who are outcasts from the school system and within their community. Forty five percent of these white youth live in single-parent households and another 6 percent are less than seventeen and do not live with either parent. For these youth, the street has replaced the home and the school as the context in which they develop their identity. The peer groups they associate with in their neighborhood supply the value models and the definitions of what these youth should think and how they should act.

The behavior of the youth is nonetheless an extension of neighborhood and societal attitudes and ideologies translated to the street. The messages of their parents, of community residents, and of political representatives at many different levels has been incorporated into a street ideology which provides further justification for racial violence.

The interplay of these different forces and the importance of the peer group as a context for the development of ethnic identity and attitudes about others can be understood by reviewing two case histories. These two youth were involved in racially motivated violence, but altered their behavior as a result of a change in peer groups. Both of these youth were students at John Dewey High School in Bensonhurst. The first was a young Italian man who used to hang out around 86th Street and Avenue X with a number of Italian youth who regularly fought African American young people around the Marlboro housing projects eight years before the interview. In his words:

> I couldn't stand black people. We used to fight with them all the time. I didn't know any better and that's what my friends were doing. We used to get together and look for some blacks to beat up. I spent most of my time on the street and had a pretty tough reputation. It all changed when I got involved with Bob DeSenna and the Council for Unity.[22] He really saved my life. I was involved in very self-destructive activities which hurt myself and other people. Luckily, nobody was ever killed. Things got real bad about eight years ago when we were headed for a race war of some kind and someone definitely would have been killed. That's when I met DeSenna who helped me to see that I was either going to kill somebody or be killed and that wasn't going to solve my problems. The council for Unity was a place where I could do positive things and feel good about myself. I was never a good student so school was never a place that I felt comfortable. But the Council showed me that you didn't have to hate and you didn't have to fight to be a good Italian. I had a black friend for the first time. It didn't happen overnight, but by the time I graduated, and I don't think I would have graduated—if I had not joined the Council for Unity,—I had a black friend whom I knew I could count on, who would watch my back, who would die for me.

Another present member of the Council for Unity related a similar story.

> I'm half Puerto Rican and half Italian. I always hung out around my neighborhood with the Italian kids. There was one other kid that is Puerto Rican. You wanted to know why I changed? I don't know. I knew a kid who joined the Council for Unity. Before that I thought only kids who were soft joined the group. Then my friend joined and he got me to go to one of their events. They did this play about

an incident that happened about eight years ago at the pizza parlor across from the school. There were racial fights between Italian kids and blacks which almost caused a race riot in the school. I saw myself in the play and where I was headed. I came to one of the meetings and that was it. The group gives you a sense of belonging, it's a family, really. And we support each other and grow as a family.

These descriptions, given by youth who were involved in racial violence, demonstrate the importance of the peer group in the formation, maintenance, and expression of attitudes towards other racial and ethnic groups. These youth were involved with neighborhood street groups comprised of youth like themselves who felt powerless in their lives and anxious about their situation, and who gained their self-identity and ethnic identity from their participation in that group. These youth were able to change their attitudes and behavior by finding a different group which supplied an alternative, positive context and a set of peers with whom to bond.[23]

This does not mean that the peer group is the only determinant of the racial attitudes and behavior of youth. Both of these young people had parents who did not condone the attitudes and behavior of the youth they hung out with on the street. There are a number of factors which impact on the ethnic and racial attitudes and behavior of young people in these communities.

In conclusion, the peer group plays a critical role in the internalization of attitudes and in facilitating behaviors based on these attitudes. Familial socialization, neighborhood sentiment, and societal messages reinforce the attitudes and posture that youth develop and adopt toward other groups. The lack of a credible deterrent to violence—a lack of neighborhood opposition to racially motivated activities, ideological messages which supply encouragement, and ineffective police enforcement against racially motivated violence—allow youth to consider acting on their attitudes without fear of punishment. The complex interaction of these factors is critical to understand if we are to decrease racially motivated violence in American society.

NOTES

1. The lack of analysis of the Bensonhurst incident is in stark contrast to the plethora of theories considered regarding the Central Park jogger case. After the white investment banker was brutally attacked and raped, numerous stories appeared in the media analyzing the phenomenon of "wilding" and examining the class background, albeit crudely, of the youths arrested for the crime.

2. Statistics on bias-motivated violence are from the Bias Unit of the New York City Police Department. The Bias Unit classifies a crime as a bias incident if it

determines that the primary motivation for the crime was the victim's race, religion, ethnicity, or sexual preference.

3. Sheatsley, "White Attitudes Toward the Negro," *Daedalus* 95 (1966): 217-38; D. Taylor, P. Sheatsley, and A. Greeley, "Attitudes Toward Racial Integration," *Scientific American* 238 (1978): 42-49; D. Kinder and D. Sears, "Prejudice and Politics: Symbolic Racism versus Racial Threats to the Good Life," *Journal of Personality and Social Psychology* 40 (1981): 414-31; and H. Schuman, C. Steeh, and L. Bobo, *Racial Attitudes in America* (Cambridge, Mass.: Harvard University Press, 1985).

4. Schuman, Steeh, and Bobo, *Racial Attitudes in America.*

5. J. Rieder, *Canarsie: The Jews and Italians of Brooklyn Against Liberalism* (Cambridge, Mass.: Harvard University Press, 1987).

6. This chapter focuses on a subsample of 79 youth who are participants in the 61st Precinct YouthDares program in Gravesend—an alternative high school program for at-risk youth and a GED program. There are two different categories of youth at the program. There are dropouts who attend the project's GED education program. These youth are in their late teens and most have juvenile criminal records, many having adult criminal records. The other group attend the project's daytime alternative high school for youth who have been thrown out of regular New York City high schools.

The 61st Precinct YouthDares program is unique in the city of New York. It is the only youth program of its kind which works with white delinquent youth in an alternative educational setting. The program participants are almost all white and reside in the surrounding communities, mostly Gravesend, Bensonhurst, Sheepshead Bay, and Canarsie. The 61st Precinct YouthDares program is a nonprofit youth agency which is not connected with the New York City Police Department. In addition to classes, the program offers workshops and counseling for the program participants.

Additionally, I held focus group interviews with five youth in a park in Gravesend, five youth in a park in Bensonhurst, and six youth in a pizzeria in Bensonhurst. The youth interviewed in the parks and at the pizzeria fit the profile of the youth in the 61st Precinct GED program.

7. Sharpton is an African American minister and political activist who organized weekly marches through Bensonhurst to protest the murder of Yusuf Hawkins.

8. Steinberg, *The Ethnic Myth* (New York: Atheneum, 1981).

9. Statistics are drawn from the annual report of the Office of Research, Evaluation, and Assessment of the New York City Board of Education, 1989.

10. From the Annual Pupil Ethnic Census, 1960-1983 from the New York City Board of Education Office of Student Information Services.

11. An attempt was made on Sharpton's life on January 12, 1991, as he pre-

pared to lead the forty-eighth march through Bensonhurst to protest the sentencing of the two defendants.

12. I first heard the term "mission" when one Bensonhurst youth brought up the subject in response to a question about race relations in his neighborhood. The rest of the youth responded with noticeable enthusiasm to the discussion of these late-night searches for individuals who "did not belong in the neighborhood."

13. M. Omi and H. Winant, *Racial Formation in the United States: From the 1960s to the 1980s* (New York: Routledge and Kegan Paul, 1987).

14. T. Sowell, *Preferential Policies* (New York: Morrow, 1990); C. Murray, *Losing Ground: American Social Policy 1950-1980* (New York: Basic Books, 1984); and N. Glazer, *Affirmative Discrimination: Ethnic Inequality and Public Policy* (New York: Basic Books, 1975).

15. Michael Levin is a professor of philosophy at the City University of New York. In the spring of 1990, he became the center of controversy when he gave several lectures and interviews in which he stated that whites have a justifiable fear of young black males because they have a higher propensity to be violent. Among other measures, Levin advocated specific subway cars for young black males—a position which resonated deeply with the youth involved in this study.

16. Bernard Goetz became known as the subway vigilante when he shot four black youth who approached him on a subway train and asked him for money. Goetz asserted that the youth were trying to rob him and that he acted in self-defense. Goetz initially received supportive statements from many prominent people including Mayor Ed Koch and U.S. Senator Alphonse D'Amato. A jury acquitted Goetz of all charges except for illegal possession of a firearm despite the fact that he shot the victims in the back and one victim was shot again while lying injured on the floor of the train.

17. *Wall Street Journal*, July 25, 1988, p. 1.

18. Mayor's Advisory Council on Community Relations, *Final Report 1989*.

19. C. Pinderhughes, "Paired Differential Bonding in Biological, Psychological, and Social Systems," *American Journal of Social Psychiatry* 2 (1982): 3, 5-14.

20. E. Erickson, *Childhood and Society* (New York: Norton, 1963); E. Erickson, *Identity, Youth, and Crisis* (New York: Norton, 1968); and J. D. Vigil, *Barrio Gangs: Street Life and Identity in Southern California* (Austin: University of Texas Press, 1988).

21. W. B. Miller, "Lower Class Culture as a Generating Milieu of Gang Delinquency," in *Delinquency, Crime and Social Progress*, ed. D. Cressey and D. Ward (New York: Harper and Row, 1969), pp. 332-48; I. Goffman, *The Presentation of Self in Everyday Life* (New York: Doubleday, 1959); R. Edgerton, *Deviant Behavior and Cultural Theory*, Addison-Wesley Module in Anthropology, no. 37 (Reading, Mass.: Addison-Wesley, 1973); J. MacLeod, *Ain't No Makin' It* (Boulder: Westview Press, 1987); and Vigil, *Barrio Gangs*.

22. The Council for Unity is an organization at John Dewey High School which was developed by Robert DeSenna. The council provides a multicultural, multi-ethnic peer group for youth who attend the school. The council promotes positive racial and ethnic identity and awareness through workshops and programs in which the youth participate. There are types of rites of passage, including an oath to the council and induction ceremonies. The organization also tries to promote multicultural awareness throughout the school and surrounding communities.

23. It is important to note that programs and organizations do exist in these communities which are attempting to deal with the problems outlined here. The 61st Precinct YouthDares Program and the Council for Unity at John Dewey are two such organizations doing excellent work with these youth. Unfortunately, funds for youth programs and recreation centers which provide youth with alternatives to the street have been slashed since the late 1970s and that trend continues. The cut in youth recreation centers and programs may well have contributed to the rise in bias violence in the last five years.

5

The Established Gang

DIEGO VIGIL

Gangs have been present in the Chicano barrios (neighborhoods) of Southern California for more than half a century. These gangs have been comprised mostly of young males, aged thirteen to twenty-five, although only a small percentage of youth in any barrio actually join. The gangs arose in the aftermath of large-scale Mexican immigration in the 1920s and resultant adaptation problems, and emerged as a street force to affect barrio life. Then, as today, because of a loosening of social control networks, the gang has functioned as surrogate family, school, and police in the absence of other controlling influences. While most of the activities indulged in by gang members parallel what adolescents and youth normally do—e.g., playing, joking, exchanging stories and gossip on personal and social events, and so on—it is the less widely accepted antisocial habits and events that have caught the public eye: the violence, drugs, and street mayhem.

The barrios in which the earliest, most firmly established Chicano gangs developed were well-demarcated settlements of Mexican immigrants. They were located in geographically isolated areas that other settlers and developers had bypassed as less appropriate for habitation, and were further isolated by cultural, racial, and socioeconomic barriers enforced by ingrained prejudices of the Anglo-American community. The isolation imposed by these conditions exacerbated the problems that barrio residents faced and, at the same time, rendered the barrios more impermeable to outside influences. The nuclei of the gangs that emerged in these barrios were comprised of street youths who saw little to aspire to in their parents' difficult circumstances and received little guidance from other adults.

From the dynamics of immigration problems and the socioeconomic and cultural upheavals which spring from them, these street youth have also shaped their own *cholo* (originally meaning a racial or cultural marginal between Indian and Spanish colonial lifeways) subcultural style. A dress, walk, talk, demeanor, and other signs and symbols syncretically reflect the mixed nature of their Mexican, American, and street experiences. This subculture also has its own set of values and norms to which youths are socialized and enculturated; in fact, "street socialization" is one of the most important forces in the formation and persistence of gangs and gang members. Generational continuity of the subculture has been fashioned by a cohorting tradition in which successive cliques in age-based hierarchical fashion replace each other to perpetuate barrio gang goals and activities.

Subsequently, Chicano youth gangs have arisen in other urban and suburban areas that are not as clearly bounded as the classic barrios. The suburban gangs (often initiated by the sons of parents who moved to the neighborhood to escape barrio conditions) typically have been formed as defensive reactions to incursions by nearby established barrio gangs. More recently, Mexican (as well as other Latino) immigrant families have begun to replace blacks and others in downtown areas of, e.g., Los Angeles and Santa Ana. In a pattern somewhat similar to that of ethnic replacement populations in the Eastern and Midwestern United States, some youths in these neighborhoods have taken on the trappings of the already existing gangs nearby. Each of these types of gangs tends to mimic (and sometimes to exaggerate) the violent and drug-using traditions, as well as the *cholo* subculture, of the established barrio gangs.

IMMIGRATION AND PLACE: TERRITORIAL CONSIDERATIONS

Barrio gangs have typically adopted a territorial-based rationale— e.g., defense of the barrio and fighting for one's "homeboys"—which both reflects and engenders several sociocultural mechanisms that ensure that there is always a cohort of youth to join in and contribute to the gang goals.[1] It is in the junior high school period when adolescent maturation begins and youths for the first time encounter age peers from other neighborhoods on a daily basis, that the gang takes on new importance. School is just one arena for the enactment of gang roles. Much of a youth's pre-gang socialization, especially street socialization, takes place when the youth is still in elementary school, and some individuals even become loosely affiliated with a barrio gang at this time. But junior high school is where intensive gang membership activity typically begins. It is usually the place where street youths from different barrios come into regular contact with one another. Transformations of puberty, and the new role demands associated with them, also occur during junior high school, with other children also willing to experiment and flirt with new role behaviors. As school diminishes in importance in their lives, street corners, friends' homes, playgrounds, and other hangouts subsequently become focal points for drinking, taking drugs, and partying with other members of the gang. Later, as contact with criminal justice authorities increases, some gang members become incarcerated in youth camps and subsequently in prisons. These gang members tend to reify the gang tradition when they return to the barrio.

The long duration of gangs in barrios throughout Southern California has created both a model and a direct impetus for the formation of other gangs in nearby areas. This longevity has also tended (along with other structural and environmental influences) to intensify antisocial aspects of the gang to the point where the possession and use of weapons, drug use, and other criminal activities have become commonplace. Long, for example, reports that former members of more recent cliques in the East Los Angeles barrios had higher usage frequencies of all drugs used by older-clique members, and had initiated the use of other drugs that the older-clique members did not use.[2] Also, in a recent study of former gang members who were continuing to hang out in their respective barrios, I found near unanimous agreement that the younger cliques are more violent than earlier ones.[3] Moreover, increasing numbers of gang youths in recent cliques report that one or more of their parents had also been active in barrio gangs. While gangs have always attracted a portion of their own barrio population, the rooted existence of gangs has borne a new normative and behavioral system to which newcomers to these neighborhoods, mainly immigrant youth, must respond.

Early gang research specified that youth gangs were common in low-income areas of the city.[4] Similarly, more recently, developments of African American and Puerto Rican gangs in New York and Chicago began in impoverished areas. Within communities where Chicanos have been heavily concentrated, this same phenomenon existed and was noted quite early,[5] and later studies show that this has persisted to the present.[6] These barrios, unlike the gang areas of eastern and midwestern cities, usually had not been settled earlier by members of other ethnic groups. Also somewhat different from the poor immigrant neighborhoods Thrasher found in Chicago in the 1920s, the classic Chicano barrios had fairly clear "turf" boundary markers. East Los Angeles and adjacent communities comprise a coterie of barrios, with dozens of barrios separated from each other by major streets, freeways, gullies and ravines, railroad tracks, waterways, and other markers. Every barrio also has a name, and the gang is also identified by the same name. (Each age-graded clique also has its individual name, but the clique's name is subordinated to the name of the barrio.)

The barrio El Hoyo Maravilla, for example, is centered in a hollow (the *hoyo* or "hole" it is named for; *maravilla* is Spanish for "wonder," so the name can be translated "The Wonder Hole"—however, the same word also refers to the four-o'clock, which once was commonly found in flower beds throughout East Los Angeles). Founded by immigrant squatters in the 1920s, its first houses were said to be "shacks . . . built of old oil cans, old tin, boxes, scrap lumber, etc."[7] By 1935, this barrio had its first gang clique; more than a dozen and a half have since been formed and dissolved. Similarly, White Fence is located in a gully across the Los Angeles River from downtown; its name was derived from a white picket fence which formerly marked part of its boundary. Its gang formed in 1944 and has also generated a string of successive cliques since then. Jardin, located adjacent to another river (Rio Hondo), evolved from somewhat less humble origins—a working-class tract-home development whose developers enticingly named it Montebello Gardens (*jardin* means "garden" in Spanish). After World War II, its prospering working-class white residents moved to other, more upscale suburban developments, and by the 1950s the area had become an isolated ethnic enclave with its own barrio gang.

Most residents of such barrios use the name—if they use it at all—simply to designate what area they live in. However, for the youngsters who form barrio gangs, the name designation has come to mean far more, a "psycho-spatial identity" with their territory or "turf." To barrio youths who have had little else to engender a sense of self-importance and control of their lives, the barrio-gang equation provides a sense of meaning and attainable goals. Control of one's turf provides protection from assaults by rival gangs and an asserted claim to access to valued resources—including local women—in the barrio.[8] Conflict with rival gangs provides an arena for the demonstration of street-learned skills, values, and loyalties.

Barrio enclaves are the products of immigration and settlement patterns. Classic barrios have specific boundary lines, although in time, the spread of urban and suburban development may diminish the clarity of the borders. Sometimes these types of barrios are founded and conveniently situated adjacent to the workplace; in short, the place to live being determined by workplace. The barrios mentioned above were close to downtown industries, packing businesses, and railway yards.[9] Cucamonga, a rural enclave, was peopled by Mexican immigrants who worked in nearby citrus orchards and vineyards, and the railroad; and Simon, once home to a now defunct gang, was a barrio that got its name from the Simon brickyard right next to it.[10]

Each of these barrios, as well as others, operated as entry ports for one after another wave of immigrants.[11] Because of this initial and continuing immigration to the barrio and the often problematic nature of adjustment and adaptation that immigrants and their families experience, there is always an available pool of youth who become "choloized" (marginalized) and thus at risk to become gang members. Cohen has aptly and correctly noted that gang subcultures are created and perpetuated because they continue to meet the needs of each generation;[12] in Southern California's barrios, the accompanying barrio tradition has also become more rooted and the gang more a barrio fixture.

Choloization, taken from the word *cholo*, which is the contemporary label for the street style in Chicano barrios, is a process of "marginalization" involving various interrelated facets which I call "multiple marginality."[13] Multiple marginality refers to being outside the mainstream of Anglo-American society and its access to wealth and power in such a way that the following differences become evident: *ecological*: visual/spatial distinctions; *economic*: underclass, secondary labor market; *social*: family strain, school failure; *cultural*: nested subcultures, syncretic *cholo*; and *psychological*: adolescent status crisis, group identity. The most established barrios and gangs, those with clear "classic" boundary lines and deep subcultural traditions, often generate conditions of social disintegration and cultural fragmentation for the most "multiply marginal" youths. Economic stresses are so extreme and cultural orientation and identity so ambivalent that little supervision or guidance comes from the home or school. Instead, these choloized youngsters become "street socialized,"[14] with their lives directed by peers and older youth from the established street gang, and they experience early antagonistic contacts with police. How this process of street socialization and attachment to the gang subculture unfolds is very important in understanding established gangs in barrios such as are found in southern California.

THE ROLE OF THE STREETS

Street socialization is an aspect of the barrio that undergirds established gangs. Socialization, the "process by which a person learns the ways of a given social group and is molded into an effective participant,"[15] is conducted, to a considerable degree, away from home, school, and other traditional institutions. The most multiply marginal individuals are often the most unsupervised and reside in crowded housing conditions where private space is limited. These youngsters are driven into the public space of the streets where peers and teenaged males, with whom they must contend, dominate. These peers and older males provide such youths opportunities for a new social network and models for new normative behavior, values, and attitudes. They also generate a need to assuage basic fears stemming from not wanting to be fair game for anyone.

Thus, one of the first goals in the streets is to determine where one fits in the hierarchy of dominance and aggression that the street requires for survival. Protection comes from seeking associates who are streetwise and experienced and willing to be friends. In turn, this prompts the youth to return the favor by thinking and acting in ways that his friends approve. The new social bonds are reinforced, a sense of protection is gained, and new behavior patterns and values are learned. Some individuals, of course, are less willing or able to seek out new friends; they might develop instead a response pattern of crazily fighting back when they are in one of those friendless and fearful situations. Nevertheless, even with this difference, most street-raised youth must come to terms with the cohort of their barrio who control the streets.

The presence of a brother or other relative in this cohort can hasten a youth's acceptance; on the other hand, it will necessitate adjustments to the kin-based relationship in the context of street socialization. For an atypical example, in one interview of a twenty-eight-year-old *tecato* (heroin addict), it was found that his father, in the same household, had been one of the original members of the local barrio gang. Upon completing the interview, the interviewer, at the informant's suggestion, queried the *tecato's* five-year-old son as to where he was from. "I'm from White Fence," said the five year old. While three linear generations of gang affiliation such as this are unusual, generational continuity of gang subcultural identity and affirmation is maintained in many families through the influence on youths of an uncle, brother, or other relative. Such generational persistence among certain barrio families helps explain why the barrio gang subculture has such deep and wide-ranging appeal and longevity.

The streets also provide such youths with opportunities for adventure and—in the absence of effective adult supervision—with the freedom to undertake those adventures. A boy can wander where he will and return when he wishes, answering to no one or, at worst, facing a spanking or berating from his often absent parents when he goes home. In this aura of freedom, the youth in the street is guided to do things of which adults would disapprove; other children are now one's reference group and their values and guidelines are adopted.[16] Experimentation with alcohol and drugs occurs, weapons are accepted as the equalizer when needed, deviant actions are taken on a dare, and bonds with similarly street-active peers who are also school classmates are intensified. Sometimes very crazy activities are undertaken—e.g., running in front of cars to hear the brakes screech, or jumping from rooftops to the ground. More mundane mischievous behaviors, such as staying out late, or skipping school, are common.

Much of this preteen bonding provides the fertile ground for later teen-years bonding when more serious gang affairs are introduced. Many of the incidents exhibiting protection, daring, managing fear, and carrying out mischievous acts are seared into the memories of such youths. This remembrance of things past is often the basis for instilling loyalty and comrade-in-arms friendships that make later gang affiliations so strong and immutable. Street socialization thus becomes the basis for entrance into the gang and the preservation of the gang lore and traditions. It is the first phase of the integration into the gang subculture that for some individuals is a steady, uninterrupted development.

The isolation and detachment from other communities has tended to make the barrio gang members more wary of outsiders. Threats and challenges are taken personally, for an infraction against one member is an affront to all. Defense of turf is a raison d'être for a barrio gang and a subcultural solution to feeling marked as fair game. Thus, bonds of mutual trust based on friendships encourage gang membership and participation for protection. Within certain areas of southern California, there exist numerous barrios, some of the classic type and others more loosely defined,[17] that have for decades been at "war" with one another. This conflict tradition is passed on through the generations, if not from grandfather to grandson as noted above, through word of mouth in the neighborhood and at school. Everyone who joins a gang, and even most who do not, know who the enemies are and how to fight them. An awareness and identification with the gang is facilitated by the customary way that past events and incidents are remembered and recalled, as a type of oral history, to build up the image and reputation of the barrio gang. Lore, legend, and even myth with specially "embossed" stories, are the vehicles with which the spoken word has helped the subculture survive.

JUNIOR HIGH SCHOOL, ADOLESCENTS, AND GANG PATTERNS

Once ties with authorities—i.e., family, schools, and police—become problematic, conditions are set for the gang to become a substitute and surrogate authority that parents, schools, and polices its own members. The modeling and mimicry that occur on the streets become more formalized in the teenage years, usually in junior high school when the adolescent status crisis results in new experimentation. Upon arriving in junior high school, the youth must react to a new set of students from other neighborhoods or barrios. Encountering this strange environment and population sets in motion other events. While adjusting to the different demands of junior high schedules and teacher expectations, he must also cope with the various groupings and cliques there that have carved out their social niches. Gangs are already evident at this level, and the schoolyard has its separate barrio gang hangouts where the youngsters gravitate. Ready-made friends and protectors are there, some of whom are already known by the newcomers and others who are new to them; as noted below, there is an initiation ordeal awaiting them. In elementary school they may have heard about these other barrio groups and are thus prepared for them, but seeing them for the first time provides an impetus for their own gang affirmation. While some individuals might have participated earlier in conflicts with rival barrios, and all are aware of such contentions, for most youths the hostilities and antagonisms are encountered for the first time in the junior high school setting.

Usually conflicts at school are not too serious, involving mostly challenging looks and staredowns, pushing and crowding someone's space. Occasionally, an arranged time and place after school are set for two rival individuals to meet and fight. Sometimes such an incident escalates, resulting in serious harm to a participant. One youngster once complained to the interviewer that a fellow gang member, known as Killer, often forced such confrontations. "He was into beating up guys and then stabbing them. His older brothers were gang members and they programmed him to do it to them because they [opponents of the brothers in the latter's earlier fights] had done it to them," he said. More serious conflict between barrios is directed by the older teenagers and *veteranos* (veterans) who have unresolved and continuing rivalries of their own; they often bring in the younger members to help them. The latter are eager to do so, but they nevertheless continue to keep up their own rivalries at school and in the neighborhood.

As conflicts increase and intensify at junior high school, an individual's reputation spreads as a known and committed gang member. This can especially create problems for a *cholo* newcomer whose parents have recently moved into the area. Even though he might not be affiliated with the established gangs of the area, he still presents himself as a *cholo*, e.g., with dress style and mannerisms, and thus an inferred gang member. One incident had the newcomer being "hit up on" (challenged) by gang members who control the school. They surrounded him and asked, "Where you from?" His response had to follow an expected (among committed gang members) routine. He stood up to the probe and stated, "I'm from [barrio name]," without hesitation. Since he was not from a rival gang, his demonstration of *cora* (heart) and *huevos* (balls)—always valued *cholo* traits—made him acceptable to the challengers, who then permitted him to hang around with the guys at school.

At the same time, most *cholo* youths' school performance is deteriorating further, a process largely due to educational neglect and isolation of ethnic minority students. Most of these youngsters enter junior high school already behind their classmates in academic achievement; their street experiences exacerbate matters and have not been conducive to good study habits. As they become more involved in and identified with the gang, and incorporate its oppositional subculture, they become increasingly disdainful of teachers and school officials—and, in the process, become budding dropouts. Thus the developments of early bonding on the streets, accompanied by school associations and experiences which solidify them, make for stronger gang ties.

This negative reinforcement, e.g., gangs acting on schools and schools on gangs, can be observed in the life of a gang member who joined while in junior high school. While learning problems for this person had surfaced in elementary years, in middle school his already poor academic record worsened. He had just begun to learn how to read in the sixth grade, having overcome a Spanish-speaking language problem coupled with poor home supervision. All this changed when he met similarly disaffected peers in the seventh grade. They all belonged to special, remedial learning classes, and instead of spending time outside of school doing homework and the like, this school bonding experience—i.e., being singled out as a different, isolated segment of the student body (here the parallel with the isolation of the barrio is magnified)—enhanced the associations that would occur on the streets. Thereafter, especially when walking home from school with his friends, he would sometimes stop at the local minimarket to shoplift and join older gang members who had been hanging out most of the day. He usually joined them at the behest of the older gang leaders, who sometimes needed to make their group appear bigger. To do so, they would have younger guys join them to increase the size of the "gang" in the eyes of onlookers, particularly rival gang members who might be cruising by.

Adolescence also is filled with other changes that these junior high schoolers must adjust to. Among them are what Erikson refers to as the "psychosocial moratorium" in which age and sex identities must be clarified.[18] For those individuals from barrio backgrounds, there are adjustments to be made which are common to all adolescents and some which are unique to the pregang grouping pattern outlined above—e.g., psychospatial defensive aspects of the turf, street socialization, and early bonding experiences. Most of the time spent in the barrio is of the usual peer networking and loose socializing that characterize most adolescent groups in any neighborhood, such as: communicating on topics of local interest, personal experiences in school or at home, early dating and courting exchanges, and the recreation and play that take up so much time.

For the barrio street youth, as noted, there are the other less common fixtures that require one's response and adjustment: How to deal with the street gang? Why must the gang dictate how to dress and act? When does the gang take over socialization? These and many other realities must be confronted and resolved during the junior high school years. Indeed, it is the presence of these forces that make gang participation so important and thus the gang a necessary coping mechanism, for it simplifies many personal conflicts.

The youth joining the gang feels compelled to do so, for to be a *cholo* and, additionally, an isolate, is to invite disaster. A *cholo* is recognized as marginal, without resources and a support network, and thus fair game and subject to manipulation. That is true, however, only if the *cholo* is all by himself. Since it is difficult to fit into established adolescent and peer groups, it is natural for a *cholo* to find a niche somewhere, namely, with others who are misfits and unable (or refuse) to belong to school clubs and sports, or even public recreation programs. Rather than belong to no one nowhere, such a *cholo* must join the gang, even though the requisites for membership are quite demanding and life threatening.

For age and sex clarifications, one is taught to think and act mature and responsible around other gang members, even if it requires antisocial activities like fighting, using drugs and/or alcohol, and opposing school and other authorities. Since many of these youths' households are mother centered, without consistent adult male supervision, the male-dominated street socialization encourages supermasculine behavior. In junior high, the early and continuing street pressures generate a strong need to "act like a man," as defined by the gang and demonstrated by the living example of former gang members. One is expected to go about showing aggression and testing his manhood through the group-patterned auspices of the gang.[19]

To aid in this adolescent adjustment, the gang has developed a cohorting, or cliquing, tradition. For example, El Hoyo Maravilla and White Fence, two longstanding classic barrios discussed above, have each generated a succession of separate age-graded cliques since their inception.[20] Such barrios thus always have at least two or three cohorts defined by age and status (and sometimes more, if some members are unable or refuse to "mature out" of the gang). There are the twelve to sixteen year olds in junior high who are just getting into the gang, the fourteen to eighteen year olds in high school—or dropouts from it—who are somewhat proven, and the eighteen to twenty year olds who are seasoned. (These age ranges are not fixed, and successive cliques may overlap in age.) Each of these cliques evolves its own name and attaches it in graffiti and spoken slogans to the barrio name. Thus, for example, a wall might bear the message, "Los Tinies del Hoyo Mara" (The Tinies of El Hoyo Mara—shortening names or using initials is common); or a group of youths, on espying known or potential rivals, might shout out, "White Fence—Monstros." In addition, there are older gang members who are known as *veteranos*, ranging in age up to middle or late twenties, or occasionally into the thirties, who play a role as titular leaders and models, sages of the street, of sorts. The latter are often those individuals who never matured out; often they have spent considerable time in and out of jail for drug use and other criminal offenses, and as a result have never expanded their social network beyond the barrio associates they made on the streets or in jail. In short, they have remained mired in the barrio because they see no other options; and their presence there has made them a strong influence especially difficult for the younger barrio cohorts to avoid.[21]

This age grading, with its informal and formal processes of socialization and enculturation, has insured that the barrio gang always has a new clique to take over the duties of defending the turf. It also makes it possible to group together in a larger force as needed when a *locura* (craziness) binge of drive-by shootings and sorties demands all-out barrio "warfare" against rivals. Every clique concentrates on its own realities and events on a regular basis, sometimes partying, taking drugs or alcohol or playing sports, but there is a coiled readiness for action if a rival barrio's threats and incursions warrant it. The barrio gang relies on such mechanisms to persuade other barrio gangs to respect them or at least leave them alone. There are also occasions when the outside threats become so critical that older, retired gang members act as ex officio *veteranos* (often relatives of the younger members) and are pressed into action, if only for defensive purposes to ready their weapons as a deterrent when drive-by shootings escalate.

Initiation into this way of thinking and acting has usually been formalized as a rite of passage. If not earlier, by junior high school each prospective gang member is initiated into the gang by being "jumped in," that is, surrounded and beaten by two, three, or more other gang members. This ordeal is a type of street ceremony, or baptism, that confirms just how interested the novitiate is in joining the gang and also provides for the older gang members to assess just how potent an addition they are allowing into the gang. Initiation serves to interrupt one's "psychosocial moratorium" and it helps to resolve whatever ambivalence still exists as to age and sex identity.[22] With this gang imprimatur the person can now state that he is "Wino" (or whatever nickname he has been given) and go on to graffiti his personal name along with the clique and barrio names, thus: El Wino, Tinies, El Hoyo Maravilla. It is interesting to note that graffiti writing starts in the pregang socialization and junior high school phases, and there appears to be a progressive improvement through the years. Practice time and the initiation event mark another phase of commitment. As a result, the graffiti improves, becoming almost artlike.

Concomitant with these developments, although often adopted earlier during pregang street socialization, is acceptance and internalization of the "*cholo* front." Signs and symbols of the streets include ways to dress, talk, walk, and act. Much of this style is based on the choloization process outlined earlier which involves a syncretism of native Mexican lifeways with those of urban Anglo-Americans into something new and different. It has become known as the *cholo* street style: dress—oversized, heavily starched khaki pants, white tee shirts or tank tops, Pendleton shirt, black or dark shoes, and the short cropped hair combed straight back; talk—innovations including terms from Anglicized Spanish, Hispanicized English, or *calo* (a type of slang created by Gypsies and diffused to Mexico); walk—a controlled, slow saunter of graceful macho motion; and act—a face and body demeanor of stoicism mixed with a calm defiance and control.

Some individuals are quite adept at this *cholo* style, if they generally learned it early, at home with relatives or on the streets, but others barely mimic the image and look fairly obvious in their pretensions; this is particularly so with the "want-to-bes," usually junior high school recruits who have had no or little street socializing. There are countless stories about prospective gang members who are confronted by experienced gang members about their "image." One Latino immigrant tells it in a manner that underscores how his "manhood" was questioned

> When I got into my first class [in junior high school], this guy sitting next to me checks me out. He looked at me [informant moves his eyes up and down to show being "checked out"] and said, "You dress like that?" By looking at me that way, up and down, he made me feel like a *chavala* [girl]."

To summarize, junior high school is the social arena where the major shift in gang involvement and behavior occurs. Aiding this transition, of course, is the adolescent tendency to seek peers for guidance and direction in fashioning a new identity. The junior high school environment adds an important dimension, with the presence of other barrio gangs providing an external force or threat to hasten gang affiliation. With initiation and the integration of the signs and symbols of the *cholo*, the youngster experiments with more serious gang patterns, such as conflicts with other gangs, and is on his way to dedicating his life to *mi barrio* (my neighborhood), a type of surrender of self to the group.[23]

With this deeper commitment, involvement, and attachment to the gang, the youngster is well on his way to problems with law enforcement, whether for gang violence, drug use, criminal acts, or any number of other offenses. Such acts are part of the activities that gang membership entails or encourages, with reinforcement also from older role models. Street socialization also includes looking up to older street leaders, especially *veteranos*, as someone to model one's behavior on. In addition to the appearance they strike for emulation, most of these leaders regularly recount "war stories" of fights and other incidents, and brag about their behavior when they were incarcerated. Much of this posturing and teaching encourages youngsters to seek approval by following in the paths of these older gang members.

Participating in a drive-by shooting of an enemy barrio, "holding" drugs for an older member, and committing a criminal act are ways to gain stature and prestige for the younger members. Getting arrested for such a deed, especially if one is incarcerated, results in even more recognition and esteem. Doing a stint in a youth authority facility thus works more as a reification of gang membership than as rehabilitation, even though the latter is the ostensible purpose for such facilities. There are two reasons why this is so. One is that the gang reward system provides new respect for one who shows his daring to commit a crime and become a proven gang member. Part of this new-found respect comes from the fact that doing time shows that one is tough and able to handle the pressures and threats of a strange and hostile prison environment. The other is that, in the words of a youth street worker, rehabilitation does not work because implicit in the meaning is to return someone to their former self. Accordingly, the former self has been choloized and street socialized, and thus by definition cannot be "rehabilitated." What needs to be done with these youngsters is to "habilitate" them, in short, to curb or prevent choloization and street socialization. In any event, the experience of "camps" and "detention facilities" operates as a mechanism for gang affirmation, as Moore has so ably documented.[24]

One of the most remarkable aspects of Chicano gangs is how continuity of group and style has withstood the challenges of time. Since at least the 1950s, the form and structure of the gang has remained the same. Stylistic innovations are selectively added, but the ubiquitous nature of the *cholo* front is a clear statement of "tradition." It is, perhaps, the processes of gang creation and persistence that revolve around street life and affairs that make it so. The fact that it was fashioned in the streets is a living testimony to the *cholos* who created it. With gangbanging and partying (drinking alcohol, taking drugs, and socializing, such as dancing or car cruising) working to strengthen and solidify gang networks, the style has become a badge of identification and resistance to established norms from both Mexican and Anglo-American sources.[25]

Especially important is how incarceration experiences have tended to insulate regular gang members from the changing styles of society, keeping them out of touch with new influences. Upon returning to the streets, they continue to dress and act as before, as if nothing had changed. They have become culture carriers of the streets without opposition. This revolving door aspect, in and out of institutions, insures that the style remains. Youngsters consider this image an important part of their street socialization and gang affiliation and desire to contribute to its longevity. For short periods—e.g., the early 1960s with the "continental" style, the late 1960s with the "hippie" look, albeit moderately so, and the 1980s with the "Stoners"—there have been some alterations. Invariably, however, a return to the traditional look won out. In short, the street style of the past has become a tradition in its own right; the *cholo* syncretic innovation seemingly has become frozen because the urban situations and conditions that sparked the style have remained the same. It also serves as a reminder that isolation from (or at least strained association with) dominant influences and institutions serves to create cultural voids and gaps, making the creation of a new culture, or subculture, the only alternative. Cultural signs and symbols are usually associated with a place, and in this instance, it is the streets.

COMPARATIVE INSIGHTS

In a comparative vein, gang research has shown that several factors are present in established gangs. Established gangs in other ethnic minority populations have shown the same tendency to mark off a particular territory, recruit from among marginalized youth there, and provide these same youth with specific goals and roles. This is particularly the case among Puerto Ricans and African Americans, who share with Chicanos many similar situations and conditions of multiple marginality. In the latter cases, once a neighborhood is recognized as a low-income port of entry, it remains so for several generations. Similarly, the presence of a marginalized youth population from which gang members are recruited remains a characteristic of such neighborhoods. There always seems to be enough young, impressionable, unattached boys who become street raised and thus at risk to become gang members. This ready-made source insures gang lifestyle continuity for subsequent decades.

Even with these similarities, however, there are important differences, some subtle, that distinguish each group's gang phenomena. Chicano barrios are more geographically marked and more likely to be the original settlement. For instance, many barrios fit better the classic mold in that they were founded in heretofore unpopulated locations in or around the urban area, locations that were bypassed by city developers, such as El Hoyo Maravilla. Similarly, rural barrios, also of the classic type, were founded close to the worksite, and in the case of Cucamonga, for example, there are almost impermeable physical boundaries of a gully, a railroad track, and a major highway to insure that there will always be a barrio. Many Chicano barrios, in Southern California and in other regions in the Southwest United States, fall into this definition of geographical markers and original settlement.

In contrast, Puerto Ricans and African Americans generally established their barrios and ghettoes in pre-existing neighborhoods in various cities.[26] Of course, these neighborhoods were rundown, dilapidated, older areas of the city, and the newcomers refashioned the older community in their own image. They also tended to continue certain street traditions. East Coast and Midwest gangs of the contemporary Puerto Rican and African American populations have also evolved in the context of previous gang traditions and lifestyles; in short, these gangs are built on past neighborhoods and past experiences. The latter forms were shaped by earlier ethnic groups, such as the Irish, Italians, Polish, other "white ethnics" (mainly southeastern Europeans), and so on. Joan Moore[27] has effectively shown that this East/Midwest tradition, which included the "numbers" racket, union corruption, and other money-making activities in league with respectable business and social establishments, was nonexistent in areas where Chicano barrios sprouted. Rather than criminal outlets,[28] Chicano gang activities have traditionally revolved considerably around conflicts with rival territories: gang fights and, more recently, drive-by shootings. In addition to longevity, there also appear to be more institutionalized gang mechanisms and routines, indeed a gang subculture, to guide some barrio youth through the demands of the streets.

In conclusion, gangs have become fixtures in the many barrios of greater Los Angeles and its environs. Within the context of immigrant adaptation and the choloization process noted as "multiple marginality," these gangs have blossomed and been nurtured by continuing strains and stresses that put a sizeable number of youths at risk to become gang members. Because of a loose, or loosening of, social control in traditional institutions, such as family, schools, and police, these youths have been cast into the streets. In this setting, they have created a street culture with attendant socialization and enculturation processes, which provide street youths with purpose and identity and enable them to fit into the gang and its subculture. The streets are the place where the subculture was formulated by youths from marginal backgrounds, who fashioned new norms and values. What began as normal male youth socializing and cohorting was reframed in the context of the streets, where survival required protection from bullies and the like.

Defense of turf from real or imagined outside threats has given these gangs a reason to indulge in conflict with nearby barrio gangs, the latter becoming the perpetual enemy. Pregang socialization (reinforced by the shifts in behavior that transpire in the junior high school) has also tended to solidify the gang network. With several phases of integration into the gang complete, the youth becomes dedicated to gang goals and routines. Many of the signs and symbols of the gang are then used to reaffirm one's involvement and commitment.

While gang activities often lead to imprisonment, it is fairly clear that incarceration to rehabilitate acts more as a reinforcement to established gang networks and processes. Choloization and the *cholos* it creates have become such a steady phenomenon that it is difficult to break the cycle of gangs that dominate the streets. At first, gangs resulted because youths were attempting to cope with the realities of the streets, but now gangs have become an additional force to affect other youths who may or may not be street socialized. In the end, classic barrios, and the gangs that have become established there, have become so entrenched that nearby loosely defined neighborhoods have reacted with gangs of their own. Conflict and violence between warring neighborhoods/barrios now characterize much of the southern California area.

NOTES

1. Joan W. Moore, James Diego Vigil, and Robert Garcia, "Residence and Territoriality in Chicano Gangs," *Journal of Social Problems* 31 (1) (1983): 182-94.

2. John M. Long, "Drug Use Patterns in Two Los Angeles Barrio Gangs," in *Drugs in Hispanic Communities*, ed., R. Glick and J. Moore (New Brunswick, N.J.: Rutgers University Press, 1990), pp. 155-66.

3. James Diego Vigil, *An Emerging Barrio Underclass: Irregular Lifestyles Among Former Chicano Gang Members*. New Directions for Latino Research and the Social Science Research Council, Public Policy Research on Contemporary Hispanic Issues (Austin: University of Texas), pp. 1-13.

4. Frederic M. Thrasher, *The Gang* (Chicago: University of Chicago Press, 1927).

5. Emory S. Bogardus, "Gangs of Mexican American Youth," *Sociology and Social Research* 28 (1943): 55-56; Beatrice Griffith, *American Me* (Boston: Houghton Mifflin Co., 1948); Ruth Tuck, *Not with the Fist: Mexican-Americans in a Southwest City* (New York: Harcourt Brace Jovanivich, 1956).

6. Celia S. Heller, *Mexican American Youth: Forgotten Youth at the Crossroads* (New York: Random House, 1966); Malcolm W. Klein, *Street Gangs and Street Workers* (Englewood Cliffs, N.J.: Prentice Hall, 1971; Joan W. Moore, *Homeboys: Gangs, Drugs, and Prison in the Barrios of Los Angeles* (Philadelphia: Temple University Press, 1978); James Diego Vigil, *Barrio Gangs: Street Life and Identity in Southern California* (Austin: University of Texas Press, 1988).

7. C. V. Gustafson, "An Ecological Analysis of the Hollenbeck Area of Los Angeles" (M. A. thesis, University of Southern California, Department of Sociology, 1940).

8. Barrio gang cliques sometimes have female counterparts; research among such Chicano gang girls suggests a great deal of ambivalence in their attitudes toward such claims by the males, with a majority rejecting the notion. See Joan Moore and John Long, *Final Report: Youth Culture vs. Individual Factors in Adult Drug Use* (Los Angeles: Community Systems Research, Inc., 1987; and especially, Joan W. Moore, *Going Down to the Barrio: Homeboys and Homegirls in Change*. Philadelphia: Temple University Press, 1991).

9. Ricardo Romo, *East Los Angeles: History of a Barrio, 1900-1930* (Austin: University of Texas Press, 1983).

10. Alejandro Morales, *The Brick People* (Houston: Artepublico Press, 1989).

11. James Diego Vigil, "Cholos and Gangs: Culture Change and Street Youth in Los Angeles" in *Gangs in America*, ed. C. Ronald Huff (Newbury Park, Calif.: Sage Publications, 1990), pp. 116-28.

12. Albert K. Cohen, *Delinquent Boys: The Culture of the Gang* (Glencoe, Ill.: Free Press, 1955), p. 63.

13. Vigil, *Barrio Gangs*.

14. James Diego Vigil, *An Ethnographic Enumeration of a Barrio in Greater East Los Angeles* (Washington, D.C.: U.S. Bureau of the Census, 1987).

15. E. Z. Dager, "Socialization and Personality Development in the Child," in *Handbook of Marriage and the Family*, ed. H. T. Christensen (Chicago: Rand McNally, 1964), p. 741.

16. Vigil, *Ethnographic Enumeration*.

17. Ibid.

18. Erik H. Erikson, "Ego Identity and the Psychosocial Moratorium," in *New Perspectives for Research on Juvenile Delinquency*, Helen L. Witmer and Ruth Kotinskey (Washington, D.C.: United States Children's Bureau Publication, 1956), no. 356, pp. 1-23.

19. H. A. Bloch and A. Niederhoffer, *The Gang: A Study in Adolescent Behavior* (New York: Philosophical Library, 1958).

20. Chicano Pinto Research Project, *A Model for Chicano Drug Use and for Effective Utilization of Employment and Training Resources by Barrio Addicts and Ex-offenders*. Final report for the Department of Labor and National Institute of Drug Abuse, Los Angeles, 1979.

21. Vigil, *Emerging Barrio Underclass*.

22. James Diego Vigil, "Group Processes and Street Identity: Adolescent Chicano Gang Members," *Ethos* 16 (4) (1988): 421-45.

23. Vigil, *Barrio Gangs*.

24. Moore, *Homeboys*.

25. Vigil, "Cholos and Gangs."

26. In South Central Los Angeles the situation is quite different in that African Americans expanded from their original ghetto into areas where mostly white working- and middle-class populations resided; the course of the establishment and evolution of black gangs in Los Angeles, however, is outside the purview of this chapter.

27. Moore, *Homeboys*.

28. As Moore (ibid.) has indicated, the sale of heroin is a partial exception to this point. Chicano gang members in the 1950s helped to build the illicit heroin trade, both as users and dealers. However, the drug dealing—although countenanced by the gang—was an individual's enterprise, rather than a gang activity.

6

Hispanic Street Gangs in Chicago's Public Schools

RAY HUTCHISON AND CHARLES KYLE

INTRODUCTION

Q: What are your worst memories from high school?
A: Seeing a student getting shot, coming out of the locker room at school.

For high school I have so many that it's like a nightmare and the gangs pressure you so much, they beat up other boys so badly . . .

This one kid in English class belongs to the gang. He always picked on other kids and me. I went for help to my counselor but was refused help. I started to cut classes. No one cared if you went or not. The gangs there are the bosses.

Although the study of street gangs and delinquent activity has long been an important area of sociological research, there has been little study of the recent surge in gang activity: while gang violence has been

This chapter is revised from a presentation at the 1987 meeting of the National Association for Chicano Studies, Salt Lake City. Santos Martinez, Maria Martha Perez, Roberto Rivera, Carmelo Rodriguez, Linda Roman, Aida Sanchez, and Bienvenida Valesquez conducted the original interviews. Our thanks to Clarissa Acevedo, Marisa Alicea, Neomi Hernandez, and Judith Bootcheck (DePaul University), Ruth Horowitz (University of Delaware), and especially Dennis Roncek (Kansas State University) and John Hagedorn (University of Wisconsin-Milwaukee) for their comments on earlier drafts of this manuscript.

featured as a cover story in national news magazines and has been the focus of investigative reports on national news networks, the *Social Science Citation Index* lists just seven citations on street gangs for the years 1983 to 1988.[1] Research on gang activity in schools is even more rare, the most notable exception being Walter Miller's 1976 report to the National Institute for Juvenile Justice and Delinquency Prevention which sounded the warning that many urban schools were terrorized by gang violence.[2] Classic studies of delinquent gangs in the 1960s mention schools only in passing, and edited collections on gangs and delinquency from the 1960s and 1970s do not contain a single article discussing gang activity in the school system.[3] And while the lack of educational and employment opportunities figures importantly in John Hagedorn's work on street gangs in Milwaukee, and Diego Vigil mentions the evolution of school friendship groups into gangs in Los Angeles, even this research does not address subsequent gang activity within the school.[4]

The control of school buildings and grounds is an integral part of contemporary street-gang activity. Public schools represent a visible symbol of control over the gang's "turf." By grouping together several hundred teenagers, junior and senior high schools provide a ready source of potential recruits and, equally important, a monopoly market for drug distribution. While patterns of drug use and drug distribution among street gangs have been addressed in several recent studies, the distribution of drugs within schools has not been studied.[5] And although street gangs may be a major factor in the decision to drop out of high school, this phenomenon is overlooked in educational research which focuses attention away from the schools and toward the supposed shortcomings of individual students, their families, and their ethnic subcultures.[6]

We examine street-gang activity within two public schools in Chicago. Our major source of information comes from student interviews conducted for ASPIRA, Inc., in 1983.[7] In 1981 the Chicago Safe School Study found that students must avoid certain places in and around school due to fear of violence and that "the presence of street gangs and the fear for personal safety because of their presence is felt throughout the system."[8] We found that street gangs effectively controlled daily activity within and around the two public schools in our study during the period 1980 to 1985. Despite public claims of school administrators that gang problems "stop at the doors of the school," our research indicates that street gangs have a pernicious presence in the school. There are at least six significant consequences of gang activity which influenced the quality of school life at the time of our study:

1. street gangs exercised control over individual schools, areas of the school buildings, and/or particular classrooms within the school;

2. street gangs controlled the extensive and lucrative drug trafficking which openly took place within the school;
3. students were actively recruited for gang membership within the school building and/or on their way to/from school;
4. students were intimidated and physically attacked by members of street gangs within the school buildings, on the school grounds, or on their way to/from school;
5. students listed gang activity as the most frequent reason for dropping out of school; and
6. school administrators acquiesced to the power and intimidation of street gangs by transferring students to other schools to insure their physical safety.

After a brief history of gang activity in Chicago, we examine the structure of Hispanic street gangs and the process of gang recruitment during the 1980s. This is followed by a discussion of the study location and research methodology. We then present examples of how gang activity—including control of individual schools and of specific areas within school buildings, gang recruitment, and trafficking of drugs within the school—influences the daily school routine, the relationship of gang activity to dropping out of high school, and, finally, in the section titled "bureaucratic acquiescence," the manner in which school officials have dealt with gang problems. In each section we address how gang activity impacts the educational process, summarize information from the ASPIRA study indicating the extent to which these activities are reported by students, and then cite examples from the student interviews.

STREET GANGS IN CHICAGO

Very little of the existing gang research focuses on Chicago. R. Lincoln Keiser's well-known study of the Vice Lords, a black gang from west side, was published in 1969. James Jacobs provides a description of Chicago street gangs in the Joliet penitentiary; they have grown in size and influence (both on the street and in prison) since that time. Ruth Horowitz's study of Chicago's Mexican community provides information on the Lions (a pseudonym), a relatively small gang confined to one southwest-side neighborhood. Irving Spergel's analyses of homicide among black and Hispanic gangs contains limited information on the structure and activity of individual gangs, and the data in this and his later report for the Chicago School Board understate the extent and seriousness of gang activity within public schools in Hispanic neighborhoods.[9] The ASPIRA study of dropouts from the two Chicago public schools which are the subject of our research revealed that problems with street gangs—

including threats of violence and physical attacks—were widespread and were the major reason given by other students for deciding to drop out of school.[10] A 1983 survey of some 330 Hispanic households in Chicago revealed that problems with street gangs were one of the most frequent complaints of Hispanics in all areas of the city.[11]

In 1983 the Chicago Police Department estimated that more than 12,000 youths belonged to 135 street gangs within the city. While street gangs are found in many, if not most, neighborhoods, gang activity is especially prevalent in Hispanic areas of the city. More than 30 of the street gangs listed in the Chicago police department's guide to city gangs are located in districts thirteen and fourteen, which include the neighborhoods where the two public high schools in the ASPIRA study are located.[12]

We believe that street-gang activity is more extensive than official reports from police, and especially school administrators, would suggest. An average of 65 gang-related homicides have been recorded by the Chicago Police Department each year since 1980, a figure which, by nature of police definition (the gang relationship must be a known motive in the crime) understates the extent of gang violence. It is well known that the Chicago gang-related crime reports are conservative. In 1984, for example, the Chicago police department reported a total of 84 gang-related homicides, yet the December 30, 1984 issue of the *Chicago Tribune* printed photographs of 97 persons between the ages of 11 and 20 killed during the year; virtually all were victims of gang violence. In 1985, there were 4,995 reports of serious misconduct and 1,120 incidents of fighting involving two or more students or involving injuries within Chicago schools; in 1987 more than 600 violent crimes were reported in and around the schools.[13]

Structure of the Hispanic Gang

Membership in Chicago's Hispanic gangs is based on geographical residence rather than ethnic background. While the majority of persons belonging to gangs in our study area are Puerto Rican, this is due to the population characteristics of the local neighborhood rather than the influence of particular ethnic subcultures. These street gangs also include Mexicans, blacks, and Anglos, reflecting the diverse population characteristics of local neighborhoods. For example, several members of the Latin Lovers (discussed in Felix Padilla's chapter in this volume) are actually white ethnics whose families live in a neighborhood which now is predominantly Hispanic.

Most of the research on street gangs, dating back to Thrasher and continuing to the present, categorizes gang involvement between core and peripheral members. While this distinction makes sense for any individual group, it is no longer an accurate guide to actual membership size. First, each gang has "chapters" in different areas of the city. Each local chapter contains subgroups differentiated by age (for most groups, the distinction is between pee-wees, juniors, and seniors), and gang membership has now evolved into an intergenerational pattern. This means that the number of "peripheral" members has continued to grow, and now includes not only active gang members from junior high school to the young adult years, but also persons in their thirties and older whose activity dates to the early 1970s. While the core group of active gang members may still consist of ten to fifteen persons, persons from other neighborhoods are associated with the gang through age grading and elaborate "gang nations."[14]

Street gangs are ranked by community workers and police as "serious," "borderline," and "minor." The serious category refers to groups which are highly visible in the community and frequently engage in violent acts; they are recognized as threatening to persons and having a highly negative impact on the community. Borderline groups are visible but engage in only sporadic acts of violence, their primary activities are hanging out together and drinking. Minor groups are rarely involved in negative activities. In 1983 BUILD, a community intervention group, ranked all but one of the fourteen groups identified in the neighborhood areas where our study is focused as "serious."[15]

In Chicago, street gangs are identified with either the Latin Disciples or Latin Kings; these larger aggregates are referred to as the Maniac Latin Disciple Nation (MLDN), and Almighty Latin King Nation (ALKN). Gang members indicate allegiance to a particular gang through hand signals, graffiti, and clothing, which incorporate symbols of either the Disciples or Kings. Yet, this does not mean that all activities are directly orchestrated by the two larger groups. In the 1980s the gang nations were renamed Folks (Disciple groups) and People (Latin King groups), indicating a symbolic departure from direct identification with (and perhaps the implied domination of) particular groups within the gang federation.[16]

The gang nations are most important in providing protection for individual gang members outside their local neighborhood—in the streets, schools, and prisons. Several members of the Latin Lovers, mentioned earlier, contend that they joined the gang for protection so they could continue to attend one of the high schools we studied. A person belonging to a gang in the Latin Disciple Nation, for example, will be protected from gang members in the Latin King Nation should the need arise.

Gang Recruitment

There are two very different processes by which Hispanic youth become involved in gang activity. One route to gang membership follows a "natural history" approach, where adolescents who associate with childhood friends and secondary groups within the neighborhood become involved in gang activity in their teen years. The second involves the active recruitment of members within the neighborhoods and schools controlled by established gangs.

The most common path to gang membership develops among groups of friends within local neighborhoods who play together when they are young, attend neighborhood elementary schools, and then are placed into larger regional junior and senior high schools where they confront groups of teenagers from other areas of the city.[17] The most serious and sustained gang activity begins when these natural friendship groups are placed in competition with one another and where conflicts based on competing claims of neighborhood (territorial) loyalty first develop. These confrontations act to solidify group cohesiveness and establish the identity of gang members.

The second process by which adolescents become involved in gang activity is very different from the natural history explanation, and relates to the active recruitment of gang members through intimidation and violence. Gang recruitment involves stopping persons in the school or on the street and demanding their gang affiliation. Any male between the ages of ten and twenty-five living in Hispanic neighborhoods is susceptible. If the individual claims that he has no affiliation he is told that he should consider joining the gang. The second time he is stopped it may be suggested that if he hasn't joined the gang it must be due to his belonging to a rival gang. Verbal harassment may proceed to physical intimidation in subsequent encounters.

In 1985 the city of Chicago unveiled a new plan to reduce gang violence through a "Philadelphia-style" intervention program employing former gang members. Despite the well-publicized efforts of the new intervention program, the *Chicago Tribune* reported a 40 percent increase in gang homicides in the first half of 1987.[18] Why has gang violence continued to escalate? And what is the impact of gang activity in the public schools?

STUDY LOCATION AND RESEARCH METHODOLOGY

Our research focuses on two public schools located in the largely Hispanic neighborhoods of West Town and Humbolt Park on Chicago's northwest side. In 1980 these communities were approximately 60 percent Hispanic; several white ethnic neighborhoods are found within each of these neighborhoods. About 60 percent of the Hispanic population is Puerto Rican; most (30 percent) of the remaining persons are of Mexican origin.[19]

Humbolt Park and West Town are located in the industrial corridor along Milwaukee Avenue, which runs northwest from the center of the city. The large-scale movement of Puerto Rican and other Hispanic families into this area began in the 1950s and has been accompanied by tremendous social disruption and displacement; between 1970 and 1976, for example, more than 1,700 housing units were lost, many because of arson, and the community was placed in the fourth stage of neighborhood decline ("accelerating decline") by HUD. The once prosperous business districts along Division Street and North Avenue have virtually disappeared, as has employment in basic industry.[20]

Information contained in this chapter is drawn from fieldwork by the two authors and from a study sponsored by ASPIRA, Inc., of Illinois to investigate the problem of dropouts in the predominantly Hispanic high schools in the West Town and Humbolt Park neighborhoods. The study, authored by Charles Kyle, involved a random sample of students from the 1979-entering cohort who were interviewed in 1983. The research revealed that only some 26 percent of the entering cohort were still enrolled in high school—including GED programs—by the middle of their senior year. The projected dropout rate of more than 70 percent for these two schools was verified in a subsequent report to the Chicago Board of Education and the Illinois attorney general.[21]

The ASPIRA study included open-ended questions where students were asked to give the circumstances for dropping out. Respondents were also asked to recount their best and worst memories from high school. This question was used in an earlier study of Mexican American students in the Southwest which found that dropouts recounted more negative elementary school memories than stay-ins, but that few youths mentioned negative high school memories. Most negative memories among high school students referred to teachers or general school experiences; no mention was made of bad memories due to street gangs, violence, or fear of violence in the first study.[22] Unless otherwise indicated, quotations in following sections are taken from the ASPIRA interviews.

GANG ACTIVITY IN THE PUBLIC SCHOOLS

Street-gang activity in the public schools ranges from the sale of drugs to acts of violence against other students. Of particular interest to sociologists, since many of these activities parallel the study of other subcultural groups, are the use of hand signals, color combinations, dress styles, and other means to represent gang identity. Also important is the pattern of symbolic violence used to intimidate other students and establish control of public areas within and around school buildings.

Control of School Buildings and Grounds

As noted above, control of public schools is important to street gangs as a visible symbol of their power. In many areas of Chicago, individual schools are known by students to be controlled by specific gangs and/or gang nations. Given the strong territorial basis of Hispanic street gangs, it is perhaps not surprising that the two schools in our study were dominated by gangs representing one of the two aggregate gang nations. In practical terms, this means that adolescents who belong to gangs allied with the gang nation are granted safe passage to and from school and within the school building; students from neighborhoods controlled by rival gangs will confront gang members each day that they come to school.

For students who do not belong to a gang, the simple act of entering the school building and attending classes may become problematic. The student is aware that the school is controlled by one of the rival gang nations. Once the student has been targeted by gang members, he (or she) may chose creative but self-defeating methods to stay in school. Several students told of cutting classes so they could arrive after gang members had gone to their classes:

> I missed because of the pressure from the gangs and I was afraid of their threats.

> I was afraid. I had been hurt by some gangs. I asked for the teacher or security guard for help. They ignore you or kick you out of school.

> Because of being harassed so in school and beat up I would stay home until later in the morning and I would miss one class every morning but I would stay for all other classes. I was just afraid and I told the teachers and my mother talked to the principal but there was nothing anyone could do for me, so I would cut the same class. The principal decided it was best to kick me out of school. I would have liked to continue my education. If you don't belong to a gang you can't survive. No one will help you—not the counselor, not the teachers.[23]

Gang members select certain areas of the school as their turf, and these are identified by other students as areas to be avoided as much as possible. One student in the ASPIRA study noticed that gang members were trailing him in school, and because he was afraid to go into the student rest rooms where gang members hung out, he decided to use the staff rest room:

> You see the things that happen in this school are very bad. Sometimes I wanted to use the washroom and was unable to because they

would follow me all over so I had to use the one by the office and then I would get in trouble with the school staff, because I did not identify the gang member. I really wanted to stay but it was either my life or my education.

When students decide to skip classes where they feel threatened, avoid certain areas of the school building, or leave school early so they do not have to confront gang members, they have acknowledged the domination of the street gang. Each of these individual actions has a corrosive influence on the educational process and symbolizes a broader lack of control over the school environment.

Drug Distribution

The relationship between street gangs and drugs is not as simple as that portrayed in the national media. Diego Vigil suggests that patterns of alcohol consumption and drug use among Hispanic gang members is similar to that of their adolescent peers, and Ruth Horowitz reports that because serious drug use may make the actions of some members unreliable, it is therefore discouraged in some gangs.[24] Although recent research emphasizes that drug dealing is but one of many activities gang members are involved in and is not always the primary purpose for gang involvement, many street gang members (including those in the schools that we studied) do deal drugs.[25]

Junior and senior high schools bring together several hundred teenagers within an enclosed environment for seven hours a day, nine months of the year. The two schools in the ASPIRA study, for example, have 2,600 and 1,600 students. This unique characteristic of the public school establishes a monopoly market for drug distribution. The fact that drugs are present in the public schools is not surprising given the widespread use of controlled substances by adolescents in the United States. But the ready availability of a wide assortment of drugs within the school is striking.

Student responses from the ASPIRA study indicated that marijuana, cocaine, speed, and heroin could be purchased from sources within the school in less than one hour. Ironically, the most difficult drug to obtain within the school was alcohol, due to inherent difficulties in storing bottles and other bulky containers. The open trafficking of drugs was scandalous to some students. As one youth told us, "drugs are all through the school like candy in a store." Youths who were lectured in class on the dangers of drug use saw the same drugs openly sold in the school building. Other students reported that they were pressured by individuals they identified as gang members to buy drugs at school. Despite the high level of drug trafficking reported by students, there were only six suspensions for the possession of drugs in the two schools under study during the first six months of the 1983-84 school year. No one was suspended or charged with dealing drugs.

Students are aware that the high volume of drug traffic could not continue without an extensive distribution network importing supplies from other countries. An assistant principal reported the fear of students of retaliation from drug suppliers:

> Kids will not tell you anything about where they got drugs. They are much more closed mouthed about this than [they are about] the gangs. They are more afraid of what can happen to them on the street if they talk about the source of the drugs than they are afraid of anything that I could do to them.[26]

One reason gang problems spread into the public schools is that street gangs recognize the potential lucrative monopoly over drug distribution. This actually encourages some gang members to attend school regularly, even if they are not active participants in the educational process. This behavior is contrary to what most educators say when they suggest that there are gangs in the neighborhood, but they don't attend school. An assistant principal from a school outside the Chicago area told us that gang members frequently protest suspensions from classes, insisting that they want to remain in school because "that's where the action is."

Gang Recruitment and Intimidation

Membership in any form of secret society is explicitly prohibited by the Uniform Discipline Code of the Chicago Board of Education (1980). Gang recruitment and intimidation within schools are further prohibited by the disciplinary code, and are felony crimes under Illinois state law (Illinois Public Act 82-564). Intimidation is defined as

> engaging in a behavior which prevents or discourages another student from exercising his/her right to education; [including] the use of coercion or force to prevent another student or to recruit another student for membership in any organization not authorized by the principal.[27]

Despite the apparently strict rules governing student membership in street gangs, many gang members attend school and actively recruit members from within the public schools. In the ASPIRA interviews, nearly 10 percent of the students indicated that they belonged to street gangs, and 20 percent said that one or more of their friends were gang members. These figures are conservative; in several interviews, students became very nervous about questions concerning gang membership and several refused to answer these questions.

Incidents involving gangs are the most frequently mentioned memories from the high school years. In the ASPIRA study, 56 percent of the male students reported that they had been asked to join a gang either in school (45 percent) or around the school (11 percent). Among the personal experiences involving violent encounters with gang members are the following:

> One day in the hall the gangs came up to me and asked what I was doing. They said if I were in a gang they would kill me right there. . . . Another time a car came up to me and started shooting.

> The gangs killed one of my best friends. In high school, I always feel afraid because the gangs hang around the school and try to recruit the current students.

Although clearly illegal and disruptive, gang recruitment and intimidation regularly occurs in junior and senior high school. Students who claim neutrality are assumed to be members of opposing gangs and face increased physical harassment. Verbal and physical intimidation is punctuated by sporadic and symbolic acts of violence, as it must if it is to be effective. More than half of the students indicated that they were afraid of being physically harmed in or around school—and an even larger number of female than male students reported a fear of physical harm.[28] Our interviews revealed the constant threat of harassment and actual physical violence *within the public schools*, as demonstrated by student comments such as the following:

> The school is full of gangs. They wanted to get in fights and I thought it best to get out of school due to these gangs. My mother told them I was going to drop out because of the gangs wanting to fight all the time.

> Not too long ago a girl was raped by three guys inside the school and she was hurt. No one did anything and I still see the boys there. . . . The gangs are not just from this area. They have guns, knives, and baseball bats. We get all of this. A few days ago a Filipino boy was stabbed several times by gang members and four other boys of his race came to rescue him but they were kicked out of school.

A student from another high school described the scene of a gang murder he observed after arriving early at the school one morning. Two gang members had been killed during the night, and their bodies laid near the entrance to the school The student related this killing to the broader pattern of gang recruitment, intimidation, and violence within the school:

If you saw the way that they killed them you'd never forget it. They slit their throats. Then they pulled the meat out of their neck. I don't know what I'll do the next time that I go to school and someone stops me in the hall and pulls my jacket open and says, "Where's your colors? I know that you're a [Latin] King. Don't you know that this is Folks [Latin Disciples] territory?"[29]

Domination of Daily School Routine

Gang activity within the public school impacts the educational process in many ways. When gangs establish control of particular floors and classrooms, other students must alter their daily routine. Some students reported that they skip individual classes where the presence of gang members make them feel unsafe; other students habitually skipped first- and last-period classes to time their arrival and/or departure from school to avoid contact with gang members. These actions result in reports of missing classes and truancy; as a consequence, students who are not gang members may be suspended by school administrators for violating school rules and even pressured to drop out altogether. The domination of daily school routines may be seen in the following examples where students explained why they cut certain classes:

Because of the gangs. They would wait for me after school to fight with me. I had to cut classes to be able to get out of school before they did.

I had problems with gangs because they want you to join and if you don't join you'd be afraid of them. The reason I dropped out was because I was so afraid of the gangs. I stopped going to school and the truant officer went to my mother and told her it was better for her to sign the papers and [for me to] drop out. That is what my mother did.

The influence of street gangs affects even such personal decisions as what to wear to school. Because particular color combinations are used to signify gang membership, students who do not belong to gangs must be careful not to dress in gang colors. This means that combinations of black and yellow, black and blue, black and green, and other colors cannot be worn to school or in the neighborhood. Students rightfully view this as an unwarranted intrusion on their free choice:

Since the first year I had problems because of the gangs, there are so many different kinds that one has to be careful the way one dresses . . .

> One time I was stopped in the hallway by two gang members. I was wearing the color of a different gang and they thought I was part of the gang.

> You can't dress different because the gang will think you belong to another gang and five or six of them will get together and beat you up. The security is not good at this school.

The informal dress code enforced by gang members may even influence decisions by school administrators. The principal of one of the high schools in our study told of collecting money to purchase a winter coat for a needy student. It then took two days to decide on a color that would not make the student an unknowing target for one of the gangs in the school.

Students also identify their membership in particular gangs by the use of hand signals (referred to as "representing" in the gang lexicon). One assistant principal commented that if a stranger walked through the halls of the high school he would think that a comedy act was under way:

> These kids walk around signaling each other with gang signs. Actually they look like third base coaches. But it's not so funny because kids come to me and say that they are afraid to go home because they've been signalled that they'll be jumped.[30]

To survive in school, other students must quickly learn the informal rules involving dress codes and conduct enforced by the street gang.

The lack of security and perception of threats to personal safety leads many students to carry weapons to school for protection. More than 40 percent of the male students and 20 percent of the female students reported that they had brought weapons with them to the school; fifteen of the students interviewed admitted that they had carried guns with them into the school building.[31] If carrying a weapon makes the individual student feel more secure—and this is a familiar argument used in debates over gun control—it is difficult to believe that this makes the school a safer environment. As one student remarked, "If someone were to check there, they would find an arsenal of guns and all types of weapons and whatever you could think of. Name it, it's there."

Bureaucratic Acquiescence

Because of the high level of gang violence and threats against other students, school administrators are sometimes forced to accept the alternative "social order" imposed by street gangs. Each instance of bureaucratic acquiescence legitimizes the authority of the street gang over the daily functioning of the school and undermines the confidence of students in school administrators. The district superintendent of one of the high schools in the ASPIRA study approved twelve transfers out of the district in a single year. In each instance, the transfers occurred because the student belonged to a gang associated with the Latin Kings; their physical well-being was threatened by attending public schools controlled by the Latin Disciples. Each time a school official authorizes a transfer for this reason, or decides upon the color of a winter jacket because of the color combinations worn by gang members, he/she is admitting that gangs actually exercise control within the public school. The only recourse that a caring administrator has to protect the life and educational future of the youth involved is to admit their school is part of the street gang's turf.

Gang pressure may force school administrators into apparently hypocritical postures of enforcing minor (bureaucratic) rules while ignoring major violations. The student who used the faculty rest room because he was afraid of using bathrooms controlled by the gang (mentioned earlier) was suspended from school and later dropped out. Another student was suspended from school because he skipped his first-period class so he wouldn't be harassed by gang members on his way into the school building. In both instances, the violation of bureaucratic rules was punished, but the gang members remained in the school.

Gang violence within the school is not always reported to the police. In 1987, the *Chicago Sun Times* reported that

> Faced with an outbreak of violence in Chicago's schools, top police and school officials Sunday agreed to reassign police to the most volatile schools. In the last two weeks, three students were shot, two students were stabbed, and a teacher raped in the Chicago Public Schools. . . . They [the police] are also expected to require school officials to report all incidents to the police, a practice not always followed now.[32]

Police officials have publicly complained of a lack of cooperation from school officials in dealing with street gangs and reporting criminal activities within the schools. One police commander was quoted in a task force report as saying,

> Some principals and district superintendents say that they have few school assaults. Even their reports to superiors say that they have few assaults. Why, then, do police officers report there are more assaults in these schools than are being reported? I think it's because some of these administrators believe a small assault statistic will impress administrators downtown. This attitude comes back to haunt them, eventually.[33]

In his study of bureaucracy, Max Weber noted that a major obstacle standing in the way of accountability is the tendency of officials to increase their intrinsic superiority as experts by keeping their knowledge and intentions secret.[34] Within the public school system there are, of course, overlapping levels of bureaucracy. Each level has a functional interest in minimizing the seriousness of gang problems. Individual teachers do not want the principal to think that their classroom is out of control; individual principals do not want school district officials to think that their school is out of control; the superintendent of schools does not want the public to think what they already know to be true: that the gang situation in the public schools is out of control.

The principal of one of the schools in the ASPIRA study remarked that gangs may present a problem to students on the grounds near the school, but do not present a problem to students within the school building.[35] After the shooting death of a gang member within a school building in 1987, the principal of the high school was quoted as saying, "We have some fights around here, but I do not believe the fights are gang related."[36] Following this in-school homicide, school administrators released figures on crime and misconduct within the public school system and the head of the school system's Bureau of Safety and Security reiterated the claim that gang activity in the schools was "on the wane" although it remains strong outside the schools: "They do not play their tricks within the schools. Once they get inside the schools, they know we've got them under surveillance."[37]

Overlooking gang problems in individual schools may prevent timely recognition of the extent of gang activities, and can lead to the outright denial of gang-related problems. While attempts to minimize gang problems are certainly understandable within the logic of public school bureaucracies, they also (in the words of the police official) come back to haunt administrators at both the school and district level.

The willingness of the majority of students to cooperate and inform officials which students are involved in major rule infractions is an important resource to the school administration in the maintenance of discipline. Street gangs have terrorized other students so thoroughly that many are afraid to inform on gang members. This dilemma—and the powerlessness of school administrators to take control of the gangs—is demonstrated by the following incident: after school officials were informed that a female student had smuggled guns into school in preparation for a "gang bang," the principal commented that

We found the guns, but what about her [the informant]? She had to return to school after helping us. She told me, "They've killed my cats, broken our front window, and set fire to my car. I want a transfer." I can't protect this kid with a police car in front of the house. She can't live as a prisoner in her own home.[38]

Street Gangs and Dropping Out

Recent studies indicate that fully half of the students in Chicago's public schools do not complete their high school education; the two schools in the ASPIRA study had a dropout rate of 70 percent.[39] The growing problem of high school dropouts is directly related to the influence of street gangs within Chicago's public schools. Joe Rosen, retired Chicago public schools district superintendent and consultant to the Network for Youth Services, conducted a 1984 survey of teachers and high school seniors at one of the high schools included in the ASPIRA study. Both teachers and students reported gang problems as being a "very important" reason for students leaving the school.[40]

Gang-related reasons were the single most common response by students in the ASPIRA study when asked about their reasons for leaving school, accounting for 30 percent of the male responses and 17 percent of the female responses. One out of four dropouts (24 percent) gave answers relating to gang pressures.[41] Some of these comments follow:

> I had it with the gangs. They would wait for me after school in the hallways. I had to run home after school. I couldn't go on that way. It was either me or them. I left the school to them. I had to leave because of the gangs.

> I left in March of 1981 because of a gang shooting in the halls of the school. I was afraid I would be killed.

> I left in October of 1982 because I didn't want to get killed by the gangs in school; the last chance I took was when the gang put the gun to my face. I left because of the fear of gangs. They wanted to kill me; I dropped out. I tried to get my transfer. One teacher called my house and I told her I was not going back to school because of the gangs.

> I do not consider myself a drop out. The reason I left school was because of the gangs. I was shot at. I talked to the principal in the high school office. He said he would take care of things. Things just got worse. The principal did nothing.

The influence of gang activity on an individual student's decision to drop out is not always this direct. The principal of one of the high schools in our study noted that after a student was beaten at the school, a group of gang members waited at the bus stop in front of school with broken beer bottles to retaliate against the other group. Although the confrontation was broken up, another teenager was murdered on a neighborhood street corner during the weekend. The principal explained, "People don't think this has anything to do with the dropout problem, but we had three students transfer out on Monday morning."

The relationship between gang violence and dropping out of school was also referred to by Horowitz when she relates why some members of the gang she studied attended a Catholic high school:

... many youths who found the gang situation too difficult at Tudor [High School] but still wanted to graduate, attended this school [St. Mark's Catholic High School]. Three Lions graduated with good grades. "Shit, I couldn't go to Tudor High for nothing. The Aces would jump me the minute I walked in. You got to be packed [carry a weapon] every day. I want to finish school, not die.[42]

Student Reaction to Gang Activity

As the comments in these sections indicate, many students are frustrated by the schools' inability to deal effectively with gang problems. Although individual students described a number of different events which led to their decision to drop out—problems with schoolwork, an unexpected pregnancy, problems with gang members—they were consistent in their complaints that teachers and administrators either did not care or were powerless to provide a safe environment. Some representative comments include:

I was suspended when the gang members put a gun in my face. The school didn't do anything about it. The boys are still there and I am out.

If I had a class problem there was no one to help, not a teacher—no one. I was disappointed with the gangs and the drugs. No one cared. They closed their eyes. From the principal to the teachers and security guard, no one cared.

These and other comments reveal a strong undercurrent of frustration with the school administration. These students understood the value of their education and they wanted to remain in school. Half of the dropouts in the ASPIRA study requested personal assistance from the research staff to get them back into school and/or to enroll them in GED classes. We do not fully agree with the students' assessment of the school; indeed, our conversations with principals and teachers indicate that most are very concerned about gang problems and have sought to minimize their influence within the school. Still, as the students recognize, school staff are relatively ineffectual in dealing with the gang problems, and street gangs continue to dominate daily activities within many public schools.

STREET GANGS IN THE PUBLIC SCHOOL

Irving Spergel criticized the ASPIRA study in his report on street gangs for the Chicago Board of Education. He notes that "the gang problem is perceived as most pervasive in District Six, which encloses the two high schools in [the] research," and that the study "supplies evidence that the community gang problem spills into the schools, but it is not clear that the gang problem is generated or aggravated by the schools."[43] While this sort of statement may lend some degree of comfort to school officials, we disagree with Spergel's conclusion. Indeed, the evidence presented here indicates that in the period under study, street gangs had a pernicious presence in the two public schools studied. As noted in the introduction, the influence of the street gang is manifest in a variety of ways, including: control of individual school buildings and/or areas of the school; control of drug trafficking within the school; intimidation and physical attacks and the active recruitment of students within the school building; the acquiesence of school administrators to the influence of the street gangs by authorizing student transfers and other actions. We believe that these factors have a direct impact on the decision of individual students to terminate their high education.

It is important to note that the public high schools in the ASPIRA study are located in areas with the highest incidence of gang activity in the city. While there is no inference that the schools are the cause of the gang problem in the neighborhood, they are clearly one of the first places that the problem is manifested. Rather than confining their activities to the surrounding neighborhood, street gangs intentionally "infiltrate" the public schools, not only for the symbolic value of expanding their turf, but also to control drug sales and gain access to recruits. This behavior is contrary to the position of Irving Spergel and others who argue that while gangs are active in the neighborhood, only a small number of youths are involved, and they don't attend school.

Escape from the pressure for involvement in gang activities may be nearly impossible for many Hispanic teenagers—indeed, Pineda's study of inner-city neighborhoods in Los Angeles describes "social forces which make gang membership almost inevitable."[44] In Chicago, some Hispanic parents send their older children back to Mexico and Puerto Rico to complete their schooling.[45] Street gangs have not penetrated the Catholic schools in the same neighborhoods, which strongly suggests that the public school's submission to the gang pressures is a significant part of the problem. But as other studies of Chicago's public schools have shown, half of those students entering high school choose to leave public schools; many have made this decision rather than face continued intimidation and threats of physical violence from street gangs.

CONCLUSIONS

Because today's street gangs are larger, more complex, and more violent than their predecessors, research from the 1950s and 1960s may no longer be relevant for contemporary gangs—the very label of "delin-quent activity" seems a quaint artifact from some bygone era. Gang pre-vention programs based on this literature may no longer be effective with inner-city youth. The most significant differences in gang activity are found in the methods for recruiting younger members to the group (begin-ning at the ages of ten to twelve), a greatly increased potential for violent and life-threatening acts, the continuity of individual gangs (which retain their identity and leadership structure even with the passing of founding members), and the continuing involvement of gang members through the adult years. Thus Chicago street gangs are taking on characteristics of the more elaborate intergenerational structure described by Joan Moore in her research on Chicano gangs in Los Angeles.[46]

The street gangs described here are at best quasi-legitimate social groupings, organized to achieve illegitimate ends, yet they acquire tremen-dous power and prestige within local neighborhoods. They also wield sig-nificant influence in the public school system, establishing zones of control within individual schools and forcing school authorities to take cognizance of gang structures in assigning students to different schools. (Even Chicago politicians have utilized street gangs as a means of furthering their own political control and influence over the voting population: in the 1983 pri-mary election, the Black Gangster Disciples distributed food baskets in black neighborhoods for then Mayor Jane Byrne's campaign, and the Latin Disciples removed posters and harassed Richard Daley's campaign work-ers in the northwest-side neighborhoods.) Nothing is more important for the successful education of high school students than the sense of a safe and secure environment conducive to learning. Yet this very basic and inalienable right is denied public school students in Chicago and other cities.

The power of street gangs within public schools and their ability to generate intense loyalty from young persons in the local neighborhood is the consequence of social forces much wider than the local community—forces which include the ready availability of handguns, decline of employment opportunities in central cities, the export of basic manufac-turing jobs to Third World countries, cuts in federal programs for central cities, and the general decline of education in the United States. Few opportunities for employment or mobility exist in these inner-city neigh-borhoods, and gang membership represents an alternative means of achieving gratification and status. There are obvious conclusions as to the economic, social, and political forces responsible for this process, but few easy answers for alleviating the problem of street gangs in the inner city.

There are some who will claim that the problem is not as bad as we have described; that while gang activity in the public schools may have been extensive in the mid-1980s it has declined in the intervening years;

that the problem is in the community and in the family and not in the school. Yet since the time of our research the number of gang-related homicides in Chicago has continued to increase, and there have been other homicides and attempted homicides within school buildings. In May 1991 the graduation ceremony at a high school in one of the southwest-side Mexican neighborhoods was disrupted by a fight between gang members which resulted in six persons being taken to the hospital.[47]

Despite the problems outlined in this chapter, it is important to recognize that there are inner-city schools which remain relatively free of the gang problems that plague other schools. In some instances these are selective academic and technical high schools which limit enrollment to the best junior high school students. In other cases public schools in even the worst gang neighborhoods have minimized gang problems by enforcing strict rules which keep overt gang activity out of the school. One of the schools in the ASPIRA study was able to reduce the level of gang activity by adopting a "closed campus" policy of not allowing students to enter or leave the school building during school hours.

As noted earlier, most studies of school dropouts focus on individual-level explanations which place the blame on individual students, their families, and ethnic subcultures. The Chicago public schools, like school systems in other cities around the country, have passed beyond the denial stage and now appear ready to confront the problem of gang activity head-on. Future research must further examine the impact of gang activity on school life and on the decision of some students to drop out of school. Increased attention should be focused on those schools which are successful in dealing with gang problems to isolate the factors responsible for success, and to insure that these procedures are implemented in problem schools. With fewer than half of the students completing their high school education, nothing less than the future of the next generation of Hispanic children in Chicago and other cities depends on this agenda.

NOTES

1. See "Gangs and Supergangs," *New Dimensions*, May 1990, pp. 20-45; "The Drug Gangs: Waging War in America's Cities," *Newsweek*, March 28, 1988, pp. 20-27; "Gangs, Guns, and Drugs," NBC news documentary with Tom Brokaw, August 22-23, 1989. Many local newspapers have run investigative series about gangs in their cities; see, for example, William Recktenwald and Nathaniel Sheppard, Jr., "Gangs," a five-part series in the *Chicago Tribune*, January 8-12, 1984.

2. Walter B. Miller, *Violence by Youth Gangs and Youth Groups in Major American Cities* (Washington, D.C.: National Institute for Juvenile Justice and Delinquency Prevention, 1976).

3. Lewis Yablonsky's description of "The 'Community' of the Violent Gang" does not mention schools; similarly Short and Strodtbeck, Spergel, and Klein contain no direct mention of schools. See Malcolm Klein, *Street Gangs and Street Workers* (Englewood Cliffs, N.J.: Prentice Hall, 1971); James F. Short and Fred L. Strodtbeck, *Group Process and Gang Delinquency* (Chicago: University of Chicago Press, 1965); Irving Spergel, *Street Gang Work* (New York: Doubleday-Anchor, 1966); Lewis Yablonsky, *The Violent Gang* (New York: Irvington Press, 1962), pp. 190-215. Among edited collections published during this period, see James F. Short, ed., *Delinquency, Crime, and Society* (Chicago: University of Chicago Press, 1976).

4. See John Hagedorn, *People and Folks: Gangs, Crime, and the Underclass in a Rustbelt City* (Chicago: Lake View Press, 1988); James Diego Vigil, *Barrio Gangs: Street Life and Identity in Southern California* (Austin: University of Texas Press, 1988).

5. See Jeffrey Fagan, "The Social Organization of Drug Use and Drug Dealing Among Urban Gangs," *Criminology* (1989): 633-69.

6. For evidence that street gangs may be a significant factor in the decision to drop out of high school, see Charles Kyle, "Los Preciosos: The Magnitude of and Reasons for the Hispanic Dropout Problem in Chicago: A Case Study of Two Chicago Public High Schools" (Unpublished Ph.D. Dissertation, Evanston, Illinois, Northwestern University, 1984), pp. 45-62. For an overview of studies which attribute these decisions to the characteristics of students and their families, see Gary S. Wehlage and Robert A. Rutter, "Dropping Out: How Much Do Schools Contribute to the Problem?" *Teachers College Record* (1986): 374-92.

7. Charles L. Kyle. *ASPIRA Chicago Hispanic Student Dropout Study* (Chicago: ASPIRA, Inc., of Illinois, 1984).

8. Edward F. Tromanhauser, T. Corcoran, and A. Lollino, *The Chicago Safe School Study* (Chicago: City of Chicago, Chicago Board of Education, 1981), p. i.

9. James Jacobs, "Street Gangs in Prison," *Social Problems* 21, (3), pp. 395-409. Ruth Horowitz, *Honor and the American Dream: Culture and Identity in a Chicano Community* (New Brunswick, N.J.: Rutgers University Press, 1983); Irving Spergel, "Violent Gangs in Chicago: In Search of Social Policy," *Social Service Review* 58 (1984); Irving Spergel and David Curry, "Gang Homicide, Delinquency, and Community," *Criminology* (1988): 381-405. In his report to the Chicago School Board Spergel notes that only 9 percent of gang-related criminal acts are reported in or adjacent to public schools (*Youth Gang Activity and the Chicago Public Schools* [Chicago: University of Chicago Press, School of Social Service Administration, 1985]).

10. Kyle, *Student Dropout Study*.

11. See Ray Hutchison, *The DePaul Hispanic Survey: A Report on Immigration, Social Networks, Language Patterns, and Ethnic Identity Among Chicago's Hispanic Population*, Research Paper No. 88-15 (Green Bay: University of Wisconsin, Center for Public Affairs, August 1988).

12. See Robert J. Simandl, "Identification of Chicago Street Gangs," Chicago Police Department, June 1983.

13. "Schools Not So Perilous, Data Show," *Chicago Tribune*, December 11, 1987, sec. 3, p. 14. See Dennis Roncek and Donald Faggiani, "High Schools and Crime: a Replication," *The Sociological Quarterly*, Winter 1985, 491-505, and Dennis Roncek and Antoinette Lobosco, "The Effect of High Schools on Crime in Their Neighborhoods," *Social Science Quarterly*, September 1983, 598-613 for information on the prevalence of crime around high schools.

14. The common designation of gang members as leaders, core members, and peripheral (or marginal) members dates from Frederic Thrasher's early work on youth gangs in Chicago and may still be found in police reports, school documents, and other sources; see, for example, Ruth Love, *Gang Activity Task Force: A Report with Recommendations for Dealing with Gang Activity in the Chicago Public Schools.* Chicago: City of Chicago, Board of Education, September 1981), pp. 1-2.

15. Information about street gangs in the neighborhoods surrounding the two high schools in the ASPIRA study is from "Youth Gangs Projected for FY83 and Hierarchical Status" (Broader Urban Involvement and Leadership Development [BUILD], Inc., Chicago 1983).

16. Prior to the use of the Folks and People labels, which cut across black and Hispanic gangs in the city, three of the Disciple groups—the Latin Disciples, Spanish Cobras, and Imperial Gangsters—used "La Familia" as an identifier for the allegiance between their groups.

17. Diego Vigil charts a similar pattern of neighborhood and school involvement in gang activity and confrontations for Chicano youth in Los Angeles; see Vigil, *Barrio Gangs*, esp. pp. 130-31.

18. *Chicago Tribune*, August 19, 1987, p. 126.

19. See Ray Hutchison, "The Hispanic Population in Chicago: A Study in Population Growth and Assimilation," in *Research in Race and Ethnic Relations*, eds. Cora Marrett and Cheryl Leggon (Greenwich, Conn.: JAI Press, 1988, pp. 193-229).

20. See Felix M. Padilla, *Puerto Rican Chicago* (University of Notre Dame Press, 1987); also Ray Hutchison, "The Hispanic Community in Chicago: A Study of Population Growth and Acculturation."

21. For information on drop-out rates at the two high schools, see Kyle, *Student Dropout Study*, pp. 12-25; Charles L. Kyle, John Lane, Joyce A. Sween, and Armando Triana, *We Have a Choice: Students at Risk of Leaving Chicago Public Schools* (Chicago: DePaul University, Center for Research on Hispanics, 1986).

22. Roberto M. Fernandez, Ronnelle Paulsen, and Marsha Hirano-Nakanishi, "Dropping Out Among Hispanic Youth," *Social Science Research*, March 1989, 21-52.

23. This student's mother stated that she had gone to the high school many times to see if she could talk to the principal or to the teachers to see if something could be worked out and to explain the problems her son was having—he was constantly coming home with torn shirts and black eyes—and the reason he was cutting the first class. She claimed that the school administrators refused to help her.

24. Vigil, *Barrio Gangs*, p. 2; Horowitz, *Honor and the American Dream*, p. 182. The literature on patterns of drug use among street gangs is summarized by Jeffrey Fagan, and several recent studies suggest higher levels of use among gang members; see Fagan, "Social Organization of Drug Use," pp. 635-37.

25. Fagan, ibid.; the *Chicago Tribune* reported on a sweep by Chicago police in a neighborhood four blocks from Humbolt Park High School were sixty members of one street gang were arrested for drug sales. Members of this and allied gangs controlled the high school throughout the 1980s. See "Gang Drug Sweep Begins; 60 Arrested," *Chicago Tribune*, March 13, 1987, sec. 1, p. 1.

26. Safe School Subcommittee meeting, Network for Youth Services, December 16, 1983.

27. CHicago Public Schools, Uniform Discipline Code, 1982, glossary.

28. Kyle, "Los Preciosus," pp. 54-55. The Boston Safe School Study reported that early 40 percent of students often feared for their safety in school or reported avoiding corridors and rest rooms; see Boston Safe Schools Commission, *Making Our Schools Safer for Learning* (Boston: Boston Public Schools, 1983). The ASPIRA finding that female students were more afraid of physical injury than were male students is in sharp contrast with other studies where males typically report greater fear of physical harm; see Dennis Rosenbaum, *Gangs and Youth Problems in Evanston: Research Findings and Policy Options* (Evanston, Ill.: Northwestern University, Center for Urban Affairs and Policy Research, 1983).

29. Quoted in Kyle, p. 75.

30. Safe School Subcommittee meeting, Network for Youth Services, December 16, 1983.

31. A study of Boston's public schools in 1983 found that 30 percent of the students admitted carrying weapons to school; half of the teachers and 40 percent of the students had been victims of school robbery, assault, or larceny; see Boston Safe Schools Commission.

32. *Chicago Tribune*, "Gang Drug Sweep Begins," emphasis added.

33. Quoted in Love, *Gang Activity Task Force Report*, p. 13.

34. Max Weber, *Economy and Society: An Outline of Interpretive Sociology* (New York: Bedminster Press, 1968), pp. 217-26; the tendency of bureaucracies to increase secrecy is elaborated by Reinhard Bendix in "Bureaucracy," in *Scholarship and Partisanship: Essays on Max Weber*, Reinhard Bendix and Guenther Roth (Berkeley: University of California Press, 1971), 129-55.

35. Comments to an investigating team from the National Commission on Secondary Schooling for Hispanics, March 25, 1984.

36. "Gang Quarrel Seen Behind DuSable Killing," *Chicago Tribune*, October 15, 1987, p. 3.

37. "Schools Not So Perilous, Data Show," *Chicago Tribune*.

38. Safe School Subcommittee meeting, Network for Youth Services, December 16, 1983.

39. Information on the relative number of dropouts across the Chicago public schools may be found in Kyle et al., *We Have a Choice*. A report from the Chicago Panel on Public School Policy and Finance gives a slightly lower figure of 43 percent (see G. Alfred Hess and Diana Lauber, *Drop Outs from the Chicago Public Schools* [Chicago: City of Chicago, Chicago School Board, Panel on Public School Finances, 1985]); also "Dropout Crisis Called Worse Than It Looks," *Chicago Tribune*, December 17, 1986, pp. 1-2). Additional information on the dropout problem in the two schools in the ASPIRA study may be found in Charles Kyle and Edward Kantowicz, "Bogus Statistics: Chicago's Latino Community Exposes the Dropout Problem," *Latino Studies Journal* 2 (May 1991): 34-52.

40. Cited in Kyle et al., *We Have a Choice*, p. 25.

41. There is a significant gender difference in the responses of male and female students; 28 percent of female dropouts reported that pregnancy and/or problems with child care were responsible for their leaving school; see Kyle, "Los Preciosos," pp. 50-51.

42. Horowitz, *Honor and the American Dream*, p. 155.

43. Spergel, *Youth Gang Activity and the Chicago Public Schools*, p. 29.

44. C. Pineda, *Chicano Gang Barrios in East Los Angeles* (Sacramento: California Board of Corrections, 1978).

45. See Marisa Alicea, "Dual Home Bases: A Reconceptualization of Puerto Rican Migration," *Latino Studies Journal* 1 (September 1990): 78-98.

46. Joan Moore et al., *Homeboys: Gangs, Drugs, and Prison in the Barrios of Los Angeles* (Philadelphia: Temple University Press, 1978).

47. "Melee at School," *Chicago Tribune*, May 26, 1990.

7

Blazon Nouveau: Gang Graffiti in the Barrios of Los Angeles and Chicago

RAY HUTCHISON

INTRODUCTION

Much of the recent research concerning street gangs in the United States has focused on the deviant aspects of gangs such as criminal activity, gang homicide, and drug use.[2] This emphasis is due both to the serious nature of social problems such as drug use and violent crime attributed to street gangs as well as the proclivity of social scientists to highlight those groups viewed as different from the middle-class mainstream (Peter Berger refers to this as "unrespectability").[3] Although street gangs have produced an elaborate subculture rich in ceremonial ritual and symbolic representation (expressed in graffiti, tatoos, clothing styles, and other cultural artifacts), there have been relatively few attempts to describe the

I would like to thank Loren Reichert (University of Nevada-Las Vegas) for his assistance in developing and printing several of the examples of gang graffiti included here. All photographs are by the author with the exception of the Insane Unknowns/Crossed Shotguns, which is by Marisa Alicea (DePaul University).

subculture of the street gang or even to deal with the complex range of gang activity within urban neighborhoods—not all of which is deviant and/or illegal. Any serious attempt to understand the role of street gangs in contemporary society requires a more thorough view of the subcultures which have arisen among minority youths in the inner city. This will require the intensive and probably ethnographic study of gang members at work, at school, at home, and in the neighborhood, in addition to the more usual sources of information concerning deviant activity.

This chapter examines one product of the street gang subculture—the seemingly omnipresent gang graffiti which have evolved in inner-city neighborhoods over the last several decades. In the following pages we will analyze and compare gang graffiti from Los Angeles and Chicago. To some, this will seem to be an academic and trivial pursuit: graffiti are typically viewed as vandalism, public nuisances to be dealt with by measures such as banning the sale of spray paint and making graffiti writing a criminal act. But gang graffiti are also rich sources of data for the urban ethnologist. They are used by police and social workers to keep track of changes in territory alliances between gangs. The analysis of gang graffiti may also be-used to learn about the structure of the gang, conflicts and alliances between particular street gangs, and possible linkages among street gangs in different cities and regions of the country.

BACKGROUND TO THE STUDY

In 1983 I had an opportunity to teach at the University of California-San Diego. As part of a senior seminar on Hispanic research, I organized a slide presentation on Mexican murals with Mario Torrero, a local Chicano artist. This presentation included several examples of gang graffiti from Chicago, and Mario subsequently encouraged me to photograph graffiti from the San Diego gangs. The following summer I spent several days in Los Angeles and San Francisco and then several weeks in Chicago systematically photographing gang graffiti. The examples of gang graffiti reproduced in the following pages are drawn from a collection of several hundred slides and negatives; most of these date from 1983 to 1985, although I have updated the collection from time to time as graffiti styles have changed; as new gangs and/or new allegiances among existing gangs which alter either the content or style of the graffiti have emerged; and to document other important characteristics of the graffiti. The examples have been selected to represent specific categories of graffiti from each location; they do not, of course, represent a random sample of all gang graffiti, either in Chicago or in the Southwest.

Although the graffiti in these locations are similar in content—presenting messages about gang identity and intergang conflict—the style of the graffiti is fundamentally different. For this reason, gang graffiti lend themselves not only to a comparative and descriptive analysis, but may also produce a more thorough understanding of gang activity and adolescent subcultures in different cities. While most researchers are aware of the graffiti and have a general understanding of what they represent, this rich source of data about street gangs and the adolescent subculture within which they have developed is missing from the contemporary literature on street gangs.

Urban graffiti have been examined by several authors. In 1974 Praeger Books published *The Faith of Graffiti*, a large coffee-table book with eighty pages of photographs of graffiti by various artists in New York City and an introductory essay by Norman Mailer. By the 1980s this graffiti had developed into the elaborate whole-car displays of subway art which Craig Castleman describes in *Getting Up*. Some of the subway graffiti artists have moved into more mainstream art and even into artistic careers, as described by Richard Lachmann.[4]

The New York/East Coast style graffiti found in these sources, however, are *not* gang graffiti: instead, as Castleman describes, individual artists sought to produce the largest number of and the most elaborate graffiti—and in more sensational locations—than other artists were capable of; the graffito was an effort to establish individual claims over artistic style (the outstanding documentary film on New York graffiti is appropriately entitled "Style Wars").[5] The purpose of gang graffiti, on the other hand, is to represent group identity and to expand the reputation of the gang, not the individual. Much of the gang graffiti in Chicago are in fact anonymous, and graffiti in Los Angeles adhere to specific style conventions which have remained unchanged for nearly two decades.

Geographers have viewed gang graffiti primarily (and at times solely) as territorial markings. David Ley and Roman Cybriwsky, for example, present a series of maps demonstrating that gang graffiti are concentrated along the boundaries of gang neighborhoods. Any discussion of the differing types of gang graffiti, and whether the graffiti in Philadelphia (where the research was done) are similar to that in New York or Los Angeles is not attempted.[6] The graffiti reproduced in the following pages convey elaborate information about gang allegiances and may be purposely designed to insult and taunt opposing gangs. Indeed, the deliberate and often complicated symbolic manipulations found in these illustrations suggests that graffiti of this type would make poor territorial markings, since only persons with intimate knowledge of street gangs could ever begin to decipher the internal messages.

Gang graffiti may be viewed as forms of artistic expression, since they follow established styles and make use of sophisticated principles of graphic design. In the last two decades graffiti have moved from the streets of New York into legitimate galleries and now are evaluated on the same terms as other art—the placement of designs within the field, use of color, and other formal criteria. Much of the gang graffiti reproduced in this chapter stand up well in comparison. Street gang members are clearly involved in something much more sophisticated and rewarding to the urban researcher than simple territorial markings.

LOS ANGELES GANG GRAFFITI

In the mid-1970s Jerry and Sally Romotsky produced a series of articles on gang graffiti in Los Angeles. Their analysis demonstrates that the graffiti in this period had developed specific lettering styles to convey information as to group membership and individual identity. Published in art magazines and graphic journals, this work emphasized the design component of gang graffiti and serves as an important backdrop to understanding the continuity of styles and conventions in the intervening decades.[7]

California gang graffito of the present day are remarkably similar to that recorded by the Romotskys almost twenty years ago; in fact the lettering styles developed by gang members in the 1960s have been appropriated by commercial artists and thus have spread to the more general adolescent subculture of the Southwest. Our discussion will focus on the presentation of gang identity, the characteristic features of *placas* produced by individual gang members, the use of distinctive lettering styles, and the merging of the street-gang subculture with the more general adolescent subculture in southern California.

Gang Names

This analysis must start with the simple observation that the purpose of gang graffiti is to represent information about the group and its members. The precise manner in which this information may be manipulated, however, is subject to infinite permutations—lettering styles change, symbols are added, individual gang members may be identified, and other information is added or deleted. Given the possible range of representation, it is significant that certain conventions emerge and that particular styles come to predominate.

In Los Angeles graffiti, gang names are typically shown in large, even life-size block letters, which may either spell out the full name or present only the initials of the gang. The use of block letters allows the artist to include other information within the graffito. The first example, from East Los Angeles, shows the initials of the gang (LES), with the name of the gang (Little East Side) written inside the body of the graffito. At the right side of the graffito is a significant addition written in Spanish: "Ese Toro Chico Boxer Somos Locos Y Que." The additional message translates "We are Toro, Chico, and Boxer [names of gang members]; we're crazy and so what"—a declaration of gang membership followed by a boast found in many examples of California graffiti.

The more elaborate examples of graffiti in Los Angeles and other southwestern cities typically include the full name of the gang along with geographical coordinates and a membership roster (information which is probably known to the police, so there is no reason to hide this from public display). These graffiti are often overwhelming in their size and complexity; the example shown in figure 7.2 is dated by the artist (8/8/83) and lists the street names of more than twenty members (The Homeboys) of the Sherman Ls (Sherman Locos, the Sherman Heights gang) from San Diego's south-side (17th Street) neighborhood. The statement "Aqui Para Big Barrio" translates literally to "here for big barrio."

These graffiti walls are frequently marked over by other gangs and contain many layers of graffiti representing several years of writing. Rival gangs often sponsor raids against their opponents' graffiti, defacing the original work and adding their own names. The illustration in figure 7.3 presents one such example where an opposing gang used a paint roller and eventually deposited the contents of a paint can over a large graffito which at one time included a roster of the 15th Street gang from the southwest side of San Francisco. In 1976 the Romotsky's noted that,

> The writing on the walls often records struggles for dominance over a given territory. Disputed walls display a multi-layered phenomenon of inscriptions which have been marked out, then re-established. . . . One group defaces the inscription of its rival by marking out its plaqueaso with asterisk-like x's and then scribbling *puto* next to it or across it.

We will compare various methods of defacing an opposing gang's graffiti when we examine Chicago graffiti in a later section.

Placas

Perhaps the most common form of graffiti produced by street gangs in Los Angeles and other southwestern cities is the *placa*. These graffiti typically display the individual's name, his/her gang affiliation, and the geographical coordinates of the gang's territory. The *placa* shown in figure 7.4 reads as follows: Lil Bobby SS 38 ST CXS *(con safos)*, representing Little Bobby of the south side 38th Street gang. To the right of the main design is

FIG. 7.1. Little East Side Gang, Los Angeles

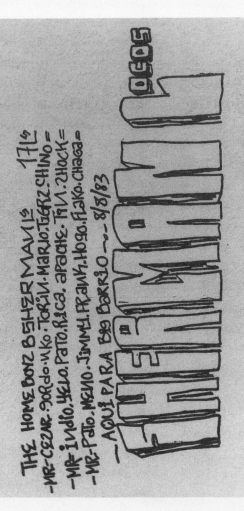

FIG. 7.2. Sherman Heights Gang, San Diego

FIG. 7.3. Fifteenth Street Gang, San Francisco

FIG. 7.4. *Placa* for Little Bobby, 38th Street Gang, Los Angeles

FIG. 7.5. Homeboy Letters, Logan Heights Gang, San Diego

FIG. 7.6. Lowriders, Logan Heights-Sherman Heights Gangs, San DIego

FIG. 7.7. Latin Disciples

FIG. 7.10. Kent City—Diesciple Nation Killers

152

FIG. 7.11. Symbolic Annihilation of Latin Disciples

FIG. 7.12. Latin Kings City

FIG. 7.13. Latin King Graffiti showing Domination of
Latin Disciples and Imperial Gangsters

FIG. 7.14. Imperial Gangsters—Modified Latin King Crown

FIG. 7.15. Insane Unknowns, Crossed Shotguns, c. 1978

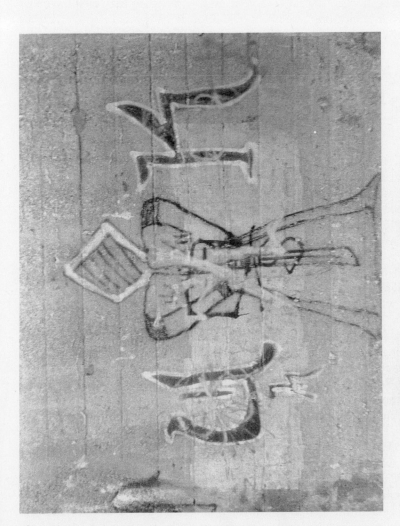

FIG. 7.16. Insane Unknowns, Ghost Figure, 1984

the number 13, which, according to the Romotskys, is a drug reference to marijuana (M is the thirteenth letter in the alphabet).[8]

The phrase *con safos* (CXS) is meant to guard the inscription from defacement by threatening evil to anyone who might deface the graffito; the translation is "the same to you." This convention may well have lost the original meaning; members of California gangs that I spoke with in 1984 did not have any specific translation for the CXS convention, even though it was regularly used in their graffiti. While the *placas* used by southwestern Chicano gangs comes closest to the individual graffito "tags" by New York graffiti artists described by Castleman and others, this form of gang graffiti is much less common in Chicago.

Lettering Style and Iconography

Three different lettering styles appear in California graffiti; these are commonly referred to as block or square letters, loop letters, and point letters. A comparison of contemporary graffiti with illustrations provided by the Romotsky's from the early 1970s indicates that these styles have been consistent for at least two decades. It is the use of distinctive lettering, and especially the point letters—now called "homeboy letters"—which makes the best California gang graffiti instantly identifiable, as shown in figure 7.5.

This graffito, from a corner grocery adjacent Chicano Park in San Diego, presents a wonderful example of point lettering from the mid-1980s along with a number of conventions found in gang graffiti in southern California. The top line, which reads Cycos, is an interesting phonetic borrowing from English (in *calo*—"gutter Spanish"—*cyco* has the same general meaning as psycho); in this context, it is a boast that we are crazy, or tough. This is followed by the street names of four gang members (Tino, Boxer, Louie, Roach). The second line from the bottom presents a linguistic transformation found in San Diego graffiti: this line reads "Ele Ache #1," which is the phonetic spelling *in Spanish* for the letters L and H (the initials of the gang's *English* name), and thus identifies the graffito as belonging to the Logan Heights gang. A similar convention is used by the Sherman Heights gang, where the initials of the gang are spelled out as Ese Eme.

The names of Chicano gangs in Los Angeles and throughout California are derived directly from local neighborhoods (Logan Heights) or more generalized geographical referents (East Side), as seen in the preceding examples. With the exception of the ubiquitous *Playboy* bunny, individual gangs generally do not have specific symbols which identify their group. The use of the skull and Panama hat in the preceding example is unusual for California graffiti; these symbols may be traced to the Mexican *Dia de los muertos* (Day of the Dead), and to the drug subculture of the barrio.

Gang Graffiti and Adolescent Subcultures

Even someone who has not visited a large American city probably is familiar with graffito images from movies and television shows and, in the last several years, music videos. In the Southwest, Chicano gangs have formed a unique subculture with specific clothing styles, language, hair styles, and the like. This is sometimes referred to as the lowrider subculture, named after the specially modified automobiles preferred by gang members and other adolescents and young adults in California. *Lowrider* magazine is circulated throughout the Southwest and in other large cities, and stylized characterizations of lowrider automobiles are sometimes found in gang graffiti, such as those shown in figure 7.6.

The subculture which has grown up around the Chicano street gangs in Los Angles and other California cities may best be viewed in *Teen Angel* magazine. This bimonthly publication reproduces the graffiti, poems, letters, and photographs sent in by gang members and other readers; regular features include several pages devoted to photographs of homeboys and homegirls, dressed in gang fashion, displaying hand signs to indicate their gang allegiance, and sometimes holding weapons. In addition to publishing poems dedicated to boyfriends and girlfriends and a regular play list of popular songs, the magazine also markets a variety of specialty products (such as *chola* bands) to a wider adolescent audience. *Teen Angel* and *Lowrider* magazines demonstrate the extent to which the cultural products of the Chicano street gang have come to permeate adolescent subcultures in the barrio.

CHICAGO GANG GRAFFITI

The graffiti produced by Chicago street gangs are identified by a more freeform lettering style and the extensive use of symbols. This results in a wider variety of images which undergo a continual process of redefinition as gangs discover new ways to improve the symbols representing their group and to insult those of opposing gangs. The manipulation of symbols and other conventions allows detailed information to be presented with tremendous economy of style and in a seemingly never-ending adaptation of new conventions. As is the case with the point or homeboy lettering style shown in figure 7.5, much of the information encoded in this graffiti is accessible only to members of this subculture. Chicago graffiti are also permeated with violent references and threats against other gangs to a greater extent than is found in the Southwest.

This section will focus on the presentation of particular icons used to identity particular gangs; the communication of allegiances and conflicts between individual gangs; the convention of "naming and killing" opposing gangs; and the manipulation of symbols representing gang identities in some of the more creative graffiti.

Gang Names and Gang Emblems

Each street gang in Chicago has adopted specific symbols or emblems which identify the group—a pointed crown for the Latin Kings, a six-pointed star and pitchfork to represent the Latin Disciples. In addition to displays of the group name and/or initials (e.g., LD for the Latin Disciples), most graffiti include many other symbols which might appear unrelated to any specific gang. The graffito in figure 7.7 is produced by the Latin Disciples: the graffito includes the letters L and D in a modified gothic design on either side of the Disciples' heart. A pitchfork is shown just to the right of the letter D. Other graffiti of the Latin Disciples may include a more elaborate "devil's heart" (shown with horns, wings, and a pointed tail) and/or a full-size devil figure holding a pitchfork.

Gang Nations and Gang Allegiances

Hispanic street gangs in Chicago are allied with either the Latin Kings or Latin Disciples.[9] The larger gang aggregates, referred to as either the Almighty Latin King Nation or the Maniac Latin Disciple Nation, provide protection on the street, in school, and in the state prison system for persons belonging to other gangs within the same nation. The graffiti of individual gangs usually incorporate symbols of either the Latin Disciple Nation (a six-pointed star, pitchfork, and/or heart with horns and devil's tail) or Latin King Nation (pointed crown and/or five-pointed star) to indicate allegiance to the larger gang nations. The use of five dots or the number five to symbolize the Latin Kings (derived from the original five-pointed crown and five-pointed star) and the number six to symbolize the Latin Disciples (from the original six-pointed star) are similar style conventions. The graffiti shown in figures 7.8 and 7.9 demonstrate the structuring of gang nations in Chicago.

The large cobra emblem in figure 7.8 represents the Spanish Cobras; the letters read Insane SC [Spanish Cobra] Nation; and the pitchfork rising out of the initials SC and at the top of the cobra's head indicate that the gang is allied with the Latin Disciples. Note that the use of "insane" is similar to "cyco" in the Los Angeles graffito in figure 7.5; the meaning of the boast is of course the same—we're crazy, so you don't want to fool around with us. The inverted KK in the bottom left corner of the Spanish Cobra graffito is street-gang shorthand for "King Killers," indicating the opposition of the Spanish Cobras to the Latin Kings.

Figure 7.9 presents a large graffito which proclaims the allegiance of the Almighty "Lords" of Palmer Street with the "Kings" of Kedzie—in other words, an alliance of the Gaylords from the Palmer Street/Palmer Square neighborhood with the Latin Kings from Kedzie Street in the Humbolt Park-Logan Square neighborhood. In the middle of the graffito two life-size Gaylord figures (modeled after a hooded Klu Klux Klan figure) are displayed wearing the Latin King's pointed crown. The graffito also indicates opposition to the Latin Disciples (both figures are holding Latin Disciple pitchforks upside down), and to the Imperial Gangsters (the tiara or rounded crown of the Imperial Gangsters is shown inverted on either side of the central emblem).[10]

Naming and Killing

A convention unique to Chicago graffiti is the simple addition of the letter K to the name or initials of an opposing gang; this immediately converts LD (graffiti written for the Latin Disciples) to LDK (Latin Disciple Killers, written by a gang from the opposing Latin King nation). Other graffiti include only the shorthand "naming of Killing" of opposing groups without any identifying information from the gang responsible. Thus a graffito which reads U-K-K/G-L-K/L-K-K (Insane Unknown Killers, Gaylord Killers, Latin King Killers) can immediately be attributed to a gang belonging to the Latin Disciple Nation, even though the group is not directly identified.

The full motto of "killer" or "killers" may also be added directly to the graffiti produced by other gangs, as was done with the overwrite of "killer" on the "Lords of Palmer St." in figure 7.9, or it may be part of the original design of a larger graffito. In the example shown in figure 7.10, the Kent City gang has declared themselves to be both Disciple Killers (as indicated by the DKs in the top line of the graffito) and part of the "Diesciple" Killers Nation (indicating an alliance with the Latin King nation).

Symbolic Annihilation

The graffito shown in figure 7.11 carries the notion of naming and killing opposing gangs a step further. In this example, the Insane Unknowns have destroyed the symbol of the Latin Disciples: the six-pointed Latin Disciple star has been broken in half; at either side of the remaining parts of the star the letters DK proclaim Disciple Killer. In the center is the name of the opposing gang (IUK or Insane Unknowns), the name of the artist (Shorty), along with an inverted Latin Disciple pitchfork. This type of graffito is a natural outgrowth of the manipulation of symbols from opposing groups, and results in many interesting variations: broken hearts displayed upside down; exploding crowns and/or stars; crowns pierced by pitchforks and shotguns, and the like. The graffiti are intended to portray the symbolic annihilation of opposition gangs.

Territorial Claims and Challenges

While I have suggested that gang graffiti have a purpose much broader
and more significant than simply territorial markers, many graffiti include
specific geographical referents, and there is one type of graffito whose
primary expression is that of a territorial claim. These large graffiti are
typically found either along the boundaries separating gang neighborhoods, or in areas adjacent gang headquarters and meeting places, such as
school playgrounds and factory/warehouse areas.

The graffito in figure 7.12 is located along a railroad viaduct which
separates the Latin King and Latin Disciple neighborhoods in Humbolt
Park; this is a strategic location since anyone driving or walking from one
neighborhood to the next will pass by the wall. The graffito proclaims
that this is "Latin King City—Come Get Us" and indicates the specific
branch of the gang which wrote the graffito, located on Kedzie and
Wabansia streets (K/W ST). To the left of the central message the notation
D-K/E-K/G-K/C-K is a reminder that the Latin Kings are Disciple-Eagle-
Gangster-Cobra Killers.

Symbolic Manipulation

Because Chicago gang graffiti make extensive use of symbols representing
individual groups and the larger gang nations, graffiti demonstrating both
an evolution of specific conventions and new, creative uses of existing
symbols appear on a regular basis. In figure 7.13, the symbols of three different gangs have been combined in a striking graphic. The pointed crown
at the top—the image boldly portrayed with just one, rather than the three
or five points more commonly drawn—identifies the origins of this graffito
with the Latin Kings; underneath, the Latin Disciples's winged heart and
Imperial Gangsters' tiara have been inverted.[11] This graffito is a remarkable
piece of graphic design; it boldly announces the domination of both gangs
by the Latin Kings.

A final example of Chicago graffito demonstrates the more creative
manipulations that come into play when gang artists begin experimenting
with existing symbols. In Los Angeles, graffiti are defaced by writing
putos or other derogatory phrases over another gang's name; similar
phrases can found in Chicago graffiti (the initials PGL, representing the
Palmer Gaylords, are sometimes altered to read Pussy Gaylords by
opposing gangs). The use of symbols to represent gang identity allows the
standard adolescent taunts and insults to enter a new realm. The inverted
Latin King crown reproduced in figure 7.14, which has an anatomically
correct phallus hanging from the base, was produced by the Imperial
Gangsters (indicated by the G perching at the base of the crown). Not
only is this an innovative graphic design, and one which has been care-

fully presented for maximum visual impact, but it also manages to convey perhaps the worst personal insult in a most effective manner.

CONCLUSIONS

Regardless of the particular city or region of the country, the content of gang graffiti is generally consistent: it is designed to convey specific messages about group identity, gang allegiances, and individual membership. The graffiti often contain specific geographical markers, identifying the group which produced the graffiti as being from (for example) the Logan Heights neighborhood on the south side of San Diego, or from Kedzie and Wabansia Streets in the Humbolt Park neighborhood on Chicago's northwest side. And while some graffiti are intended specifically as territorial markers, this is not the exclusive or even the main purpose of contemporary gang graffiti.

While this chapter has examined certain common elements of gang graffiti, more striking are the very different styles and conventions which distinguish graffiti in the Midwest from that of the Southwest. Some of the significant variations discussed in this chapter include lettering styles, the use of symbols, the naming and killing of opposing groups, and the extent of integration within a more general adolescent subculture.

Los Angeles gang graffiti make use of distinctive lettering styles which have become standardized over time. More than one writer has referred to these graffiti as "barrio calligraphy," and one lettering style—point letters—has come to be know as "homeboy letters," making use of the slang term referring to gang members. The use of these lettering styles is confined to California and Texas; they are not used in Chicago, where the graffiti show an eclectic and often freeform lettering style.[12]

Each Chicago gang has a specific symbol (or group of symbols) to identify the group; in many instances the symbol is an extension of the gang's name (the Latin King crown and the Spanish Cobra emblem, for example), although other symbols may have only a tangential relationship to the group's name and identity (the Latin Disciple pitchfork and devil figure, the Insane Unknown ghost figure). Street gangs in Los Angeles, San Diego, and other southwestern cities do not use symbols, and the names of the gangs are usually taken from the surrounding neighborhood (Sherman Heights, Maravilla, and the like).[13]

Because Chicago street gangs make more extensive use of symbols, the city has a wider variety and more creative use of graffiti than is found in the Southwest. The common procedure for defacing graffiti in California is to mark through or paint over them. Chicago gangs, on the other hand, seem constantly on the lookout for new methods to alter and deface their

opponents' graffiti: adding your symbol on top of the symbol of an opposing gang indicates that you have domination over the other gang; revers-
ing their symbol transforms a message supporting one gang into one
opposing that group. Symbols are combined in evermore complicated
designs to indicate gang allegiances and opposition; adding the letter K to
the graffiti of another gang declares that you are "killers" of the first group.
Inevitably, gang members discover ways to disgrace the symbols of the
opposing group, as when the Latin King crown is converted into a large
phallus. This sort of manipulation and invention is not possible in the California graffiti.

One very significant difference between the Chicago and Los Angeles gangs is the degree to which gang activities—and the cultural products
of this activity, such as graffiti—have become part of a larger adolescent
subculture. Emory Bogardus's early research indicates that street gangs
have existed in Los Angeles's Mexican barrios for more than half a century.[14] Over time the graffiti have evolved specific lettering styles and carefully organized *placas;* the gangs themselves have become integrated into
the local neighborhoods; and certain elements of gang culture have
merged into the more general adolescent subculture. Thus walls of gang
graffiti may include drawings of lowrider automobiles, and store owners
in the local neighborhood may stock clothing styles preferred by members of the gangs.

In Chicago, no such well-defined Mexican, Hispanic, or youth-gang
subculture has developed, in large part because the major barrios were
not settled until the 1960s and there has not been sufficient time to develop
and then formalize particular conventions. As a consequence, lettering
styles appear freeform and vary greatly from one gang and from one
region of the city to the next. Mario Gonzalez, a Chicago artist, notes that
specific lettering conventions have now developed which differentiate the
graffito of Mexican gangs in different neighborhoods of the city. And
although gang members are very much a part of the local neighborhood,
as Ruth Horowitz reminds us, the more general adolescent subculture
does not appear to have borrowed as extensively from gang traditions.[15]
But gang graffiti are a living and evolving art, and it remains to be seen
if—and when—the Chicago graffiti will become more formalized and
develop the same sort of stylistic conventions observed in Los Angeles
and other southwestern cities.

DIRECTIONS FOR FUTURE RESEARCH

This study represents only a small selection of graffiti from Midwestern and Southwestern cities, and from only one segment of gangs

(labeled here as Hispanic) within these communities. Not included are examples of gang graffiti showing age divisions within each gang, female groups associated with each of the larger gangs, walls to commemorate gang members killed by other groups, or graffiti produced by black street gangs. Each of these subjects could well be the topic of a separate research paper should other urban ethnologists wish to sort through the graffiti and, in the best tradition of Robert Park's earliest students, "get the seat of their pants dirty."

The comparative analysis of gang graffiti suggests a number of areas for further study. These concluding remarks present topics which appear to offer special promise for the urban ethnographer.

Gang Graffiti and Artistic Traditions

It was noted in an earlier section that gang graffiti share many of the characteristics required for something to be labelled as "art": there is a specialization of roles so that particular individuals may be recognized as artists; particular stylistic conventions have developed which are recognized by individual practitioners; and these styles are independent of any particular artist—they may well outlast any given artist. Not only do gang graffiti meet these preconditions, but it is also possible to observe how style conventions change over time as new artists come along and as ideas are borrowed from other areas of the country.

The photographs shown earlier, both presenting the ghost figure of the Insane Unknowns, illustrate these characteristics of gang graffiti. The first example dates from the late 1970s, and was produced by the original graffito artist of the gang; this piece of graffito was referred to as the "crossed shotguns" by gang members, police, and persons in the local community who were familiar with this wall before it was demolished in 1980. As a play on the group's name, the central emblem along with the space for the group's motto above and below the emblem are left blank—the group must remain unknown. The artist was killed in gang warfare in 1979. While the Insane Unknowns retained the ghost symbol, the style changed in the mid-1980s as a new artist (known by the street name of Psycho) began to produce the graffiti. The new emblem, shown in the second example, is a more powerful graphic image, but it lacks the haunting, mysterious quality of the original.

Although any gang member may write graffiti, most Chicago gangs have one member who specializes in producing larger graffiti. While research has long categorized gang membership into core and peripheral members, additional attention might be given to other more specialized roles within the gang. Most Chicago gangs have a distinct structure, including a president, vice-president, treasurer, secretary, war counselor, and enforcer. Several of these positions are at least nominally elective offices; some gangs actually kept minutes of their meetings in earlier years. While many researchers and police officials reject the idea that these offices have any significance, the fact that the position of the graffiti artist is so well defined suggests that the more general question as to role specialization within the gang may be a rewarding area for study.

Diffusion of Graffiti

The popular media have made much of the spread of street gangs from large cities to smaller communities, and of linkages between gangs in different cities (see Joan Moore's chapter in this volume). Gang graffiti offer excellent source material to examine the extent of these linkages; the graffiti shown here question whether such connections exist (note, for example, differences in lettering styles and iconography between Los Angeles and Chicago). This is not to say that gang members from Chicago do not end up in Los Angeles, and vice versa. One Chicago gang—the Party People— began using homeboy letters in the late 1980s; they are not, however, directly linked to any Los Angeles gang. Despite the introduction of several community murals by artists demonstrating the techniques of East Coast graffiti in both the Mexican and Puerto Rican barrios, the gangs appear to have hung on to the "home-grown" graffiti traditions. If there was a significant linkage among street gangs in these different locations, we would expect to find greater borrowing of styles and conventions from each area.

Gang Graffiti and Violent Subcultures

One need spend only a short time in Chicago to notice a very significant characteristic of the gang graffiti produced in the Mexican and Puerto Rican barrios of the Midwest. In addition to the symbolic "killing" of opposing groups, a common feature of these graffiti, there are other frequent and direct references to gang violence. Boasts such as "Vicious— Folks We Kill for the Thrill"; "Animal Killers"; "Five Popping—Six Dropping"; "Killing for a Living"; "King Cobra Rest in Hell", are common in much of the graffiti across the city. The Diesciple Killers Nation graffiti reproduced in figure 7.10 is an example of this type of message.

The question of why Chicago graffiti emphasize such dramatic and violent messages is intriguing. The extraordinarily high rate of homicide among Hispanic street gangs in Chicago may be part of the explanation. Carolyn Block's research on homicide patterns in Chicago's Hispanic community indicates that the risk of becoming the victim of a gang homicide was three times greater for Hispanic males aged fifteen to nineteen than for black males and nearly five times greater than for Anglo males in the same age group.[16] The constant reference to violence in the Chicago graffiti may well be an accurate reflection of adolescent life in Hispanic neighborhoods of the city.

In any case, Chicago gang graffiti have not been subjected to the same degree of standardization and routinization observed in the Southwest, where the graffiti and other gang artifacts have over time become an accepted part of the barrio subculture. This suggests that as Chicago street gangs become more institutionalized and develop intergenerational structures similar to those described for Chicano gangs in Los Angeles, and as the level of gang violence in Hispanic neighborhoods decreases and stabilizes, some of the more overt violence displayed in the Chicago graffiti may disappear or, more likely, evolve into a new convention.

Language Use

An interesting pattern in the graffiti presented here is the fact that Spanish—and especially *calo*, or gutter Spanish—is commonly used in graffiti in California, but is rarely encountered in Chicago. This pattern cannot be explained by differences in language patterns between the two cities; language studies indicate that a majority of adolescents in both communities prefer to use English.[17] Among Hispanic adolescents in urban communities the use of Spanish is often considered to be a negative marker of recent immigration, so perhaps it is not unusual that the street gangs would use English.[18] Further comparisons might be made to language patterns found in Hispanic gang graffiti in Miami, New York, and other cities, as well as to the significance of linguistic transformations such as the ELE ACHE and ESE EME graffiti produced by the Logan Heights and Sherman Heights gangs in San Diego.

Commercialization of Gang Subcultures

A significant amount of gang activity is embedded within conventional commercial activity in the local community: gang members purchase customized sweaters and silk-screened tee shirts from local sports shops; elaborately embroidered gang emblems, copied from drawings submitted by gang members, are produced by the same companies that produce high school letters; mail order stores in California and Texas carry clothing styles favored by gang members; and gang members customizing their automobiles—lowriders—purchase specialized products from auto parts dealers.[19]

Similarly, cultural products of the street-gang subculture have been appropriated by commercial artists and others; the best-known example is probably the homeboy lettering which appears on record albums by the Eagles (the best-selling rock group of the 1980s) and Jackson Browne. Gang graffiti have been favored for background shots on music videos and television movies for many years, and movies geared toward an adolescent audience, such as *Beat Street* (shot in New York), *Bad Boys* (Chicago), and *Lost Angels* (Los Angeles) have purposely used graffiti and/or mural backdrops. *Teen Angel* magazine has made a successful (and very profitable) bridge between the street-gang subculture and a more general Hispanic adolescent subculture in the Southwest, and, more recently, MTV has popularized gang graffiti and slang to a national audience. There is an interesting question as to the long-term effect of street gangs and their cultural products on adolescent subcultures more generally. Alternatively, does the commercialization of gang culture make gang activity somehow more acceptable and legitimate? The recent emergence of Rap and Hip Hop musical styles are a further indication of this trend. The cover to a 1990 album by Kool Moe Dee shows the rap artist wearing a blue sweat suit with a BK monogram standing in front of a jeep with the front tire resting on a red handkerchief. This may be the first Crips record: the British Knight monogram also signifies "Blood Killers" and the red handkerchief shows disrespect to the Bloods.

Joan Moore's study of Los Angeles gangs suggests that the integration of street-gang subculture with the local community has resulted from the long interaction between gangs, gang members and their families, and the local neighborhoods. Ruth Horowitz's study of a Mexican gang in Chicago further emphasizes that gang members are an integral part of the local community.[20] Should we expect gang graffiti in Chicago to develop more elaborate conventions and routinized lettering styles, as has occurred in Los Angeles? And will this ultimately produce images which are less violent and therefore more acceptable to the wider adolescent subculture in the city and suburbs?

Gang Graffiti and Street-Gang Culture

Gang graffiti represent only a small part of what I have called the cultural production of the contemporary street-gang subculture. Other symbolic creations such as hand signals, tatoos, gang jackets, and hairstyles seem especially appropriate for further study. It is perhaps significant that there are regional differences in these cultural products as well: while the hand signals of Los Angeles gangs, for example, have been taken from the deaf alphabet and represent the initials of the group name, in Chicago hand signals have been developed in a somewhat haphazard fashion by gang members. In Chicago, the Latin King symbol of three fingers extended upward means "I love you" in sign language; the Latin Kings in Los Angeles, in contrast, sign the letters LK to represent the gang.[21]

Street-gang subcultures include elaborate ceremonial rituals (such as gang funerals) and actively create and modify the symbolic representation of gang identities in tatoos, clothing styles, and the like. In some areas of the country street-gang subcultures may already have been adapted by significant portions of the more general adolescent subculture. Yet there are important variations in this subculture from one city to another, suggesting complicated and diverse patterns of borrowing which complicate any simple statement as to the spread of gang activity from one area to another. Just as graffiti serve as a barometer of gang activity and changing patterns of gang allegiances, the study of other cultural artifacts of the street-gang subculture may produce further insights into the origins and patterns of gang activity across the United States.

NOTES

1. *Blazon* refers to "the part of heraldry which attempts to describe in accurate terms the armorial bearings in the late middle ages" (Gerard J. Brault, *Early Blazon: Heraldic Terminology in the Twelfth and Thirteenth Century with Special Reference to Arthurian Literature*. Oxford: Clarendon Press, 1967], p. 7). *Blazon Nouveau* refers to the study of heraldry in the modern city—thus the study of gang graffiti and gang emblems.

2. See, for example, Marjorie S. Zatz, "Los Cholos: Legal Processing of Chicano Gang Members," *Social Problems* 33 (1985); G. David Curry and Irving Spergel, "Gang Homicide, Delinquency, and Community," *Criminology* 26 (1988): 381-403; Jeffrey Fagan, "The Social Organization of Drug Use and Drug Dealing Among Urban Gangs," *Criminology* 27 (1989): 633-65.

3. Peter Berger, *An Invitation to Sociology* (New York: Anchor-Doubleday, 1963).

4. See *The Faith of Graffiti*, documented by Mervyn Kurlansky and Jon Naar, text by Norman Mailer (New York: Praeger, 1974); Craig Castleman, *Getting Up: Subway Graffiti in New York* (Cambridge: MIT Press, 1982); Richard Lachmann, "Graffiti as Career and Ideology," *American Journal of Sociology* 94 (1988): 229-50.

5. *Style Wars* (New Day Films, 1984).

6. David Ley and Roman Cybriwsky, "Urban Graffiti as Territorial Markers" (*Annals* of the Association of American Geographers 4 (1974): 491-505).

7. See Jerry Romotsky and Sally R. Romotsky, "California Street Gangs: Wall Writing in L.A." (*Print* 28 [1974]: 60-65); "Placas and Murals" (*Arts in Society* 11 (1974): 288-289); "Plaqueasos on the Wall" (*Human Behavior* 4 [1974]: 64-70). Their most thorough treatment of the subject is found in *Los Angeles Barrio Calligraphy* (Los Angeles: Dawson's Book Shop, 1976) and the accompanying collection of seventy-five slides from Environmental Communications, Venice, California.

8. Romotsky and Romotsky, *Los Angeles Barrio Calligraphy*, p. 49.

9. Despite the frequent Hispanic identifier for many Chicago gangs—Latin Eagles, Puerto Rican Stones, Latin Kings, Spanish Cobras—the gangs are not segregated by ethnicity or race. Street gangs are territorially based and may include Mexican, Puerto Rican, black, and even white members, depending on the ethnic composition of the local neighborhood. Because Chicago is one of the most segregated cities in the country, "black" gangs do tend to be mostly black, and the "Mexican" gangs from the Pilsen-Little Village area (18th Street and 26th Street) are mostly Mexican. Hispanic gangs from the northwest side of the city, however, tend to have a remarkably diverse membership.

10. This is a significant graffito announcing the alliance between the predominantly white Gaylords and the Latin Kings, two northwest-side gangs in the spring of 1984. In return for protection of their gang members within the state prison system, the Gaylords agreed to provide drugs and weapons to the Latin Kings. The graffito has also been defaced by the C-Notes, who have overwritten "killer" on the Gaylords, inserted a "K" after the Kings, and added their emblem (a dollar sign) to the field.

11. This sort of graffito, where the symbols of several different groups have been combined into a single graphic, has an interesting history. By 1980 it was common to add crowns, cobras, and the like to your own graffito when appropriate (e.g., a cobra figure wearing a Latin Gangster crown). The next stage of evolution involved placing inverted symbols of other gangs underneath your own graffito; first this was added to existing graffiti, and later a single piece of graffito might be produced showing, for example, an upright Latin King crown with an inverted Imperial Gangster crown from the same circular base. In the late 1980s the more complicated graphics, combining symbols indicating multiple allegiances and opposition, began to appear.

12. There are at least two exceptions to any general statement comparing these lettering styles: First, many Chicago gangs make use of gothic lettering, particularly for the large name walls and territorial markers, although this tendency diminished during the 1980s as new and more complicated symbolic manipulations spread across the city. Second, the Party People, a gang located in the heart of the 18th Street/Pilsen Mexican barrio, began to incorporate homeboy letters in the late 1980s (I first photographed graffiti of this type in 1987). Members of this gang now use this style exclusively; significantly, other Mexican gangs in the neighborhood have not followed their lead.

13. Most of the Chicago graffiti shown here come from the Wicker Park-Humbolt Park neighborhoods on the northwest side of the city, where the gangs are ethnically mixed. Mexican gangs in the 18th Street (Pilsen) and 26th Street (Little Village) barrios typically have names derived from street names—the Two-Six gang, Cullerton Boys, Racine Boys, and the like—a pattern more similar to that of gang names from the Southwest. Only one northside gang, the PBCs (Paulina-Berry Community), has a specific geographical referent in their name.

14. Emory S. Bogardus, "Gangs of Mexican-American Youth," *Sociology and Social Research* 28: 55-56.

15. Ruth Horowitz, "Community Tolerance of Gang Violence," *Social Problems* 34 (December 1987): 437-450.

16. Carolyn Rebecca Block, "Lethal Violence in the Chicago Latino Community" (in Anna Victoria Wilson, ed., *The Dynamics of the Victim-Offender Interaction*, Anderson Publishing Company, forthcoming).

17. For information on language patterns in Chicago, see Ray Hutchison, "Language Use Among Hispanic Groups in Chicago," in Lucia Elias-Olivares and Mary Ellen Garcia, eds., *Spanish in the United States* (Mouton, forthcoming); for language patterns in Los Angeles see D. E. Lopez, "Chicano Language Loyalty in an Urban Setting," *Sociology and Social Research* 62 (January 1978): 267-79.

18. For a description of the peer group pressure on Mexican and Mexican American adolescents in the United States to use English, see Letticia Galindo, "Spanish Language Maintenance and Shift Among Chicano Adolescents in Austin, Texas," in Elias-Olivares and Garcia, eds., *Spanish in the United States*.

19. For many years the baseball cap of the Pittsburgh Pirates has been a favorite item of clothing for the Latin Kings: the colors (black and yellow) are the same as those worn by the Latin Kings, and the letter P represents an inverted D (for Latin Disciples). A recent article in the *New York Times* discussed how sports jackets and team emblems have increasingly been appropriated by gang members across the country; see "Raiders Chic: A Style With Sinister Overtones" (*New York Times*, March 4, 1991).

20. This does not mean that others in the community support the actions of gang members. Horowitz reminds us that most gang members have grown up in the local barrios, live at home with their parents and/or their own families, and are known on a first-name basis by others in the neighborhood. Joan Moore, *Homeboys: Gangs, Drugs, and Prison in the Barrios of Los Angeles* (Philadelphia: Temple University Press, 1978); Horowitz, "Community Tolerance of Gang Violence."

21. Differences between the deaf alphabet and the gang signs commonly used in Chicago are responsible for at least one gang-related murder; a deaf mute teenager was approached by gang members and apparently signed "I love you" to indicate he meant no harm. The gang members mistook this for the Latin Kings' symbol and shot him.

8

The Working Gang

FELIX PADILLA

"I'm going to work," Rafael said. "I have to go and make me some bread." The day is April 17, 1989. I had just finished having lunch with Rafael in a local restaurant. Rafael is a member of a Puerto Rican youth gang in Chicago that I have been studying for over two years. He was responding to one of the questions I would ask him as we departed from the restaurant.

"Where can I drive you?," I asked. Of course I knew that he was headed to the usual street location where he had been dealing drugs for several years. After dropping him off, Rafael and a friend boarded a car, which appeared to have been waiting for his arrival. They drove away from the vicinity only to return thirty minutes later carrying a large amount of merchandise he would try selling on this day.

Once back in the neighborhood, he would position himself alongside other dealers to earn a day's pay. Rafael, as well as his co-workers, were employed by one of the distributors in his gang. Like other workers, they were expected to be at the job for a certain amount of time.

Rafael's work relations with the gang are a clear illustration of the business side of the organization. This is a topic which remains unveiled despite a fairly extensive scientific and journalistic literature on youth gangs. In the main, most accounts about gangs and drugs tend to consider "all" teenage drug dealing as an innate activity of the gang. However, this approach overlooks many cases of teenage drug dealing that are not affiliated with or sponsored by the gang.

There are some young men who simply establish drug-dealing

173

networks or crews comprised of several members, but these are not gangs. They lack a formal organization and leadership stratum. Members are not expected to invest time in attending formal meetings. Nor do they pay any form of dues. Members of the network or crew do not consider this group a gang. In other cases, young people who are not affiliated with the gang manage to develop street-level dealing operations on their own. There also are instances of street-level dealing being carried out by gang members working on their own. I will demonstrate below that these three cases are unlikely to materialize where street-level dealing is controlled by a gang, though individuals continue to make attempts to establish these forms of individual undertakings.

The scholarly and journalistic writers do not make a distinction between the times when drug dealing represents a gang activity and a large portion of the earnings go to the organization and the times when drug dealing is an endeavor carried out by nongang members working only for themselves. The discussion that follows will focus primarily on street-level dealers who work for the gang, and who receive a salary for their labor. It also will touch on the experiences of several youngsters who are independent dealers, but who are still part of the gang's occupational structure. They purchase their merchandise from the gang's distributors, utilize the gang-controlled turf for retailing, and are required to pay weekly organizational dues.

The following questions will be considered. What are the reasons for the gang becoming a business organization? What does the gang look like as an entrepreneurial establishment? That is, what are its defining characteristics as a business enterprise? Which cultural elements are used by youngsters for cementing and reinforcing business relations among themselves? What is the gang's occupational structure? How does the gang generate income for itself?

Information for this chapter comes from a two-year study that I have been conducting of a Puerto Rican youth gang in Chicago. I have given the gang the fictitious name of the Diamonds. The neighborhood that serves as the Diamonds' turf is located five miles north west of the downtown area. For the last twenty years, the neighborhood has been racially and ethnically mixed, comprised of Latino (i.e., Puerto Ricans, Mexican Americans, and Cubans) and white residents. Puerto Ricans, who comprise the largest group among Latinos, often refer to this neighborhood as *Suburbia* (pronounced "sooboorbia"). Living there is perceived as a measure of social prosperity and improvement. Census reports confirm this perception. In 1980, almost 40 percent of workers were employed in white-collar occupations. Only 18 percent had incomes below the poverty line and the unemployment rate was 9 percent.

THE DIAMONDS BECOME A BUSINESS GANG

The history of the Diamonds dates back approximately twenty years, a relatively short period when compared to other Latino youth gangs in Chicago. At first, the Diamonds was a musical group. Members played their music on the street or in local night clubs. In 1970, a member of the musical group was mistaken for a gang member and was killed by a gunshot fired by a youngster from a rival gang. This incident sparked the reorganization of the group into a violent gang. For the next six years the Diamonds provoked fights with other groups. During most of this time, the membership of the Diamonds was quite small. The organization did not divide itself into different sections. Some members used drugs, but in the late 1970s a major change occurred in the thrust of the operations of the gang. It began taking on a businesslike character. No longer were retaliation and violent behavior the mainstays of the organization. Money making through drug dealing came to represent the gang's chief activity. Several factors account for this change.

Controlled Substance Act

One gang member named Carmelo described one change:

I remember this older guy from the neighborhood who wanted me to sell for him. He asked several of us to be his dealers. He was offering good money, but I was afraid. I didn't know what he was about. We knew that he was doing something, because all these people used to come to his house all the time. But he never dealt with us before, and then all of sudden he wanted us to work for him. I said no to the guy.

The event that precipitated the development of the gang into a business was the 1971 passage of the Illinois Controlled Substance Act. It carried heavy criminal penalties for adult heroin and cocaine dealers. Well aware that juveniles could always beat the penalties of the newly instituted law, adults who for the most part had controlled drug distribution and dealing up to this point, began enlisting some members from the Diamonds and other gangs to work the streets of particular neighborhoods. Some youngsters like Carmelo refused the job offers. Others agreed. It did not take them or leaders of the gang long to realize that they could profit substantially by controlling neighborhood drug dealing. In other words, these youngsters began to ask the question, why can't we develop our business?

Gang leaders began thinking about the gang as a wholesaler or investor. It would purchase the merchandise itself and hire its own members, especially the younger ones, to sell at the street level. Because the Diamonds viewed themselves as landlords of several *puntos* or blocks in the neighborhood, the only thing still missing for developing a business operation was the necessary capital with which to purchase large amounts of drugs.

They began pulling their money together. Sometimes two or three of the older members (or leaders) would "go into business." Sometimes the group was larger. At other times, leaders would request that all members make an investment of a certain amount and use this sum for purchasing the drugs with which to open the business.

High Demand for Drugs

The rise of the business side of the gang also was ignited by the increasing demand for drugs, particularly cocaine. The increasing popularity of drug use during the 1970s and the still blossoming international cocaine trade created a situation in which demand outstripped the supply. One distributor recalls the times when, as a street-level dealer, he would sell his merchandise so easily that some customers at times were left without goods. This was the time when the demand was greater than the supply.

Author: How would you compare selling now to years ago?

Carmelo: I was dealing in the streets back in 1974 or so. We did not have the organization that we have now. Now we deal through the gang. So, that was one difference.

Author: What was another difference?

Carmelo: I think it was the amount of reefer and coke, but mainly reefer that were out in the streets. Cocaine was expensive, but reefer, everybody wanted reefer and we were making all kinds of money.

Author: How was that possible?

Carmelo: Like I told you. There was a lot of stuff out there. There were times when I would get my supply in the morning and then go back in the afternoon and get some more. My supplier wanted me out there all the time because the stuff was selling real fast. There were times when I had to turn some of my customers on to somebody else, something I never wanted to do, but if I didn't have the stuff it was better that they cop from other guys. That way they would not want to stop using it. That's what kept us going. Yeah, but, man, that was good, today, well, you seen how that is.

The Nation Coalition

When the business side of gangs grew too large, it had to be better organized. That is when gang nations were built. "My understanding of what the nation means is that we are supposed to respect other groups from the same nation," replied Rafael when I asked him to explain the meaning of the concept. He added that

> gangbanging is nothing really hard to do. In my neighborhood, you have to hang out a lot. Our chief wants us there a lot so nobody else would try to take our neighborhood from us. And we have boundaries, and a little bit of the neighborhood we share with others from the same nation, but of a different affiliation. And we have our territory and if they were to come into our territory, we wouldn't start trouble by getting loud and stuff like that. We all respect each other pretty much, and it's alright.

At a more general level, Rafael was describing the moderate and congenial relations established by rival gangs in Chicago during the early 1980s. Peaceful relations were facilitated by the division of city areas into two gang nations or alliances, People and Folks. Suburbia's various gangs came under the auspices of the latter. No one is really certain of the lineage of the nation alliance, but rumors have it that the alignment was created from formerly rival gangs that were jailed together in 1981. It is also believed that jailed, former leaders of these two parent groups continue to play a significant role in dictating the policies and practices of street gangs in Chicago.

Theoretically, the nation approach was aimed at reducing significantly the degree of intergang violence that had been so common during the 1970s. As indicated by Rafael above, nation gangs were discouraged from invading each other's territories, and agitation and harassment were not to be brought upon coalition members. Indeed, the nation coalition contributed immensely to solidifying the business operation of the gang. "Respect for each other's territories" also came to mean the sharing of the drug consumer market. Each gang was permitted to operate its business from a relatively safe turf or marketplace, selling only to those customers who voluntarily frequented there. No longer was the gang involved in efforts to take over other turfs, hoping to expand its business boundaries beyond its immediate setting. The new nation approach called for the development of a particular gang's business enterprise in its own turf, improving the image and reputation of the business, and making it more attractive to consumers.

Since drug use was so widespread, the most rational business decision was to share the market. It was no longer necessary to fight over turfs. This also freed the neighborhood of gangbanging and provided a fairly safe "shopping area" for prospective customers. A neighborhood that was known for its ongoing gangbanging activities tended to scare off customers.

Members of the Diamonds are committed to mutual understanding and harmony with other gangs but have not abstained entirely from conflict and fighting. In fact, members of the Diamonds believe that the nation alliance has broken down as gangbanging among nation gangs is becoming routine. But the significant point is that when first started, the nation alliance reduced intergang violence substantially and enabled some gangs to establish their organizations as sound business enterprises.

Perceptions of Conventional Work

Youngsters' image of "traditional" jobs was perhaps the leading force that helped to transform the gang into a business venture. These young men began turning to the gang in search of employment opportunities, believing that available conventional work would not be sufficient for delivering the kinds of material goods they wished to secure. One youngster indicated,

> There are some jobs that people can still find, but who wants them? They don't pay. I want a job that can support me. I want a job that I could use my talents—speaking, communicating, selling and a definite goal that I'd be working towards as far as money is concerned.

These young people have a pessimistic appraisal of and outlook toward jobs in the regular economy. They have become increasingly convinced that those "jobs available to them" are essentially meaningless, and far from representing the vehicles necessary for overcoming societal barriers to upward mobility. Although these youngsters have been socialized with the conventional cultural belief in achieving material success, they refuse to accept the conventional means to become successful. That is, they do not accept the "American achievement ideology," reflected in middle-class norms, and shown by Horowitz, Kornblum and Williams, and others to be widely supported by ethnic and racial minority parents and teenagers.[1] The ideology stresses that success in school leads to the attainment of managerial and professional jobs, which in turn pave the way for social and economic advancement. The youngsters' own school experiences and contact with the job market, as well as the futile and frustrating efforts of adults around them to achieve social advancement through menial, dead-end jobs, contradict the American achievement ideology. These young men do not believe in the power of education to serve as the "great equalizer." Nor do they perceive conventional jobs as leading to a successful, meaningful life.

These views reflect the tension between culturally defined goals and the ineffectiveness of socially legitimate means for achieving them that Robert Merton first described and subsequent gang studies confirmed.[2] They point to the absence of avenues and resources necessary for securing rewards which society purports to offer its members.

The decision by members of the Diamonds to sell drugs was informed by their assessment of available opportunities in the regular economy as well as their high level of aspirations. Drug dealing did not arise in deliberate violation of middle-class normative aspirations. The gang represents a "counter organization" geared to achieving things valued by the larger society and countering forces weighing heavily upon their lives. In effect, these youngsters transformed the gang into an income-generating business operation in an unconventional economy in order to "make it" in conventional American society.

SOCIAL AND CULTURAL COMPONENTS OF THE ETHNIC ENTERPRISE

Two questions need to be addressed at this point. First, what are the distinguishing characteristics of the gang that enable it to function as a business organization? Second, what social and cultural devices did the youngsters use for organizing the gang into a reliable money-making enterprise?

The gang has developed its own culture. The gang does this in the same way that the family unit teaches its young the norms, skills, values, beliefs, and traditions of the larger society—and the ways to communicate and reinforce that culture. At the heart of the gang culture is a collective ideology that serves to protect all the members. Collectivism also serves as the major determinant of the gang's efficient development as a business operation. The members' response to their shared conditions and circumstances is collective in the sense that they form a partnership.

For the young people I studied, collectivism translates into an ideology of strength. These young men share a belief that their capacity to earn a living or improve their life can only be realized through a "collective front." In the views of a youngster by the name of Coco, "we are a group, a community, a family—we have to learn to live together. If we separate, we will never have a chance. We need each other even to make sure that we have a spot for selling."

The collectivist nature of the gang can be said to be an extension of the traditional Puerto Rican family. In Puerto Rican immigrant society, as well as in other societies from which many other ethnic and racial groups originated, the family served as the cornerstone of the culture, defining and determining individual and social behavior. Ties between families were cemented by the establishment of *compadrazco* (godparent-godchild) relationships. Relatives by blood and ceremonial ties, as well as friends of the family, were linked together in an intricate network of reciprocal obligations. Individuals who suffered misfortunes were aided by relatives and friends. When they had re-established themselves, they shared their good fortunes with those who had helped them.

That the gang is rooted in the norms of family life and tradition can be observed from the various descriptions of the gang offered by the youngsters I studied.

> Tony: My grandmother took care of me for a long time. I guess this was part of the Puerto Rican tradition at one time. Your grandmother took care of you while your mother and father were away working. Sometimes grandmothers did not believe that their son or daughter were fit to be parents so they took the responsibility of raising their grandchildren. My grandmother is my life. Anybody who messes with my grandmother ' has to mess with me. The same thing with my aunt.
>
> Author: Which aunt are you referring to?
>
> Tony: This is my mother's sister, which is really weird because they are the same blood but treat me so differently. My aunt is the mother I never had. We are really closed. She is the person that I go to when I need someone to tell something to. She always listens to me.
>
> Author: And why does she always listen to you?
>
> Tony: My aunt is this wonderful woman, she's about 35 years old, who is really together. When I'm with her I feel like I can tell her anything that is in my mind. That's what family is all about. This is all in the blood. She cares because she is family. When you have a family, even if it's your aunt or uncle, you know you belong. You will always have someone looking out for you.
>
> Author: In the last interview, you talked a little about the family as it related to the gang. How similar is the gang family to what you're describing now?
>
> Tony: They are very similar. You see a family is like a fist [he pointed to his fist, clenching it and opening it to show that when it's opened it represents five fingers separated from one another]. I know that the five fingers of your hand are supposed to be related, however, what would you prefer having, a hand with five fin-

gers or a closed fist? When the fist is closed the fingers are insep-
arable; when the fist is opened they stand at a distance from one
another. I prefer the closed fist. That's exactly how our gang is—
we are very closed. To be in our gang you need to have heart. To
have heart means that you are truly committed to each other; that
you'll do anything for another member because he is part of your
family.

In addition to stemming directly from a Puerto Rican family tradition, ethnic solidarity served as another cultural element, used by the
youngsters for cementing their business relations. As Puerto Ricans, they
expressed feelings of a primordial tie, of blood kinship, said to unify them.
This, in turn, provided the basis for trust. As one youngster put it: "The
fact that I knew that what I liked was at another person's house—they
would talk to me about things like, 'we're going to listen to Salsa music,
we're going to have *arroz con gandures* [rice and pot pies]' and some other
stuff, I would get more attractive to that than to other things."

Part of the collectivist, communitarian foundation of the gang was
also shaped by a base of local consumers or people who are referred by
friends. Their willingness to become faithful customers, to continuously
purchase available goods, i.e., drugs and stolen merchandise, is viewed by
gang members as an indication of membership. These customers become,
in the opinion of one youngster, "one of us." The same young man also
said: "People from the neighborhood know that they can get smoke, cane,
and other things from us. It's risky going to other places. So they protect
us. We are safe with them. So we think of them as part of the business."

The significance of collectivism for gang members can be also
extracted from their views about the idea of individualism. These youngsters are not in agreement with the view that the successful exercise of
individual effort in pursuit of economic and social mobility is applicable to
them. To them, individualism means placing oneself at a precarious position. How can they exist or survive without one another? They are fully
aware that they do not possess the traditional resources, such as money
and high levels of formal education, that are used by members of the middle class to negotiate and advance their individual life chances. They
believe that individual effort represents a step toward obliteration. As
directly put by one youngster, "By ourselves, we are nobody. We can be
had without no problem." Another's remarks were just as straightforward: "This is not a game that you can win by yourself. If you want to win,
you do it as a team. If you want to lose, play alone."

Individual success honors those who have achieved it. Failure, and
economic failure in particular, stigmatizes those who suffer it. Such failure
can only make those who have "failed" the objects of criticism or scorn. It

can also be taken to mean that they are inadequate or deficient. The individualization of "success" and "failure" in American society is unacceptable as far as these young men are concerned. For this reason, collectivism is perceived as capable of giving gang members a special sense of purpose and ability—the driving force with which to pursue economic and social success.

RULES OF COLLECTIVISM

The gang adopted explicit rules aimed at enforcing communitarian behavior and discipline among its members, which was translated into economic activity. Individuals who decided to work on their own were fully aware of the severe penalties associated with such behavior if it led to problems with the "law." For example, members who are apprehended by the police for selling drugs or stealing on their own may not be entitled to receive the amenities accorded to others who engage in collective action. One youngster, who spent six months in jail, describes the consequences of working alone. "I was left to rot. My people didn't come for me. We were all warned about doing shit by ourselves. I was one who paid for not listening."

Additionally, sullen individual action can lead to severe physical harm, in particular the brutal punishment embellished in one of the most traditional rituals of the gang: the Vs. As explained by one youngsters, Vs stand for "violations," which are beatings dispensed to individual members for violating certain rules of the gangs. They are often used in special ceremonies, like initiations or withdrawals of members. During these occasions an individual must walk through a line comprised of other members. The number in the line could range from ten to fifty. The line walk usually lasts three to five minutes and the individual must try to defend himself from the onslaughts of those making up the ranks of the line. If an assault causes the individual to fall, he must return to the beginning of the line and start again. If he gives up, he cannot be excused from the penalty, or accepted as member, or allowed to leave the gang. The most devastating of the Vs are those involving members wishing to quit the gang and those who violate gang rules. One young man described the violations performed during cases when a member leaves the gang:

> There are no rules when they give you a V out. They can use whatever they want on you, they can kick you wherever they want, they pull you on the floor, they can punch you wherever they want, you can't fight back. You just stand there and cover up what you can cover up, and hope that they don't hit one of your weak spots.

I was informed of many instances when individuals who violated certain rules were given severe beatings. The case of Frankie is one example.

I came out all bruised up and had a broken rib, and that was about it. I just had lumps and bruises all over my face and on my back. It was a lot on my back. But it wasn't as hard really as I thought it would be, so it went pretty fast and I just hope for the best. I wanted to come out alright [sic], alive, at least.

It is to the advantage of individuals to function from the collective perspective of the gang rather than on their own. As gang members, drug dealers are offered a fairly safe marketplace from which to sell their products. The gang's turf, the location in the neighborhood where drug transactions tend to occur, is to be used by members only. In cases when a particular turf has developed a reputation for carrying stocks of reliable and good merchandise, as is true for the turfs of the section of the Diamonds I studied, youngsters can be assured of having an on-going clientele and a profitable business.

Another advantage of a collectivist approach to doing business is found in the symbolic messages this action tends to communicate, particularly to "outsiders." For example, the presence of a group of dealers on a street block or corner, usually taking turns to insure that everyone has an opportunity to make a sale, serves to discourage possible robbery attempts. Customers, users, and others not associated with the gang recognize the danger in trying to burglarize or stick up a group of dealers who are members of a particular gang. In addition, the gang provides individuals with a "reputation," serving as a defense against possible customer snitching. Customers and other individuals would be afraid and hesitant to reveal information about a particular dealer who is viewed as belonging to a particular gang. There is a widespread understanding that to snitch against one is tantamount to revealing information about the entire gang. This is an act youngsters in the streets recognize will provoke retribution and physical violence.

The gang, as representative of a collective unit, carries another advantage. It provides customers with a reputable source from which to purchase drugs and other items. In doing so, it contributes significantly to cementing seller-customer relations. Knowledge about the gang, its territory, its affiliated dealers and overall reputation present customers with the background information necessary for trusting that the merchandise they buy is authentic and good. Customers feel confident that they are not being sold a fraudulent product, or what street-level dealers call "junk."

Finally, the collective approach to selling drugs provides youngsters with protection against police invasion and apprehension. The youngsters I studied worked in groups or crews of at least three members. This work arrangement served as a reliable shield to keep each worker alert and informed of the different predators and threats around them. Otherwise, having to conduct an illicit business from an open and highly visible location, like a street corner, makes arrests a distinct possibility.

Occupational Character

The gang, as a business, is built around a fairly elementary occupational structure. Several leading jobs are found within this structure: drug suppliers/distributors, cocaine and marijuana dealers, and those involving several forms of stealing. This occupational structure, like in other business establishments, is developed in a hierarchical basis, representing a pyramid of power, prestige, authority, and information. One's position on the pyramid is correlated with one's access and possession of these attributes.

At the top level of the gang's occupational hierarchy stands the cocaine and marijuana suppliers or distributors. The number of suppliers/distributors is limited, for the smaller the number the larger the profit. Members of the Diamonds referred to their distributors/suppliers in terms of "leaders," "older guys," or simply "main heads." They thought of the distributors as individuals who had paid their dues by remaining with the gang for a very long period of time. In the process they would have gained knowledge about the drug distribution network and accumulated the necessary money for purchasing bulk quantities of drugs. Distributors hold a virtual monopoly over the purchase and supply of drugs sold by members of the Diamonds.

Author: Who did you purchase your stuff from?

Carlos: I usually bought it from my gang leaders.

Author: So there was a distributor within your gang?

Carlos: Yes, every gang has at least one distributor. There are times when a section may not have one, well these guys then buy from another distributor from the larger gang. My guess is that the older guys took trips to Florida, or meet people half-way. I heard some guys going downtown for the stash. Some of these people were into real estate, restaurants. But it's through some business and the owner of the business was handling the stuff. But this was all done by the older guys, the younger ones never got into this, they couldn't.

Author: I heard you refer to the distributor as the "older guys."

Carlos: Yes, it is the older ones who know what life is all about, who are making money and living a nice life. They are into communicating with one another and making money. But not the youth.

Distributors exercise great influence over street-level dealers through their control over drug sources. A single distributor may have as many as fifteen to twenty youngsters working for him on a regular or periodic basis. The money paid to each youngster, as well as the amount of drugs that he gives on consignment, depends on the type of relationship that is established. If he believes that an individual is not making him money, he will sever the relationship by refusing to supply him. Along with their monopoly over the supplies of cocaine and marijuana, the ability to hire and fire employees gives these distributors a considerable amount of influence over youngsters working at street-level dealing.

The distributor epitomizes success within the gang. He seduces newer members. He is not an illusion or fantasy. Rather, he embodies the dream which the larger society has denied Puerto Rican youngsters. And, in the mind of the youngsters, the distributor represents the one position within the business infrastructure of the gang that they want.

I would see my prez and other heads, you know, two or three cars, and this and that, and they still got jobs, money, you see a bankroll in their pocket, and they be asking you what you want to eat. And this and that, and you be like, "I want to make this money and that money, I want to be like you." And he'll be like, "Ok, well I'll go buy an ounce of reefer, right, cause you ain't got the money to do it." And you know you can't do it.

Since successful drug distribution requires a great deal of secrecy, information about top-level distributors is limited. Contact between the distributor and street-level dealers is restricted to sporadic episodes, most likely involving occasions of drug dispersion and money collection. Distributors are rarely seen on the corners where drugs are presently sold.

Distributors belong to a fairly closed and exclusive club. The few individuals who remain with the gang long enough to achieve this level of job mobility are usually expected to create a new section of the gang in a different area of the neighborhood. They also might be appointed to oversee an existing section that was viewed by the leadership as nonproductive. One young man provides a precise account of the nature of the distributor's job:

In my section, the big guys would never change. They were the distributors, the people everybody wanted to be like but couldn't. They had the control and were not going to give it to anyone. If you got big like them, you had work with another section. They didn't let you compete with them. Why should they? They were going to lose money. But I guess it's not a bad idea to create your section—it's only yours.

In effect, most workers within the Diamonds's job hierarchy occupied the position of street-level cocaine and marijuana dealers—the job directly beneath the distributor/supplier. In most cases dealers sell both drugs, though the preference is toward the cocaine business for its larger profits. Dealing cocaine and marijuana requires possessing available cash in order to purchase the drug from the supplier. Otherwise, youngsters work_ as sellers for the supplier who "fronts" them a certain amount of drugs—dealers receive a small percentage of the profits. There are other times when the supplier uses gang members to sell cocaine and marijuana by hiring them to make "drops" or "deposits" of specific amounts to individuals outside of the neighborhood. The profits from this job are usually small.

Because of the relatively small profits made by those working for distributors or dealers, the ultimate goal of street-level dealers is to become independent businessmen. That is, they want to amass the necessary amount of dollars to acquire and sell the product without having to share the profits with the distributor. As "independents," the youngsters know very well that the return for their investment and labor will always be higher.

Author: How long did you stay in drug dealing?

Gustavo: I'm still doing it to this day.

Author: What was your biggest profit when you were working for the man?

Gustavo: My biggest profit a week was about $100.00 to $150.00 a week. The profit I was making for the guy was sometimes $1,000-2,000.

Author: So you were making very little.

Gustavo: That's right. He was making all the money. There were Saturdays when I would be counting the money that I was going to take him and there were times when on a Saturday he would make $2,000.

Author: Now that you're on your own, how much money do you make?

Gustavo: It varies. If I go and buy $800 worth of cocaine I can make $1,600—a one hundred percent profit. If I package the stuff myself into quarter bags I can make more. Any profit to me is good, as long as it's over $100. But you see, I don't make that kind of money because I don't have the money to buy that quantity.

Author: What has been the most you've ever made?

Gustavo: I bought $400 and took out that plus another $400. And I sold that on a Wednesday, Thursday, and Friday.

Similarly, as independents, dealers determine which drugs to sell, favoring cocaine over others even though the penalties for selling it are more severe. "The money is in cocaine," indicated a youngster as he described the difference between selling cocaine and marijuana. He also stated, "I have spent a lot [of] time working the streets, selling reefers and pills, but I know that I can double whatever I make in these jobs by selling cane."

Dealers from the Diamonds tend to sell both cocaine and marijuana to local consumers, though other buyers come from the "outside." In the majority of the cases, the outside buyers are young, middle-class whites, who have learned through different ways and sources about a particular corner or street block where cocaine can be readily purchased. The thing drug dealers like most about outside buyers is that they tend to become habitual customers, making purchases throughout the course of the week.

Author: You were telling me about some of your customers, and you mentioned how people from the neighborhood are not steady. What do you mean by that?

Carmelo: Friday is the big day. It's pay-day. That's when most of people come out to make their kill. Actually, the whole weekend is when we sell a lot to people from around here.

Author: And you would not consider that to be steady!

Carmelo: Well, I guess. But, you see my white customers come around all the time. These people have money all the time and don't care about spending it. They come around on a Monday or a Thursday, whenever.

Author: So are you saying that people from the neighborhood make larger purchases that last for the entire week?

Carmelo: Are you kidding? No, they buy a few hits, that's all.

Author: What happens to them during the the week?

Carmelo: We work out different things. Sometimes I just give them the stuff and they pay me on Friday. Or, they bring something that they use to trade. For example, I had a guy give me this expensive watch one time. Another left his VCR. So there are different ways that we use.

Marijuana is the most readily sold drug among the youngsters I studied. Not surprisingly, the job of marijuana dealer is the one found most often within the occupational structure of the gang. Marijuana is usually sold to local clients for a very low price. Members of the Diamonds working in marijuana dealing indicated that the common use and popularity of the drug is correlated with customers' perception of it as being relatively mild, pleasurable, and easily manageable. One dealer provided what he believes to be the reasons why users or customers prefer marijuana over other drugs like cocaine.

> Because people have the opinion that cocaine is dangerous. And marijuana you just smoke it, it's like smoking a cigarette, you just smoke and get high and that's it. There's not a real big affect on you, you don't get addicted to it. You know, some people do, but they, it's controllable, it's not as bad as cocaine—you get hooked. . . . You know, you get rid of marijuana fast. Marijuana goes better than cocaine.

Youngsters also believe that the legal penalties for dealing marijuana are less severe than those for dealing cocaine. This suggests another explanation for their widespread involvement in marijuana sales. From the dealers' perspective, there is no sign of any significant enforcement apparatus and no cases of severe punishment for possessors of marijuana.

Finally, at the bottom of the gang's occupational hierarchy are those youngsters who make money through stealing. The large number of youngsters involved in acts of stealing are the newer members, called the "Pee Wees" or "Littles." In many cases, stealing represents a "special mission" that Pee Wees are instructed to carry out to demonstrate their loyalty and commitment to the gang. Although these efforts are geared to "proving themselves," they still manage to generate a profit. For other youngsters, stealing becomes a way of life. They work in crews of three or four, and the major item they target is cars. These youngsters become extremely proficient in stealing cars and make a substantial amount of money, though not as much as that generated from drug dealing.

MONEY-RAISING CAPACITY

Similar to other business organizations, the gang's survival depends on its capacity to develop and maintain a sound financial base. Funds are needed to meet a wide range of organizational needs, such as purchasing weapons, making rent payments, bailing members out of jail, and paying for attorney's fees. The gang's finances are managed primarily through two major sources: one is the organization's own centralized fund, referred to by youngsters as the "box," and the other represents the private funds of the drug supplier/distributor(s) within the gang.

The centralized fund or "box" is established through membership contributions or dues, paid periodically (i.e., weekly, biweekly) to the gang's treasurer. As one youngsters put it: "Without the kitty [box] we would had [sic]disappeared a long time ago. We needed all kinds of money to get people out of jail because for a while we were doing some heavy gang-banging. We were paying about $10-15 a week." The significance of membership dues in terms of maintaining the gang is also described in detail by another young man:

Author: How often did you pay dues in your gang?
Hector: We pretty much paid twice a month. We were paying ten dollars per crack. To me that was a lot of money.
Author: What would have happened if you didn't pay?
Hector: But we had to pay—if we didn't the organization would stop. There were times when the president would give us time to raise the money, but we always had to pay. And I guess when you're part of the gang, you care for it. So if you care about the gang, you always find the way to get your hands on some money. It's like if you care for your girlfriend, you always find a way to make her happy. With the gang, you had to find the money to it happy.

Money for the centralized fund was also secured through other means, for membership dues could only raise a very limited amount. Included in these activities were the stealing and selling of weapons, car parts, and the like. While recalling his early days in the gang as a new-comer, one youngster described his working relationship with senior gang members to whom he was assigned:

The older guys would always bring me and tell me to go steal or sell this or that. And that this would bring money for me, but most of the money had to be taken to the box for dues. They would tell me that the money would be used for getting me out of jail or any trouble that I might get into later.

A similar account was given by another youngster: "In our gang, we collected dues. Everybody had to pay. Several times I worked together with other guys pulling some jobs, we stole a car and stripped it. The guy in charge took most of the money for the box because we were empty. I guess we didn't mind that much."

The other mode for generating funds for the box is through contributions made periodically by the distributor/supplier. Because the supplier has a vested interest in the maintenance or survival of the gang, there are times when he uses his own funds for resolving certain gang-related matters. The supplier understands quite well that without his monetary donation, the gang might well fall apart. Similarly, he understands that without the gang, he could lose his business. Contributions made by the distributor are geared to protecting his workers, his street-level dealers. If they are apprehended by the police, he puts up the money for getting them out of jail. In the following exchange, Carlos provides a graphic picture of the role of the distributor as a provider toward the wellbeing of the organization and its members.

Author: How often did the distributor use his money to get members out of jail?

Carlos: Many. We had some times when they pull the money out of their own pockets and one of us would get bailed out. Or sometimes to pay a hospital bill or for someone who got really busted out.

Author: And why did the distributor do this?

Carlos: They would do it really out of their good-will, for the devotion they got for their own gang. And they want everybody in the hood; they figure the more of us who are out there, the better for them.

Author: What were the other reasons the distributor used his money to get people out of jail?

Carlos: One thing you have to understand that is they got their money back. The guy paid him double. It's like an investment because the guy would have to pay him two times what it cost to get him out of jail in the first place.

Author: Did you ever see this happen within your gang?

Carlos: Yes, I saw this happened several times. I even saw it where the big guy borrowed the money and charged double for getting this guy out. He needed money to pay his rent and went and got this money from some other other guy and bailed this other one out.

Author: You said earlier that one reason the big guys get others out of trouble situations is to demonstrate to everybody else that they are devoted to the gang and they care for the gang. Elaborate on this.

Carlos: They want to show everybody in the gang that they are devoting everything they have into the gang to make it better. And to take, how can I say it, "look what I did for you," kind of thing. And they they tell everybody, "that's why I'm leader and that's one reason I want all of you to look up to me."

DISCUSSION

In this chapter I have provided a basic sketch of the leading components of the business youth gang. It is clear from the presentation that this kind of enterprise is quite complex. There were many factors contributing to the formation of the gang as a business operation. The examples provided indicate how external forces and conditions combined with internal cultural group dynamics to give rise to systematic and highly organized business relations among gang members.

In addition, although the description presented in the chapter suggests that the gang does indeed provide youngsters with an alternative to unemployment, it is also the case that this form of labor is highly exploitative. The street youth gang of Suburbia is far from representing a progressive cultural response to youth labor exploitation. On the contrary, it serves to reproduce that exploitation and oppression.

There are several reasons for this. Contrary to public belief, street-level dealers make little money selling drugs or through stealing. In most cases, these youngsters represent another type of minimum-wage labor. The saturation of the market with mass amounts of drugs as well as the fast rise of so many gangs involved in drug selling have increased availability of drugs and decreased the cost. Youngsters' profit margins are quite small. One youngster explained this turn of events in a very interesting way. "I was planning to make enough to go legit. I wanted to do something with the money I was going to make. I know an older gang member who owns a car wash. I wanted something like that. But as I told you, I worked hard and yet I'm still standing on the corner." Another youngster put it this way:

> I guess when we joined the gang, we would see the prez and chief with so much gold and [we'd] think we're going to be the same. But then we have to face the hard facts. There is not much for most of us. But by then, you're too involved, you're a member, people see you and know you now. So you stay—you continue dealing, what else can you do?

In effect, street-level drug dealers are a cheap and permanent labor force used by a few suppliers or distributors within the gang to maintain and enhance their business interests and profits. Although the wages received from selling drugs may be higher than those earned "turning hamburgers at McDonald's," in the the case of the street-level dealer upward mobility is highly unlikely. It is to the advantage of the supplier to maintain the subordination and dependency of their street-level dealers. Distributors/suppliers establish the wages of street-level dealers. Suppliers also maintain a large number of youngsters employed, establishing a very real competitive setting and compelling dealers to operate according to the rules established by suppliers.

Additionally, street-level dealing can be regarded as exploitative labor in that the occupation itself is "sporadic, having high peaks and droughts, and is full of uneven demands on [their] time."[3] Manning and Redlinger, 1983:283). The large majority of the youngsters I studied indicated "working the block" or "standing on the corner" for a good part of their day, for there was not any established time for "making a deal." A transaction could occur at 6:00 A.M. or 12:00 midnight. In addition, competition from other dealers contributed directly to the amount of time youngsters invested working the streets or corners. As one former dealer put it:

> We used to work very long hours. There were other times that we would have to work long past 12 midnight because we got some of these people coming in on Fridays or Saturdays at 2 or 3 in the morning telling us that they just came out of after-hours and they needed it now and they would pay more for it. These were some desperate folks. But you had to deliver otherwise you would lose your clients.

Moreover, the extreme danger of drug dealing adds to the persisting strenuous nature of the occupation. These young people are the ones who do the dirty work of the business, which is often accompanied by physical harm or even death. For youngsters caught doing the gang's dirty work the common consequence is stigmatization by the larger society. Re-entering school is difficult. Obtaining employment in the conventional economy is almost out of the question.

NOTES

1. Ruth Horowitz, *Honor and the American Dream* (N.J.: Rutgers University Press, 1983); William Kornblum and Terry Williams, *Growing Up Poor* (Lexington, Mass.: Lexington Books, 1985).

2. Robert K. Merton, *Social Theory and Social Structure* (Glencoe, Ill.: The Free Press, 1957); Richard A. Cloward and Lloyd Ohlin, *Delinquency and Opportunity* (New York: Free Press, 1960); Joan Moore et al., *Homeboys: Gangs, Drugs, and Prison in the Barrios of Los Angeles* (Philadelphia: Temple University Press, 1978); Horowitz, *Honor and the American Dream*; Diego Vigil, *Barrio Gangs: Street Life and Identity in Southern California* (Austin: University of Texas Press, 1988).

3. Peter K. Manning and Lawrence J. Redlinger, "Drugs as Work," in *Research in the Sociology of Work*, eds., Ida H. Simpson and Richard L. Simpson (Greenwich, Conn.: JAI Press, 1983), p. 283.

9

Gang Organization and Migration

JEROME H. SKOLNICK
RICKY BLUTHENTHAL
THEODORE CORREL

Although many of us long for the good old days of safe streets, gang kids and street crime are scarcely a novel feature of the urban American landscape. The benchmark study of the urban gang is still Frederic Thrasher's of 1,313 Chicago gangs, first published in 1927.[1] The disorder and violence of these gangs appalled Thrasher. He observed that the gangs were beyond the ordinary controls of police and other social agencies, beyond the pale of civil society. He saw "regions of conflict" that were "like a frontier." He described gang youth as "lawless, godless, wild."

Of these youthful gangsters, only 7.2 percent were "Negro." Located in economically disadvantaged neighborhoods, the Chicago gangs of the 1920s were composed of children of immigrants—mostly Poles, Italians, and Irishmen, mixed with Jews, Slavs, Germans, and Swedes. Their moral posture seems scarcely different from today's black youth. "Stealing, the

For support we wish to thank the California Department of Justice, Office of the Attorney General; the U.C. California Policy Seminar; the National Institute of Justice; and the Guggenheim Crime Seminar. Points of view or opinions expressed here are those of the authors and do not represent the official position or views of the agencies or foundations which supported the research.

leading predatory activity of the adolescent gang," Thrasher wrote, "is regarded as perfectly natural and contains no more moral opprobrium for the gang boy than smoking a cigarette." Today's youthful gangsters sell illegal drugs, particularly crack cocaine, with similar moral abandon. And armed with semi-automatic military weapons, they are capable of far greater injury to themselves and others.

It was in light of these concerns that we began our research on street drug dealing, particularly cocaine trafficking, in the summer of 1988. Our data are based on more than one hundred interviews with inmates and wards in five California correctional institutions—two adult prisons and three California Youth Authority facilities—in both Northern and Southern California conducted during 1988 and 1989. Despite Joan Moore's admonitions in this volume against "correctional research" we found considerable consistency between ethnographic research on drug-selling gangs and what we learned from the correctional research interviews.[2]

During our second research year we expanded our research question from the relation between California gangs and drug dealing in California to the issue of why gang members migrated to sell drugs in other areas in the United States, as well as to other parts of California. By late 1988 police departments all over the country, from Shreveport, Louisiana, to Kansas City, Missouri, to Seattle, Washington, were reporting that California gang members were extending their operations. Law enforcement agents have often convened to discuss this issue.[3]

From the perspective of criminological theory, two polar and conflicting theories seem plausible as explanations of gang member migration. At one pole is the organized crime infiltration or "mafia" theory.[4] Under it, street gangs have evolved into sophisticated organized crime groups who consciously evaluate and target particular markets. Members are assigned territories to work, while maintaining strong economic and filial links with the host gang.

The symbolic association theory lies at the other explanatory pole. In that view, a young man from the old neighborhood, who may or may not have been an active gang member, migrates to a new city and sets up a new gang, with few or no links to the old gang; he uses the Los Angeles gang name because of its panache. Based on our data, we argue that neither of these theories accurately captures reality. The relation between gangs, drugs, and gang migration is neither as organized as the first model suggests nor as disconnected as the second does.

Instead, we propose that the data we have developed best fit what we are calling a "cultural resource" theory. This posits that although gangs do not sell drugs—individuals do—some gang organizations generate values, understandings, and trust relationships which facilitate but do not direct drug selling or the migration of members. Southern California gangs, we conclude, are organized horizontally, stressing values of neighborhood, loyalty, and the equality that obtains among members of a family. Gangs of this type are "cultural gangs." By contrast, northern California gangs are organized vertically, with status in the gang dependent upon successful role performance in criminal activity.

This theory may also be applicable to Eastern U.S. gangs, such as the Jamaicans, and helps to explain a puzzling and otherwise inexplicable finding: that San Francisco Bay-area gangs don't travel or travel very rarely—even to Sacramento—in contrast to Los Angeles-based Bloods and Crips, who sell drugs from Shreveport, Louisiana, to Seattle, Washington, as well as in Sacramento. We believe that our research has uncovered an interesting and perhaps surprising paradox: that gangs which were initially culturally organized for social purposes can draw upon more resources to support migration to sell an illegal product than "entrepreneurial" gangs organized for the specific purpose of selling drugs. To understand why that is so it will be useful to review last year's (1989) findings supplemented by our interview findings from this year (1990).

THE CONTINUED RISE OF THE ENTREPRENEURIAL GANG

Our most recent research partially supports one of the principal findings of our first report: California urban drug-selling gangs can usefully be divided along "cultural" versus "instrumental" lines and, at least among African American Los Angeles gangs, there is a dynamic movement from the former towards the latter. Our major thesis is as this occurs, the developing entrepreneurial activities of Los Angeles gang members are supported by the resources of traditional gang membership, which includes horizontal organizational loyalty norms and favored status. This foundation is especially important in shoring up migratory selling. By contrast, vertically organized entrepreneurial gangs do not enjoy these resources.

Cultural gangs, as we described them in *The Social Structure of Street Drug Dealing*, typically hold respect, fraternity, trust, and loyalty to gang and neighborhood as bedrock values. These gangs are strongly grounded in neighborhood or territorial identity and tend to extend across generations. Criminal activities have traditionally been a contingent feature of the southern California cultural gang. As Joan Moore explains, "In the poverty environment, small scale extortion was (and is) fairly common among teenagers to obtain public consumption ends."[5] Klein's earlier study of an East Los Angeles gang shows similar delinquency patterns—theft, truancy, status offenses such as incorrigibility—as a minor part of gang life.[6]

While the cultural gang routinely engages in criminal activities including the black market, gangs exist prior to and independent of the illegal activities in which they are engaged. The criminal acts do not define either the identity of the gang or its individual members. Instrumental gangs, by contrast, are business focused with financial goals paramount; hence we employ the term "entrepreneurial gangs." In these gangs, members enter the gang for instrumental (economic) reasons, fealty of gang membership tends to depend on economic (usually drug-related) opportunities offered by leaders, and the gang is motivated by profits and the control of markets. These gangs tend to be viewed by their members as "organizations," and are considered as a strict business operation.

The cultural gang is a tightly knit primary group, an extended family, in the interpretation offered by members. The entrepreneurial gang is like a business organization. Gang members may enjoy recreational activities together, similar to the way employees and managers of a small business do, but these activities are contingent, not central. A sociologist would say that the cultural gang operates within a symbolic interactionist framework, responding to previously developed social norms, while the entrepreneurial gang is purposively rational, valuing instrumental and strategic action.[7]

How each gang type employs violence is central to understanding their different institutional frameworks. Cultural gangs employ violence predominantly as a symbolic aspect of gang loyalty and identity. Entrepreneurial gangs may employ violence with comparable savagery, but with different goals. That is, the entrepreneurial gang employs violence for the purpose of controlling their drug-selling territory or enforcing the loyalty norms of the operation, rather than for gang or social identity per se. The Los Angeles sheriff's department investigated ninety-six homicides in 1988. They identified only seven as "drug related." The remainder were classified as "gang related."[8] The infamous Crips and Bloods gangs apparently do most of their violence over matters of honor.

In *The Social Structure of Street Drug Dealing* we observed the dynamic movement of African American Los Angeles gangs from symbolic interaction to the purposive rationality: "[T]he situation of the Los Angeles gangs . . . seems to be changing, indeed dynamically so, as the values associated with drug marketing come to dominate members."[9] And we continued, noting the specific importance of such attributes as initiative and ambition in African American gangs and explained why these gangs are particularly likely to transform their role in the marketing of cocaine.

Since crack cocaine appears to be the most profitable drug, and since crack cocaine is sold mainly by African American street dealers, the sale of that drug seems to have blurred the distinction between the cultural and the entrepreneurial gang. In Los Angeles, African American cultural gangs, which were never as tightly identified with the neighborhood as Latino gangs, are increasingly becoming instrumental in their relationship towards drugs. These gangs seem to prize individual initiative and ambition as indicia of status. As a result, African American cultural gangs seem increasingly to look like gangs instrumentally designed for the sale of drugs.[10]

Our recent research suggests that the movement from the symbolic interactionist to the purposively rational mode has affected Latino gangs as well, although probably not as strongly as it has African American gangs. In our current research, we found that both environmental factors—such as law enforcement efforts and increased drug-selling competition—as well as the internal dynamics of the gangs are propelling this move towards professionalization and entrepreneurship. It is also clear this change has become more pronounced over time. We note and elaborate on the movement here because of its important policy implications.

It is clear from our interviews as well as from common sense that the changing role of urban gangs in street drug dealing is occurring against a dynamically changing community backdrop. The urban neighborhoods affected by gang, drug, and violent activity have come under intense public and police scrutiny, and related law enforcement efforts. The media have focused on such neighborhoods across the country—neighborhoods that have reportedly become saturated with the drug "epidemic"; and, particularly for Los Angeles, have had violence escalate to a level "comparable to Beirut."

In actuality, Los Angeles has come to occupy perhaps the pre-eminent position in the United States for the importation of cocaine.[11] As we stated in our previous report, the price of cocaine fell precipitously from $60,000 to $12,000 a kilo. Some of our most recent interviews suggest that just in 1992 this price has fallen still, to $9000 or $10,000 a kilo.

Our current research confirms these public perceptions about the changing arena within which urban Los Angeles drug selling occurs. Our most recent inmate and ward respondents were almost unanimous in citing an increase in law enforcement efforts and pressure, an all-around tightening of the drug trade, and a major increase in the incidence of violence. Across the board, from Modesto to San Diego, the respondents reported that law enforcement has stepped up their efforts to curtail the drug trade and gang activity.

Most importantly, there was near unanimity that these efforts were having an impact on their drug business, and this was particularly true for Los Angeles. The interviewees were similarly in agreement on the tightening pressures of the illegal drug trade, citing such factors as the precipitous decrease in the cost of drugs and an increase in the number of drug dealers, the conspicuous success of many of those already involved in the drug trade, and the escalation of violence. It is clear, in other words, that seller participation in the Los Angeles urban drug market is perceived to have become markedly more difficult, more dangerous, and less lucrative in the last three years.

If we think of gang values and organization as potentially facilitative of drug marketing, the factors discussed above significantly affect the role of gangs in the Los Angeles drug business. Based on our interviews, we conclude that these factors have bolstered the power and position of the Los Angeles gangs, and we believe that this is fueling a transition from the cultural towards the entrepreneurial gang.

DRUG SALIENCE IN CULTURAL GANG MEMBERSHIP

One strong indication of the shift from the cultural to the entrepreneurial gang is a change that seems to be occurring, at least in Los Angeles, in the ambition of youths who seek to join gangs. Some of our interviews for our earlier report suggested that individuals were being attracted to gangs not for what they represented to others in the neighborhood, but rather for what they represented in opportunities for drug dealing.

Whereas simply joining the gang and attaining one of its more respected stations used to be the paramount, sometimes the only goal, it now seems that youths are increasingly interested in joining the gang for the economic benefits conferred by such membership. Since 1985, these economic benefits have largely been attained through access to the world of drug dealing. In the words of one young gang member:

"People joining, I figure myself, they join the gangs, because in the gangs, I guess if you got a gang behind you, you stronger. It's easier to distribute cocaine if you got a lot of people to sell to or to sell for you."[12]

Complementing this shift in the motivation of youths is a loosening of gang-membership criteria in favor of one's involvement in the drug trade. Position in the drug business is increasingly becoming accepted as the new passport to status in traditionally cultural gangs. Our previous research showed that even within cultural gangs one could attain the status of "homeboy" through adoption if one successfully sold drugs for another higher ranking homeboy, or even just brought drugs to the set. One of the respondents reported how this adoption mechanism worked:

"If they sold dope for me, that would be my homeboy, and if he's my homeboy then he's everybody's homeboy. Something happen to him, it's all our responsibility."[13]

Drug-Dealing Benefits of Cultural Gang Membership

In *The Social Structure of Street Drug Dealing* we reported that being a member of a gang facilitated drug dealing success.[14] This facilitation was apparent in myriad ways. Gangs, for example, offer a rich source of shared marketing information. Information about who sells for what price, and who has drugs available is routinely communicated along gang lines. The gang member can also rely on his homeboys for protection and concerted retribution if anything were to happen to him inside or outside his gang turf. Gang members, furthermore, enjoy easy access to and control of territorial markets. They can sell drugs in their own neighborhood without intruding upon the turf of others. In return, they can exclude others from selling on their turf. This territorial monopoly is backed by force since the gang automatically protects against outside intruders. Finally, there is a well-developed and virtually sacrosanct sense of trust inhering in the homeboy relationship, so that gang members are expected not to betray other members to the police or rival gangs.

Our current research confirms that the above advantages still benefit gang-affiliated dealers. It appears, moreover, that the benefits of gang membership have actually, and even significantly, increased over time. This is a second indication that traditionally cultural gangs are reorienting towards the drug trade. The reorientation is further evidenced in several observations.

First, the ready trade of drug-dealing information within gangs has mushroomed and solidified into a full-blown apprenticeship system for those just entering the drug trade. This provides benefits both for the new inductees as well as for the more established dealers. Older gang members often not only introduce younger members to drug dealing but also routinely offer these younger members prepackaged drugs on consignment, to be sold for easy "double-up" profit.[15] This economic "good will" gesture is, if need be, accompanied by instruction in such things as the standard quantities of drugs to be sold, the going prices, whom to sell to and whom to avoid, the best locations to sell, and the best way to avoid being caught by police. In turn, the older gang member/dealer can count on a steady peddler of his contraband. He can also call on the younger member to perform various illegal tasks—ranging from holding drugs to working shifts in a rock house to carrying drugs between locations—to further insulate the older dealer from police scrutiny.

Second, the type of drug-dealing information being exchanged within gangs has expanded to encompass the new out-of-town and interstate drug-trafficking operations. Information on the least risky and competitive out-of-town locations is now transmitted through the gang, as well as information on law enforcement presence and tactics in the various new locations.

Third, the web of support expected of and provided to fellow gang members has expanded beyond mere protection, and it has become increasingly economic oriented. Such provision of support for fellow gang members is expected on demand, and includes such things as lending money, fronting drugs, and providing guns for a "mission." In several of our most recent interviews we were told that the provision of this sort of support has gone beyond loans to include an expectation of outright gifts, usually of money or drugs, but even of clothing or automobiles.

These gifts seem to be given under two circumstances. When an apprentice drug dealer has performed particularly well he might be rewarded with gifts; or if a gang member is sent to prison, largess is expected both to keep him well-equipped there and to ease his transition back into the drug business upon his release. When a gang member fails to provide such support, his reputation and standing are diminished:

"If you was my homeboy and I asked you for [some money] and he says "no I can't," but you know he got it, and he refusing to assist another one of his homeboys, he got to go. Either somebody's going to rob him, kill him, or kick him off the set."

Yet gang support, we found, does not stop here. It now also includes an expectation—in addition to the fronted or free drugs and cash—of bail money. Gang members can also count on a relatively secure immunity from being ripped off, or "being jacked" as it is called, by fellow gang members. Finally, as always, gang members enjoy a special priority in obtaining drugs from their fellow members. Thus, gang membership offers one of the most secure and reliably consistent supply of drugs.

Expanded Control of Drug-Dealing Territories

The ultimate drug-dealing benefit conferred on gang members has been expanded cultural gang control of drug-selling territories. This control appears to have intensified. It deserves independent consideration as a direct indication of the shift from the cultural towards the instrumental gang. Respondents speak to the new authority of the gangs in regulating local drug peddling:

"In our neighborhood, can't just anybody come up there and sell drugs and stuff. If you not a enemy of ours, and you on the cool side, everything's alright. But other than that the homeboys, they keep a tight lock on the neighborhood. They don't let everybody come up there . . ."

At the same time, no respondents reported that "sets" completely controlled the supply of drugs in the neighborhood. Sets, by virtue of their power in the neighborhood might enjoy de facto control over drug supply, but this has never been reported as an explicit aim or accomplishment of a set.

The New Ambition of Cultural Gangs

Against these developments in the Los Angeles drug market we found an interesting and paradoxical countertrend to the unabated rise of entrepreneurial values. Although the values of the cultural gang consistently protect and facilitate gang member participation in drug dealing, it now seems that the ascendance of drug dealing is undermining the cultural understandings of the gang. We note the emergence of this conflict in several important ways.

As we reported in *The Social Structure of Street Drug Dealing*, participation in cultural gang violence, or "gangbanging," traditionally has been one of the primary means for younger gang members to accumulate respect and position within the gang. While the continued importance of engaging in such violence should not be underestimated, our research does pick up a subtle change in orientation. Youth engage in gang-related violence not simply to enhance their position within the gang, but also their prospects in the drug trade.

Attaining status in the gang by assisting and participating in the drug-dealing activities of older gang members now seems to have taken on an independent significance for younger members. "Coming up" in the gang now has as much to do with the money one earns from selling drugs as the overt violence committed in fealty to the gang. One older gang member reflected on this diminution of older gang member's involvement in the gang in favor of full-time drug dealing:[16]

"Like, . . . some of them [fellow gang members] see themselves as high rollers . . . they done got too old, so they not really into gang banging anymore. It's the younger generation that's comin' up. The people my age [twenty], they kickin' back now, they out selling drugs and kickin back now; they lookin' to the future."

Gang Migration

Against a background of escalating violence, declining drug prices, and intensified law enforcement, Los Angeles-area gang-related drug dealers are seeking out new venues to sell the Midas product—crack cocaine.

According to Frank Storey, head of the FBI's field office in Kansas City, Missouri, Bloods and Crips "have set up crack operation there and in forty-five other cities, including Tulsa, Omaha, Denver, and St. Louis."[17] These operations have also gone beyond urban areas. As a recent *New York Times* headline proclaims, "Drug Gangs Are Now Operating in Rural States."[18] Our research confirms such reports. Respondents claim to have either participated in or have knowledge of Blood or Crip crack operations in twenty-two states and at least twenty-six cities.[19]

In fact, it appears difficult to overstate the penetration of Blood and Crip members into other states. As one Crip respondent put it:

> "Everywhere you go, you know what I'm saying, any where you go, you're gonna see some people from L.A. If they got, you know, a dope house out there, or a dope street out there, you gonna see somebody . . . you'll run into somebody on that street from L.A."

Further, every respondent that belonged to a L.A.-area Blood or Crip set reported either travelling themselves or having knowledge of individuals in his set who did. This finding has led us to conclude that travelling or going "out of town," as it is commonly referred to by gang members, has become an intrinsic part of the decisional fabric of the Los Angeles drug business. That is, just as drug dealers decide whether to "curb" sell or "house" sell; to have partners or sell alone; or to sell "weight" or just rock, they also decide whether to migrate or stay put.

It is difficult to pinpoint precisely when migration became an institutionalized aspect of drug dealing. A recent Justice Department report on the expansion of crack operations into rural states dates the phenomenon as beginning in 1988. Among our respondents, one reports having travelled to several states as early as 1981-1982, but of course, he was selling cocaine as powder. A more accurate estimation, based on our interviews, is that the most ambitious and skilled drug dealers may have started as early as 1985, but most didn't begin until 1986 or 1987. This development appears to have had a significant impact on African American Los Angeles gangs. Travelling to sell drugs is one more indication of the transformation of gangs from a 'cultural' orientation to an instrumental or entrepreneurial orientation. Or as one respondent explained, "Back in the earlier days, you know, the values of drugs was never overriding the values of gangs."

WHY TRAVEL?

Like an object poised between a closing door and a magnet, Los Angeles-area gang members experience push and pull pressures to abandon the streets of Los Angeles. What pushes? Competition is one factor. It is widely reported that the Los Angeles-area drug market is either already saturated or fast becoming so.[20] With a reported gang membership population of eighty thousand, it is easy to understand why and how competition would reduce crack prices in Los Angeles. A respondent describes the economic pressure:

"There's competition, man. Like, say I'm selling my ounces for, like, seven fifty. Man, I'm making a killing. This motherfucker comes from L.A., you know what I'm saying, with ounces for five fifty. . . . Next thing you know, everybody . . . trying to sell at five fifty, I'm going to lower my prices down. You know what I'm saying. Or, you know, like, I'm giving out a big five O sale. And my five O is *big*. And he come with a bigger five O . . . So I got to bigger mine, you know what I'm saying?"

One respondent offered an overabundance of supply explanation for lower prices:

"Four ounces gonna cost you on street value today, like $2500. Back then, four ounces would cost you like three or four thousand dollars." ["Why has the price come down?"] "Because it's so easy to get now. It's coming in so much large quantity that everybody's gettin' it, everybody wantin' to make they money, you know."

Price reduction has made drug markets outside of Los Angeles much more attractive. As one respondent commented:

"Out of town where nobody else ain't at . . . that's where the money's being made because there's too much competition in Los Angeles. It's got too many dope dealers in Los Angeles competing against each other. So they take it out of town. The profits are better. Here you can sell an ounce for $600, over there you can sell it for $1500."

If competition serves as one of the propelling factors, intensified law enforcement is another. When drug selling in a neighborhood becomes too extensive and too visible, a concentrated police response is often the result. One respondent describes gang member perceptions of and reaction to a police response:

"Probably my neighborhood would get hot or something like that, you know. The law would be death on the neighborhood. ; They just crack down and come like every other day . . . just make a whole sweep and just take everybody to jail. You know all the time you look up and see the police. You can't be in that neighborhood without the police coming. So you go somewhere else."

In sum, both competition and police pressure motivate migration. None of our respondents suggested, however, that anyone committed to selling drugs is about to seek out an honest job. Instead they look for business opportunities elsewhere. As one respondent summarily explained,

"You get too known, it get too competitive, it get too hot . . . a lot of police crack down. Then again, the people just want to make money. They say, "It's too much competition here, hey man, let's go out, like to Iowa, Iowa and Utah.""

The Pull to Travel

The pull to travel is best understood as a pursuit of higher prices, although there are other advantages to travelling which will be discussed later. Ultimately, the draw to travel is simply the flip side of the declining street value of crack in Los Angeles.

"The gangs are gettin' bigger, they gettin', I'd say, more sophisticated to selling drugs. . . . They expanding their organization out of town. First it was just in the L.A. area and in their neighborhood. Now they takin' it out of town because there's more money to be made there."

As this respondent suggests, areas adjacent to Los Angeles, and other cities in California first experienced the effects of this pursuit of higher prices.[21] One respondent related his experience in these areas:

"You can charge a lot more, you know, like when I went to the San Fernando Valley, what they was charging for $50, you know what I'm saying? I'd give it to them for $20 [in my neighborhood]."

Apart from the higher prices that Los Angeles-area gang drug dealers can exact from out-of-town markets, there are four additional advantages to migration.

1. Gang members can exploit a reputation for violence, thus diminishing threats from local out-of-town drug dealers. Two respondents explained the attitude that local dealers take towards Los Angeles visitors:

"Because other cities, they consider L.A. a crazy city which it is. You know what I'm saying? . . . Like Chicago, like cities with gangs not like us, they look at us like, 'you motherfuckers is crazy', . . . you get a lot of respect."

2. Los Angeles travelers perceive themselves as enjoying access to more resources—money, firepower, and skill—than local competitors. Respondents offered the following comments regarding this advantage:

"We faster than they are, we from the city, see. So they would have to watch us first, because we knew what we were doing. It's like if a businessperson were to go to a slower town and start up a business putting computers in. They had to learn from us."

3. Los Angeles travelers have access to larger quantities of cocaine than local dealers. One respondent described the out-of-town drug market in the following way: "Out there [Minnesota], it's quick to sell, it didn't even take us a week [to sell seven kilos]. We sold by the ounce, the quarter key, the half key. The dealers from out there started buying from us."

4. Los Angeles travelers have developed more sophisticated arrest avoidance techniques than local police usually encounter. A respondent gave us an example of one technique he used while selling in Las Vegas, Nevada:

"The police was trying, but they couldn't do nothing about it [drug sales]. They got some police out there called 'nasty boys,' they wear all black. You can't see them coming unless you really look out. So we said, 'yeah, that's a slick idea.' So we got to wearing all black so they couldn't see us, so they didn't know what was going on."

Stay at Homes

Despite the compelling inducements and the many advantages gang members enjoy when they do migrate, many members travel selectively within California, or not at all. Respondents indicated four reasons for declining to sell drugs outside Los Angeles.

Foreign Prisons. Respondents discussed the quality of prison life. They fear doing time in prisons outside of California. In California, gang members already retain ties to inmates, while they do not in other venues. As one respondent put it:

"They [inmates in other states] are gonna fuck with us . . . They've never been to Los Angeles County. They got them hinky, honky, motherfuckers up there, man. Fucking kill off my fucking ass or something, man."

Sentence Severity. Respondents fear that in some other states and in the federal system sentences will be higher than they are in California for comparable offenses. Some states merited explicit identification. "I'd hate to get caught in Texas or Alabama or Mississippi with a cocaine charge."

Others were opposed to travelling regardless of the destination: "That's dangerous, you're talking about a lot of time. And if you just do it in California you're cool."

Distance from Friends and Family. Respondents expressed a fear of the unknown, of leaving the security, familiarity, and recognized relationships of the neighborhood. One respondent, discussing others who declined to leave the neighborhood, addressed their timidity in somewhat disparaging terms: "They is addicted to the 'hood, you know what I'm saying? They don't want to leave home . . . move away from the 'hood, you know?"

Other respondents explain their disinclination to travel not so much as timidity, but as caution in anticipation of the dangers of the unknown; as well as a lack of confidence in those who claim to know the dangers of the outlying territory: "I always wanted to be around my 'hood . . . I want to know where I can run to. I don't like following a motherfucker hoping he knows where he is going, I want to know where I'm going."

Satisfaction. Some respondents reported that some gang members were satisfied with the income derived from drug selling operations in Los Angeles. Almost all consider travelling, but don't feel that the pressures warrant the risk associated with travel.

Making the Move

Whatever the pressures to leave the comfortable environs of Los Angeles and strike out to sell in unfamiliar venues, travelling usually does not commence following anything like a formal meeting and strategic planning by informed associates. According to our respondents, all inclinations to travel of course begin with the expectation of acquiring income, even wealth, from the new local drug trade. But these are the travels of provincials, not cosmopolitans. The unaccustomed drug income offers many of them their first opportunity to travel outside their state, city, and even neighborhood. Indeed, the idea of selling drugs out of town may be activated from ordinary extended family visits to distantly located relatives: "A family member probably say something, like you know. . . . Drugs is out here . . . they got drugs here but not a lot of drugs, like out there in South Central."

As the operation expands it usually becomes more sophisticated, depending on actual market opportunities, plus the skill and ambition of the gang member who "discovers" it. Generally, the longer the travelling phenomenon continues, the more sophisticated it becomes as Bloods and Crips begin to develop an extensive network of contacts in cities and counties throughout the nation.

Among those who do decide to travel, plans are usually made according to the network of the individual planning to migrate and the word on the street about the potential of a market. That is, most of those who venture out of South Central choose a locale either because a trusted homeboy is already on the scene or he hears from a trusted homeboy that money can be made out there. The former mode is illustrated by a respondent who describes his introduction as follows:

"Yes, I had people who was already out there, already knew the ropes and shit, you know, what's going on, and shit, because if you just go out there and you don't know a damn thing you'll go to jail quick."

Three respondents reported that they chose an out-of-state destination based upon what they had heard on the street. One of them related the conversation as follows: "'Hey, what's been goin' on homeboy? I been out here and here . . .' 'What's been goin' on out there?' '. . . There's money out there.' 'Where about?' And he tell me . . .' "

Or they were recruited to sell drugs for someone else out of town:

"Well my homeboy tell me . . . one of my big homeys come over there and say, 'Yeah, I just got this spot from this, you know, base head. You know, we got a spot over there from a base head.' So we go over there and make money."

Occasionally, risk-accepting homeboys who are feeling the heat or the competition in South Central decide, like immigrants seeking a promised land, to venture somewhere, anywhere, that seems to promise economic opportunity and adventure. One reported that he had been selling in Arizona. Did he have connections there? His answer:

"Nah, we just got on the airplane. Paid them the money, went out and got on a airplane." ["You didn't know anybody, have any prior information?"] "Didn't know nothing. Just looking for, you know, the dope . . . the dope smokers, you know."

Although the homeboys are, in one sense, provincials, in another they are sophisticates. They know the culture of, and feel comfortable within, the confines of an inner-city's drug-dealing world. If a homeboy has neither contacts in a particular city or information about the nature of its drug market, he often understands how to scout it out:

"We went out there and got our own area. We had to peep things out first. There's ways to go about it. Go out there, get with some girls or something, talk to girls, find out information. We have all this jewelry and the flashy clothes and the loud sound in the car and we'd just ride around different high schools. And people, say like in Kansas, they see that and they like 'Oh man, you know they from LA, they from LA, from California' and they come to you."

Once the expansion decision has been made, the issue shifts to the potential hazards posed by illegal drug transfer. Few respondents counted occasional transportation of drugs across state lines as extraordinarily difficult. But those who transported drugs on a regular basis invested considerable thought and energy into avoiding capture. One respondent mailed his cocaine to a P.O. box or an address, since police were using dogs at airports. Others usually drove or flew with or near the drugs to the out-of-state locale. Tactics to avoid arrest varied.

"We had it like this [when we flew]: the guys would dress ordinary . . . like off the street. The police got hip to us. So we started dressing good—the fancy clothes, the big jewelry—so the police would get us and the girls would go through. The police would say 'hey, you're drug dealers' and hassle us; the girls would dress ordinary and get through."

As the remarks of the above respondent illustrate, an elaborate and well-conceived transportation plan must be developed for most ongoing crack operations. Drugs must be dispatched to the new market and proceeds returned to Los Angeles. One group of travelers began training their runners or couriers:

"Most likely the runner be a female, an older woman, in her thirties. We'd have a woman, and she'd have to get trained—I guess you would call it trained—we just told her how to do it, then she would do it if she wanted to . . . We was paying our runner $9,000 -$10,000 a month."

Through these various methods our respondents were transporting as little as an ounce to as much as six to ten kilos a month to cities in Nebraska, Missouri, and Louisiana.

Once there, crack operations varied in quantity of drugs sold, frequency of visits, and nature of selling (e.g. curb selling vs. house selling). Typically, Los Angeles-area gang members will adopt the selling practices used by locals. Thus, in Detroit, travelers generally sold out of houses, while in Minnesota travelers sold at the curb.

Eventually, at the high end, these operations, aided as they are by modern communications technology, can become quite sophisticated. As this occurs, they come more closely to resemble the organized crime model. One advanced drug entrepreneur describes his operation as follows:

"I got a beeper, okay, you know, with a beeper service. I got a beeper that's, you can be in Cleveland and get beeped from out here [Los Angeles]. It's what you call 'round the world' beeper, one for LA, one for all around. So . . . if I had to go do something—pick up some money or something, or take someone stuff out there—they'd just call."

In one gang, members had established out-of-town spots in five cities. They then began pooling their money together: "All the home boys put all their dope together, and send it like that; then all the money come back and then it's how much everybody should get . . ."

Operations such as this are well organized, low profile, and if possible, nonviolent. These characteristics, exhibited among high-level dealers, are also manifested among more casual travelers. In particular, efforts to maintain peace with other Los Angeles gangs and local drug dealers and low profiles with regard to law enforcement agencies is shared by all travelers, irrespective of their ambition and sophistication.

Taken together, these characteristics may represent the "new rules of drug dealing." In sharp contrast to the rules prevailing in Los Angeles, Bloods and Crips are not interested in gangbanging with one another or with locals when they are out of town.

"As for that Crip and Blood thing, that's not going on outside of town."

"Everybody trying to keep a low profile. Everybody like, 'there's enough out here for everybody. Just don't step on nobody's toes'. We never got into it. It's all about money; money come first. You can gangbang anytime."

Indeed, gang members will leave a locale rather than risk conflict with another set, even a rival.

"If you go out of town, and you a Crip set and there another Crip set, then you have to move out; that's respect. If we go out to a state and there's Bloods out there, then we choose if we want to leave or not. But most likely we'll leave because we don't want to be shooting a fight with no others, in no different state, because we out there to do one thing: make money . . . We're out there to sell drugs not for the killing."

These instrumental values implicit in the new rules of drug dealing are not easily apparent to younger gang members, who are socialized to the traditional Los Angeles gang rules. They, in effect, need to be resocialized to understand and conform with the emerging entrepreneurial goals of distant markets.

Gang Organization and Migration Patterns

The willingness to assume risk is not the primary difference between northern (entrepreneurial) and southern California (cultural) gang-related crack-selling operations. And as Bruce Johnson et al., have pointed out,

> inner-city minority youths working in the illicit cocaine economy are selling their labor, sales skills, and willingness to risk very substantial prison penalties. The willingness to take such risk is the only service which middle class persons value and pay for [when buying drugs].[22]

A more important distinction is in organizational structure. The Los Angeles cultural gang is horizontally organized while the Northern California gang is vertically organized. The only purpose of Northern California "gangs" is to facilitate profitable criminal activity. The distinctive features of these gangs are: (1) members consider them a business organization; (2) the business is drug dealing; and (3) as a consequence of (1) and (2), the use of violence is limited to intentional violence, directed towards protection or promotion of business interests. In addition, such organizations have a vertical structure. There are three elements of vertically organized crack operations:

First, one person usually controls the supply of drugs to a turf. As one respondent put it: "There's always a big man somewhere around. As far as being in a dope gang, there's always a big man." Several respondents referred to specific turfs as being run by one or a small group of individuals. One respondent reported playing such a role in his turf:

"I was passed the torch from my brothers, as far as leadership. I have some O.G. homeboys, but they in jail. Everybody in Hunter's Point [San

Francisco] pretty much listens to me. I had that respect coming to me from my brothers, and I had it coming to where I could say 'we goin' do this, that'."

Second, this person determines who can sell drugs in a turf, that is, he determines, in a organizational sense, membership. According to one respondent:

"The whole Acorn [in Oakland] don't get along. Now it's different. [When] Larry P. was running the whole Acorn, we didn't fuck with him. Larry P. was like 'Man, tell your fool, I catch you down here, you or any of your boys down here selling some more dope, fool, and it ain't any of mine, I'm going to break arms or whatever.'"

Third, within the organization, several roles are created and filled on the basis of age and expertise. One respondent described his introduction and matriculation through an organization.

"Around ten, that's when they started liking me, hooking me up. I keep their dope on me when the police come and shit like that. Gradually I got hooked up and I started selling dope for them, my older partners, my OGs. And then I grows up and my little partners, they look up to me. They started getting hooked up with me. And it goes on and on like that."

While the above sounds relatively efficient, the vertical structure of most crack operations generates competition within the organization. There are only a limited number of "spots" at each level of the organization. As a consequence, distrust, betrayal, and sometimes violence occurs among members.

"In Oakland . . . , when you in the dope game you can't really trust nobody, you can't trust nobody; even you motherfucking brother . . . I started feeling I couldn't trust him [his father] and he couldn't trust me. Even though he was my father, we was blood. Then came the point when I was getting so big on my turf and he was hearing about it and I was crossing so many of his partners that he had people come and jump me. So you really can't trust nobody in the dope game."

One respondent reported ripping off fellow turf members to rise up. In general it seems a truism that "The next man is tryin' to come up off the next man." Indeed, one respondent reported:

"I didn't want to get that high up. I done seen too many folks be called big dope dealers, die. They feel like they kill him, they can move up. It's tight to get up there. You need to do a lot of stepping to get up there."

This intraturf competition poses serious problems for those in leadership. Typically, two methods are employed to maintain the leader's authority. The first involves rewarding members with drugs, luxury items, or clientele. As pointed out in our previous report, "the fealty of membership depends on the opportunities offered by leaders, usually those who can claim a reliable connection to a source of drugs."[23]

Members are also rewarded with clientele. According to one respondent, "My big partners, they be tellin', like 'yea, we want you all to go to such and so house.' They be givin' us their clientele so we could come up."

At the other end of the spectrum, authority is maintained by physical coercion, which in extreme cases may result in deadly violence. One respondent who "employed" thirty or so people described how he maintained fealty.

"They [his little partners] be trying to come up for themself. But we didn't play it like that. You worked for me or you didn't work for nobody. You get caught buying some dope, you better buy it from me. They were like sneaky little motherfuckers though. They make their little money and then they go buy like two ounces from somebody else, while I get another count.

["What would happen if you caught them?"] "They get fucked up. They ain't going to get killed, but they'll get beat up. Take their car, take their jewelry, slap their bitch in the face, spit on them. "Get on fool, why don't you get with another group. You can be as dead as they are." They like, 'that's okay man.' They be scared to leave."

In sum, vertically organized crack operations generate intraturf competition, which sometimes results in violence. This occurs both as low-level dealers attempt to displace higher level ones, and horizontally, as "the next man trys to come up off the next man."

This competitive attitude extends to rival crack,selling operations and is the primary cause of violence. As one of our respondents reported, "Gangbanging for the people of the Bay area isn't really like Los Angeles— it's a little turf dispute. What we're fightin' over is money and power . . . I wouldn't say it's gangbanging."

As we reported in our earlier research, "the frequency of instrumental gang violence depends on territorial stability."[24] Northern California crack-selling operations may be summarized as businesslike, hierarchical, and dependent upon the liberal use of coercive mechanisms against both internal and external competitors.[25]

SOUTHERN CALIFORNIA GANGS:
THE HORIZONTAL STRUCTURE EXPLORED

Northern and Southern California gangs do not deal drugs differently. Both employ curb- and house-selling techniques to distribute their product. Both rely on violence to protect their "market share" and guard against rip-offs from desperate crack users. However, the attitudes and behaviors that Southern California drug dealers hold towards members of their own gangs is markedly different than those of their Northern California counterparts.

Southern California gangs instill in members trust, loyalty, and identity. In many ways they serve to create whole individuals and thus play an important role in the lives of members regardless of whether they sell drugs or even actively remain in the gang. Many respondents described what the gang gave them:

> "Well a gang, it like gives you something, it gives you something on the inside. You feel, when you join a gang, you feel like somebody. Especially in South Central, people feel like if you not a movie star or a professional sports player, you nothin'."

Further, drug dealing within the gang is optional. The gang doesn't sell drugs. Individuals or groups do. According to our respondents: "[Gangs] didn't have nothing to do with selling no drugs. That's just something you do on your own. You straight gangbang. You ain't got to get into the drug deal, you know."

Finally, southern California gangs eschew the concept of leadership. The gang, whether in myth or actuality, maintains an ideology of participant democracy: "There's not really one designated leader. You just all together. If a person has an idea, or suggestion, then we look into it. Follow through with it. But there's not a designated leader." The implication of course, is that the structure of the gang is more horizontal. People still "come up" in the drug trade and within the gang, but this occurs not as a consequence of competition with other members, but with age, experience, and knowledge.

CONCLUSION: A THEORY OF GANGS
AND GANG MIGRATION

Although gang migration has attracted government and media attention, many aspects of it still remain opaque.[26] One explanation for why gangs migrate is that the desire for greater or renewed profits motivates dealers to travel to other states. This presupposes a transfer of drugs from "old markets" (i.e., Los Angeles, San Francisco, New York, Miami, Philadelphia) to "new markets" (i.e., Seattle, Phoenix, Kansas City, St. Louis, cities in Tennessee). While partially correct, this line of reasoning doesn't answer why some "old markets" generate gang migration and others don't.

Nor does an explanation grounded in the skill and focus of law enforcement. That line of argument implies that Los Angeles police are more effective than those in San Francisco and Oakland and other target cities; and that New York and Miami police treat Jamaicans differently than indigenous African Americans. There is little evidence to suggest that is the case. Police in all cities we have studied have evolved and are developing a variety of sophisticated enforcement structures—buy-bust teams, neighborhood police units, tactical units, undercover units—to address drug selling. Gangs everywhere try to avoid police apprehension.

Arrests for selling crack have increased dramatically in New York City, from three thousand per month in 1986 to six thousand per month in the fall of 1988.[27] Similar figures can be found in Los Angeles, Miami, San Francisco, Kansas City, and Seattle. Street drug sellers experience law enforcement pressure all over the country.

As the rise in arrests and enhanced police activity was occurring, the price of cocaine was perceptively dropping in all of these cities. According to Terry Williams, the price of a kilo in New York fell from $60,000 in 1980 to $20,000 in 1988.[28] A similar price decline is chartable in San Francisco, where a kilo sold in 1989 for $12 to $13,000. So street sellers also experience market pressures. All of these—the increased number of drug dealers and the increased supply, the decline in price, the pressure of law enforcement—serve to encourage travelling to "new markets."

At the same time, migration seems to occur mainly among Jamaican, Haitian and Dominican gangs on the east coast and African American street gangs in Los Angeles.[29] And only Jamaicans and southern California gangs apparently travel regularly to the midwestern United States. Both the Dominican and Haitian operations appear to be regional, albeit large, markets. Why should that be?

We conclude that the cultural and structural organization of gangs, rather than law enforcement or market pressures, offers the most compelling explanation of why members of some gangs migrate while others do not. Los Angeles crack-selling operations appear to be horizontally organized (although this may be changing). San Francisco gangs, on the other hand, are vertically organized. And according to Williams and Johnson, New York's crack operations are also vertically organized.

These two different structures of crack dealing express conspicuously different values—one promoting trust and loyalty among equals, the other promoting competition and deadly ambition within a local hierarchical structure. Horizontally organized cultural gang structures, we conclude, furnish the individual gang member with resources—access to source of drugs, confidence, belief, courage, attitudes toward risk, a certain amount of trust—which facilitate venturing into new marketing territories. By contrast, vertical structures, with leaders, engender opportunism within the organization. Trust and cooperation are more limited.

To be sure, as Southern California gangs move into new territories their adventuresome and entrepreneurial members implicitly recognize that their operations do not permit the continuation of the cultural gang values so familiar to them in Los Angeles. Nevertheless, cultural gang values and understandings offer support. Thus, the data from our interviews suggest that the symbolic values implicit in the cultural gang nurture drug marketing migration while, paradoxically, purposive, rational, entrepreneurial values do not.

NOTES

1. Frederic M. Thrasher, *The Gang: A Study of 1,313 Gangs in Chicago* (Chicago: University of Chicago Press, 1927, 1963 ed.), p. 3.

2. See, for example, Terry Williams, *The Cocaine Kids: The Inside Story of a Teenage Drug Ring* (New York: Addison-Wesley, 1989). Correctional research surely has its limitations but so does ethnographic research. The correctional researcher may tend to see and talk with gang members most involved in criminal activity—but the ethnographer may be close to those least involved. Every research perspective has its shortcomings.

3. Bob Baker, "FBI, Police of 9 Cities to Plan Battle Against Gangs that Sell Drugs," *Los Angeles Times*, June 23, 1985.

4. For a discussion of how organized crime infiltrates casinos, see Jerome H. Skolnick, *House of Cards: Legalization and Control of Casino Gambling* (Boston: Little, Brown, 1978).

5. Joan Moore et al., *Homeboys: Gangs, Drugs and Prison in the Barrios of Los Angeles* (Philadelphia: Temple University Press, 1978), p. 39.

6. Malcolm W. Klein, *Street Gangs and Street Workers* (Englewood Cliffs, N.J.: Prentice Hall, 1971).

7. Jurgen Habermas, *Toward a Rational Society* (Boston: Beacon, 1970), p. 93.

8. Interview with Lt. Ron Herrara, Los Angeles sherrif's office.

9. Jerome H. Skolnick with Theodore Correl, Elizabeth Navarro, and Roger Rabb, *The Social Structure of Street Drug Dealing* (Office of the Attorney General, FORUM, Bureau of Criminal Statistics, Sacramento, 1988), p. 3.

10. Skolnick et al., *The Social Structure of Street Drug Dealing*, p. 21.

11. According to local DEA spokesman Ralph Lochridge, "This seizure [20 tons of cocaine] should put to rest any further speculation that Los Angeles is, in fact, the major pathway for cocaine entering the country." Reported by Michael Connelly and Eric Malnic in the *Los Angeles Times*, September 30, 1989, p. 24. Note the dramatic increase in currency flowing through Los Angeles banks, 1985-1988— $4 billion a month to $21 billion—with Los Angeles rivaling Miami as the money-laundering capital of the United States.

12. Skolnick et al., *Social Structure of Street Drug Dealing*, p. 6.

13. Ibid., p. 8.

14. Ibid., p. 11.

15. "Doubling-up" is the standard street term for receiving a quantity of drugs on consignment, the street value of which is roughly double the amount required to be returned to the supplier.

16. The age-risk curve is partially but not completely explanatory.

17. Larry Martz, "A Tide of Drug Killing," *Newsweek*, January 16, 1989, p. 45.

18. Julie Johnson, "Drug Gangs Are Now Operating in Rural States, Justice Dept. Says," *New York Times*, August 4, 1989, p. A1.

19. These cities and states are: Alabama; Alaska; Arkansas; "a small town near Phoenix" and Phoenix, Arizona; Denver, Colorado; Indianapolis, Indiana; Iowa; Kansas; Shreveport, Louisiana; Detroit, Michigan; Minnesota; St. Louis and Kansas City, Missouri; Las Vegas, Nevada; New York City; Cincinnati and Cleveland, Ohio; Oklahoma; Portland, Oregon; Tennessee; Texas; Utah; Seattle and Tacoma, Washington; and Milwaukee, Wisconsin.

20. Aldore Collier, "To Deal and Die in LA," *Ebony Special Issue: War! The Drug Crisis*, August 1989, 110.

21. According to our respondents, Los Angeles-area gang-related drug dealers have travelled to sixteen California cities. Those cities are: Bakersfield, Chino, Claremont, Fresno, La Verne, Modesto, Montclair, Oakland, Ontario, Paris, Redlands, Rialto, Riverside, Sacramento, San Diego, and Stockton. There is little question that our figure is a gross underestimate since we were primarily concerned with out-of-state travel and did not routinely ask respondents about intrastate travel.

22. Bruce Johnson et al., "Drug Abuse in the Inner City: Impact on Hard Drug Users and the Community," in *Drugs and the Criminal Justice System*, ed. Michael Tonry and Jones Q. Wilson (Chicago: University of Chicago Press, 1989), p. 28.

23. *Social Structure of Street Drug Dealing*, p. 3.

24. Ibid., p. 9.

25. Both *The Cocaine Kids* by Terry Williams and "Drug Abuse in the Inner City" by Bruce Johnson et al. describe a vertical organization of crack selling very similar to the picture which emerges from our interviews of northern California drug dealers.

26. The Department of Justice recently released a report on the migration of gangs and crack to rural states, and on NBC's "Gangs, Cops and Drugs," the second hour of the program was devoted to exploring the gang migration phenomenon.

27. Johnson et al., "Drug Abuse in the Inner City," p. 51.

28. Williams, *Cocaine Kids*, p. 7.

29. Johnson et al., "Drug Abuse in the Inner City," p. 23.

10

Gangs in More- and Less-Settled Communities

DANIEL J. MONTI

A theory about gangs and corrigible public policies about gangs presume the existence of good comparative information about gangs. Such information does not exist today and, indeed, never has existed. Much research into gangs is based on a few groups that have been observed in a particular community for a period of time.[1] This work can be informative, even compelling. Nevertheless, it cannot provide a satisfactory basis for developing broader descriptions and explanations of gang organization and behavior. Our observations of individual gangs are too fragmented to allow us to construct a theory about gangs in general.

Sociologists appreciate the importance of good comparative information about gangs. Indeed, the first sociological study of gangs was Frederic M. Thrasher's work which was published in 1927 and involved over 1,300 different groups. His was not an easy undertaking. There were many practical problems to overcome in a study of so many groups spread over dozens of neighborhoods. It was time-consuming and difficult work made not substantially easier by the use of multiple investigators. The information collected for Thrasher varied considerably in quality, and this made piecing together a comprehensive picture of gangs difficult to accomplish. It was no surprise that subsequent researchers undertook less ambitious studies involving only a few gangs, and perhaps only one gang, or a small geographic area.

Gangs from different communities probably look and behave differently. There has been little research that would enable one to identify those differences and to indicate how great or important they can be, however. That is why "theories" about gangs have the look and feel of a cake that went into an oven missing some important ingredients and came out half-baked.

Case studies of individual gangs or of gangs in a particular neighborhood usually are good vehicles for exploring the relation between gangs and the community where they are found. Efforts to develop taxonomies of gangs in which "types" of gangs are linked to certain social and psychological phenomena usually provide a much less clear picture of the relation between gangs and their surrounding community. This could be justified, in part, by the idea that only certain "types" of communities were expected to have gangs.

Frederic Thrasher assumed that gangs were found in a particular type of community called "gangland." In Chicago, gangland was attached to the city's industrial areas. It was a slum inhabited largely, but not exclusively, by foreign immigrants. This kind of community was likely to produce gangs because of its mix of people and problems. Communities lacking this particular mix were not expected to have gangs. Thrasher did not bother to look for gangs in other places. He was satisfied to describe gangs found in the most run-down parts of Chicago.

Thrasher's work had a profound effect upon the study of gangs. A mix of certain kinds of people, specific social and economic factors, and geography were taken to represent or signify a particular type of community: gangland. That community and the culture it supported were presumed to provide a haven for gangs. Subsequent researchers specified the relation between the kind of people prone to creating gangs and the social and economic conditions thought to encourage such tendencies.

Much attention, of course, continued to be focused on newly arrived immigrants from southern and eastern Europe. These newcomers had been the primary object of Thrasher's attention. The supposed lack of fit between their foreign customs and the dominant American culture was conducive to creating a "disorganized slum" where peasant institutions failed to help people adapt to a modern urban world.

There were gangs in areas populated by newcomers and characterized by poverty and poor housing. Gangs also appeared in neighborhoods where one set of low-income persons was replacing another. Some researchers, however, objected to the idea that all such communities were "disorganized slums." Whyte and Suttles, among others, showed how well integrated gangs were in communities that had a coherent structure and much resiliency. To accommodate such observations researchers spoke of gangs in "stable slums."

Central to much early thinking about gangs was the idea that they would pass out of existence as the newcomers became more acculturated to an American way of life. Some especially troublesome members of a particular ethnic group might find the attraction of criminal enterprises too difficult to ignore, but most would find a secure social and economic niche in American society. As time passed it became painfully obvious that not all newcomers were moving into the mainstream of American society and, indeed, had become stuck in something called the "underclass."

Walter Miller has described very well the intellectual origins of the "underclass" explanation of gangs. It is, he maintains, "a variant of Cloward and Ohlin's blocked opportunity theory of the 1960s. A new class of persons seems permanently locked out of technical and service jobs that would provide chances for upward mobility and locked into neighborhoods plagued by a host of social problems. The "sense of community formerly found in lower-class neighborhoods has weakened, alienating . . . [youth] from the society at large [and] . . . higher-status members of their own ethnic groups." The creation of gangs is "a response . . . to the unavailability of legitimate employment and . . . fulfillment in their local communities."[2]

The idea that gangs emerge from an underclass stuck in a disorganized slum has great appeal and much relevance in contemporary debates about "the gang problem." Yet, as Miller states, it overlooks the possibility that this "new" class is merely an extension or elaboration of long-standing patterns of lower-class life in cities. To the extent that this is true it may not be accurate or fair to characterize such communities as "disorganized." They may have sources of stability and strength that go unnoticed by outsiders. Gangs composed of "underclass" youth may be found in "stable slums."

If one adopts the language appropriated from past and present gang researchers, it is possible to push contemporary gangs into a crude set of categories that reflect the joint influence of demographic and social factors. Youth from recent Vietnamese and Chinese immigrant groups have formed gangs. The former, however, do not have as stable or viable a community base upon which to build.[3] For this reason, perhaps, Vietnamese and Chinese youth gangs are organized and behave somewhat differently from one another. African American and Hispanic youth who form gangs, on the other hand, come from populations that have been in the United States for some time. Although both populations have many impoverished members, their communities are thought to be different. African American communities are far more likely to be viewed as disorganized, and their gangs are thought to be organized and behave differently from

Hispanic gangs.[4] Hispanic communities are said to have strong traditions and a viable institutional base. Newcomers are more readily absorbed into an ongoing and successful social enterprise.

The strength of this formulation is that it allows one to compare gangs emerging from communities with different demographic, social, and economic profiles. Unfortunately, it has several important shortcomings. Implicit in the formulation is the long-standing view of gangs as a product of poor or minority persons living in some sort of slum. It does not help us to account for the persistence of white gangs, the emergence of female and racially mixed gangs, or the involvement in gangs of persons who are not poor. Nor does it provide for the possibility that gangs might be found in city neighborhoods that are not slums or arise in suburban communities.

All of these limitations and omissions really play to a single theme: the gang as a deviant group found in a community that is somehow not quite right. If gangs were found in a variety of settings, including areas that were anything but slum-like, then we would have to change rather substantially our thinking about the functions gangs serve in the community and their contribution to its stability. It is likely that such a change in thinking is warranted. Persons who have studied various forms of communal or organizational unrest in Europe have shown that disorderliness is more likely an extension of a community's customs than a rejection of its habits and members' values.[5] Gang-like behavior would fall comfortably within the range of activities ordinarily included in such a discussion.

My object in this chapter is to determine whether gangs do arise in a variety of community settings, including areas in cities and suburbs that are not slums. Then an effort will be made to identify in what, if any, ways gangs in different areas vary in their organization and behavior. Finally, it will be suggested that gangs contribute more to the creation and maintenance of a workable social order in cities than is commonly supposed by American researchers.

MORE- AND LESS-SETTLED COMMUNITIES IN ST. LOUIS

The communities studied for the purposes of this research are found in the city of St. Louis and several of the suburbs just north and west of the city. The preliminary findings reported here are based on interviews with hundreds of young persons from those communities.[6] The communities themselves vary a great deal. Some have names, others do not. A number are only a few square blocks in size and have two or three hundred residents. Others occupy one or two square miles and have thousands of res-

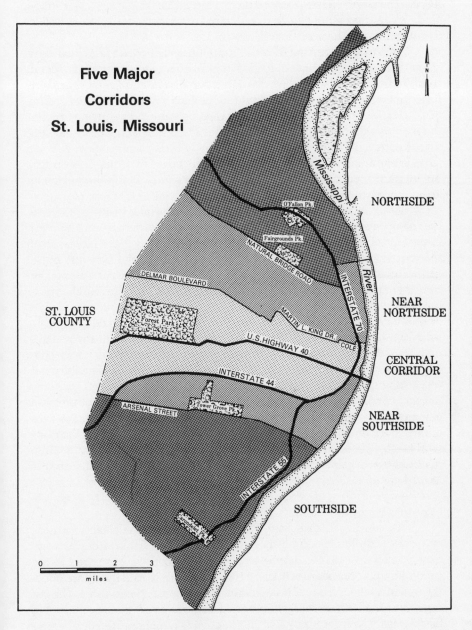

FIG. 10.1. Five Major Corridors: St. Louis, Missouri

idents. The nineteen suburban municipalities included in the present study share a common school system, but they are serviced by different police departments and local governments.

The Missouri portion of the metropolitan area changed a great deal after 1950. The city of St. Louis lost more than half its population and much of its industrial base. Much of this population and business activity found its way into St. Louis County immediately west of the city. Some pushed farther out. By 1990, the major changes were over and only a comparative trickle of people and businesses were moving substantial distances within the metropolitan area.

While all parts of the St. Louis area were unsettled during this period, not all parts were affected in the same way or came out of the changes in an enviable position. Touched most negatively were areas that today have the largest concentrations of African American people. Parts of the city that had been predominantly black became overwhelmingly so. Parts that had an established minority population experienced great increases in that population. The suburbs stretching west and north of the city of St. Louis received many new African American residents. This was especially true of the municipalities described here as the Near North Suburbs, which are among the closest to the city.

Many middle-class African American households moved to the suburbs beginning in the mid-1960s in an exodus that mimicked the one initiated by whites in 1950. Less well-to-do whites and blacks also left the city, however, and it is people in the latter category who have become the most recent migrants into the Near North Suburbs.

The information displayed in table 10.1 shows the effect of these changes as of 1980. St. Louis was left with a minority population that was almost as large as the white population but somewhat younger and less well-to-do. The Near North Suburbs had a substantial minority population, but that population's income, educational, and occupational profile looked comparatively strong. Predominantly white portions of St. Louis weathered the changes relatively well, at least in comparison to those sections that became predominantly African American.

The housing stock across the city was old, but the Near Southside and Southside had retained more of this housing. Those areas had not experienced as much clearance or demolition work as compared to the predominantly black areas in Near Northside and Northside. More housing in white areas also was occupied by the owners and cost more. The per capita income in these areas, while not great, was larger than that found in black areas. The Near Southside and Southside had more people of working age, and a greater share of those persons were working. These areas also tended to have a slightly better-educated population and people in higher-status jobs.

TABLE 10.1
Demographic Profile of St. Louis City and Some Suburban Municipalities, 1980

	Near North Suburbs St. Louis County	Northside St. Louis City	Near Northside St. Louis City	Central Corridor St. Louis City	Near Southside St. Louis City	Southside St. Louis City
Total Population	33,647	77,599	110,714	42,110	61,368	161,246
Households: Total	12,420	24,496	38,093	20,648	24,463	70,750
Married Couples	6,226 (50%)	10,481 (43%)	11,829 (31%)	4,227 (21%)	9,425 (39%)	33,680 (48%)
Other Families	2,838 (23%)	7,630 (31%)	13,256 (35%)	2,742 (13%)	5,280 (22%)	9,439 (13%)
Nonfamily	3,3256 (27%)	6,385 (26%)	13,008 (34%)	13,679 (66%)	9,758 (40%)	27,631 (39%)
Percent Black	64%	82%	95%	47%	26%	1%
Age of Persons: 0-17	11,277 (31%)	26,693 (34%)	35,490 (32%)	7,173 (17%)	16,783 (27%)	32,529 (20%)
18-44	14,737 (40%)	28,235 (36%)	36,279 (33%)	18,136 (43%)	24,461 (40%)	55,738 (35%)
45-64	6,683 (18%)	14,474 (19%)	22,193 (20%)	7,373 (18%)	11,386 (19%)	36,169 (22%)
65+	3,951 (11%)	8,198 (11%)	16,753 (15%)	9,428 (22%)	8,738 (14%)	36,810 (23%)
Income: Per Capita	$6,461	$4,753	$3,955	$8,493	$5,760	$7,288
Household, 15,000 or less	5,616 (45%)	14,745 (60%)	27,840 (73%)	13,460 (65%)	15,169 (62%)	38,063 (54%)
Education: 0-8 years	4,378 (21%)	11,663 (29%)	21,469 (35%)	6,216 (22%)	11,740 (33%)	36,364 (33%)
12 years	6,507 (32%)	11,538 (29%)	14,723 (24%)	6,137 (22%)	8,922 (25%)	33,521 (31%)
16+ years	2,908 (14%)	2,393 (6%)	2,919 (5%)	7,674 (27%)	4,598 (13%)	9,794 (9%)
Occupation: Total employed	15,091	27,165	33,513	18,059	24,743	69,586
Manager/Professional	3,030 (20%)	3,180 (12%)	4,087 (12%)	6,511 (36%)	4,849 (20%)	12,060 (17%)
Technical/Sales	4,715 (31%)	7,677 (28%)	8,489 (25%)	5,415 (30%)	7,116 (29%)	25,226 (36%)
Service	2,757 (18%)	6,950 (26%)	10,560 (32%)	3,253 (18%)	4,784 (19%)	10,189 (15%)
Other	4,589 (30%)	9,359 (34%)	10,378 (30%)	2,880 (16%)	7,994 (32%)	22,111 (32%)
Housing: Total Units	13,018	27,444	45,349	25,479	29,077	74,602
Occupied	12,329 (95%)	24,483 (89%)	38,058 (84%)	20,568 (81%)	24,299 (84%)	70,640 (95%)
Rented	3,554 (29%)	9,780 (40%)	24,536 (65%)	17,077 (83%)	14,376 (60%)	31,887 (45%)
Median Rent, monthly	$252	$197	$167	$206	$170	$188
Built before 1940	4,036 (31%)	13,899 (50.6%)	27,546 (61%)	12,807 (50%)	20,301 (70%)	47,857 (64%)
Average Value of Owned Home	$30,000	$21,581	$18,327	$72,130	$30,792	$35,377

Stuck between these different areas was the city's Central Corridor. Its population decline had been steeper in both relative and absolute terms than those of the northern and southern thirds of St. Louis. On the other hand, the changes had left its remaining population more racially mixed, wealthier, more educated, better employed, and more expensively housed. There were not as many children or families as in other parts of the city. The redevelopment of St. Louis as a postindustrial city took place in this part of town, and the profile of its population is consistent with that fact.[7]

The Near North Suburbs lost modest portions of their resident population (i.e., between 1.5 to 21 percent) during the 1970s. All areas experienced substantial increases in their minority population. Several went from 1 or 2 percent black to 20 and 30 percent black. In cases where the minority population already was established (i.e., between 26 and 38 percent), minority representation grew to 79 and 86 percent. By 1980 nearly two of every three residents in these townships was of African American descent. These changes were comparable to the minority increase in Northside's population which was 46 percent black in 1970 and 82 percent black a decade later.

The Near North Suburbs had some strong features despite these changes. Half of the households consisted of married couples. Only 23 percent had a different kind of family structure, usually an unmarried or divorced female with one or more children. There were many children, but the population of working-age people was substantial as well. Most of these people were working, and only the Central Corridor had a larger share of its residents working in professional jobs or holding a college degree.

The housing stock in these suburbs generally was occupied by the owners and in the same price range as housing in south St. Louis. The median rents were higher. The Near North Suburbs in 1980 looked sounder than many portions of the city, which is why so many black persons moved there. During the 1980s there was reason to believe that the social class composition of the migrating black households took a downward turn, because the school district had an infusion of children who qualified for many state and federal assistance programs. Nevertheless, the population retained many of the features that it had in 1980.

It is possible to compare in a rough way the several areas that have been discussed. Each no doubt has its own strengths and weaknesses. However, it would seem that the Central Corridor of St. Louis emerged from this tumultuous period with a stable mix of people and some financial strength. It would not likely become an area known for neighborhoods with many families or children, but it would have a peculiar vitality.

The next most-settled area would consist of the southern portions of St. Louis City. Most parts retained strong neighborhoods with many traditional households and children. The growing population of elderly persons was a concern, and it was not a wealthy area. Nonetheless, this section of St. Louis generally would be considered settled and stable. The northern sections of St. Louis would be seen as the most problematic. The people who live there generally are not well-to-do, and many of the households do not have two adults heading them. The educational and occupational profile of the population is not one that would make it competitive in a postindustrial labor market.

The Near North Suburbs underwent some large racial changes in their populations after 1960. Today they are experiencing some changes in the social class composition of their resident population. These changes have created tensions and introduced to the schools a number of youngsters with problems. On the other hand, the population has retained many of the strong features that distinguished it in the past from the predominantly African American sections of St. Louis City. The Near North Suburbs are relatively more settled and stable than the northern portions of the city.

Racial change is only one of several things that can unsettle a community, and a racially homogeneous community can show more signs of instability than one with a mix of persons from different backgrounds.[8] The assumption here is that there is something about a community, rather than the color of the people who live in it, that lends it to becoming a site for one or another type of gang. "White gangs" and "black gangs" would be expected to behave similarly, if they lived in similar circumstances.

Gangs and Community Organization

Based on information acquired through many interviews, it is clear that gangs can be found operating in all parts of St. Louis City and County, and that less-settled areas have more gangs than more-settled areas. Not all communities, however, have produced their own home-grown gangs. Three things and activities have allowed, even encouraged, gangs based in one community to carry on their activities in other places: the automobile, drug dealing, and school desegregation.

The impact of school desegregation on the genesis and spread of gang members and activities is not well documented. John Hagedorn has proposed that minority youngsters transferred to new schools as a result of Milwaukee's desegregation program formed gangs in order to protect themselves in an unfamiliar setting.[9] Unfortunately, there is little else in the social scientific literature to support this claim.

A little more will be said about this issue in the present chapter, but only in the context of the city public school district's efforts to move children from one to another part of town. Probably all school districts involved in a desegregation exchange program with the city have received some gang members. Testimony presented before the Missouri State Advisory Committee to the United States Commission on Civil Rights in the spring of 1990 indicated as much.[10] Youngsters from city gangs have created problems in their host schools and recruited new members while at school. Some of the new recruits are white. Most come from the ranks of formerly unattached youngsters from the gang's home territory.

School desegregation, drug sales, and the automobile have made gang members more mobile. This makes it difficult to determine the exact number of gangs, their size, and the scope of their territory. Virtually all known gangs have a home territory or base in the community. Most have extended their claims of sovereignty to one or more public schools in or around that home territory. Shifting students to different schools makes the gang's potential territory more dispersed, but even the home territory of city gangs has been known to change. Thus, the connection between gangs and the communities where they are found is bound to be more complex than it may have been years ago.

The recent upsurge in gang activity for the St. Louis area began in the mid-1980s. That was when law enforcement officials began to notice groups of young men carrying out delinquent acts and buildings being marked with graffiti. This activity occurred in the city but also appeared in the Near North Suburbs and several other communities. Virtually all of the original groups disappeared by the late 1980s. Some members were arrested or killed, but most of the groups apparently were unstable. New groups appeared almost as soon as the first collection disappeared. Those newer groups were the ones studied for the research project described in the present chapter.

There were approximately thirty-six gangs in the city of St. Louis as of July 1990. Not included in this count were an unknown but growing number of nascent gangs composed of younger children in North St. Louis and teenage gangs in South St. Louis. The groups composed of younger black children were literally popping up all over the northern parts of St. Louis during the 1989-1990 school year.[11] Included in the count of thirty-six were better-established groups composed largely, but not exclusively, of teenagers or young men in their twenties. The slightly older gangs had established reputations for fierceness and, in most cases, a merchandising operation for illegal drugs.

A pattern emerged when the distribution of gangs was arranged next to the list of communities described earlier. The most settled (or resettled) part of St. Louis in 1990 was the Central Corridor, and it had only two gangs based exclusively in it. Another three gangs claimed a portion of this area as part of their home territory, but those portions were located on the borders of the Central Corridor.

The next most-settled parts of St. Louis in 1990 were Near Southside and Southside. No fewer than nine youth gangs had most or all of their home base in these areas. One was exclusively black. Another had a Laotian membership. A third was racially mixed. The remaining six had only white members.[12]

The least-settled parts of St. Louis City consisted of the Near Northside and Northside areas. Twenty-five gangs called different neighborhoods within these parts of town their home territory. Another three gangs were located on the boundary line separating the Near Northside from the Central Corridor. A majority of these twenty-eight groups were based on the Near Northside.

The Near North Suburbs were said to be more settled than the northern parts of St. Louis but not as settled as the city's central and southern areas. These communities had approximately fourteen gangs. That number of gangs fell between those of the southern and northern sections of St. Louis.

At least eleven gangs were composed of young men in their teenage years. Members were found in the junior high school and/or the senior high school. There were an additional three gangs composed of young women in their teenage years. Only one of these groups seem to have continued beyond the junior high school level. Excluded from this count of fourteen were a small number of groups composed of younger children who were not yet affiliated with the established groups in a formal way.

It is apparent from the present analysis that more-settled areas have fewer gangs than less-settled areas. It is equally clear, however, that gangs can develop in any community. A brief discussion about the way these different areas are organized may help us to understand why this is so.

The types of groups people create for themselves complement other aspects of their lives. One is not likely to find a chapter of the Knights of Columbus in a community populated by persons who are Jewish, for example. Nor will the residents of a well-to-do suburb likely form a self-help group for homeless persons. Youth gangs may not be found in retirement villages, but they may form in communities with many children or other kinds of groups that are closely identified with a small neighborhood. This is precisely what has happened in St. Louis.

The author conducted a survey of all voluntary associations and service agencies in St. Louis during the late 1970s. It was a crucial moment in the city's history, because the massive shifts in population that had begun in 1950 were coming to an end. The 1980 census figures presented a picture of who had come to live in different parts of St. Louis. The survey data provided some clues to how these persons organized their lives.

There were over 2,800 voluntary organizations and service agencies in St. Louis at one point during the late 1970s (see table 10.2). In excess of

TABLE 10.2
Distribution of Voluntary Organizations and Service Agencies
in the City of St. Louis, 1976-1977

Area of City	Churches	Community Groups	Government Agencies	Schools
Northside	12.4	7.5	5.6	13.4
Near Northside	59.3	22.1	14.6	32.8
Central Corridor	18.0	43.0	65.1	19.8
Near Southside	2.6	9.8	5.3	11.7
Southside	7.6	17.6	9.3	22.3
TOTALS	838	1455	301	247

one-third of those formal groups were located in the Central Corridor. The overwhelming majority of them (i.e., 71 percent) served a dispersed clientele. Most of these groups did not cater to a local or neighborhood constituency but to the whole city or metropolitan area. The organizational culture of the Central Corridor did not lend itself to the growth and spread of small, aggressive neighborhood groups. That would have included gangs.

The more-settled southside areas of St. Louis had a comparatively small share (i.e., 21.6 percent) of the voluntary organizations and agencies found in the city. Many more of these (i.e., 55 percent), however, were dedicated to serving persons within that area. The organizational culture of this part of St. Louis was not as cosmopolitan as the Central Corridor's and would have supported more energetic neighborhood groups. The six youth gangs located in this general area provided some support for this argument. The defensive character of five of these gangs, which is described below, was even more indicative of this area's organizational and social climate.

The combination of economic decline and racial change had an especially unsettling effect on the whole northern third of St. Louis. African American families and individuals moved or were displaced from neighborhoods in the Central Corridor and Near Northside. Some areas were redeveloped. Other areas became temporary passageways for migrating people. Black St. Louisans nudged their way into neighborhoods formerly closed to them and overwhelmed areas where they already had a presence. By the early to mid-1980s the biggest changes associated with black migration were completed and life for these people began to settle down. They started the difficult chore of rebuilding their communities.

The area in which they lived had many organizations. Indeed, over 40 percent of all voluntary organizations and agencies in the city were located somewhere in the northern portions of St. Louis. This part of town had more schools and government agencies than the southern end of St. Louis, but that might have reflected efforts to provide more services to a population that needed help. The Near Northside and Northside also had a large share of the city's community groups. Most of these groups, like those in south St. Louis, were designed to serve a local or neighborhood constituency. The big difference came in the number of churches found in the more unsettled parts of St. Louis. The Near Northside and Northside in 1977 had nearly 72 percent of all the churches to be found in St. Louis. The southside areas had only 10 percent of the city's churches. Denominational differences accounted for the great variation. Churches in the more-settled areas served good-sized congregations and belonged to the Catholic Archdiocese, Lutheran Synod, or Episcopal Church. Churches in the less-settled northside areas were small and did not belong to a well-integrated confederation of churches.

The neighborhoods bound together in north St. Louis were not disorganized. If anything, they were overorganized in the area of religion. There was less diversity in the organizational base of north St. Louis than other areas. (Only 25 percent of its organizations were oriented toward a nonlocal constituency.) A successful form of organization was widely replicated in an environment that did not allow for many successes. Small groups divided up the available territory and competed vigorously for limited resources, including parishioners. The unsettled condition of north St. Louis, coupled with the religious customs of its new residents, encouraged successful groups to be mimicked; the new groups filled the social vacuum left in the wake of massive population shifts. Larger denominations survived, but they did not flourish. Smaller churches flourished, but did not prosper. They were unable to consolidate available resources, coordinate or sustain political activities for too long, or articulate a broader vision for the community.

The proliferation of gangs in north St. Louis during the 1980s bears a striking resemblance to the earlier growth of small churches in the same part of town. The creation of gangs was not the result of social disorganization, but the discovery by young persons of a type of voluntary organization that gave them a relatively secure anchor in a community beginning to rediscover itself after thirty years of disruption.

Comparable data about organizations in the Near North Suburbs did not exist. Persons familiar with the area, however, had no difficulty accounting for the rise of gangs during the 1980s. They pointed to three related factors: the increasing presence of "troubled households" with children familiar with city gangs; the hostility with which many black youngsters were greeted when their numbers increased in district schools; and traditional rivalries among the townships comprising the district.

Black youth gangs in the Near North Suburbs made their first appearance in the early to mid-1980s. This was about the same time that city gangs were making their presence known. According to reports pulled together by area police departments, there were approximately twenty-two gangs operating in the Near North Suburbs at that time. Three of these were composed of young women. One-third were composed of youngsters from different townships. Several townships had more than one gang in them.

The early gangs were brittle and fell away fairly quickly. When the newer gangs emerged during the late 1980s, some changes had occurred. These groups were less likely to cut across municipal boundary lines. The number of groups coming from the same town declined dramatically. The groups were better organized.

One can draw several preliminary conclusions about gangs in more- and less-settled communities on the basis of the discussion so far. First, gangs developed in parts of St. Louis City and County that were quite different. They appeared in both relatively settled and unsettled communities, in places with obvious problems and places that appeared in good shape. Second, most gangs came from areas heavily populated with minority citizens. There were noteworthy and understandable exceptions to this pattern, however. Third, and finally, gangs were found to fill an important hole in the communities where they developed. How well they filled it probably varied with the community in question.

Gang Organization and Behavior in Different Parts of St. Louis

Gangs in less-settled communities are not particularly stable. Changes occur in their number, size, territory, name, allegiances, structure, and behavior. Some changes can be attributed to the natural growth and development of the gang. Other changes are better accounted for by the instability of the groups in question. Much of the time it is not easy to determine which explanation should be applied.

There were nineteen known gangs located on the Near Northside and Northside of St. Louis in 1988. Interviews with members and other knowledgeable persons, including police officers, provided information about each gang's organization (table 10.3) and behavior (table 10.4). It was not possible to acquire all the desired information about each group.

All nineteen gangs had an exclusively black and male membership. Seven had girl auxiliaries. The size of gangs varied considerably. Five had fewer than twenty members, and five had more than thirty members. The remaining groups had between twenty and thirty members. Three gangs were reported to have experienced no increases or loss of membership in 1988. One gang only lost members, while twelve only gained members.

The last three gangs experienced both increases and losses in membership. All the members of known youth gangs were of the same race and sex, but there was considerable variation in the age of members. In only two gangs did the age of the youngest and oldest member differ by four years or less. The age span was five to six years in another eight gangs, and seven or more years for the remaining gangs for which information was available.

Gangs in other cities have members of varying ages, but members typically are divided into age-graded sets.[13] This was not the case for St. Louis gangs in less-settled areas. Regardless of their age, all members belonged to the same group. No distinction appeared to be made among members on the basis of their age. It was not immediately apparent why this happened or that the pattern would be maintained. Once gangs grew larger or older perhaps they would institute an age-graded structure as gangs in other cities had.

The gangs were not particularly well organized. Most had one or more leaders and at least one person who was identified as the group's "enforcer." There were no other established roles in the gangs. The gangs had no strict hierarchy, no officer corps or formal rules for developing a "gang policy," and no set custom for initiating or removing members.

Members in at least half of the known gangs routinely shared money made from legal or illegal means with some or all of their fellow members. Only two gangs were known to share money or some other valued item with persons who lived in the gang's territory. There was no organized system of pooling resources save that tied to the acquisition and sale of drugs.

Part of the apparent instability of gangs was attributable to their age. Most had not been in existence before 1984 and still were in the process of expanding and contracting. Only eight gangs had stable borders. Of the remaining eleven gangs, five experienced some growth in their territory, five saw their territory contract, and one gang abandoned its home base only to re-establish it in another neighborhood two blocks away.

Contributing to the impression of instability within gangs was the fact that ties between gangs were unstable. Only one gang in this area was not fighting other groups in 1988. Five gangs were fighting as many as four or five other groups. Other gangs fought at least one or two other groups. On occasion these different conflicts were being waged simultaneously. Such ongoing battles actually help the gangs, because gangs typically acquire much of their identity by fighting each other.

Gangs also tried to forge more hospitable ties, but these ties were not especially strong. Three-quarters of the known gangs in 1988 had built an "alliance" with at least one other gang. The alliances tended to be brittle and evanescent, however. Gangs on good terms did not necessarily

TABLE 10.3
Organization Traits of St. Louis Youth Gangs, 1988

Name	Race of Members	Sex of Members	Estimated Number of Members	Age of Members	Have Girl Auxil.	Gangs Tied To	Gangs Fighting Against	Territory Expanding/ Contracting	Gaining/ Losing Members	Have Established Leaders	Have Enforcer(s)	Members Share Profits	Profit Donated to Community
North Side Punks	Black	Male	25	13-22	No	3	0	Expand	Gain	Yes	Yes	D/K	D/K
North Side Players	Black	Male	8	13-18	No	0	2	Contract	Lose	Yes	No	No	No
North Side Posse	Black	Male	20	13-18	No	2	2	Contract	Gain	Yes	No	D/K	No
Slattery Boyz	Black	Male	10	D/K	No	0	3	Neither	Neither	Yes	Yes	D/K	No
The Cochran	Black	Male	25	14-20	Yes	2	3	Neither	Gain	Yes	Yes	Among Some	D/K
Vaughn Taking Over	Black	Male	60	14-19	No	0	5	Contract	Gain	Yes	Yes	D/K	D/K
Jeff Vander Lou Posse	Black	Male	30	12-22	No	2	3	Expand	Gain	Yes	No	Among Some	D/K
Fila Boyz	Black	Male	25	13-21	No	0	5	Neither	Gain	No	No	D/K	D/K
West Side Mob	Black	Male	90	15-22	No	1	1	Neither	Gain	Yes	Yes	D/K	D/K
West End Mob	Black	Male	60	15-39	No	1	1	Contract	Both	Yes	Yes	Among Some	D/K
West End Boyz	Black	Male	12	12-18	Yes	5	4	Neither	Gain	No	No	No	No
The Right Stuff	Black	Male	6	15-18	No	1	1	Expand	Gain	Yes	Yes	Among Some	No
Hardy Boyz	Black	Male	28	15-21	No	1	5	Both	Both	Yes	No	Among Some	No

TABLE 10.3 (continued)

Name	Race of Members	Sex of Members	Estimated Number of Members	Age of Members	Have Girl Auxil.	Gangs Tied To	Gangs Fighting Against	Territory Expanding/ Contracting	Gaining/ Losing Members	Have Established Leaders	Have Enforcer(s)	Members Share Profits	Profit Donated to Community
West Side													
Rockers	Black	Male	60	14-19	Yes	2	3	Neither	Neither	Yes	Yes	Yes	No
Boyz of Destruction	Black	Male	60	13-22	Yes	4	4	Neither	Gain	No	Yes	Yes	Yes
38 Boyz	Black	Male	20	15-20	Yes	2	3	Neither	Neither	No	No	Among Some	No
Show Me													
State Rockers	Black	Male	15	13-17	No	1	3	Expand	Gain	Yes	Yes	No	No
Eastgate Boyz	Black	Male	30	12-19	Yes	4	2	Expand	Gain	Yes	Yes	Among Some	Yes
Pershing Boyz[1]	Black	Male	20	12-19	Yes	0	3	Contract	Both	Yes	Yes	No	No
Thunder Katz[1]	Black	Male1	30	12-20	No	6	5	Expand	Gain	Yes	Yes	Among Some	No
Peabody Boyz[1]	Black	Male	20	14-21	No	2	1	Expand	Both	No	Yes	Among Some	No
South Side Posse[2]	Black	Male	150	11-18	Yes	3	3	Neither	Both	Yes	Yes	Among Some	No
South Side Gangsters[2]	Black	Male	55	13-23	Yes	3	0	Expand	Both	Yes	Yes	Among Some	No
Nigger Beaters[3]	White	Male	5	15-19	No	0	5	Neither	Neither	No	No	N/A	N/A

KEY: D/K = Know
N/A = Not Applicable
[1] Located in Central Corridor.   [2] Located on Near Southside   [3] Located on Southside

TABLE 10.4
Delinquent Behavior of St. Louis Youth Gangs in Home Territory, 1988

Name	Use Safe House	Use Weapons	Use Guns	Commit Assaults	Commit Robbery/ Burglary	Steal or Vandalize Cars	Sell Drugs	Fence or Barter Stolen Goods	Use Profits on Drugs, Guns, or Cars	Fight/ Practice Intimidation	Practice Extortion	Commit Drive-Bys Shootings	Use Graffiti
North Side Punks	Yes	Yes	Yes	Yes	Yes	Yes	Yes	Yes	Yes	Yes	Yes	Yes*	No
North Side Players	No	No	No	Yes	Yes	No	No	No	No	Yes	Yes	No	Yes
North Side Posse	Yes	Yes	No	Yes	Yes	Yes	Yes	D/K	Yes	Yes	Yes	Yes*	Yes
Slattery Boyz	D/K	Yes	Yes	Yes	D/K	D/K	Yes	D/K	Yes	Yes	D/K	Yes*	Yes
The Cochran Vaughn	Yes	Yes	Yes	No	No	Yes	Yes	Yes	Yes	Yes	D/K	D/K	No
Taking Over	Yes	Yes	Yes	Yes	No	No	No	D/K	D/K	Ywes	No	Yes	Yes
Jeff Vander Lou Posse	Yes	Yes	Yes	Yes	Yes	Yes	Yes	D/K	Yes	Yes	No	No	Yes
Fila Boyz	Yes	Yes	Yes	Yes	Yes	D/K	Yes	D/K	D/K	Yes	No	Yes*	Yes
West Side Mob	Yes	Yes	Yes	Yes	Yes	Yes	Yes	D/K	Yes	Yes	Yes	Yes	Yes
West End Mob	Yes	Yes	Yes	Yes	Yes	Yes	Yes	Yes	Yes	Yes	Yes	Yes	Yes
West End Boyz	Yes	Yes	No	Yes	No	No	No	No	Yes	Yes	No	No	No
The Right Stuff	Yes	Yes	Yes	Yes	Yes	Yes	Yes	Yes	Yes	Yes	Yes	Yes	Yes
Hardy Boyz	Yes	No	Yes	Yes	No	Yes	Yes	Yes	Yes	Yes	No	Yes	Yes
West Side Rockers	Yes	Yes	Yes	Yes	No	Yes	Yes	No	Yes	Yes	Yes	Yes	Yes
Boyz of Destruction	Yes	Yes	Yes	Yes	Yes	Yes	Yes	Yes	Yes	Yes	Yes	Yes	Yes
38 Boyz	Yes	Yes	Yes	Yes	Yes	Yes	Yes	Yes	Yes	Yes	Yes	No	Yes

TABLE 10.4 (continued)

Name	Use Safe House	Use Weapons	Use Guns	Commit Assaults	Commit Robbery/ Burglary	Steal or Vandalize Cars	Sell Drugs	Fence or Barter Stolen Goods	Use Profits on Drugs, Guns, or Cars	Fight/ Practice Intimidation	Practice Extortion	Commit Drive-Bys Shootings	Use Graffiti
Show Me State Rockers²	Yes	Yes	Yes	Yes	Yes	Yes	Yes	No	Yes	Yes	Yes	Yes	No
Eastgate Boyz	Yes	Yes	Yes	Yes	Yes	Yes	No	No	Yes	Yes	Yes	Yes	No
Pershing Boyz	Yes	Yes	Yes	Yes	Yes	Yes	No	No	Yes	Yes	Yes	Yes	Yes
Thunder Katz¹	Yes	Yes	Yes	Yes	Yes	Yes	Yes	D/K	Yes	Yes	No	Yes	Yes
Peabody Boyz¹	Yes	Yes	Yes	Yes	Yes	Yes	Yes	No	Yes	Yes	Yes	Yes*	Yes
South Side Posse²	Yes	Yes	Yes	Yes	Yes	Yes	Yes	Yes	Yes	Yes	Yes	Yes	Yes
South Side Gangsters²	Yes	Yes	Yes	Yes	Yes	No	Yes	No	Yes	Yes	Yes	Yes*	Yes
Nigger Beaters³	No	Yes	No	Yes	No	Yes	No	No	No	Yes	No	No	Yes

KEY: D/K = Don't Know

* = Drive-by, but no shooting

¹ Located in Central Corridor ² Located on Near Southside ³ Located on Southside

cooperate on things other than fighting a common enemy. Gangs on poor terms sometimes collaborated on things such as wholesale drug sales. The important point would seem to be that there were no permanent alliances among these gangs.

Much of the time gang members spend with each other is occupied by leisure activities such as "hanging out," partying, and drinking or consuming other drugs. A second major set of activities engaged in by individual members or sets of gang members is more explicitly delinquent in character. These are the activities that draw attention to the gangs and create problems in the community.

Those acts most publicized by the media are drive-by shootings and the sale of drugs such as crack cocaine. Fourteen gangs in 1988 were associated with selling drugs within their home territory, and ten gangs did drive-by shootings. At least one other gang sold drugs only outside its own territory, and another four gangs engaged in drive-bys only as a show of force.

Drug selling was not something associated with all gangs, and not all members of gangs that were involved sold drugs themselves. The gangs treated drug distribution in much the same way as earlier ethnic immigrants organized associations to protect certain trades in which their members had a substantial interest. Trade associations provided a protective umbrella under which individual entrepreneurs conducted their business in an assigned area. The association might dun its members a certain percentage of their profits and provide them with goods at discounted prices, but it did not produce or sell anything on a retail level. It coordinated the trade, organized and restrained competition among association members, and protected them from outside competitors.[14]

Most gang members who sold drugs did so on an intermittent basis and usually to acquire spending money. The number of members who sold drugs on anything approaching a regular basis was small, perhaps no more than two or three persons. Even these persons, gang members reported, spent or loaned most of the money they made. As indicated earlier, gangs had no organized system for sharing profits or accumulating wealth. Some gangs were involved in a great deal of drug dealing, but the business was not as well-organized as it could have been.

Gangs failed to sell drugs in their own territory for several reasons. First, they might not have been developed well enough to carry out such an enterprise (e.g., the Northside Players and Vaughn Taking Over). Second, individual members may have been so involved with consuming drugs that the gang could not organize such an effort (e.g., the Pershing Boyz). Third, the gang may have wanted to keep its home territory free of drug selling so that police would not bother the group (e.g., the Eastgate Boyz).

There was no apparent connection between selling drugs outside of one's home territory and the willingness to fight or conduct drive-bys. Virtually all gangs fought groups outside of their home territory. Only half sold drugs outside that territory, however. Whether the creation of a more expansive drug-selling territory preceded, followed, or bore no relation to a gang's willingness to fight or conduct drive-bys was not clear in 1988.

All gangs fought and carried out a serious campaign to intimidate outsiders with threatening displays of force. Some gangs also tried to intimidate persons living in their home territory. Most gangs permitted, even encouraged, members to commit assaults, robberies, and burglaries inside their territories. They also stole or vandalized vehicles. A majority of the gangs practiced extortion against area residents. Virtually all kept "safe houses" in their territory where they hid contraband and stolen items; but only a few fenced or bartered these goods. With few exceptions, the gangs marked their territory with graffiti. Members in all but two gangs used weapons such as clubs, chains, and knives when committing some delinquent acts. Members in all but three gangs used guns on one or another occasion.[15]

Much of what has been said about gangs in less-settled parts of St. Louis also applies to the minority gangs located in the Central Corridor and Near Southside (i.e., the Thunder Katz, Peabody Boyz, South Side Posse, and South Side Gangsters). These gangs were composed of minority youth whose families lived in public housing sites or neighborhoods to which they had been moved after being displaced from yet another place. The Thunder Katz was the only city gang in 1988 that had age-graded sets. Members of the Thunder Katz from the LaClede Town public housing site have been moving north in the city and out into the county as officials closed down the development. The gangs in the Near Southside neighborhoods are firmly planted there and remain active, though somewhat out of place.

The other gang located in south St. Louis in 1988 was not out of place. Its name was the Nigger Beaters, and it was composed of white youths from a high school that had begun to receive black gang members from other parts of the city. The Nigger Beaters, as its name implied, had a well-defined but limited goal. Members did not buy or sell drugs or do most of the illegal things that black gangs did. Its members were well integrated into the neighborhood, and were not viewed as dangerous by area businesses and residents. Their group originated in response to the threat posed by incoming black students. The threat, which had both symbolic and real elements, was manifested first in one high school. By the end of 1988, however, it was clear that groups like the Nigger Beaters were forming at schools and neighborhoods in other parts of south St. Louis.

There were five known youth gangs in south St. Louis as of 1990. Four had an exclusively white membership. The fifth had begun that way but gradually accepted some black youngsters who moved into the gang's territory. Three of the gangs, including the one that is integrated today, were formed to protect white students from black gang members sent to their public school, along with the other minority youth, as part of the city's desegregation plan. The other two gangs appear to have sprung up rather naturally in the course of efforts by local young men to defend themselves against roving groups of other whites.

The genesis of such groups was predictable. Whites did not like black people moving into "their" neighborhoods or attending "their" schools. Young white males took up the challenge posed by new African American students and residents. The Nigger Beaters and the groups that followed them were classic examples of reactionary communal groups intended to protect the traditional rights and customs of a people under attack by "outsiders."[16]

All neighborhood-based gangs have a defensive or reactionary quality to them. The predominantly black gangs in less-settled areas have less of this quality. While they go to great lengths to defend their turf against outsiders, it is not clear what customs or traditional prerogatives they are trying to uphold, and they are just as likely to turn against other residents in their home territory. Given the unsettled nature of the community in which they are found, perhaps it is understandable that minority gangs have less interest in protecting local residents and we have difficulty identifying a set of customs that these gangs might defend. For whatever reasons, however, contemporary gangs in less-settled areas have less claim to the tradition of communal groups that seek to protect rather than exploit the community of which they are part. White gangs organized to fight against the influence or presence of outsiders in their established community are more closely identified with this tradition.

It is hard to speak of tradition in a community that has experienced unsettling changes, particularly when one is talking about youth gangs. By the spring of 1990, some things about gangs in St. Louis City had changed. The most prominent changes came in the number and distribution of gangs. Nine of the twenty-four known gangs in 1988 had been disbanded or absorbed by other gangs (i.e., the North Side Players, Slattery Boyz, West End Mob, The Right Stuff, West Side Rockers, 38 Boyz, Show Me State Rockers, Pershing Boyz, and Nigger Beaters). One gang (i.e., the North Side Posse) divided into three sets after sharply increasing their membership and disagreeing over a few drug transactions. (There was some feuding among the three sets, but they still identified with the original group.) Four new gangs organized themselves under the banner of the Los Angeles-based Hoover Crips (i.e., Redbud, 49 Crips, Rolling 60s, and

49 Hoovers). The remaining twelve new gangs were relatively independent. They had allies and/or contacts with gangs in other cities, but they were not part of a local confederation of gangs.

Three of the new gangs were composed of young women. Graffiti identifying at least one (i.e., the Switch Blade Sisters) had appeared in late 1988, but the existence of the group remained unverified until 1989. The other female gangs (i.e., El Control and West Side Possettes) were independent groups that had close ties with different male gangs. The young women in the latter two gangs held drugs and weapons for their male allies. The one thing that all three groups had in common was a willingness to fight. If members were engaged in other delinquent activities, it had not come to the attention of the police.

By 1988, many black male gangs had established ties with either the Crips or Bloods. The local gangs served as the wholesale distribution network for drugs controlled by the two Los Angeles-based gangs. By 1990, several local gangs had taken the name Crip or Blood and added it to their title (e.g., the Cochran Crips, North Side Crips, Bloods of Destruction, and U. City Bloods, formerly the Eastgate Boyz). The ties between local gangs and Los Angeles gangs had become stronger. Several new groups took the Crips name from their inception (e.g., Strodtman Crips and Delmar Crips). It was likely that one or more members from each local group doing business with the Crips or Bloods had spent some time in Los Angeles. The number of local gang members who had been formally initiated as a Crip or Blood, however, probably was quite small.

There was one known Laotian gang in south St. Louis. Not much was known about it. However, it originated in part because of hostility Laotian immigrants received from local black youth. There were strong suspicions, but no evidence, that this group was engaged in rather sophisticated criminal activities based in the local Asian population.

Gang Organization and Behavior in the Near North Suburbs

It was noted earlier that the Near North Suburbs were relatively more settled than north St. Louis but less settled than south St. Louis. The population and community of the Near North Suburbs were similar in some ways to those of north St. Louis and similar in other ways to the population and community of south St. Louis. It was not much of a surprise, then, to find that gangs in the Near North Suburbs had features common to gangs in north and south St. Louis. They had real pride in their neighborhood and were relatively protective of it even as they developed a rapacious business that clearly hurt some persons in their community.

There were fourteen community-based gangs in the Near North Suburbs as of the spring of 1990. Twelve of these groups had a fixed territory that corresponded to municipal boundary lines. One gang was affiliated with a much larger organization based in Chicago, and its members were spread among several townships. The fourteenth group was composed of young men from the same town, but its members proclaimed no particular status as a community-based gang and were involved only in selling drugs. Three gangs whose members did claim territorial loyalties were composed exclusively of young women.

The long-standing rivalries among townships comprising the Near North Suburbs were reinforced, albeit unintentionally, by the policies of the school district that serves the Near North Suburbs. Young children attended elementary schools with many youngsters from their own community, and they brought to school the community loyalties they had learned in their neighborhoods. There were children at every elementary school who were active gang members or serious about claiming some gang affiliation. Youngsters from all the municipalities were brought together at the junior and senior high schools.

The schools became sites where both the social and economic activities of gangs were played out and reinforced. New challenges were laid down and old scores were settled. In the junior and senior high schools, gang members also planned criminal activities and sometimes carried them out. Notwithstanding their frequent disagreements and almost constant posturing, however, there was no question that all groups had a right to be there. This softened the tone of disagreements and reduced the need for groups to establish their sovereignty in the schools.

Junior and senior high school gang members in the city had a more difficult time. Many students in and out of gangs were transported to schools all over the city and county as a result of desegregation plans. The effect of all this moving around on city gangs was to continually expose members to new and threatening situations far away from the comparative safety of their home territory. New and unstable combinations of gangs were routinely invented without much thought given to the consequences. There was little chance for gangs to reach some accommodation over their right to be at a particular school, much less their common use of the facility. The situation faced by city gang members was far less stable than that faced by gang members in the Near North Suburbs. Gang fights in city schools were more routine and more likely to involve substantial violence.

Other things done by gang members in schools were likely to happen more often and be more severe in the city than in the Near North Suburbs. Included would be extortion, intimidation, drug and weapon use, the encroachment of nonstudents into the school, and general disruptiveness. All of this can be traced back to the unsettled character of the schools and the gangs themselves.

The size of gangs in the Near North Suburbs was determined by the number of children in each municipality that had a gang. More populous townships had larger gangs. The membership in these groups generally was larger than that in city gangs. The two largest community-based gangs in the Near North Suburbs had in excess of one hundred members. The membership certainly was more stable. Children grew up knowing where they lived and the gang they eventually would join, if they chose to become a member. The number of persons who maintained friendly contacts with each gang in the Near North Suburbs also was greater. These "affiliates" were not routinely involved with gang activities; but they did "hang" with gang members from their community and would come to their aid in a fight with another gang, particularly if the other gang was invading their community.

Recruitment of would-be gang members was done informally in the Near North Suburbs. Few, if any, children were intimidated or bullied into becoming a gang member, as was often the case in city gangs. The interpersonal and family ties developed in each township were the basis for gang membership. This was true in the city as well, but the friendship and family networks, with few exceptions, were not as well-developed in north St. Louis.

There were many young children who played at being gang members. While much of this play and imitative behavior had a game-like quality, the children took it seriously and appreciated the significance of what it meant to be a gang member. It was through often rough group play, the wearing of colors, and flashing of signs that children explored the role of "gang member" and identified themselves as potential recruits.

The self-selection process continued at the junior and senior high schools. Membership was not mandatory, but some status was conferred upon persons who became members. The degree of involvement exhibited by members varied. At a bare minimum, persons claiming some affiliation with the gang were expected to "go down" with other members in fights with other gangs. There were exceptions to this, however, and a member could find ways to avoid a particular fight without losing any prestige in the gang. This was most likely to happen when someone had a friend or close acquaintance in the other gang. Such a relationship was much less likely to emerge between members in different city gangs.

The gangs in the Near North Suburbs had a segmented age structure similar to that found in gangs from communities with a tradition of gang activity. There were up to four age-graded sets in the larger gangs, and they corresponded to the members' school status. Membership peaked among youngsters twelve to fourteen years old.

Many gang members were involved in criminal activity on an intermittent basis. Relatively few engaged in criminal activity on a daily basis. Virtually every child interviewed was aware of the criminal activities engaged in by gang members; but they also knew students not in gangs who committed crimes.

Junior high school students graduated from less profitable criminal enterprises such as burglary and moved into drug dealing with little effort and personal or financial risk. Comparatively few stole cars in an organized way. The risks probably were not much greater than selling drugs, in part because there was a good market for stolen autos among reputable dealers in Missouri and Illinois.

Senior high school students who elected to acquire money through illegal enterprises did so almost exclusively by selling drugs. Given their mobility and sophistication, there was almost no limit to how much money they could acquire. The work at this level entailed far greater financial and personal risks, however. A number of persons in and out of the gangs were paid for their cooperation and assistance in this activity. By no means did all gang members sell drugs. Nor did those who sold do so every day. Most moved in and out of the trade, depending on how much money they needed to meet their normal living and entertainment expenses or needed to save for a larger item such as a car.

The drug trade was not so well organized as many persons suspect. Members of the same gang cooperated in buying quantities of drugs and selling them on a retail basis. Persons who did not sell served to protect those who did or punished individuals who reneged on a deal. They were paid for these services. Persons who did sell competed against each other in the same territory. Most of the municipally based gangs had close ties to the Crips or Bloods, and it was from representatives of those organizations that local members purchased the drugs they sold. Some local gangs were better organized than others; but only one local gang appeared so well organized that a few of its senior members invested their profits in more conventional enterprises.

There were individuals who sold drugs on their own. One has the impression that most of the drug dealing was organized through the gangs, however. The gang became a medium through which this business was conducted, supported, and legitimated. Indeed, by the time youngsters reached high school age, the economic function of gangs was at least as important as their social function.

It should be noted that gangs whose members sold drugs differed in several important ways. None, so far as I have been able to determine, condoned drug sales to children for the purpose of consumption. Some gangs also prohibited the involvement of children until they were teenagers. Other gangs integrated anyone over eight years of age into their operation. Most gangs condoned the selling of drugs to any adult; but a few gangs sold drugs only to white people. Girl gangs were not known for selling drugs, though individuals girls did sell or assist boys in their efforts. By the time youngsters entered junior high school, it was the boys who went out and earned money and the girls who were given presents and money for dating and engaging in sexual intercourse with the boys. (Some did this with several boys simultaneously.) Both acquired status in the eyes of many peers for such activity.

Formal alliances between gangs were rare. It was common for some gangs to be "close" to others or to be viewed as traditional rivals. The views of which gangs were close to each other or distant depended, in part, on the age of the children providing the information.

It was apparent from interviews that relations between gangs in the area were brittle and fluid. The municipally-based group was the organizational building block for the different combinations or unions identified by all the youngsters. Individual friendships and family ties drew whole groups into fairly stable unions. The physical proximity of towns helped to accomplish the same end. Individual antagonisms were not likely to rupture such unions, but such disagreements did keep traditional animosities heated and could, if left unaddressed, set two relatively ambivalent groups against each other.

The distribution and sale of illegal drugs added another dimension to contacts among gangs. Representatives of the Crips or Bloods probably were the primary source of drugs sold by individual gang members. Gangs aligned with the Crips bought drugs from Crips, though individual members may have had other contacts. The same was true for gangs connected with Bloods. It was possible that one or more members of a municipally-based gang were also members of the Crips or Bloods, or they were extremely close to one or the other group.

The Crip or Blood identity was important, but not so important as the identity that came from one's community attachment. This caused some interesting conflicts for individual members with Crip or Blood ties when their town fought persons from their Los Angeles-based gang. In general, the member avoided becoming involved in the fight if at all possible. When avoidance was not a viable option, the member in question "went down" with his neighborhood gang.

The municipally-based gangs simply were reasserting their dominance and expressing their desire to limit the amount of violence or at least have it occur outside of their community. The only nonlocal gang that seemed to have established a successful bridge across several different towns was the Gangster Disciples.

In light of the failure of the Crips and Bloods to successfully take over the territories of municipally-based gangs, it was most unlikely that a strong union of local gangs would be fashioned. Municipally-based gangs continued to serve as the wholesale distribution outlets for drugs pushed by Crips and Bloods. Individual members of the local gangs continued to seek and hold a companion membership in either the Crips or Bloods, but their primary allegiance remained with the neighborhood group.

The organization of municipally-based gangs militated against the formation of a strong union or hierarchy among gangs. These groups took their primary identification from the town or neighborhood and drew their members from that same place. The larger municipalities had different sets, and these sets aligned themselves with different Los Angeles gangs. In general, however, the fragmented character of municipal life in the area was echoed in the gangs. It was no easier for the youngsters to coordinate gang activities than it was for their elders to coordinate public services.

COMPARING GANGS IN MORE- AND LESS-SETTLED COMMUNITIES

Early researchers expected to find gangs in slums. They allowed for the possibility that gangs in "stable" slums might differ from those in "unstable" slums, but there was no doubt where such groups were to be found. The research described in this chapter was based on the idea that gangs could be found in a variety of communities, not just slums. That idea proved true, and gangs in the St. Louis area were found in communities that were relatively settled and in communities that were comparatively unsettled. The term "slum" could have been applied to only a portion of the unsettled communities, and even then one could have argued about the assignation.

If it was once the case that only slums had gangs, that no longer is true. Gangs can develop in a variety of communities. Moreover, the mobility of contemporary youth gangs has stretched their ideas about what constitutes a home territory and made even well-to-do suburban areas sites for some gang-related activities. The expansion of gangs' territorial horizons has been promoted by public policies that move inner-city youth to suburban school districts.

The gangs found in different communities share some common features, but there are some important dissimilarities. The dissimilarities appear in the way gangs are organized, what they do, and how they relate to the community with which they are most closely associated. If we are to develop corrigible public policies about gangs, we must understand that not all gangs are the same. The first step in acquiring such understanding is to describe the differences among gangs and to show how those differences are related to the kinds of communities in which the gangs emerge.

All gangs are built around friendship and family groups found in a relatively compact geographic area. These groupings vary in size and exclusivity. How large or exclusive these groupings become depends on the community where they are found. The groupings in unsettled areas are larger but not especially exclusive. Those found in more settled areas are smaller and more exclusive. Each has its own peculiar strengths and weaknesses.

Gangs in less-settled areas (i.e.. North St. Louis) have more potential recruits, but the family and friendship ties among them are not likely to be strong. This introduces brittleness to such gangs that makes them more vulnerable to outside attacks and seductions. It also makes it easier to replace members who, for whatever reason, have been removed from the area. Such gangs do not have especially close ties to area institutions and residents. They compensate for this by constructing elaborate routines for socializing would-be recruits and admitting or expelling members.

Gangs in more-settled areas (i.e.. central and south St. Louis) have fewer potential recruits, but the family and friendship ties among them are likely to be strong. These groups are probably less vulnerable to outside attacks and seductions, but are more fragile when members are removed from the area. These gangs will have close contact with area institutions and residents. They will have less need for elaborate or exotic rituals to help them identify who should belong to the gang and who should not. Unlike gang members from less-settled parts of town, these persons already know who has "heart" and who does not.

Gangs in relatively settled communities (i.e., Near North Suburbs) combine features of gangs in more- and less-settled areas. The number of actual and potential members can be fairly substantial, but many will know each other pretty well. The size of the gang may vary quite a bit over a period of time, but it should be able to be sustained despite these changes. The ranks of "affiliated" members could be large, and persons may select the frequency and type of contact they want to sustain with more active members. Identification with the gang may be high; and the gang certainly identifies with the community where it is found.

The most routine behavior engaged in by gang members is hanging out together. Next in order of frequency and popularity is fighting. After these two activities comes a list of delinquent acts that includes everything from peace disturbance and loitering to drug dealing and murder. All the members of a particular gang do not engage in all of these activities together. Only a few may sell drugs, for instance, on anything approaching a routine basis. However, the gang provides a supportive environment in which these acts are carried out and a companion set of ideas that allows individual members to justify their behavior.

Gangs in less-settled areas (i.e. north St. Louis) do most everything and are more likely to blend violence in with whatever activity in which they are engaged. Their environment is viewed as being vulnerable, and these groups both exploit that vulnerability and take serious steps to insulate themselves from it. Groups of career criminals are more likely to develop and thrive in these communities.

Gangs in more-settled communities (i.e. central and south St. Louis) are much less likely to engage in serious delinquent acts or to sustain such activities over a long period of time. Their environment is viewed as being relatively invulnerable, even when that may not be true. In any case, these gangs do not exploit the vulnerability of their community and are more likely to defend its integrity.

Gangs in relatively settled communities (i.e.. Near North Suburbs) engage in most, if not all delinquent acts frequently associated with that type of group. They also are quite capable of continuing these activities for long periods of time and of mixing violence in with these activities. They will exploit the vulnerabilities of their community but much more of their delinquent behavior is carried on outside their home territory and against persons in areas where opposing gangs are located.

The relationship between a gang and the community where it is found can be a close and supportive one. Alternatively, it can be distant and threatening. Much about that relationship is implied in the way a gang is organized and the way it behaves in and out of the neighborhood.

Gangs in less-settled communities (i.e., north St. Louis) are not well integrated into the daily routines of the institutions or residents that share the area with them. The gangs are distant and threatening. They are much more likely to exploit the weaknesses of area residents and groups than are gangs in other kinds of communities.

Gangs in more-settled communities (i.e., central and south St. Louis) are well integrated into the daily routines of area, residents and institutions. Their relationship with the larger community is likely to be close and supportive. They are unlikely to exploit the weaknesses of area residents and institutions. In fact, the defense of local customs and the protection of area residents are primary objectives of these gangs. That is why they often enjoy considerable support from area residents.

Gangs in relatively settled communities (i.e., Near North, Suburbs) have a more complex relationship with residents and institutions in their home territory. There are occasions when the gang can be quite threatening and exploit at least a portion of the local population. Much of the time, however, the gang is recognized as a legitimate group and its members are not avoided or shunned. These gangs have a sense of pride and ownership in their, community, but they are not above causing problems for area, residents or frightening them.

CONCLUSIONS

The general view of gangs is that of a deviant group found in communities with severe problems. Both parts of this formulation were challenged in the present study. What follows is a brief discussion of how St. Louis gangs, and communities that have gangs, appear to violate some basic assumptions made by researchers over the years.

To begin, it is clear that gangs can be found in a variety of communities. Gangs may be more prevalent in areas that are "unsettled," but they will arise in relatively settled and even quite stable neighborhoods. Communities that have substantial numbers of poor and less-educated or securely employed residents, more run-down housing, and young minority citizens tend to have more gangs; but gangs also are found in areas with fewer of these "problems." Indeed, gangs can arise in communities with substantial strength and a varied organizational base.

Precisely how gangs fit into that organizational base is not known. However, it is clear that gangs can mimic or build on the adult groups and institutions in their area. Particularly relevant to this point would be the way gangs multiplied and filled the available social landscape of north St. Louis or made their territorial boundaries consistent with the municipal boundaries of the Near North Suburbs. Black youngsters attending public school in those suburbs found themselves categorized on the basis of their municipality, and they quickly learned to organize themselves on that basis just as generations of white youngsters had before them. The confusing and changing pattern of school assignments in the city of St. Louis, the absence of fixed neighborhood boundaries, and the mobility of some residents made such territorial designations difficult to create or sustain in the city.

Exclusively or predominantly white gangs in south St. Louis had long-standing loyalties to certain neighborhoods and schools. This made it easier to organize gangs, identify eligible members, and rally support for their posturing against outsiders. They had quite a bit in common with gangs in the Near North Suburbs for this reason, despite the fact that the suburban gangs were composed of black youngsters whose families in some instances had not lived in the area a long time.

Gangs in north St. Louis had a more difficult time identifying and holding a particular territory as their own. The most prominent exceptions to this were several gangs located in public housing sites. These groups had an identifiable and secure home base. There was movement in and out of these sites, to be sure. It was not so great as in some northside neighborhoods, though, and never enough to raise doubts about the physical integrity of the home base.

Notwithstanding the continuing mobility of some black persons in St. Louis, the African American population as a whole became more settled during the 1980s. It probably is not a coincidence that the number of gangs in north St. Louis did not begin to grow until that time, because it is difficult to organize a population for good or ill when it is almost constantly in motion. The formation of gangs in north St. Louis and the Near North Suburbs occurred as black St. Louisans were ending nearly three decades of forced and voluntary migration across the metropolitan area. The emergence of youth gangs in this case, therefore, is better explained as an expression of community reorganization than disorganization. The formation of youth gangs in predominantly white areas during the late 1980s coincided with the efforts of residents to sustain their communities, not tear them down. The presence of gangs might better be taken as a sign of a community's underlying or growing strength rather than as a sign of weakness and depravity.

Gangs and members of gangs often behave in an uncongenial and destructive manner. Their disagreeable and illegal actions can be condemned by community residents and outsiders, but they also can be understood as devices by which young persons establish a more secure social and economic niche for themselves in an environment not known for its security or congeniality. Moreover, it is not always the case that gangs are treated as outlaw groups in their home territory. They can be tolerated and even accepted as part of the community's organizational landscape, providing muscle to the customs and habits of area residents and institutions. In short, gangs contribute more to the creation and maintenance of a workable social order in cities than is commonly supposed by American researchers.

There probably are other dimensions on which gangs from different communities can be compared; and the present analysis reflects little more than a superficial treatment of the variables that seemed relevant in the St. Louis case. Nevertheless, the evidence presented in this and previous essays suggests that gangs fit into the communities where they are found. They complement their social setting, even when they do not flatter it. Gangs are a social creation and can only be understood in the context of the worlds where they are created and operate. Like most social creations, gangs are not infinitely flexible. There are limits beyond which they cannot be stretched and places where they are not likely to be found. The search for those places and the comparative data about gangs that such a search will yield are the necessary first steps in any effort to develop a theory about gangs and policies that will not make gangs more threatening than they already are.

NOTES

1. See for examples: Gerald Suttles, 1971, *The Social Order of the Slum* (Chicago: University of Chicago Press, 1943); William F. Whyte, *Street Corner Society* (Chicago: University of Chicago Press, 1965); Joan Moore et al., *Homeboys* (Philadelphia: Temple University Press, 1978); James Diego Vigil, *Barrio Gangs*

(Austin: University of Texas Press, 1988). Also see the work of Cummings, Vigil, Pinderhughes, and Padilla in this book.

2. Walter Miller, "Why the United States Has Failed to Solve Its Youth Gang Problem," in *Gangs In America* ed. C. Ronald Huff (Newbury Park: Sage Publications, 1990), p. 279.

3. Ko-Lin Chin, "Chinese Gangs and Extortion," in *Gangs In America*, ed. Huff, pp. 129-45; James Diego Vigil and Steve Chong Yun, "Vietnamese Youth Gangs in Southern California," in ibid., pp. 146-62.

4. James Vigil, *Barrio Gangs*; John Hagedorn, *People and Folks* (Chicago: Lake View Press, 1988).

5. Charles Tilly, "Collective Violence in European Perspective," in *Violence in America*, eds. Hugh Graham and Ted R. Gurr (Beverly Hills: Sage Publications, 1979), pp. 83-118.

6. The origins of this research project are described in my 1991 article entitled "The Practice of Gang Research" which appeared in *Sociological Practice Review* 2 (1) (January 1991): 29-39. Young men and women were interviewed in various public locations, homes, schools, and police department offices. None of the persons was in any trouble. All had submitted to interviews voluntarily. All interviews were conducted privately, except those with elementary school-aged children where a counselor was present. All interviews were tape recorded unless the subject objected. All subjects remained anonymous.

7. D. Monti, *Race, Redevelopment, and the New Company Town* (Albany: State University of New York Press, 1990).

8. Ibid.

9. Hagedorn, *People and Folks*.

10. Hearings before the Subcommittee on Gangs and Drugs, Missouri State Advisory Committee to the United States Commission on Civil Rights. (Kansas City: Regional Office of the U.S. Commission on Civil Rights, May 1990).

11. Police officials estimated there were forty-four gangs as of August, 1990, but they made no list available of the names, locations, or activities of those groups. No doubt their number included the Crips and Bloods from Los Angeles and perhaps the Vice Lords and Disciples from Chicago. Members from these gangs were operating in St. Louis but probably not as community-based groups. I cannot account for the remaining discrepancy between the police estimates and my own. I strongly suspect, however, that both estimates were conservative.

12. At the time that this chapter was written the author was aware of predominantly white gangs in approximately half of south St. Louis. Further interviews were being conducted in order to determine how many other gangs might have been operating in the other half of south St. Louis. It was most unlikely, however, that many more would be discovered because black St. Louisans had yet to make any inroads into neighborhoods in that part of south St. Louis.

13. Hagedorn, *People and Folks.*

14. See the earlier chapter by Padilla. S. Cummings, *Self-Help In Urban America* (Port Washington, N.Y.: Kennikat Press, 1980); I. Light, *Ethnic Enterprise in America* (Berkeley: University of California Press, 1972).

15. The variety and pervasiveness of delinquent acts committed by gang members was impressive. Some evidence of the effect of gangs on delinquent acts, if not the direct involvement of members in such acts, was provided by the St. Louis metropolitan police department. Summarized in table 10.5 are the number of Part 1 crimes (e.g., homicide, rape, robbery, assault, burglary, larceny, vehicle theft, arson, stolen property, vandalism, embezzlement, fraud, forgery, prostitution, sex offenses, drug and liquor offenses, gambling, weapons, peace disturbance, and other assorted acts) committed in the territories of each of the twenty-four known gangs between 1984 and 1988. Obviously, not all of the reported crimes would have been committed by gang members. This fact notwithstanding, one can see that serious crimes inside gang territories increased substantially during this period. Indeed, reported crimes inside gang territories generally increased much more than in the police district where the gang was located.

There were several exceptions to this pattern. The territories of the North Side Players, Slattery Boyz, Pershing Boyz, and Eastgate Boyz all showed no increases in crime or substantial decreases in crime. The first three gangs were in the process of breaking up in 1988 or were having difficulty sustaining themselves in the face of attacks by other gangs. The Eastgate Boyz worked hard to keep crime down in their own territory because they did not want to be bothered by the police. One could have expected fewer reported crimes in these areas.

The point remains that areas with a substantial gang presence were likely to have witnessed substantial increases in crime. Gang activity might not have accounted for all of the increases, but something was happening in those areas that coincided with the rise of gangs. Areas without a gang presence did not experience such dramatic increases in reported crimes. Whatever was occurring in gang areas was not occurring in areas that did not have gangs.

16. Tilly, "Collective Violence in European Perspective."

TABLE 10.5
Total Reported Crime by District and Gang Area, 1984-1988

	1984	1985	1986	1987	1988	Percent Change 1984-1988
District 1	6,903	6,251	6,862	6,681	6,910	+ 0%
District 2	6,145	5,614	6,269	6,050	6,800	+ 11%
Nigger Beaters	29	48	56	78	61	+110%
District 3	15,582	15,316	17,135	18,252	18,521	+ 19%
Peabody Boyz	454	505	583	619	543	+ 20%
South Side Posse	645	591	542	708	748	+ 16%
South Side Gangsters	1,082	1,034	1,263	1,420	1,329	+ 23%
District 4	7,557	8,667	8,868	8,819	9,193	+ 22%
Vaughn Taking Over	229	284	271	336	338	+ 48%
The Cochran	97	95	180	215	260	+168%
District 5	6,778	6,765	6,537	7,333	7,751	+ 14%
North Side Players	171	164	116	149	152	- 11%
North Side Posse	1,183	1,199	1,208	1,387	1,394	+ 18%
Slattery Boyz	65	58	46	45	63	- 3%
District 6	7,686	8,105	9,313	9,950	10,465	+ 36%
North Side Punks	717	739	824	1,029	882	+ 23%
District 7	9,372	9,761	10,645	11,492	12,414	+ 32%
West Side Rockers[1]	393	483	508	570	620	+ 56%
38 Boyz[1]	94	86	90	76	107	+ 13%
Boyz of Destruction[2]	807	783	977	916	919	+ 14%
Hardy Boyz[3]	175	170	191	184	222	+ 27%
Pershing Boyz	309	305	272	349	310	+ 0%
Eastgate Boyz	87	71	70	53	62	- 29%
Show Me State Rockers	429	371	453	424	438	+ 2%
Westend Boyz	218	278	253	295	300	+ 38%
The Right Stuff[3]	175	205	203	202	257	+ 47%
West End Mob	740	807	909	1,021	1,030	+ 39%
District 8	6,964	6,858	7,622	8,433	8,583	+ 23%
West End Mob	741	806	908	1,021	1,029	+ 39%
West Side Mob	414	470	459	528	499	+ 20%
District 9	8,700	9,311	8,917	10,506	10,490	+ 21%
West Side Mob	414	469	458	528	499	+ 20%
North Side Posse	394	400	403	462	465	+ 18%
Slattery Boyz	22	19	16	14	19	- 14%
Fila Boyz	210	250	138	248	240	+ 14%
JVL Posse	402	427	399	535	599	+ 49%
Thunder Katz	420	497	645	826	811	+ 93%

[1] Territories Overlap   [2] Territories Overlap   [3] Territories Overlap

PART III

WHAT CAN BE DONE
ABOUT GANGS

11

Moral Panic and the Response to Gangs in California

PATRICK JACKSON
with CARY RUDMAN

An old French witticism— the more something changes, the more it remains the same—appears to capture the main drift of the legal response to gangs in California during the past decade. Legislative activity has been intense, particularly in the late 1980s. A few new criminal laws were passed, but most changes have simply meant meaner, lustier, and tougher existing laws due to their enhancement or expansion. But even with these numerous changes, what has remained virtually unchanged since the retraction of social programs in the 1960s is revealed in the present policy responses to gangs, which are overwhelmingly devoted to gang suppression and incapacitation, buttressed by a theory of human motivation stressing deterrence.[1]

In the 1980s, when the question of what to do about gangs intensified and became part of the agenda of public problems, this approach became firmly institutionalized in the Gang Violence Suppression program. A major purpose of legislative change in the Golden State as it concerned gangs was therefore to enhance the ability of criminal justice officials to crack down on what was perceived as an inextricably connected problem of gangs, drugs, and violence. This essentially law enforcement approach continues as the major one as of this writing.

This is a study of the response to gangs in the 1980s. It examines laws and policies developed in response to actual and perceived problems related to gangs. The materials for study include gang or gang-related legislation from 1981 through early 1991 in a state (California) reputed to have one of the most serious gang problems in the United States.

This study is part of a broader inquiry into how the social control response to gangs has developed. In this chapter we take a preliminary step in this direction by focusing on state laws. Our concern here is with state-level legislative activity.[2] In the discussion we take up the question of the efficacy of existing laws and possible alternatives.

PUBLIC PROBLEMS AND THE RESPONSES TO GANGS

In the 1980s gangs found themselves in the limelight of media attention. Gangs or gang members became celebrities and/or villains of a sort in nationwide newscasts, talk shows, most major newspapers, *Time*, and *Newsweek*; they were the topic of numerous federal, state, and local government hearings, select committees, reports, and the full-length movie *Colors*. Going further than newspaper coverage of gangs, the movie *Colors* provided a graphic and spectacular portrait of many of the major aspects of gang violence to mass audiences.

As is true of many social problems, the policy response to the perceived problems of gangs presumed a more or less accepted definition of what a gang was. It is therefore of some interest to define the parameters of what a gang is said to be. We can begin by quoting Miller, who notes the inherently problematic nature of defining a "gang": "At no time has there been anything close to consensus as to what a gang might be—by scholars, by criminal justice workers, by the general public."[3]

The image of gangs that figured prominently in mass media and the discussions at public hearings was of groups who use juveniles, high-power weaponry, and motor vehicles to traffic drugs. These gangs were characterized either as instrumental groups or vaguely defined youth street gangs whose overriding purpose was to make large amounts of money through the distribution and sale of crack and other drugs. The level of participation in such gangs was portrayed as very high, with individuals driven in good part by the potentially great amount of money that could be made. Gangs' large membership included poor and minority youth with few other employment alternatives and who placed little value on human life.

Public concern about gangs and existing laws was heightened because media coverage depicted vulnerable youth:

Because the law treats minors more leniently than adults, children and adolescents are a natural choice for exploitation by older narcotics dealers, who use them as lookouts, salesmen and couriers.[4].

Schools then became defined as a site for the recruitment of potential gang members as well as places for gangs to sell drugs to youth.

Moreover, community concern about gangs and associated problems spread from Los Angeles and other large cities with gang problems to other cities across the country. One reason for this was the known exportability of the drug market, particularly crack. Rock houses could be readily set up and fortified in smaller cities. The crackdown on trafficking in south central Los Angeles and the saturation of that market also helped to spread the drug trade to Northern California, Oregon, Washington, Tulsa, Kansas City, St. Louis, and elsewhere (see chapter 9 in this volume). Thus, for example, in Sacramento the unveiling of the Final Report of the Mayor's Task Force on Drug Abuse was accompanied by Police Chief John Kearns's statement that

> With the added pressure being put on gangs dealing drugs in the Los Angeles area, we're going to see a further increase of their dealing drugs in Sacramento.[5]

Slightly predating the release of the report was a *Sacramento Bee* article, which reported the direct and indirect effects of already existing problems in the state's capitol:

> Entire Sacramento neighborhoods are now at risk of becoming the Northern California rendition of south-central L.A. because of the rock cocaine plague and the gangs that brought it here.
> Residents of some areas . . . contend with almost daily drive-by shootings, brawls, fights and vandalism, not to mention the devastation wrought by those hooked on rock: prostitution, child abandonment and abuse, theft and drug-induced insanity.
> A similar situation exists in Portland, where 300 gang-related incidents have been reported since May 1987.[6]

Public concern about gangs has also been fueled by the death of innocent bystanders, the intimidation of potential witnesses to gang-related activities, reports of increasing gang violence in schools, gang graffiti, drug-related commitments to local facilities, and drug-related arrests. In addition, the growth of gangs was viewed as potentially uncontrollable without adequate law enforcement. Gangs were thought to be more heavily armed than police, and police were strapped by limited resources due to shrinking local budgets.

Very briefly, the problem as defined in the public agenda has not been solely one of gangs. Integral to the threat involved is a coalescence of presumed evils: gangs involved in the sale and distribution of drugs, coupled with the use of violence. Subsumed within the image of gangs presented are large numbers of poor, minority gang members enticing or pressuring children to do their evil deeds. Within the image of drugs there is the ready likelihood of its abuse due to its highly addictive quality, and the secondary problems associated with addiction. Violence includes the use of powerful weaponry and automobiles to deal with competition over turf and to generate money to feed a drug habit, and other vagaries of the drug trade. To place the importance of these images in historical perspective we examine the rise of gang violence suppression.

Gang Violence Suppression

By the mid-1970s large caliber and semi-automatic or automatic weaponry was increasingly a part of gang-related conflict in California, but the perception of gang violence largely remained confined to poor communities.[7] By the early 1980s, however, there was an increase in drug trafficking through southern California, which was pronounced in south central Los Angeles, where rock houses and the effects of addiction to crack became well known.[8] Initially, the legislative response to gangs, consistent with years of past experience, was to rely on local law enforcement agencies to control gangs through special enforcement policies (e.g., gang units, special task forces, and arresting known gang leaders). These efforts were periodically supplemented by federal funding.

In June of 1981, then attorney general (and subsequently governor from 1983 to 1990) George Deukmejian issued a special task force report on youth gang violence in California. The report contained a number of suggested law enforcement techniques to deal with gangs as well as legislative strategies to curb the criminal activities of youth gangs. It also brought statewide attention to a recently discovered gang problem.

One of the legislative task force recommendations became law and serves as a model, along with its shortcomings, of the 1980s legislative approach to eliminating the problem of gangs. The Gang Violence Suppression (GVS) program was created in 1981 (effective January 1, 1982) to enhance efforts by district attorneys to prosecute perpetrators of gang violence by using operational and organizational techniques used in California and other states.

Responsibility for the GVS program was placed in the governor's Office of Criminal Justice Planning (OCJP), which serves as the major state conduit to fund and monitor a variety of gang- and drug-related state and federal programs. As originally created, GVS was to provide financial and technical assistance exclusively for district attorneys' offices. However, throughout the decade GVS was amended to provide financial and technical assistance to law enforcement agencies, county probation departments and community-based organizations (1982), and school districts and county offices of education (1986).

In passing the initial GVS program, the legislature acknowledged that the gang problem needed a more intensive law enforcement focus. Consequently, additional resources were provided to local prosecuting agencies to specifically target gang members for prosecution. Thus the increasing recognition of a "gang problem" was accompanied by the allocation of more resources for law enforcement agencies and probation departments to enhance the enriched (police, prosecution, and probation) "law enforcement approach" to solve the gang problem.

In a gesture of political compromise, and perhaps as an acknowledgment that approaches other than law enforcement might positively affect the gang problem, a community-based gang prevention component was included in amendments to the GVS program. Four years later, amid reports of substantially increased gang activity, school-based components were added to provide support to both an enhanced law enforcement approach (by requiring the schools to cooperate with law enforcement agencies) and an enhanced community-based prevention approach (by requiring the schools to coordinate with appropriate community-based organizations).

The GVS program, as well as myriad other state laws and programs directed at gangs and drugs, mirrored the federal government's approach by providing far more resources and technical assistance to enforcement strategies than for prevention/education strategies. As of the late 1980s, for every dollar spent on education, prevention (or, in the case of drug addiction, treatment) combined, three were spent on law enforcement.

Criminal Law Changes Through 1987

In addition to the GVS, the legislature reacted to the problems of gangs, violence, and drugs by passing a variety of laws through 1987 which, with a couple of exceptions, enhanced the penalties for a myriad of pre-existing drug and weapons offenses and violent crimes. The highly publicized triad of gangs, drugs, and violence provided the major focus of virtually all the gang-related legislation generated during the 1980s.

The perception of a problem of gangs, drugs, and violence increased throughout the 1980s. The state legislature, much more reactive than proactive, enacted legislation aimed at all three ingredients of the so-called epidemic, hoping in the process to eliminate drug abuse and drug- and gang-related violence. The year 1988 signalled a turning point in legislation, for reasons discussed below; changes in 1988 are discussed separately from other criminal law changes that occurred prior to this year.

Given the public perception of gangs, the legislative response centered on various aspects of perceived gang-, drug-, and violence-related behavior, including weapons, drive-by shootings, rock houses, and the use of minors and schools in the drug trade. Even though many of the laws do not mention gangs specifically, they were intended to directly or indirectly respond to or rectify gang-related problems.

Juvenile Court Waiver. One way to get at problems of gangs was to focus on penalties for youthful gang members who might use their juvenile status to evade serious punishment. In 1982, two laws relating to waiver from the juvenile court were amended to deal with armed gang violence as well as drive-by shootings. These permit the juvenile court judge to define a youth as an inappropriate object of rehabilitation if the youth commits or attempts to commit a felony with a firearm, or attempts to intimidate witnesses and influence testimony given to law enforcement officials. The amendments also permit judges to allow members of the public to attend juvenile hearings when the youth is sixteen years of age or older.

Drugs. Increased penalties for drug-related offenses were also developed. A 1983 law enhanced the sentence for possession for the sale, transportation, or manufacture of a narcotic or PCP by one year if the value of the drug exceeds one-half million dollars, two years if it exceeds two million dollars, and three years if it exceeds five million dollars, where it can be shown that the person had induced another to traffic in narcotics or PCP. Another law broadened the list of offenses that triggers a provision requiring drug offenders to pay a fifty dollar fee as a part of any fine assessed upon conviction.

A 1985 law enhanced the punishment for the offense of manufacturing any controlled substance from two, three, or four years in prison to three, five, or seven years. Another denied probation to individuals convicted of possession for sale of fifty-seven grams or more of a substance containing cocaine or methamphetamine. A 1987 law revision also added fifteen years to a heroin- or cocaine-related offense if the weight of the drug confiscated is over one hundred pounds.

Drugs, Minors, and School. Perhaps one of the most frightening aspects of gangs is their perceived targeting of vulnerable youth at school. A 1983 law provides for a prison term of five, six, or seven years if an adult sells or gives controlled substances to a minor under age fourteen on a schoolyard or playground during school hours or during the hours in which any school-related program is being conducted. The previous terms were three, four, or five years. This law was also modified in 1988. Another law passed in 1990 restored a stiffer penalty for juveniles and adults of up to six months in county jail (rather than only ten days), juvenile hall, ranch, etc., for possession of more than one ounce of marijuana on school grounds (K through 12). A final law imposed as a condition of probation, unless the court finds it inappropriate, the performance of forty hours of community service for any minor found guilty of unlawfully possessing a controlled substance on the grounds of a K through 12 school during school hours.

As of 1984 the principal of a school has been permitted to exclude an "outsider" from the school grounds if the principal has a reasonable basis for concluding the outsider's presence or acts would result in the distribution or use of harmful or controlled substances. The seriousity of the offense was raised from a mere infraction to a misdemeanor.

Using Minors in Drug Trafficking. Lawmakers also sought to remove legal roadblocks to the effective prosecution of adult gang members who use minors for drug-related work. In 1985 one amendment changed a past law that prohibited using or hiring minors who "knowingly" transport, sell, furnish, etc. controlled substances by deleting the provision that the minor "knowingly" transported, etc., those controlled substances. The change also added amphetamine and methamphetamine in the provisions, making it a misdemeanor (with a mandatory ninety-day jail sentence) to be under the influence of heroin and cocaine. It also prohibited a sentence of probation for committing certain drug offenses (e.g., sales of over an ounce of heroin; using a minor to commit offenses related to PCP) or using minors to manufacture, compound, or sell cocaine or methamphetamine, or of selling 28.5 grams or more of methamphetamine.

Rock Houses. In 1985 a new law specifically forbidding rock houses was enacted. The law specified that it is a felony, punishable by three, four, or five years in prison, to control or manage a structure and knowingly allow it to be fortified as a "rock house," and gain excessive profits from its use as a "rock house." The same punishment was prescribed for someone who uses a rock house to sell or possess for sale heroin, cocaine, or PCP. Persons convicted under the latter provision are ineligible for probation except under unusual circumstances.

Drive-by Shootings. A 1987 law provided that a person who, while committing a felony, inflicts great bodily harm or causes the death of another by a firearm discharge from or at an occupied motor vehicle proceeding on a public street or highway is ineligible for probation except in unusual cases. Another 1987 law provided that any person who is convicted of a felony (or an attempt) in which that person discharged a firearm at an occupied motor vehicle, and which causes great bodily injury or death, is to be punished by an additional term of five years. Both laws were urgency measures that became effective September 26, 1987.

Seizure and Forfeiture. In 1983, a law passed which expanded the existing law of seizure and forfeiture of money and other things of value to include trafficking in PCP or methamphetamines and drug traffic conspiracy. It allowed the tracing of drug-trafficking assets during the last five years if there is at least one conviction of a specified drug-trafficking offense. It also permitted trucks, boats, or planes to be seized. Another law provided that the expense of seizing, eradicating, or destroying any controlled substance or its precursors is recoverable from any person who unlawfully cultivates or manufactures them, or any person who aids and abets or profits from the manufacture or cultivation on property owned, leased or possessed by the defendant. Recovery may be obtained through a civil action or as a part of a criminal action. Moreover, civil action is not contingent upon criminal conviction.

Victim Intimidation. A major problem for law enforcement officials is gaining the cooperation of citizens to prosecute gang members. A 1982 law made victim intimidation a felony offense (it was previously a misdemeanor) punishable by imprisonment in state prison for two, three (the base term), or four years. Moreover, when such an act or intent is accompanied by, among other things, force or threats of force, that fact can be considered a circumstance in aggravation of the crime in imposing a term of imprisonment. Previous law also allowed anyone to serve a subpoena; the law change in 1982 prohibited criminal defendants from serving a subpoena in an action related to their case.

Firearms. A 1983 law raised the maximum sentence for unlawfully carrying a concealable firearm without a license from six months in jail and a fine of five hundred dollars to one year in jail and a one thousand dollar fine.

Criminalizing Street Gangs, Enhancing Parental Responsibility, Etc.: 1988 and 1989

The ineffectiveness of both the GVS approach and the modification or creation of new criminal laws that occurred through 1987 (described above) in curbing the problem of gangs, drugs, and violence was abruptly thrust into public view in 1988. Extensive media coverage followed a drug- and gang-related drive-by shooting in Westwood Village, Los Angeles—a popular, affluent, movie and restaurant area frequented by tourists, and adjacent to the University of California, Los Angeles. This shooting resulted in the death of a young, innocent, female bystander with an affluent background, named Karen Toshima, on January 30, 1988. Perhaps no other incident placed the public problem of gangs, drugs, and violence more forcefully on the public agenda than this one did. Moreover, the high level of attention devoted to gangs, violence, and drugs in the media and other public forums was sustained for months afterward.

The Toshima death catapulted the widely discussed problem of gangs, drugs, and violence into the state legislature's crime agenda. Gangs were perceived as pivotal in the explosion of drugs and violence. Attorney General J. van de Kamp noted that the "media feeding frenzy" on criminal gangs "has created a powerful election year awareness of law enforcement's needs in city halls and in the state Capitol." He argued that law enforcement should "strike while the iron is hot" and capitalize on publicity about gang violence. "Indeed, negotiations are under way ... and I believe they'll lead to the announcement of a strong, bipartisan package on street gangs in the next week or so."[9]

Adding to the sense of urgency, on June 15, 1988, the state's reconvened task force on street gangs declared that the increased violence fueled by rock cocaine made parts of Los Angeles more deadly than the wartorn Middle East. Robert Philibosian, who chaired the reactivated State Task Force on Gangs and Drugs, said that "It is more dangerous to walk down the streets of South Central Los Angeles than it is the streets of Beirut."[10] Officials, including the Los Angeles police chief and sheriff, along with Philibosian, later identified 100,000 gang members as contributors to a problem that Philibosian said "has reached crisis proportions statewide."[11]

The year 1988 was an extraordinary one for California lawmakers, who hammered out some of the most controversial crime-related legislation of the 1980s. They created a new law criminalizing street gangs, enhanced parental responsibilities for minors, and surrounded schoolyards with sentence enhancements for cocaine dealers.

Drugs and Schools. As one part of an overall legislative package on gangs, drugs, and violence, the Juvenile Drug Trafficking and Schoolyard Act of 1988 provided that any person eighteen years or older convicted of the sale, possession for sale, transportation or manufacture of cocaine or cocaine base upon school grounds, or within one thousand feet of a school, would receive a sentence enhancement of three, four, or five years in state prison. The law provided for an additional full and separate three-, four-, or five-year enhancement if the offense involves a minor who is a least four years younger than the defendant. These terms are to be imposed in addition to any other provision of law without restriction.[12]

Drive-by Shootings. This 1988 law provided for a five-year enhancement for discharging a firearm from a motor vehicle in the commission of a felony where, with intent to inflict great bodily injury or death, the defendant does inflict great bodily injury or cause death. This law also specified how the drive-by shooting enhancement relates to sentencing and multiple enhancements.

Criminal Street Gangs. One of the most controversial laws passed in the 1980s is known as the Street Terrorism Enforcement and Prevention Act (STEP), an urgency measure which became effective September 23, 1988, and operative until January 1, 1992. The law has been renewed and extended until January 1, 1997. It created a distinctively new law worthy of greater description. Under previous law there were no provisions which made the commission of criminal offenses by members of street gangs a separate and distinctly punishable offense. This law did, and it had a sentence bite as well.

By way of background, the legislative findings and declarations were that

the state of California is in a state of crisis which has been caused by violent street gangs whose members threaten, terrorize, and commit a multitude of crimes against the peaceful citizens of their neighborhoods. These activities, both individually and collectively, present a clear and present danger to public order and safety and are not constitutionally protected. The Legislature finds that there are nearly 600 criminal street gangs operating in California, and that the number of gang-related murders is increasing. The Legislature also finds that in Los Angeles County alone there were 328 gang-related murders in 1986, and that gang homicides in 1987 have increased 80 percent over 1986. It is the intent of the Legislature in enacting this chapter to seek the eradication of criminal activity by street gangs by focusing upon patterns of criminal gang activity and upon the organized nature of street gangs, which together, are the chief source of terror created by street gangs. The Legislature further finds that an effective means of punishing and deterring the criminal activities of street gangs is through forfeiture of the profits, proceeds, and instrumentalities acquired, accumulated, or used by street gangs.[13]

The main portion of Penal Code Section 182.22(a) stipulates that

Any person who actively participates in any criminal street gang with knowledge that its members engage in or have engaged in a pattern of criminal gang activity, and who willfully promotes, furthers, or assists in any felonious criminal conduct by members of that gang, shall be punished by imprisonment in the county jail for a period not to exceed one year, or by imprisonment in the state prison for one, two or three years.

Some critical legal terms include "pattern of criminal gang activity," defined as

> the commission, attempted commission, or solicitation of two or more of the following offenses [specified below], provided at least one of those offenses occurred after the effective date of this chapter and the last of those offenses occurred within three years after a prior offense, and the offenses are committed on separate occasions, or by two or more persons.[15]

The offenses included assault with a deadly weapon, robbery, unlawful homicide or manslaughter, the sale, possession for sale, transportation, manufacture, etc. of controlled substances, shooting at an inhabited dwelling or occupied motor vehicle, arson, victim or witness intimidation, and grand theft of a vehicle, trailer, or vessel.

The criminal street gang is defined as

> any ongoing organization, association, or group of three or more persons, whether formal or informal, having as one of its primary activities the commission of one or more of the criminal acts enumerated [above], which has a common name or common identifying sign or symbol, whose members individually or collectively engage in or have engaged in a pattern of criminal gang activity.[16]

This law also provides one-, two-, or three-year enhancements for misdemeanor offenses committed with the specific intent to promote criminal conduct by gang members; and one-, two-, or three-year additional and consecutive enhancements for felony offenses. Moreover, a person convicted of a life felony can not be paroled until a minimum of fifteen years have been served.

The STEP Act was subsequently incorporated into numerous laws and further enhancements were added (see below.) In 1990 the first conviction of a gang member using the new law was obtained in San Fernando, California.

An abatement provision also was included as a part of the STEP Act, which relates to the building or place used by gang members. It states that

> Every building or place, other than residential buildings in which there are three or fewer dwelling units, used by members of a criminal street gang for the purpose of the commission of the offenses listed or any offense involving dangerous or deadly weapons, burglary, or rape, and every building or place, other than residential

buildings in which there are three or fewer dwelling units, wherein or upon which that criminal conduct by gang members takes place, is a nuisance which shall be enjoined, abated, and prevented, and for which damages may be recovered, whether it is a public or private nuisance.[17]

Procedures to abate are specified and numerous restrictions apply.

Juvenile Waiver. This 1989 law amended the Welfare and Institutions Code to include as grounds for lack of fitness for juvenile court proceedings, and, after a hearing, remand to the adult court, those juveniles sixteen to seventeen years old who have been charged with a felony under the STEP Act, discussed above .

Enhanced Parental Responsibility. This 1988 law amended the penal code section related to contributing to the delinquency of a minor to read:

For purposes of this section, a parent or legal guardian to any person under the age of 18 years shall have the duty to exercise reasonable care, supervision, protection, and control over their minor child.[18]

This revised law subsequently was applied to the parent of a youth who was involved in a youth gang, in violation of the STEP Act. The case has generated considerable national attention and the involvement of the American Civil Liberties Union. Questions presently surround the meaning of "reasonable" and persist because the law would hold one person responsible for another person's behavior. This law was passed as a part of the legislative package including the STEP Act.

A 1989 law created an enhancement of one, two, or three years for carrying a loaded or unloaded firearm while committing any criminal street gang-related offense in violation of the STEP Act. The enhancement term is to be served consecutively to the committing offense.

Drugs and Weapons. This 1988 law added an additional two-year (base) prison sentence enhancement to offenders convicted of committing a felony while using a firearm if the offense involves specified controlled substance offenses. Also, a person who is a principal in the commission of a specified controlled substance offense and who knows that another principal is armed with a firearm shall be punished by an additional term of one, two, or three years in state prison.

Assault Guns. This 1989 law is the historic Roberti-Roos Assault Weapons Control Act of 1989, which represented a major defeat for the National Rifle Association. This law had broad-based support due in part to the mass killing of children in a Stockton, California, schoolyard by a man who subsequently committed suicide; support for it immediately grew among those concerned about the high-power weaponry enjoyed by gangs.

The law defines thirty-three categories of semi-automatic weapons as "assault weapons"; provides felony penalties for their manufacture, importation, sale, giving, or lending; and prescribes a variety of consecutive sentence enhancements for being armed with or using an assault weapon, or assault with an assault weapon or machine gun.

Graffiti Removal. A 1988 law required the California Youth Authority (CYA) to establish and monitor a three-year pilot project in Los Angeles County, administered by the probation department, for the removal of graffiti. Minors and adults may be required as a condition of their probation to repair, remove, clean, or reconstruct any damage or defacement resulting from the application of graffiti to public property. The CYA is required to report to the legislature on the pilot project and the legislative analyst is to study the potential for tax credit or incentives to encourage the donation of paint and graffiti-removal products.

Resolutions. One 1988 resolution established the Joint Committee on Organized Crime and Violence and requires the committee to report to the legislature by November 30, 1988, on methods of curtailing the problems of organized crime, gang violence, and drug abuse. A 1989 resolution recognized April 14 to 16, 1989, as Statewide Days of Prayer for gang violence victims.

Transportation of Controlled Substances. A 1989 law increases the term of imprisonment for transportation of specific controlled substances to three, six, or nine years in prison from three, four, or five years, if the controlled substances are transported for sale from one noncontiguous county to another.

1990 and Beyond

There were no gang-related laws passed in 1990. A variety of laws or policies were considered but not passed, due in part to a state budget crisis. There were at least twenty bills pending as of June 18, 1990, in the California Assembly and Senate. As of the beginning of the 1991 session all of them had died in committees. They deserve a brief look since they may portend the future direction of legislation in California related to gangs.

• AB 2993 (Eaves), would make it a felony for a person participating in a criminal street gang to prevent or dissuade any witness or victim from attending or giving testimony at any proceeding or in assisting law enforcement or prosecution activities.

- AB 3484 (Epple) would provide that any person participating in a criminal street gang is liable for the expense of an emergency response by a public agency to a scene of any incident caused by the criminal activity.
- AB 3485 (Epple) would broaden the definition of buildings abatable under the STEP Act.
- AB 3939 (McClintock) provides that any minor fourteen or over charged with a violation of the STEP Act, who has a prior conviction for a violation of the act, or who possessed a firearm in violation of the act, will be punished as an adult.
- AB 4170 (Hunter) would require offenders convicted of any criminal offense committed as a part of an initiation procedure to receive prison sentences of five, seven, or nine years.

SUMMARY AND DISCUSSION

One general finding of this review is that the major legislative response to gangs, which climaxed in the passage of the Street Terrorism Enforcement and Prevention Act of 1988, coincided with the coalescence of a variety of social images related to gangs (including violence and drugs) on the crime control agenda. Viewed in combination, the image of gangs, violence, and drugs evoked an intense public and legislative reaction, one much greater than would likely have been the case had each been considered separately. The sustained media coverage following the death of Karen Toshima, viewed in the context of pre-existing developments, played an important role in facilitating the passage of some of the most extreme gang-related legislation in the country. In short, new laws were a reaction to the definitions and social images of gangs provided by law enforcement, the media, and other groups.

While it is too early to assess how successful these recent legal responses to gangs have been, they clearly are not a panacea. The problem of gangs has continued, if not grown, during the 1980s and into the 1990s. The old solutions of either denying the problem, of giving the police and prosecutors the responsibility for the problem, or of making it "invisible" by sending gang members to prison, has not made it "go away."[19] The stupendous increase in the number and rate of offenders imprisoned in California (and elsewhere), including gang-related offenders, has not lowered crime.[20] Police reactions to gang members, consistent with Hagedorn's recent study and earlier ones examined elsewhere,[21] may reinforce antisocial tendencies. Some of the earliest thinkers about gangs realized the potential adverse consequences of the present response; more recent inquiries repeat it.[22] Contemporary public policy must recognize the potential negative consequences of official reactions to the public problem of gangs.

This review of legislative changes in laws and programs suggests that there has been a extremely heavy emphasis placed upon law enforcement solutions to the perceived problems of gangs in California. This is also true of strategies for dealing with gangs today in many other states. By the mid 1980s there was some acknowledgment that alternative solutions were also worth trying. By the end of the decade, with the availability of federal funds, the broadening of the policy response to incorporate more treatment and prevention seems somewhat more likely.

The evidence to date suggests that the nature of the reaction to the "gang problem" in California is similar to other instances of what has been referred to as "moral panics." Where a perceived threat of an individual or group greatly surpasses their actual threat the setting is ripe for the characterization of it as a "moral panic":

> When such discrepancies appear between threat and reaction, between what is perceived and what this is a perception of, we have good evidence to suggest we are in the presence of an ideological displacement. We call this displacement a moral panic.[24]

The question of whether the societal reaction to the perceived threat of criminal gangs, drugs, and violence has greatly surpassed the actual threat posed by them is not one that can be easily answered. Greater evidence would be needed, for example, on the actual nature of gangs and changes in gangs and gang activity over the time period in question. With this qualification, it may be appropriate to characterize the response to gangs in California as a moral panic, an overreaction, or even what Huff refers to as a "misidentification."[25] However, at least on the surface, the focus of legislative changes has been upon the perceived behavior of mostly poor, young, and minority males, which is similar to past inquiries finding support for the idea of a "moral panic."[26]

REDIRECTING POLICY

At the same time there were numerous criminal law changes in California in the 1980s, sociodemographic changes with ramifications for crime and the development and persistence of gangs were also underway. While the evidence is not yet entirely in, it appears that the old ways of making the public problem of gangs go away through defining it as a criminal justice problem could not and did not work in this changed environment. The term most frequently used to call attention to underlying changes in society with direct implications for gangs is that of the "underclass."[27]

One important structural reason for the continuing existence of youth gangs, and the older ages of gang members, is the growth of an underclass in society. As Hagedorn has pointed out, older studies of gang formation and desistance noted that the spontaneous development of gangs and the eventual departure of gang members from the gang was intimately bound up with the assimilation of immigrant groups into middle-class society. What the persisting problem of gangs of today reveals, however, is the absence of the assimilation of certain members of society because avenues of mobility have disappeared or shrunk considerably. Not surprisingly, the average age of gang members has therefore increased.

Viewed in this light, existing policies for the elimination or reduction of gangs (through the use of deterrence or incapacitation strategies) are bound to fail because youth in some communities may have no alternative choices. Moreover, locking up gang members may well sever existing ties to the community, accelerate the spread of gang influence, and provide a continuity between socialization in the community and the prison. Spergel and Curry's recent assessment of alternatives for dealing with gang problems found that while suppression interventions were among the most widely used strategies to deal with gang problems,

> strategies of community organization and social opportunities were associated clearly and strongly with perceptions of agency effectiveness and a reduction of the gang problem, particularly in terms of perceived greater effectiveness of city or urban area efforts.[28]

In light of the foregoing, we suggest an alternative policy goal that might be called one of "informed restraint" in the official response to gangs.[29] Such a policy would recognize that the use of draconian means for dealing with gang problems—such as mass arrests or lengthy incarceration for gang membership—are likely to fail or have negative consequences (particularly, the growth or persistence of gangs and related undesirable consequences). This appears to describe the present situation in California and some other states. Under a policy of informed restraint, officials would resort to the use of the least-restrictive alternatives (rather than a ready resort to deterrence and incapacitation strategies), and this would be informed by careful study of their operation and consequences. There is a notable absence of study of the present alternatives to the control of gangs.

The informed use of least-restrictive alternatives would be combined with the development of social alternatives that provide avenues of escape from an underclass existence. One of the major difficulties facing such a proposal will be the development of social alternatives. Gangs as such may have to be recognized as a social grouping worthy as a social policy, which has not been highly successful in the past. It may also be useful to broaden policy to include groups who—based on past experience—have been at greater risk of having gang-related problems. Immigrants who have arrived in the United States during the past decade may be such a group.[30]

Moreover, creative legislators would have to be willing to empower local communities with the wherewithal to develop positive alternatives, and communities would have to have a sustained determination to take advantage of them and/or develop their own. Some program alternatives do exist.[31] There are, to be sure, some communities that once had serious gang problems and no longer do.[32] While fiscal constraints may seem overwhelming, a recognition of the fiscal costs of existing law enforcement, and especially correctional policies for dealing with gangs and gang members (suppression and incapacitation), might be a beginning point for the debate over alternatives.[33]

NOTES

1. Cheryl L. Maxson and Malcolm W. Klein. "Agency Versus Agency: Disputes in the Gang Deterrence Model," in *Evaluating Contemporary Juvenile Justice,* ed. James R. Kluegel (Beverly Hills: Sage Publications, 1983); P. G. Jackson, "Theories and Findings About Youth Gangs," *Criminal Justice Abstracts* 21 (1989): 313-29.

2. It should be noted in passing that numerous local or private laws and rules have also been developed, in whole or in part in response to gangs, ranging from ordinances prohibiting cruising in Modesto to rules that forbid the wearing of presumed gang attire (Raider's jackets, etc.) on a private establishment that caters to youth in Sonoma County. We make no attempt to summarize these here.

3. W. M. Miller, "Violence by Youth Gangs and Youth Groups in the United States" (Washington, D.C.: U.S. National Institute of Juvenile Justice and Delinquency Prevention, 1975), p. 115.

4. *Sacramento Bee,* June 27, 1988, "For Kids, Death's Part of the Game, Money's the Prize."

5. *California Probation News,* July 7, 1988, "LA Influence Spreads North."

6. *Sacramento Bee,* June 28, 1988, "Reeling from Gangs, Cities Hunt for Answers."

7. Miller, "Violence by Youth Gangs."

8. M. Klein and C. L. Maxson, "Rock Sales in South L.A.," *Social Science Research* 69 (1985): 561-65.

9. "Time's Right to Control Gangs, Van de Kamp Says," *Sacramento Union,* May 10, 1988.

10. *Sacramento Bee*, June 15, 1988, "Gangs Make LA Worse than Beirut, Task Force Says."

11. *New York Times*, June 29, 1988, "Officials Say California is Plagued by 100,000 Gang Members."

12. Another law related to school grounds and drugs made a modest change. Under previous law it was a felony for someone eighteen years or older to sell, prepare for sale, or give away any controlled substances to a minor under the age of fourteen while on the grounds of any elementary or secondary school or public playground. This law raised the age limit to apply to selling any controlled substances to a person under the age of eighteen if the defendant is at least five years older than the minor.

13. Penal Code Section 186.21, Deering's Penal Code, 1990, p. 53.

14. Ibid.

15. Penal Code Section 186.22 (E), p. 54. Ibid.

16. Penal Code Section 186.22 (F), p. 55. Ibid.

17. Penal Code Section 186.22 (A), p. 56-57. Ibid.

18. Penal Code Section 272, p. 6. Ibid. A case prosecuted under this law will be heard by the California Supreme Court during 1992.

19. J. M. Hagedorn and Perry Macon, *People and Folks* (Chicago: Lake View Press, 1988), p. 158.

20. Hagedorn notes:

> Incarceration as a method of breaking up gangs is perhaps the worst single policy at the disposal of public officials. Yet it remains the chosen policy, even though our data and other research strongly suggests that use of incarceration to deter gang participation can easily backfire. (*People and Folks*, p. 162)

21. P. G. Jackson, *In Search of Gangs and Public Policy*. Report prepared for the Crime Prevention Unit, California Attorney General's Office. Sacramento, Calif., 1988, pp. 320-22.

22. Hagedorn, *People and Folks*.

23. I. A. Spergel and G. D. Curry, "Strategies and Perceived Agency Effectiveness in Dealing with the Youth Gang Problem," in *Gangs in America*, ed. C. Ronald Huff (Newbury Park: Sage Publications, 1990), p. 299.

24. S. Hall, C. Critcher, T. Jefferson, J. Clarke, and B. Roberts, *Policing the Crisis: Mugging, the State, and Law and Order* (New York: Holmes and Meier, 1978), p. 29.

25. Huff, *Gangs in America*, p. 313.

26. See, e.g., M. Zatz, "Chicano Youth Gangs and Crime: The Creation of a Moral Panic," *Contemporary Crisis* 11: 129-58.

27. For a brief discussion of the concept in the context of gang research see Moore et al., *Homeboys*, Philadelphia: Temple University Press, 1978 (1988: 6-8). She suggest that it means people who are "permanently excluded from participation in mainstream occupations. They survive, somehow, by a combination of economic resources" (p. 7).

28. Spergel and Curry, "Strategies and Perceived Agency Effectiveness," p. 308.

29. Jackson, *In Search of Gangs and Public Policy*.

30. Jackson, "Theories and Findings About Youth Gangs," p. 324.

31. Lynn Curtis, *American Violence and Public Policy* (New Haven: Yale University Press, 1985); Lynn Curtis, "Race and Violent Crime: Toward a New Policy," in *Violent Crime, Violent Criminals*, eds. N. A. Weiner and M. E. Wolfgang (Beverly Hills: Sage Publications, 1989); E. Currie, *Confronting Crime* (New York: Pantheon Books, 1985); Spergel and Curry, "Strategies and Perceived Agency Effectiveness."

32. W. M. Miller, "Why the United States Has Failed to Solve Its Youth Gang Problem," in Huff, *Gangs in America*.

33. Jackson, "Theories and Findings About Youth Gangs," p. 323. Background for this review relied in part on Quicker (1982) and Hardman, whose works were inadvertently omitted from the citations.

12

Gangs and
Civil Rights

ROBERT A. DESTRO

INTRODUCTION

The task of this chapter is to set out briefly which of its myriad subtopics are relevant to the topic of gangs. Given the resurgence of gang activity around the country, its demographics, and the illegal and increasingly brutal nature of the activity (which prompts renewed public and academic interest in "gang control" efforts), it should come as no surprise that the civil rights issues which are relevant happen to be some of the most complex and controversial of the lot.

Considered together, gangs and civil rights have all the ingredients for an explosive sociopolitical combination: both make attractive issues

B.A., 1972, Miami University, J.D., 1975, University of California, Berkeley; Associate Professor of Law, Columbus School of Law, The Catholic University of America, Washington, D.C. The author would like to acknowledge the invaluable research assistance provided by two student researchers at the Columbus School of Law: Thomas P. Moran, J.D. 1989, whose research contributed significantly to the materials on STEPA and RICO, and Paul Kouroupas, Class of 1992, who helped with everything else.

for politicians and political operatives seeking to draw attention to problems which will resonate with terrified urban residents; both are legally difficult and quite complex (i.e., there are no "easy" answers in either field); and though neither is well understood by either the public or those charged with the duty to make public policy, nearly everyone can be counted on for a relatively predictable instinctive reaction about what to do about gangs.

The goal of this chapter is to highlight—as fairly as possible—the multiplicity of interests necessarily included in, but not always identified as, "civil rights" issues related to gangs. The intent is not so much to resolve them (which would be impossible in any event), or even to attempt an exhaustive discussion of the most important ones; it is, rather, to suggest that a feel for context and a sense of proportion is—or ought to be— critical in all law-oriented discussions of civil rights policy, especially those relating to gangs. The "facts"—individual, social, and political, including particularly the unpleasant or inconvenient ones—are, after all, the backdrop against which policy develops. And this is so even if, in the end, the law seems out of touch with "reality," however defined.

The first part will set forth the working definitions of the two main terms utilized in this chapter: "gangs" and "civil rights." The second part sets out an analytical framework in which to view the civil rights aspects of gang control policy and legislation, and the third part suggests that the problem for lawyers (and law professors) is not so much with "gangs" as such, but with their propensity to engage in collective criminal conduct. The chapter concludes with the observation that, to the degree that the law retains a traditional criminal law focus on illegal conduct, it will avoid the most significant civil rights problem of all: a decision to base surveillance, arrest, conviction, or punishment on factors other than guilt.

WORKING DEFINITIONS

What Is a Gang?

In General. The term "gang" is notoriously imprecise, but there is no question that it has a generally pejorative connotation. Whatever a "gang" does, the common understanding of the concept is that, at the very least, it is unsavory. The term itself, however, potentially describes a multitude of groups, from the Democratic or Republican parties (especially in convention) and fraternal organizations whose funny hats and other regalia trumpet their group identity, to unruly groups of fraternity pranksters out to have a little, not-always-inexpensive "fun" at someone else's expense, and business associates who make and execute plans to fix or manipulate commodity prices.[1]

While it may be unwise for the authorities to ignore antisocial and sometimes illegal behavior by any of these groups, it happens more often than the authorities are likely to admit. The reason is rarely stated explicitly, but it is safe to assume that the nature of the group in question or the behavior involved leads law enforcement authorities to conclude (validly or not) either that there is no continuing threat to public safety, or that prosecution would simply not be worth the cost, given the risk of acquittal or light sentence. The real social concern about "gangs" is with those groups a lay person might describe as "real criminals." Among these are the gangs about which we are concerned here; from the street toughs who mug and rob passersby on a regular basis to integrated criminal enterprises whose reach extends even into the prisons, groups such as the Mafia, the Crips and Bloods, the Jamaican Posses, and the Tong. The public is *scared*. In the words of the California State Task Force on Gangs and Drugs: "Some communities are literally held captive by the violence, intimidation and decay. . . ."[2]

The practical problem for lawyers may, as a result, be summarized as follows: even though all groups which can be characterized as "gangs" share a common characteristic, joint action for a common purpose, the concern of "gang control" laws cannot really be either group identity or joint action *per se*; for too many legitimate associations would be caught in the net. The problem appears to be various types of behavior which, because of their nature or extent, are so antisocial that a collective purpose to engage in them is simply intolerable.

So it is important at the outset to be clear about what is at stake when recommendations for laws and policies designed to address the "gang problem" are drafted. When an association of individuals is formed for noncriminal purposes (e.g., social, economic, or fraternal), rules governing associational activity will be scrutinized by the courts to determine the nature of the group's activity and what, if any, legitimate governmental interests justify regulating it.[3]

When the common purpose of any group or association, whether termed a "gang" or something else, is illegal however, the law has a legitimate right to take whatever steps are appropriate to control the illegal behavior.[4] Where the government wants to go farther, to regulate the noncriminal activities of the members of the group or their eligibility for public employment or housing benefits, for example, the burden on the government increases. It must produce evidence sufficient to stand up in court[5] that those to be singled out for special treatment because of membership in an illegal group: (1) are active members of the illegal organization; (2) that they know of the illegal aims or activities; (3) that they have a specific intent to carry out or further the gang's illegal purposes; and (4) that their activities or association with a criminal enterprise is incompatible with the purpose of the program in question.[6]

The California State Task Force on Youth Gang Violence, for example, has found that "[a] uniform definition of gangs is needed" because "valid data collection is unavailable and interagency cooperation is hindered" without one. "For consistency," it suggested the following clarification of the meaning of the term "gang" and suggested that it be used "as the uniform statewide definition of youth and adult gangs in California":

> A gang is a group of people who interact at a high rate among themselves to the exclusion of other groups, have a group name, claim a neighborhood or other territory *and engage in criminal and other antisocial behavior on a regular basis.*[7]

As useful as this definition might be in developing a "statewide gang information system,"[8] it captures only a part of the problem for law enforcement purposes. While the groups most often thought of as gangs generally operate on the fringes of society ("interstitially" in Thrasher's definition[9]), and the criminal or antisocial behaviors with which society is concerned may cluster demographically on the margins, neither the occurrence of gangs nor criminal behavior are limited to that demographic region.[10] The law's legitimate concern is any sort of collective or group-directed illegal activity, whether on the streets of a neighborhood, in the cell blocks of prisons, in the sales territories of the international drug marketplace, or in the corporate boardroom.[11]

By the same reasoning, not all groups which "interact at a high rate among themselves to the exclusion of other groups, have a group name, [and] claim a neighborhood or other territory" are actual or even potential criminals, even if they do engage in "anti-social behavior on a regular basis."[12] "Antisocial" is not the same as "criminal."[13] As Dolan and Finney note: "Most social gangs aren't looking for trouble when they first take shape. . . . The trouble erupts when one or more of their social activities starts to get out of hand."[14]

In legal parlance, sociological definitions of the term "gang" tend to be both overinclusive ("overbroad") and underinclusive (discriminatory). If sociologically useful definitions are adopted for criminal law purposes, they are in danger of being held unconstitutional because, in plain English, they are not specific enough.

The courts do not look kindly upon criminal statutes which utilize broad language to describe the activities to be prohibited; for, by definition, the enforcement of criminal laws will adversely affect the lives, liberties, or property of the individuals or groups to which they are applied. Notwithstanding their utility for other purposes (such as data gathering), the adoption of broad statutory definitions of criminal behavior may result in a judicial determination that, for constitutional purposes, the definitions are "vague, indefinite and uncertain." ambiguities render the statute "vague and overbroad" in legal parlance, and this violates the most basic precepts of due process of law.[15] For nearly identical reasons, statutory ambiguities are resolved in favor of lenity.[16]

The practical result is that any definition of "gang" which is to be useful for legal purposes must be keyed both to the specifics of the criminal code and to empirically verifiable patterns of gang conduct. That such a limiting definition is necessary as a matter of constitutional law was underscored by a unanimous eight-member United States Supreme Court in *Lanzetta v. New Jersey*. *Lanzetta*, decided in 1939, involved a 1934 New Jersey statute which provided that:

> Any person not engaged in any lawful occupation, known to be a member of any gang consisting of two or more persons, who has been convicted at least three times of being a disorderly person, or who has been convicted of any crime in this or in any other State, is declared to be a "gangster"; provided, however, that nothing in this section contained shall in any wise be construed to include any participant or sympathizer in any labor dispute.[17]

Mr. Lanzetta and his co-defendants were convicted and sentenced under this statute to the state prison for five to ten years at hard labor. Their crime was "being a 'gangster'."[18] For them, the question who is a "gangster" (i.e., a "gang" member), was more than an interesting sociological question; it meant the difference between freedom and imprisonment.

After canvassing several dictionary definitions and the work of Herbert Asbury and Frederic Thrasher,[19] the Court reversed Lanzetta's conviction because "[i]t is the statute's definition of the offense—["being a gangster"], not the accusation under it, that prescribes the rule to govern conduct and warns against transgression":[20]

> That the terms of a penal statute creating a new offense must be sufficiently explicit to inform those who are subject to it what conduct on their part will render them liable to its penalties, is a well-recognized requirement, consonant alike with ordinary notions of fair play and the settled rules of law. And a statute which either forbids or requires the doing of an act in terms so vague that men of common intelligence must necessarily guess at its meaning and differ as to its application, violates the first essential of due process of law.[21]

The logic of the Court's decision is apparent when one looks critically at the separate elements of the "offense" of being a gangster under the statute in question. A "gangster" was any person:

1. not engaged in any lawful occupation;
2. known to be a member of any gang consisting of two or more persons; and
3. having at least three convictions of being a disorderly person, or conviction of any crime in New Jersey or in any other state.

But one could certainly be engaged in the types of criminal activities with which New Jersey was then apparently concerned without meeting the conditions listed above—that is, one could *behave* like a gangster, but not *be* one for criminal law purposes. All that was necessary to escape was (1) lawful employment (as an attorney, for instance), (2) secret association and cooperation with a gang of organized criminals, and (3) a clean criminal record to date. Thus, all one had to do was have a decent job, be discreet, and, above all, not get caught.

By the same token, one could legally be a gangster under New Jersey's law, yet not currently be engaged in any criminal activity. In effect, one would be penalized for being an unemployed person with a criminal record who hangs around with a "known" group of friends. Clearly, the New Jersey statute at issue in *Lanzetta* was overinclusive, underinclusive, vague ("known"? by whom?) and ambiguous.[22]

The real problem was in New Jersey's approach; it was attempting to criminalize a sociological concept rather than human behavior. If there is a conclusion that can be drawn from all this, it is that social science definitions and legal definitions cannot always be the same. Definitions which are useful for descriptive social science purposes may, for precisely the same reasons, be unconstitutional as legal ones. The question which remains to be examined is whether legislative drafters and gang task forces have learned much since *Lanzetta*. The answer depends, in part, on how one reads *Lanzetta* itself.

Current Approaches: STEPA, RICO, and the Continuing Criminal Enterprise. If one assumes that it is possible to translate a sociological concept as amorphous as "gang" into a criminal statute specific enough to pass constitutional muster, the task after *Lanzetta* is not to give up on punishing membership in gangs, but to be more specific about what is meant when speaking of "gang control." The two most important pieces of legislation currently on the books and directed toward that end are California's Street Terrorism Enforcement and Prevention Act [STEPA], and the federal Racketeer Influenced and Corrupt Organizations Act [RICO]. Both are designed to enhance the penalties provided by existing law for collective criminal conduct.[23] Another useful descriptive device is the concept of the "continuing criminal enterprise" adopted in the Comprehensive Drug Abuse Prevention and Control Act of 1970. The act creates the crime of being the head of a criminal enterprise and enhances otherwise available penalties accordingly.[24]

None of these statutes, however, defines "gang" in accordance with the desire of the California State Task Force on Youth Gang Violence for a "uniform statewide definition of youth and adult gangs."[25] Given the nature of the term, the quest for a uniform definition will inevitably be met with frustration in the context of criminal law. Nonetheless, the necessary conceptual compromises are minor, basically exchanging flexibility and certainty for uniformity. That this is an improvement over the definition in *Lanzetta* is obvious, and it is certainly preferable to no gang control legislation at all.

STEPA defines a "criminal street gang" as "any ongoing organization, association, or group of three or more persons, whether formal or informal, having as one of its primary activities the commission of one or more of the [following] criminal acts . . .":

> Assault with a deadly weapon or force likely to produce great bodily injury,
> Robbery,
> Homicide or Manslaughter,
> Drug Trafficking,
> Shooting at an inhabited dwelling or occupied motor vehicle,
> Arson,
> Witness Intimidation, or
> Grand Theft of any vehicle, trailer or vessel.

In addition, it must be found that the group has "a common name or common identifying sign or symbol," and that its "members individually or collectively engage in or have engaged in a pattern of criminal gang activity."[26]

For purposes of the statute a "pattern of criminal gang activity" is defined as

> the commission, attempted commission, or solicitation of two or more of the [above-listed] offenses, provided at least one of those offenses occurred after the effective date of [STEPA] and the last of those offenses occurred within three years after a prior offense, and the offenses are committed on separate occasions, or by two or more persons.[27]

Persons subject to prosecution for gang violence under STEPA are those who are known members of gangs and who have exhibited a prior criminal background, and "gang-related means that the suspect or victim of the crime is a known member of a gang."[28]

In the few cases decided to date, the California courts have been strict in their insistence that the statute be strictly construed against the state:[29]

> The elements of the offense of participation in a criminal street gang are: (1) the existence of a "criminal street gang"; (2) defendant's "active" participation in that gang; (3) defendant's knowledge that "its members engage in or have engaged in a pattern of criminal gang activity"; and (4) defendant's willful promotion, furtherance, or assistance "in any felonious criminal conduct by members of that gang."[30]

The California response to the overbreadth problem identified in *Lanzetta* is to define "criminal gang behavior," and leave the task of defining the term "gang" to the sociologists.

Because state laws are inadequate to the task of controlling the highly sophisticated multistate criminal enterprises engaged in drug trafficking and other forms of organized crime or criminal gang behavior, Congress enacted the Racketeer Influenced and Corrupt Organizations Act, usually known by its acronym, RICO, as Title IX of the Organized Crime Control Act of 1970.[31] It is not limited in its coverage to what is commonly considered "organized crime," and may be used against any group or association of individuals who engage in the requisite predicate acts, such as street or prison gangs. RICO has been used successfully in New York, for example, against the Chinese street gang known as the Ghost Shadows and the Hell's Kitchen murder-for-hire gang, The Westies.[32]

RICO provides substantial criminal and civil penalties for engaging in a "pattern of racketeering activity" within a ten-year period, and defines such a pattern in a manner similar to, but broader than, STEPA: "any act *or threat* involving murder, kidnapping, gambling, arson, robbery, bribery, extortion, or chargeable under state law and punishable by imprisonment for more than one year.[33] The final catch-all provision, which includes all state offenses punishable by imprisonment for more than one year, is particularly sweeping because of the sheer number of crimes which fit this description. In addition to its broad sweep, it is particularly relevant to note, for present purposes, Congress' mandate that RICO be "liberally construed to effectuate its remedial purposes."[34] Taking Congress at its word, the courts have allowed a very expansive reading of the statute, resulting in a large number of indictments and convictions for a wide range of activities, ranging from street gang activity to federal securities fraud.[35]

One of the most effective aspects of RICO is its provision for civil remedies, including injunctions, treble damages, divestiture of illegally gained property, and attorney-fee awards brought in the name of either the United States or "[a]ny person injured in his business or property."[36] The breadth of the statute, coupled with the courts' liberal construction, are the aspects of the statute which have engendered considerable critical commentary.[37]

The Comprehensive Drug Abuse Prevention and Control Act of 1970 creates the crime of being the head of a "continuing criminal enterprise." According to the statute,

> a person is engaged in a continuing criminal enterprise if—
>
> (1) he violates any provision of [the Act] the punishment for which is a felony, and
> (2) such violation is a part of a continuing series of [narcotics trafficking] violations . . .
>
>> (A) which are undertaken by such person in concert with five or more other persons with respect to whom such person occupies a position of organizer, a supervisory position, or any other position of management, and
>> (B) from which such person obtains substantial income or resources.[38]

Once again the pattern is to define the "enterprise" in terms of the commission of specified criminal acts which are committed in cooperation with a specified number of persons, here five or more. STEPA, by contrast, requires only three persons to constitute a "criminal street gang," and RICO, the broadest of all, defines "enterprise" to include "any individual, partnership, corporation, association, or other legal entity, and any union or group of individuals associated in fact although not a legal entity." Other relevant statutes focus on the circumstances surrounding the events leading up to the conviction, and increase punishment for specific types of conduct such as the use or concealment of a weapon in the course of a crime.[39]

Which Rights: Civil or Criminal?

Distinguishing Criminal and Civil Rights. The term "civil rights," properly understood, encompasses a wide range of topics touching on individual and collective political, liberty, and "human rights" interests. For purposes of this chapter, the most important of these are freedom of association, freedom of communication, freedom to travel freely, and freedom from discrimination on the basis of race and national origin. The term "civil rights" does not, for present purposes, include the rights of individuals generally associated with the administration of criminal justice, such as the right to counsel, warrant requirements and associated limitations on state investigative and search and seizure powers, the right to a jury trial and confrontation of witnesses, and other important constitutional guarantees specifically designed to protect individuals who have become the targets of criminal investigations or charges.[40] While these, too, are important interests, and each, like its civil counterparts, rests upon not only the written guarantees of constitutional and statutory law, but also upon "natural law," a structure of judicial decisions, and administrative guidelines, policies regulations and practices any substantive discussion of these topics would go far beyond the scope of this chapter.

As applied to the phenomenon of "gangs," the civil rights which concern us here serve as a type of filter. The process accepts as its starting point a given characteristic of gang-related policy and runs it through a series of tests to determine what, if any, civil rights problems can be identified. The first part of this chapter utilized this process, using only one "filter"—Due Process—to examine the constitutional issues related to defining the problem. Expanding the definition of "civil rights" casts the net more broadly, and the potential that the inquiry will flag a civil rights problem increases accordingly.

This observation is equally true with respect to the manner in which provisions of gang control policy is scrutinized. To the extent that only the text of the law is examined (the narrowest approach, and known by lawyers as an examination of the law "on its face"), few violations will be found; but the ones which are found may be significant enough to invalidate the policy without requiring evidence of how it works in practice. If, however, the focus turns to the broadest, and perhaps the most pertinent point of reference—the manner in which it is applied in the day-to-day workings of the myriad subunits and employees of the local, state, and federal governments—the potential for finding violations increases exponentially as a function of the number of persons having operational responsibility. This is so because sensitivity to the civil rights concerns of individuals and communities is not so much a function of positive law (though that helps too) as it is a state of mind which requires respect for one's social and civic duty. Since government employees, from social workers to the state's attorney are the most common point of contact between the citizen and the government, it is to their activity (or neglect) that we must look to find the most intractable problems.

A Dual Inquiry. Any civil rights inquiry is necessarily a dual one, but the dual nature of the gangs and civil rights inquiry is particularly important. In the jargon of civil rights law, collective or societal concerns are generally discussed, if at all, under the catch-all category of "compelling state interest." This is an unfortunate tendency in any event given the importance of the topic in constitutional law,[41] but with respect to criminal gangs, the propensity of most legal scholars to subsume the interests of individual citizens into a relatively amorphous concept of "state interest" does not do justice to the personal interests of individuals who are affected personally by gang activity.

Thus, the first inquiry concerns the rights of individual citizens and their families to be protected from intimidation and harm. While this may seem obvious, it is far too often the missing variable in "rights" discussions in the field of criminal law.[42] That this is the least-obvious inquiry to many, if not most, students of constitutional law rests upon a number of factors, not the least of which is the belief that, in the words of David Luban, "the goal . . . in criminal defense is to curtail the power of the state over its citizens. We want to handicap the state in its power even legitimately to punish us, even if the result is that justice is not served in an individual case. The goal is political: 'impeding justice in the name of more fundamental political ends, namely keeping the government's hands off people.'"[43]

This is certainly a laudable political goal as a matter of general political theory, but in the present context it misses the point that people truly are being held hostage—if not worse—in their own homes and neighborhoods. Stories of innocent victims hit by stray bullets or attacked because they were in the wrong place at the wrong time are not uncommon.[44] In this regard, the first finding of the California State Task Force on Gangs and Drugs bears repeating: "Some communities are literally held captive by the violence, intimidation and decay resulting from drug-trafficking by gangs."[45]

Since law and politics are supposed to reflect a balancing of individual and community interests, and it certainly cannot be that the losses which crime victims suffer is irrelevant either to the definition of the offense or the degree of punishment,[46] both criminal and civil law must take into account the particularly dangerous nature of the gang problem. RICO and STEPA, however imperfect the drafting might be, are good examples of legislation which attempts to meet that need. After all, among the purposes to be accomplished by the federal Constitution was to "establish Justice, insure Domestic Tranquility, provide for the common defense, promote the general Welfare, and secure the Blessings of Liberty to ourselves and our posterity."[47]

United States Supreme Court Justice Antonin Scalia's dissenting observation on behalf of four members of the Court in *Booth v. Maryland* captures the essence of the problem which arises when the interests of society-in-the-abstract are "balanced" against the interests of a real defendant:

Many citizens have found one-sided and hence unjust the criminal trial in which a parade of witnesses comes forth to testify to the pressures beyond normal human experience that drove the defendant to commit his crime, with no one to lay before the sentencing authority the full reality of human suffering the defendant has produced which (and not moral guilt alone) is one of the reasons society deems his act worthy of the prescribed penalty.[48]

For those whose lives are affected by the violence, fear, and uncertainty for the security of house, goods, and (most importantly) self and posterity, the most important role of the state is to "insure domestic tranquility" through the operation and enforcement of the criminal and civil sanctions designed to promote order and regularity in community life. This is indeed one of their "civil!' rights; the ordinary citizen has nowhere else to turn.[49]

The second inquiry, into the civil rights of gangs and their members, is both more specific and more familiar to those acquainted with civil rights discussions. It is nevertheless difficult because it involves an overt balancing of individual and associational interests against the individual and collective security interests of those who live and work in a community in which a gang and its members operate.

IS AN "INDIVIDUAL RIGHTS" PARADIGM ADEQUATE TO THE TASK?

Introduction: A Question of "Balancing"?

Most discussions of civil rights are bipolar, pitting the interests of a faceless "state" against those of individuals or groups whose identifying racial, ethnic or cultural characteristics, legal status or associational choices are, for largely irrational reasons, disfavored by members of the general public. Discrimination on the basis of race, religion, and national origin fit neatly into such a framework.

More difficult are issues where government policy lines are drawn ("discriminate") on the basis of factors which are both "rational" and which, upon examination, have some relationship (even if only an assumed one) to the attainment of legitimate public purposes. Among these are restrictions on otherwise protected communication interests (e.g., graffiti, symbolic attire or gang "colors"), restrictions on personal mobility or association, parental responsibility laws, and civil forfeiture laws. Notwithstanding either the seemingly absolute language of several constitutional provisions,[50] the rhetoric of many civil libertarians critical of such balancing, there are few, if any, rights which are construed to be absolute in the face of what are perceived to be compelling community needs.[51]

Nowhere is this balancing process beset with more difficulty—and controversy—than in the individual liberty aspects of criminal justice. It is in this arena that public and private interests in crime prevention, apprehension of criminals, the administration of justice, and penology clash head-on with explicit constitutional guarantees designed to protect individuals from discrimination on the basis of race or national origin, and from intrusion or interference in the realm of intrafamily relationships, travel, associations with others, and communications with others.

When homes, jobs, businesses, and neighborhoods (including those which lie within the walls of a prison or jail) lie within the territory of a "gang," or when the organization, secrecy, and group cohesiveness of a gang complicates the already difficult task of law enforcement or penal officials, not just the legally enforceable liberty rights of gang members are at stake. Ordinary citizens have the same—if not more substantial, given the circumstances—rights to privacy and the integrity of the home, to maintain the emotional and physical well-being of oneself and one's family, and to go about their lives without fear.

In fact, the civil law provides civil remedies for violation of rights both to those alleged to have committed crimes and to their victims. All are equal before the law, and the case reports are filled with state and federal cases filed by convicted criminals seeking protection of their rights. Unfortunately for crime victims, most criminals are judgment-proof. Nevertheless, the civil and criminal justice systems do, at least in theory, provide complimentary and cumulative protection for the civil rights of all citizens.

A Proposed Analytical Structure

Up to and including the issues-identification stage, applying an individual liberties analysis to gang-related questions is not a particularly difficult task.[52] From that point on, the civil law backdrop and bipolar nature of civil rights analysis complicates the picture. Perhaps the easiest way to illustrate the process is to utilize a standard sociological definition of "gang" such as the one suggested by the California Task Force on Youth Gang Violence (quoted in the text at note 7) as the basis from which to extrapolate the issues under each of the criteria. According to that definition, the gang is a group of people:

1. who interact at a high rate among themselves;
   a) freedom of association—to "belong" to the group
   b) freedom of travel (territorial questions)

c) freedom to assemble peaceably as a group

d) rights of associational privacy, including the right *not* to belong to the group

2. which excludes other groups;

a) exclusivity of private or "fraternal" organizations

b) self-definition

c) nondiscrimination on the basis of race, national origin, and culture

3. which has a group name;

a) self-identification

b) communication of group identity via graffiti and other means such as uniforms and distinctive clothing

4. which claims a neighborhood or other territory;

a) travel restrictions as conditions of parole or probation; restrictions on freedom of movement of neighborhood residents

b) graffiti control; rights of private and public property owners

5. and which engages in criminal and other antisocial behavior on a regular basis.

Freedom of Communication, Assembly, and Association

In relevant part, the First Amendment to the Constitution of the United States provides that "Congress shall make no law . . . abridging the freedom of speech, or of the press, or the right of the people peaceably to assemble."[53] Its relevance lies in its express protection of speech, press, and assembly, as well as the right of freedom of association, which has been implied from its terms. Not only are gangs as free as anyone else to assemble "peaceably," they are also free, subject to the rights of property owners and others, to hang signs announcing the existence of their group, to wear distinctive clothing which identifies them as members of a gang, and to associate with one another as much or as little as they please.

Problems arise when the gang has an established record of criminal activity. Just what can the authorities, including the police, do? The short answer is that it depends upon two factors: (1) for immediate action, the focus is whether or not they have reasonable suspicion to believe that a crime is being or has been committed,[54] and (2) for general regulatory policy, the question is whether (as in the definition of "gang") the policy is narrowly drawn, with sufficient clarity to give notice of the type of illegal activity prohibited.

As currently understood by the Supreme Court, freedom of association can be best understood as encompassing three separate analytical constructs. The first is association related to expression or religion, which is protected by implication from the First Amendment itself. This type of association, which would include political party or church membership, is subject to analysis under the high standards of constitutional review appropriate to speech, press, and religion cases. The second is association related to close, personal relationships, held by the Supreme Court to be protected by the right to privacy which is implied from the Bill of Rights and Fourteenth Amendment. The standard of review for these cases is also quite high, but the nature of the relationship is critical; if the Court has not singled it out for special protection, the state need only show a rational reason for regulating it in the public interest. (The Court's refusal to extend the right to privacy to include consensual homosexual activity in the privacy of the home falls into this category.[55]) And last, there are other forms of association, including association for economic or purely social purposes, which are protected only to the extent that regulations must be rationally related to some legitimate governmental purpose.

The specific associational issues which arise in the context of gang control legislation fall into all three categories. Criminal conduct, for example, clearly falls into the "unprotected" category: the state need only show that the conduct is criminal and it is not protected. If the conduct in question f its into a "protected" category, association involving legitimate expression (e.g., display of gang insignia), or activities within what is known as the "zone of personal privacy" (e.g., laws imposing liability on family members), further analysis is required before a final judgment can be made concerning the legitimacy of criminalizing such conduct.

Assuming that one could get beyond the definitional problems and write a statute criminalizing "gang membership," the freedom of association question would be posed as follows: Is it legitimate to make "membership" in a gang a crime? There are only a few cases which deal with the issue of "mere" membership in an unlawful organization, and these date back to the loyalty-oath era where one's "mere" membership in the Communist Party was enough (for some) to raise questions concerning one's loyalty to the United States.[56] The Supreme Court appears to have held that, while membership *per se* is not enough to impose disabilities on the member, membership in an organization which engages in or encourages illegal activity raises legitimate questions which would support the decision of public authorities to make further inquiries.[57]

As applied to gangs involved in criminal activities, such inquiry becomes a practical necessity for reasons related both to the individual rights of the person accused of crime, and others having an interest in seeing that justice is done (e.g., victims, neighbors, taxpayers, etc.). Since the Constitution does not permit "innocent" association to be criminalized, at least some degree of knowledge of the gang's illegal activities and the specific intent to further the gang's purpose must be demonstrated before any enforcement efforts may be undertaken with respect to a given individual.[58]

Given the types of initiation requirements often imposed on gang members and their high degree of social cohesiveness, it is doubtful that many novice gang members remain naive about ongoing patterns (as opposed to extent or frequency) of criminal conduct. Nevertheless, criminal law requires proof of a reasonable suspicion of illegal activity (usually before a judge) before the authorities may act. It is this constitutionally based need for precision and proof in all matters involving the administration of criminal justice which explains why statutes like California's STEPA are phrased in terms of specific acts, rather than association with a "gang," however defined.

Even more interesting questions (at least to this writer) lie on the "public interest" side of the equation. Police and other law enforcement personnel need and use data on gangs, their members, and their activities to establish patterns and profiles which are useful tools of the trade. As might be expected, the extent to which the police may rely upon established patterns in gang territories as the reasons upon which they seek to defend against claims that criminal procedure rights have been violated varies in accordance with the facts of each case.[59] Gang membership is generally relevant, but, standing alone, it is not determinative. For this reason, the collection and storage of data on gang members can raise potentially serious questions about invasion of privacy and unconstitutional surveillance, a concern expressly noted in the legislation implementing California's STEPA.[60]

In addition to law enforcement needs, the rights of others—potential witnesses, for example—make further inquiry into a gang member's association with a gang relevant to the non-gang member's safety. The Illinois Court of Appeals has noted in another context that

[c]ommon life experience teaches us that gang members often protect one another, and consequently the implication that the jurors' safety might be in question is legitimate. . . . Furthermore, experience with criminal trials teaches that a juror's daily association in the neighborhood where the crime occurred would be a common reason for a peremptory challenge [to the juror's qualifications] with or without gang activities in the area.[61]

Perhaps the most controversial provision of STEPA is that which makes it a misdemeanor for parents to fail "to exercise reasonable care, supervision, protection and control over their minor children" who may be members of gangs. California Penal Code §272, as amended in 1988, provides a range of criminal penalties for what is commonly known as "contributing to the delinquency of a minor"; and specifically imposes a duty of parental surveillance:

For purposes of this section, a parent or legal guardian to any person under the age of 18 years shall have the duty to exercise reasonable care, supervision, protection, and control over their minor child.[62]

While not specifically directed at gangs, Section 272 reflects the California Legislature's findings that there is evidence that "gang involvement begins at an early age . . . [and that] parents of gang members lack appropriate parenting skills."[63]

The first gang-related case brought under this provision involved a mother who was charged because she allegedly condoned her son's membership in a street gang by posing for a photograph in a gang tee shirt and allowing her children to pose for pictures while displaying weapons.[64] Though the case was eventually dropped when it was found that the woman had taken courses designed to help in her attempts to bring her children under control, the thought of punishing parents for failure to control their children provoked considerable commentary.[64]

There is no question that California's approach seeks to regulate the parent-child relationship, and that this relationship is a type of association which has been held to be deserving of special constitutional protection.[65] Though the California legislature expressly stated that "nothing in this section is intended to disrupt the family unnecessarily or to intrude inappropriately into family life, to prohibit the use of reasonable methods of parental discipline, or to prescribe a particular method of parenting,"[66] there is no question that courts will eventually be forced to sit in judgment of parents caught in extremely difficult situations.

There are no reported decisions to date on the application of this statute to the parents of gang members, but it is not uncommon for juvenile courts to exercise considerable oversight of parental decision making and conduct alleged to have a harmful impact on children, especially in cases affecting their health and education.[67] California thus joins a number of other states in holding parents legally responsible for failure to supervise their children.[68] The difference—and it is a substantial one—is that the liability imposed is a criminal one. Nevertheless, the prevailing attitude of the Courts is well stated by the Supreme Court of Connecticut in *Watson. v. Gradzik*:

> The court cannot accept the defendants' premise that the fundamental right to bear and raise children has been interfered with merely because a parent is held responsible for his child's torts. With the right to bear and raise children comes the responsibility to see that one's children are properly raised so that the rights of other people are protected.[69]

The last inquiry derived from the First Amendment is whether or not attempts to control the dress or graffiti of gang members violates their right to freedom of speech. Since graffiti is "pure" speech, and wearing a gang's "colors" is, at very least, communicative activity, there is no question that blanket attempts to control such activity will raise serious constitutional problems: a more "targeted" approach is necessary. This is underscored by an unreported decision of the California Court of Appeals in *Renteria v. Dirty Dan's, Inc.*[70] Though *Renteria* did not involve a governmentally imposed dress code, and hence no constitutional question, the California court did hold that a dress code enforced by five topless bars which denied admission to persons wearing motorcycle gang insignia was illegal under California's Unruh Civil Rights Act.[71] Setting aside the court's gratuitous observation that "[i]mposing a topless bar dress code is the ultimate oxymoron,"[72] the case does raise a serious issue: to what extent must it be shown that there is an actual threat of violence or danger before steps may be taken to reduce the threat of gang violence?

It is in this context that the individual rights paradigm which influences contemporary constitutional decision making begins to come under considerable strain. Gang members wear colors to advertise their affiliation with the enterprise and cohesiveness. Experience shows that gang members and rivals identify one another by colors, graffiti, and hand signs[73]— all of which are communicative activity which, if innocent, are protected by the First Amendment. The problem is that innocent people also get caught wearing the "wrong" colors—and sometimes get killed for it.[74]

In the case where the message of the garb or graffiti either suggests illegal activity (including threats) or is written on private or public property, the law may intervene to control it.[75] The unresolved question is how much latitude the courts will permit in the absence of evidence of prior illegal behavior. The California court's decision in *Renteria* indicates that it likely will be narrow, even though the current Los Angeles district attorney has noted that the wearing of the wrong colors may itself provoke murder, and school boards around the country are considering flat bans on "gang clothing" as an attempt to prevent trouble and intimidation before it begins.[76] The reason: in cooperation with the police, school officials have noticed children as young as early middle school age "as gang wannabes from the larger community."[77] How many deaths, muggings, or other violent acts will it take before a "compelling" interest is found by judges? One suggestion is found in the testimony of Captain Barry King of the Los Angeles County Sheriff's Department before the State Task Force on Youth Gang Violence:

We have to make the judiciary more sensitive to the kinds of concerns gangs pose. The judges don't understand totally what the gangs are all about. They think, as probably many of us do, that we are dealing with the same gangs we had when we were younger, the less violent, more of a social kind of interaction. They don't realize that there's tremendous amounts of underground money, tremendous amounts of violence.[78]

Freedom from Discrimination on the Basis of Race and National Origin

As cultural subgroupings, ethnic and racial homogeneity in youth gangs is quite common. In fact, it is the rare gang which is truly "interracial."[79] It is difficult, if not impossible, therefore, to apply traditional civil rights analysis to gang control legislation which is carefully drawn to regulate only illegal behavior. By definition, legislation directed at street gangs will have an impact on minorities which is likely to outweigh its impact on the majority community, and the Supreme Court has held consistently that in order to establish a constitutional violation, governmental acts must be intentionally discriminatory.[80] As a result, one must focus on the far more common scenario: the day-to-day operation of gang control policy.

The most pervasive problems of discrimination in the administration of criminal justice lie in the area of official discretion: when to arrest, whom to arrest, decisions to charge or plead, and the myriad other decisions made daily by police officials and prosecuting attorneys. When these rest on racial factors, they are unconstitutional; for the state bears the burden of showing that its decisions are untainted by race discrimination.[81]

To the extent that gang activity is widespread within a given ethnic or racial community, any attempt to control the gang activity will be seen (by some) as racially motivated. If such bias can be proved or is apparent from a fair reading of the facts, it cannot be tolerated on grounds of either fairness or good police practice. If there is suspicion, and police-community relations do not permit resolution of allegations of racially motivated police tactics, the isolation of those who live in gang-controlled neighborhoods will simply increase. California has wisely recognized that suspicion of law enforcement motives is not conducive to success in the task of gang control, and has developed mechanisms, which operate in conjunction with STEPA, to support community-based programs designed to address gang-related problems.[82]

It is notable that race discrimination by the authorities is not limited to the targets of police attention; sometimes the police themselves are the victims. Discriminatory assignment and promotion policies which assign officers to gang, immigration, or drug-related cases on the basis of race, ethnicity and language proficiency, rather than their professional qualifications or experience, have been found to be illegal under Title VII of the Civil Rights Act of 1964.[83]

CONCLUSION

In the final analysis, the problem of "gang control" (with the emphasis on "control") is one of law enforcement and the administration of criminal justice. While understanding the structure, patterns, sociology, and demographics of gangs is extremely useful for those charged with law enforcement, sentencing and penology,[116] the essence of the law enforcement task is to prevent and punish criminal behavior.[84]

It makes little difference in the context of criminal law whether the public officials can arrive at a consistent definition of the term "gang"; for gangs *per se* are not, and as a practical matter cannot be, illegal. For purposes of criminal law, the only thing absolutely required is that laws regulating criminal behavior, collective or individual, are specific, and give clear notice of what behaviors are unacceptable. Not only does this avoid the vagueness and overbreadth problems which would cast doubt on the laws' constitutionality, but it eliminates the most significant civil rights problem of all: a decision to base conviction or punishment on factors other than guilt.

And it is in this framework that the civil rights issues affecting gangs should be seen. The law has no legitimate concern with the speech, association, travel, dress, or other matters of a personal nature as long as there is no attempt to violate or evade the law. To the extent that gang members abide by the law and respect the rights of other members of the community in which they live, there is no problem with their behavior.

Problems do arise, however, when those who enforce the law act in a lawless manner. Discrimination based on race or national origin, for example, has no place in society, much less in the administration of justice. Excessive zeal in rooting out lawless behavior on the part of gangs can also lead to violations of individual rights, justifiable suspicion of police motives, and an overall breakdown in respect for the law.

The balance is a difficult one to maintain, if it can ever be established. Tempering concern for the public interest with a well thought-out balancing of collective and individual interests requires careful planning, training, and, above all, open communication between those who enforce the law, and those who must live under it. Such a balance is, in the final analysis the essence of civil rights.

NOTES

1. In fact, the Racketeer Influenced and Corrupt Organizations Act, better known as RICO, was patterned after antitrust legislation. RICO is discussed in some detail in the text accompanying notes 23 to 39.

2. California Council on Criminal Justice, State Task Force on Gangs and Drugs, Final Report (State of California: Sacramento, January 1989) p. 16.

3. See, e.g., *Roberts v. United States Jaycees*, 468 U.S. 609 (1984) (commercial associations); *Moore v. City of East Cleveland*, 431 U.S. 494 (1977) (familial relationships); *NAACP v. Button*, 371 U.S. 415 (1963) (professional relationships for the advancement of a political and social agenda).

4. In *Roberts v. United States Jaycees*, note 3, which involved the Jaycees' refusal to admit women members, the Supreme Court held that the state may even intervene in the membership selection decisions of associations which have as one of their major goals "expressive" activity; that is, activity which merits First Amendment protection. Such intervention may take place, however, only when there is a "compelling state interest of the highest order" and the regulation is the least restrictive means of attaining the government's purpose. Where the activity the state seeks to regulate is illegal—in *Roberts* discrimination on the basis of sex was prohibited—it is arguable that the state has already met its burden of proof. See *Oregon v. Smith*, 494 U.S. 872, 110 S.Ct. 1595 (1990).

5. Cf. *Brandenberg v. Ohio*, 395 U.S. 444 (1969); *Dennis v. United States*, 341 U.S. 494 (1951); *Schenk v. United States*, 249 U.S. 47 (1919). See generally Nowak, Rotunda, and Young, *Constitutional Law* 3d ed. §§16.40-16.44 (West: St. Paul, 1986), pp. 946-65 (freedom of association and nonassociation).

6. Cf. *United States v. Robel*, 389 U.S. 258 (1967). Compare text at note 30.

7. California Council on Criminal Justice, State Task Force on Youth Gang Violence, Final Report (State of California: Sacramento, January, 1986) (hereafter, California Task Force on Youth Gang Violence Report), pp. 8-9 (emphasis added).

8. Id. at 9. Section 13825 of the California Penal Code, adopted in 1988, required the State Office of Criminal Justice Planning to produce a "study regarding the implementation of a computerized data base information system to monitor gang violence and drug trafficking activities, as . . . relative to gang violence in California" by July 1, 1990. Among the items to be examined were: "The guidelines to be required to ensure that the data base is uniform" and "the type of safeguards to be used to ensure that the personal privacy rights of the subject of the information are not violated [and] [w]hether or not additional safeguards are needed to ensure that only information relating to criminal activity is placed in the system" Calif. Penal Code §§13825(a)(4, 7, 8).

9. See Thrasher, F. M., *The Gang*. J. F. Short, Jr. abr. ed. (Chicago: University of Chicago Press, 1963), p. 46.

10. See, e.g., C. Scattarella, "Gangs Exploding the Myth—Losing Children To Gangs Is Not a Problem for Just Uncaring or Poor Families; A Loving Upbringing May Not Be Enough Protection," *Seattle Times*, October 28, 1990 (final ed.), p. A1; T. Daunt, "Gangs in Suburbia; Thousand Oaks: With a Low Crime Rate and High Average Income, the City Seems an Unlikely Place for Youth Gangs Such as The Houston Hoods," *Los Angeles Times*, September 16, 1990 (Ventury County ed.) Metro, p. B1.

11. See, e.g., *Abell v. Potomac Insurance Company*, 858 F.2d 1104 (5th Cir., 1988) (RICO applied to claim of federal securities fraud).

12. California Task Force on Youth Gang Violence Report, at 9.

13. See E.F. Dolan and S. Finney, *Youth Gangs* (New York: Julian Messner, 1984), chapters 3, 6; M. D. Lyman, *Gangland* (Springfield, Ill.: Charles Thomas, 19—), pp. 15-17 (discussing the definition of the term "organized crime"), pp. 95-96 (discussing the definition of the term "youth gang"); Thrasher, *The Gang*, chapters 4-9.

14. Dolan and Finney, *Youth Gangs*, p. 51.

15. See *Lanzetta v. New Jersey*, 306 U.S. 451, 458 (1939) discussed in the text accompanying notes 17 to 22.

16. See, e.g., *Liparota v. United States*, 471 U.S. 419 (1985) (prosecution for illegal possession of food stamps); *United States v. Nofziger*, 878 F.2d 442 (D.C. Cir. 1988) cert. denied, 493 U.S. 1003, 110 S.Ct. 564 (1989) (prosecution of former presidential adviser under the Ethics in Government Act).

17. 306 U.S. 452 (1939). Quoting Laws of New Jersey, 1934, §4, ch. 155. Justice Frankfurter did not participate in this case.

18. Every violation of the statute was punishable by a fine not exceeding $10,000 or imprisonment not exceeding twenty years, or both.

19. Id. at 454-455 and nn. 3-5.

20. Id. at 453, citing *Stromberg v. California*, 283 U.S. 359, 368 (1931) and *Lovell v. Griffin*, 303 U.S. 444 (1938).

21. Id.

22. Compare cases cited at note 16 ante.

23. Cal. Penal Code §§186.20 to 186.27 (West Supp. 1989); and 18 U.S.C. §§1961-1968. It also bears noting here that several states have followed the Congressional lead, and have enacted state laws closely patterned after RICO. Discussion of their specific characteristics and provisions is beyond the scope of this chapter. See, e.g., Fla. Stats. §§895.01-895.06 (West 1989); Ga. Code §§16-14-1, et seq.; Ill. Rev. Stat. ch. 56 1/2 §§1651-1660 (narcotics racketeering); Ind. Code §§35-41-6-1, et seq.; La. Rev. Stats. §§1351 et seq.; Ore. Rev. Stats. §§166.715 et seq.; Pa. Corrupt Orgs. Act., Pa. Stats. §911.

See also Cal. Penal Code §12021.5 (adds a two-year term to sentence in street gang convictions where a loaded or unloaded firearm is carried on the person or in a vehicle).

24. Pub. L. 91-513, 84 Stat. 1265 (1970); and 21 U.S.C. §848(a)(1), see part I(A)(2)(b)(2).

25. See note 7.

26. Cal. Penal Code §§186.21(f) (operative in 1993) (West Supp. 1989). Cal. Penal Code §§186.21(e)(1-8) (West Supp. 1989). Section 186.22(e)(1-7), operative January 1, 1993, omits grand theft of vehicles, trailers and vessels. Cal. Penal Code §§186.21 (f), 186.22 (f) (West Supp. 1989).

27. Cal. Penal Code §§186.21 (e), 186.22 (e) (West Supp. 1989).

28. Cal. Penal Code §§13826.3 (a,b) (West Supp. 1989).

29. See In Lincoln Rudolph J., 223 Cal. App. 3d 322, 272 Cal. Rptr. 852 (2d Dist., 1990) (juvenile proceeding; insufficient evidence to find criminal street gang involvement); In re Leland D., 223 Cal. App. 3d 251, 272 Cal. Rptr. 709 (1990) (same; insufficient evidence that gang to which juvenile allegedly belonged was engaged in "pattern of criminal gang activity" within meaning of STEPA). Compare *People v. Superior Court* (Robert L.), 213 Cal. App. 3d 54, 261 Cal. Rptr. 303 (1989) (mandating a reconsideration of a juvenile court's refusal to transfer a minor for trial for murder as an adult in a "drive-by" shooting case where evidence of gang involvement was strong).

30. In re Leland D., 223 Cal. App. 3d 251, 327, 272 Cal. Rptr. 709, 854 (1990).

31. 18 U.S.C. §§1961-1968. Pub. L. 91-452, 84 Stat. 941 (1970).

32. See respectively, *United States v. Turkette*, 452 U.S. 576 (1981). *United States v. Tom*, 787 F.2d 65 (2d Cir. 1988) and *United States v. Louie*, 625 F. Supp. 1327 (S.D.N.Y. 1985). *United States v. Coonan*, 839 F.2d. 886 (2d Cir. 1988).

33. 18 U.S.C. §1961(5) (emphasis added). See *H. J., Inc. v. Northwestern Bell Telephone Co.*, 492 U.S. 229, 109 S.Ct. 2393 (1988) ("pattern" requirement mandates showing both a relationship and a continuity among the predicate acts) and 18 U.S.C. §1963(a).

34. Section 904(a), Pub. L. 91-452, 84 Stat. 941 (1970).

35. See, e.g., *United States v. Salerno*, 481 U.S. 739 (1987) (Mafia); *Abell v. Potomac Insurance Company*, 858 F.2d 1104 (5th Cir., 1988) (RICO applied to claim of federal securities fraud); *United States v. Ferguson*, 758 F.2d 843 (2d Cir. 1985), cert. den. 106 S.Ct. 124 (1985) (Black Liberation Army; armed robbery); *United States v. Bagaric*, 706 F.2d 42 (2d Cir. 1983), cert. den. sub nom *Lagarusic v. United States*, 464 U.S. 840 (1983) (Croatian terrorists; bombings).

36. See, e.g., *Caplin and Drysdale, Chartered v. United States*, 491 U.S. 617, 109 S.Ct. 2646 (1989) (divestiture of funds as affecting defendant's ability to employ counsel; Sixth Amendment). See 18 U.S.C. §1964.

37. See generally G. E. Lynch, RICO: The Crime Of Being A Criminal, Parts I & II, 87 Colum. L. Rev. 661 (1987), Parts III & IV, 87 Colum. L. Rev. 920 (1987); M. Goldsmith, RICO and Enterprise Criminality: A Response To Gerard E. Lynch, 88 Colum. L. Rev. 774 (1988); D. W. Gartenstein and J. F. Warganz, Note: RICO'S "Pattern" Requirement: Void for Vagueness?, 90 Colum. L. Rev. 489 (1990); M. Headley, Comment: *Sedima v. IMREX*: Civil Immunity for Unprosecuted RICO

Violators?, 85 Col.L.Rev. 419 (1985). An important question, which remains open at this writing, is whether or not RICO liability may be imposed where neither the "enterprise" nor the "pattern of racketeering activity" had any profit-making element. *United States v. Ivic*, 700 F.2d 51, 58-65 (2d Cir. 1983) (enterprise or predicate acts must have financial purpose); *United States v. Flynn*, 852 F.2d 1045, 1052 (8th Cir. 1988), cert. denied, 488 U.S. 974 (1988) (enterprise must be directed toward economic goal). *But see McMonagle v. Northeast Women's Center, Inc.*, 868 F.2d. 1342 (3d Cir., 1989), cert. den., 110 S.Ct. 261 (1989).

38. Pub. L. 91-513, 84 Stat. 1265 (1970). 21 U.S.C. §848(a)(1) and 848(c).

39. STEPA, Cal. Penal Code §186.21(f), 186.22(f). RICO, 18 U.S.C. §1961(4). See, e.g., Cal. Penal Code §12021.5 (adding a two-year term to sentence in street gang convictions where a loaded or unloaded firearm is carried on the person or in a vehicle, but giving the judge discretion to vary the term by one year for aggravating and mitigating circumstances).

40. References are to U.S. Constitution Amendments VI, IV, VI and VII, and VI (1791). See also Amendment V (1791) (double jeopardy, self-incrimination, indictment by Grand Jury, due process of law); Amendment VI (compulsory process, venue, notice of charges); Amendment VII (no re-examination of facts found by jury); Amendment VIII (excessive bail).

41. See *Oregon v. Smith*, 494 U.S. 872, 110 S. Ct. 1595 (1990). *See also*, S. E. Gottlieb, *Compelling Governmental Interests: An Essential, but Unanalyzed Term in Constitutional Adjudication*, 68 B.U.L. Rev. 917 (1988).

42. *Compare, Payne v. Tennessee*, 111 S. Ct. 2597 (1991) with *South Carolina v. Gathers* 490 U.S. 805, 109 S.Ct. 2207 (1989); *Booth v. Maryland*, 482 U.S. 469 (1987).

43. T. L. Shaffer, *American Legal Ethics: Text, Readings, and Discussion Topics* (Matthew Bender, 1985), pp. 180-82, quoting D. Luban (ed.), *The Good Lawyer* (New York: Rowman and Allanhed, 1983), pp. 83-127.

44. See, e.g., M. Copeland, "Colors Held Hostage: Gangs Have Usurped the Color Spectrum. Now How You Mix Colors Could Be a Matter of Life or Death," *Chicago Tribune*, September 5, 1990 (North Sports Final ed.) "Style," p. 16 (noting that "When Angel Agosto took a shortcut home last summer he had no idea he was in the wrong place at the wrong time and wearing the wrong colors."); J. W. Fountain, "Gunfire Taking Deadly Toll on Children," *Chicago Tribune*, September 5, 1990 (North Sports Final ed.) "Chicagoland," p. 1 (recounting the death of six-month-old Rashonda Flowers by a stray bullet).

45. California Council on Criminal Justice, State Task Force on Gangs and Drugs, note 2.

46. *Payne v. Tennessee*, 111 S. Ct. 2597 (1991).

47. U.S. Constitution, Preamble (1787).

48. *Booth v. Maryland*, 482 U.S. 469, 519-20 (1987) (Scalia, J., joined by Rehnquist, C. J., White, and O'Connor, J J. dissenting).

49. See *Rivera v. United Auto Workers Local 179 UAW-CIO Bldg. Corp.* 266 Cal. Rptr. 262 (1990) [ordered not published, Cal. Rules of Ct. 976] (denying tort cause of action based on failure to provide adequate protection for visitors against owner of building in gang-infested area which rented the building for a party unrelated to its business).

50. *E.g.*, U.S. Constitution Amendment I (1791) ("Congress shall make no law respecting an establishment of religion or prohibiting the free exercise thereof, or abridging the freedom of speech, or of the press, or the right of the people peaceably to assemble, and to petition the Government for a redress of grievances."); U.S. Constitution Amendment XIV, §1 (1868) ("No State shall make or enforce any law which shall abridge the privileges or immunities of citizens of the United States; nor shall any State deprive any person of life, liberty, or property without due process of law; nor deny to any person within its jurisdiction the equal protection of the laws.")

51. The Supreme Court of the United States has never construed the First Amendment as broadly as its language appears to allow, much to the chagrin of justices such as the late Justice Hugo Black who believed that "no" law meant precisely that: no law.

52. For purposes of clarity, and in the interests of brevity, the main civil rights topics to be addressed in this section will be discussed from the perspective of individuals who belong to gangs. Where appropriate, mention will be made either in the text or in the notes to the application of the principles discussed to victims of crime.

53. U.S. Constitution Amendment I (1791).

54. *Compare, e.g., People v. Rahming,* 795 P. 2d 1338 (1990) (mere proximity of gang members wearing colors to rival gang members' residence was insufficient for police stop), with *State v. Whitaker,* 58 Wash. App. 851, 795 P. 2d 182 (1990) (failure to prove that search was based purely on status of gang leader).

55. *Bowers v. Hardwick,* 478 U.S. 186 (1986).

56. See, e.g., *Shware v. Board of Bar Examiners,* 353 U.S. 232 (1957); *Konigsberg v. State Bar,* 353 U.S. 252 (1957), affirming decision to deny petitioner bar admission on grounds that he did not cooperate with the investigation when he refused to answer certain questions pertaining to his membership, 366 U.S. 36 (1961).

57. See *Konigsberg,* 353 U.S. at 273-74 (fact of past membership is not sufficient grounds to refuse admission to bar because of disloyalty or lack of good character). The Court narrowed the scope of permissible inquiries in a later series of cases. See *Baird v. State Bar,* 401 U.S. 1, 6 (1971); In re Stolar, 401 U.S. 23 (1971).

58. Such knowledge must be shown to exist. See, e.g., *State v. McGowan,* 789 S.W.2d 242 (Mo. App., 1990) (evidence established that defendant met with other members of the gang to plan confrontation with rival gang, that he was armed with a revolver which he carried when other gang members went to provoke a

fight, and remained in the area while the gang shot indiscriminately in a populated area); *State ex rel. Juvenile Department of Multnomah County v. Holloway*, 102 Or. App. 553, 795 P. 2d 589 (1990) (failure to prove that a minor aided and abetted gang-related homicide); *Commonwealth v. Stern*, 393 Pa. Super. 152, 573 A.2d 1132 (1990) (prosecutor's reference to past gang activity was proper as showing intent and motive for murder).

59. See, e.g., *People v. Christopher B.*, a Minor, 219 Cal. APp. 3d 455, 268 Cal. Rptr. 8 (1990) (what constitutes an "arrest" by member of a gang task force in case where gang members were wearing colors and congregated in a large group and one member dropped a bag of cocaine); *Commonwealth v. Wolcott*, 28 Mass.App.Ct. 200, 548 N.E.2d 1271 (1989) (suspect's rights violated when expert in gang violence case was unqualified to testify).

60. See, e.g., *People v. Gonzalez*, 188 Ill. App. 3d 559, 544 N.E.2d 1044 (1989) (prejudicial evidence regarding gang affiliation held irrelevant under the circumstances). A number of states, including California, have state constitutional provisions which were adopted with informational privacy in mind. E.g., Ariz. Const. part. 2, §8; Fla. Const. art, 1, §23; Wash. Const. art. 1, §7. See note 12 for a discussion of STEPA.

61. *People v. Williams*, 177 Ill. App. 3d 787, 532 N.E.2d 1044 (3d Dist. 1988) (rejecting claim of racial discrimination in the prosecutor's exclusion of a neighborhood resident), citing People v. Carradine (1972), 52 Ill. 2d 231, 287 N.E.2d 670 (witness to homicide preferred six months of imprisonment for contempt rather than testify against local members of the Blackstone Rangers gang).

62. Cal. Penal Code §272 (Deering 1990), as amended by 1988 Cal. S.B. 15 (emphasis added). See also, Cal. Welf. and Inst. Code §300(b) (Juvenile Court has jurisdiction where "[t]he minor has suffered, or there is a substantial risk that the minor will suffer, serious physical harm or illness, As a result of the failure or inability of his or her parent or guardian to adequately supervise or protect the minor") (effective until January 1, 1992); §601 (habitual truancy); §602 ("Any person who is under the age of 18 years when he violates any law of this state or of the United States or any ordinance of any city or county of this state defining crime other than an ordinance establishing a curfew based solely on age, is within the jurisdiction of the juvenile court, which may adjudge such person to be a ward of the court."]

63. Cal. Penal Code §13826(d,e) (West Supp. 1989).

64. Myrdans, "Mother is Charged Because a Son Is California Street Gang Suspect," *New York Times*, May 4, 1989 p. A18; "Mother of Rape Suspect Charged with Aiding Gang," *Chicago Tribune*, May 3, 1989 (final ed.), News, p. 4. R. W. Welkos, "Mother Seized Under Gang Law Cleared," *Los Angeles Times*, June 10, 1989 (Home ed.) pt 1, p. 1; Reuters, "Poor Parent Charge Dropped For Mother of Gang Member," *New York Times*, June 10, 1989 (late ed. final) Sec. 1, p. 12. See, e.g., Editorial, "Holding Parents Responsible for Teens," *Chicago Tribune*, May 9, 1989 (North Sports Final Ed.) p. 22; E. Goodman, Editorial, "Sins of the Kids:

Should Parents Pay . . .", *Washington Post*, May 9, 1989 (Final Ed.), p. A23; S. H. Pillsbury, Op-Ed, "How Many Parents Can We Prosecute?; Gang Problems, Like Drug Abuse, Won't East Without Participants' Self-motivation," *Los Angeles Times*, May 10, 1989 (Home Ed.), Metro, Part 2, page 7; Editorial, "Parents and Crime," *Christian Science Monitor*, May 10, 1989, p. 20.

65. *Moore v. City of East Cleveland*, 431 U.S. 494 (1977) (familial relationships); *Pierce v. Society of Sisters*, 268 U.S. 510 (1925); *Meyer v. Nebraska*, 262 U.S. 390 (1923).

66. Cal Welf. and Inst Code §300(j).

67. See sources cited at note 62. See generally *Prince v. Massachusetts*, 321 U.S. 158 (1944). Though there were no reported cases at the time this essay was written, it is unsurprising that, in the time between submission and publication, Section 272 was ruled unconstitutional by the California Court of Appeals. *Williams v. Reiner*, 2 Cal. Rptr. 2d 472 (Cal. App., 2d Dist. 1991). Because the California Supreme Court agreed to review the case in April, 1992, 6 Cal. Rptr. 2d 638, 826 P.2d 1125 (1992), the "final word" on the constitutionality of Section 272 has yet to be written.

68. See, e.g., Illinois Parental Responsibility Law, Ill. Stats. ch. 70, §§51-57 (holding parents or legal guardians liable for actual damages up to $500.00 for the "willful or malicious acts of such minor which cause injury to a person or property."). See, generally, Annotation: Parents' Liability For Injury Or Damage Intentionally Inflicted By Minor Child, 54 A.L.R.3d 974 (1990); Annotation: Validity And Construction Of Statutes Making Parents Liable For Torts Committed By Their Minor Children, 8 A.L.R.3d 612 (1990); Annotation: Liability Of Person Permitting Child To Have Gun, Or Leaving Gun Accessible To Child, For Injury Inflicted By The Latter, 68 A.L.R.2d 782 (1990).

69. 373 A.2d at 192, quoted in *Vanthournout v. Burge*, 69 Ill. App. 3d 193; 387 N.E.2d 341 (3d Dist., 1979).

70. 198 Cal. App. 3d 1447, 244 Cal.Rptr. 423 (1988) (designated for nonpublication in the official reports pursuant to Cal. Ct. R. 976).

71. Cal. Civil Code §§51 et seq. (Deering 1990).

72. 198 Cal. App. 3d 1447 at n. 5.

73. M. D. Lyman, *Gangland*, pp. 100-104. See also P. Mott, "Breaking Ties That Bind; Gangs: Four Former Members Recall the Difficulties They Overcame In Getting Away to Start New and Independent Lives," *Los Angeles Times*, September 4, 1990 (Orange County ed.), part E, p. 1; L. Sahagun, "Gang Homicides Increase 69% in L.A. County Areas; Violence: Authorities Blame Heavy Firepower, Impact Of Poverty and Appeal of a 'Trendy' Image," *Los Angeles Times*, August 21, 1990 (Home ed.) p. A1 (noting that gang killings in unincorporated portions of Los Angeles County soared 69% during the first eight months of 1990, a period during which all violent crimes in the same region rose 20%).

74. E.g., M. Copeland, "Colors Held Hostage: Gangs Have Usurped the Color Spectrum. Now How You Mix Colors Could Be a Matter of Life or Death," *Chicago Tribune*, September 5, 1990 (North Sports Final ed.) "Style," p. 16 (noting that "When Angel Agosto took a shortcut home last summer he had no idea he was in the wrong place at the wrong time and wearing the wrong colors").

75. See sources cited at note 5. Compare *Los Angeles City Council v. Taxpayers for Vincent*, 466 U.S. 789 (1984) (rejecting challenge to ordinance forbidding posting signs on public property). See generally 18 U.S.C. §1964 (RICO civil remedies); Cal. Penal Code §186.22(a) (permitting a court to enjoin certain gang hangouts and activities as a "nuisance which shall be enjoined, abated and prevented, and for which damages may be recovered . . ."). See also Thompson, "Los Angeles Seeks Ultimate Weapon in Gang War," *Wall Street Journal*, March 30, 1988, p. 18 (noting that the city of Los Angeles had obtained an injunction prohibiting trespassing, graffiti, littering, blocking streets and sidewalks, or doing anything to annoy, harass, or intimidate residents of the area where the Playboy Gangster Crips were selling crack cocaine.)

76. I. Reiner, Guest Editorial, "Slain Over a Baseball Cap," *New York Times*, May 18, 1989 (Late City Final ed.) p. A31. Compare *Tinker v. Des Moines School Dist.*, 393 U.S. 503 (1969) (wearing of black armband by student to protest Vietnam war is protected speech), with *Bethel School Dist., No. 403 v. Fraser*, 478 U.S. 675 (1986) (school may regulate "offensive" speech by student where unrelated to political viewpoint and school authorities could reasonably conclude that the speech would "undermine the school's basic educational mission").

77. S. Hubler, "Redondo Beach Schools Expand Gang Clothing Ban," *Los Angeles Times*, September 13, 1990 (Valley ed.) p. B14 (noting that the ban included a prohibition on "the presence of any apparel, jewelry, accessory, notebook or manner of grooming which, by virtue of its color, arrangement, brand name and logo or any other attribute, denotes membership in gangs").

78. California Task Force on Youth Gang Violence, Report, note 7.8 at p. 38.

79. Dolan and Finney, op. cit. note at 39.

80. See *Washington v. Davis*, 426 U.S. 229 (1976).

81. Compare *Holland v. Illinois*, 493 U.S. 474, 110 S.Ct. 803 (1990); *Batson v. Kentucky*, 476 U.S. 79 (1986).

82. See Cal. Penal Code §§13826.6 (community-based organizations), 13826.62 (urban programs), 13826.65 (school districts).

83. See, e.g., *Gallegos v. Thornburgh*, 52 BNA Fair Empl. Prac. Cas. 343 (D.C. 1989); *Pere v. F.B.I.*, 714 F. Supp. 1414 (W.D. Tex. 1989); *Muni v. Meese*, 115 F.R.D. 63 (D.C. 1987).

84. Prison gangs are also a serious problem as well, but given the unique nature of the prison setting, full discussion is beyond the scope of this chapter. See generally *Thornburgh v. Abbott*, 490 U.S. 401 (1989); *O'Lone v. Estate of Shabazz*, 482 U.S. 342 (1987); *Bell v. Wolfish*, 441 U.S. 520 (1979).

13

Public Policy and Gangs: Social Science and the Urban Underclass

SCOTT CUMMINGS
DANIEL J. MONTI

INTRODUCTION

In this concluding chapter, we examine the limits and constraints affecting social science contributions to public policy dealing with gangs. In the opening chapter, Monti traced the intellectual and theoretical roots shaping contemporary research on gangs. Of particular importance were the contributions of Frederic Thrasher. While his ideas continue to influence social science research on gangs, political and economic changes within American cities have given them new structure and form. Changing economic conditions in cities have also altered the nature of American urban policy, and transformed social programs dealing with the poor and members of the nation's underclass.

Two general themes are developed in our concluding chapter: (1) the uncertain role of social science knowledge in the policy formation process, and; (2) the apparent drop in public concern over the special problems of the urban underclass. The specific relevance of these themes to social science research dealing with gangs is critically analyzed. We also examine the absence of social programs dealing with young people attracted to gangs and gang activities. Based upon the evidence and arguments presented by the authors in this volume, we suggest that social program strategies dealing with economic development, education, and job training will be the most effective policy interventions directed toward gangs. We draw heavily upon underclass theory to support this latter observation.

Over the past decade, public policy in American cities has dramatically shifted toward greater reliance upon private sector initiatives. Federal programs and funds targeted for inner-city problems have been sharply reduced or eliminated. During the 1980s, expenditures allocated to nondefense programs steadily dropped as both a percentage of the gross national product and in absolute dollar figures. Major targets for budget reductions included social security, Medicare and Medicaid, higher education and student loans, aid to disadvantaged school districts, unemployment insurance, housing assistance and grants for urban development, grants for job training and creation, financial aid to the poor and the elderly, grants for urban social services, and legal assistance to the poor. Because the beneficiaries of these programs are disproportionately located in the nation's cities, urban areas have been most severely affected by the recent transformations in public policy.

Since the contemporary gang problem has been largely defined as an inner-city, minority issue, social science research on the topic, and social programs dealing with urban youth, have been directly influenced by the privatization of public policy. "Privatizing" generally refers to the popular movement to halt or reverse the growth of governmental institutions producing and distributing public goods and services.[1] The movement to privatize urban services, and the budget cuts accompanying it, reflect widespread dissatisfaction with welfare state liberalism and declining concern over the alleged beneficiaries of liberal policies: the urban underclass.

During the presidency of Ronald Reagan, very low priority was assigned to federally sponsored urban programs. Reagan's critical attitude toward the welfare state, carried forward by the Bush administration, affected the type of knowledge produced by the social science research community and the types of programs directed toward minority youth. Research dealing with the special problems of the urban underclass has received little or no financial support during the era of privatism. Changes within the American economy and spiraling federal deficits have influenced social science research in a manner that has undermined the liberal policy agenda, and reinforced conservative interpretations of urban poverty and what is required to alleviate it.

The Politics of Underclass Research

The concept of an urban underclass and its relationship to contemporary youth gangs is laced with controversy. Earlier in this volume, Moore argued that deleterious changes within many urban economies partially explain the increasing prevalence of gangs in America. She contends that illegal activities among many youngsters must be understood in light of declining opportunities within a city's regional economy. In another recent volume of new research findings dealing with gangs, Huff observes that underclass theory is one of the two most important perspectives shaping contemporary research on gangs.[2] Despite its popularity, however, many social scientists are not enthused about the policy applications of underclass theory,[3] and question its theoretical utility in the study of gangs.

Clearly, wholesale application of Wilson's version of underclass theory to describe the history, growth, and development of gangs in American cities has limitations.[4] We know, for example, that gangs are not exclusively drawn from minority populations. We know that gangs are not exclusively comprised of young people drawn from the very lowest strata of society. We also know that many gangs have long-standing cultural traditions, and are deeply rooted in the fabric of community life and culture. Having acknowledged these limitations, we are also convinced that Wilson's treatment of the emergence of a permanent underclass in American cities has important ramifications for development of effective public policies dealing with gangs.

In *The Truly Disadvantaged*, Wilson criticizes liberal social scientists: (1) for their failure to discuss problems of the underclass candidly out of concern with being labeled "racist," or accused of "blaming the victims" of oppression, and; (2) for their tendency to avoid using the "underclass" altogether for fear of creating negative stereotypes about the urban poor.[5] Wilson believes that the problems facing many inner-city residents are much too serious to be camouflaged by ideological rhetoric. He also thinks that effective public policy directed toward urban problems must focus upon jobs, economic development, and related structural factors not currently part of the conservative political agenda. Agreeing with many of Wilson's observations, we think that underclass theory is pertinent to our summary observations in a number of ways.

First, we are inclined to agree that liberal social scientists have failed to deal with the problems of the urban poor in a politically effective manner. Further, it seems apparent that changing economic circumstances have: (1) dramatically altered research dealing with urban problems, and; (2) sharply increased the seriousness and magnitude of the gang problem. In many respects, the liberal policy agenda and its academic "brain trust" have failed the urban poor. The production of social science knowledge can be viewed as part of a larger complex of economic and political institutions. Malchup observed:

> The production of knowledge is an economic activity, an industry if you like. Economists have analyzed agriculture, mining, iron, and

steel production, the paper industry, transportation, retailing, the production of all sorts of goods and services, but they have neglected to analyze the production of knowledge.[6]

State-supported research is only a small part of what Malchup calls the "knowledge industry." The amount of dollars allocated by federal knowledge-producing programs (e.g., NSF, NIE, NIMH, etc.) is a small component of this larger industrial complex. Further, the amount of money received by individual social scientists through these special programs is minuscule in comparison to funds received by medical scientists and engineers, for example.[7] One of the largest knowledge-producing sectors of the economy is higher education. The resources consumed by public universities, in particular, overshadow the investments made by the federal government in special research programs. Research within higher education, however, seldom serves the interests of the urban underclass.

Fiscal uncertainty within the public sector has negatively affected not only federal but also university research programs. Most institutions of higher education have experienced major cutbacks in recent years. Declining levels of public revenues and severe budgetary cuts have negatively affected many social science programs, especially those located within urban universities. By and large, the decline in state and federal funds for university research programs mirrors larger economic changes taking place in many American cities. Most important to stress, however, is the fact that economic restructuring has enhanced the production of certain kinds of knowledge and sharply curtailed the production of other types.

Knowledge which is useful to private business has been given special priority during the era of privatization. Consistent with these economic trends, the knowledge produced by liberal social scientists has encountered a serious erosion of marketability. The current political climate has produced an easy and asymmetrical relationship between individual social scientists, the research process, and the market forces shaping the production of knowledge.[8] Shifting trends in public policy have had a direct impact upon the research and academic programs traditionally concerned with the urban underclass.

By dismantling public sector institutions and programs, the privatization movement has simultaneously reinforced the interests and initiatives of the private sector, and strengthened those programs within higher education that endorse their values and policies. The immediate question facing social scientists concerned with urban problems is how to respond to the shift in public expenditures away from underclass programs and policies. Chubin and McCartney minced no words when they recently observed that if social scientists want to play ball in the current political climate, they will have to accommodate themselves to the private agenda established during the Reagan-Bush era:

> The new . . . criterion of utility is what research can do for the private sector. Thus, the effort at NSF to reclaim the social science percentage of survey research, which is widely used in the private sector, can be seen as an effort to accommodate social science to new political priorities.[9]

Not only has there been limited demand for underclass research in the private marketplace and in the federal grant economy, it has also had limited appeal and utility in the social policy marketplace. Social science research dealing with urban problems was in great demand during the creation of the policies and programs comprising the failed War on Poverty.[10] In more recent years, however, the public policy market for research activities favorable to the interests of the urban underclass has largely evaporated. These changing conditions have directly impacted research dealing with gangs, and the policies directed toward them.

Miller recently observed that gang problems apparently rank very low on the nation's domestic policy agenda. After examining the *Catalogue of Federal Domestic Assistance Programs*, he concluded that:

> The 1989 edition lists 1,139 grant programs under approximately 535 major subject categories. Youth gangs are not listed as a major or a minor category. Of the 1,139 listed programs, the term *gang* appears in descriptions of four programs, or about one-third of one percent of all programs; of these, two involved gang control as such, another a conference on gangs, and a fourth a program on drug abuse prevention and education as it relates to you youth gangs. . . . The 1990 federal budget allocates about $10 billion to drug programs administered by the Office of National Drug Control Policy. There is no Office of National Gang Control Policy.[11]

Miller contends that gang research and the dearth of social programs to deal with them reflect the absence of political power among the urban underclass. He thinks the wide disparities between priorities and resources explain the inability of the underclass to influence policy debate over gangs. As summarized by Miller: "Gang control is a low national priority in large part because those with good access to resources put a low priority on gang problems and those who put a high priority on gang problems have poor access to resources."[12]

Like most serious problems experienced by the urban underclass, the gang issue has been removed from the national policy agenda. Consistent with the administrative transfer of many social programs to state and local government, cities have been left to deal with their own problems. Miller observes:

> The nation has failed to develop a comprehensive gang control strategy. The problem is viewed in local and parochial terms instead of from a national perspective. Programs are implemented in the absence of demonstrably valid theoretical rationales. Efforts to systematically evaluate program effectiveness have been virtually abandoned. Resources allocated to the gang problem are incommensurate with the severity of the problem. There is no organizational center of responsibility for gang problems anywhere in the United States.[13]

The Economic Roots of the Gang Problem

As the authors appearing in this volume indicate, there are more youth gangs in operation today than in the 1950s, a watershed period in public recognition of the problem. More importantly, gangs today appear more violent and more inclined toward criminal activities than at any prior point in recent history. As Huff observes, contemporary gangs are also appearing in small to medium-size cities, areas that previously reported fewer problems with youth violence and drug traffic.[14] Despite their increasing presence, however, we have available fewer and fewer resources to understand their growth and development, and less will to treat the causes that produce and sustain them.

Consistent with underclass theory, we think the increasing prevalence of gangs in nearly every American city is related to the same recessionary and industrial changes transforming urban and public policy. Over the past two decades, tremendous changes have occurred within the American economy. Basic industry in the United States is being dismantled, and we are in the midst of what Bluestone and Harrison call a period of "deindustrialization."[15] In the face of greater production capabilities and efficiencies from other nations, and the growing internationalization of markets, the American economy slipped in the 1970s to eleventh place in rate of productive growth. The loss of competitive positions in a number of world markets, and the growing number of shutdowns and job losses in previously strong industrial cities, has impacted minorities and women most severely.

The most immediate consequence in American society produced by the dismantling of basic industry is rising levels of unemployment and underemployment. By and large, the areas hardest hit by these devastating economic trends were cities, especially those located in the industrial Midwest, mid-Atlantic, and Northeastern states. As the economic climate of those areas continued to deteriorate, the tax and revenue base of state and local government also eroded. O'Connor argues that as crises develop within the American industrial order, serious destabilization will simultaneously emerge in the public sector.[16] During the past decade, both Reagan and Bush have presided over the worst federal deficits in recent American history. While levels of unemployment have been partially stabilized, the erosion of economic opportunities for those residing in many cities continues.

There is little doubt that William Wilson is correct when he observes that a relatively permanent underclass has emerged in many American cities. It is our contention that the modern gang problem can be better understood through examination of the profound changes taking place within the American industrial and postindustrial cities. While the ethnic and racial characteristics of gang members receive considerable attention in the media and popular press, the policy significance of this focus is limited. Wilson argues that race relations in many American cities reflect the structure of inequality in the larger society and are a response to the employment opportunities available within a region's urban economy.

Following this line of reasoning, Wilson contends that the special problems of the urban underclass can be more effectively addressed through public policies based upon economic rather than racial premises:

> Policy programs based on the premise that the recent rise of social dislocation, such as, joblessness in the inner city, is due to current racism will be significantly different from policy programs based on the premise that the growth of these problems is due more to nonracial factors.

By agreeing with Wilson, we are certainly not dismissing the continued presence of racial discrimination in the urban labor market. And we recognize that the problems accompanying gang violence disproportionately affect the residents of minority communities.

Nonetheless, we are pursuaded by Wilson's observation that underlying economic dynamics strongly contribute to the expansion of the urban underclass, and think that his arguments have direct relevance to gangs and public policy. Wilson contends that the economic problems of the urban poor have escalated, despite major progress in the civil rights arena. We agree, therefore, with recent analyses of the gang problem that link the expansion of such to deindustrialization and economic restructuring. Hagedorn, for example, maintains that: ". . . changed economic conditions have altered the maturing out process and have contributed to the institutionalization of gangs as a means for young adults to cope with economic distress and social isolation."[18]

Earlier in this volume, Moore advanced a similar interpretation when she argued that deindustrialization directly influenced rising patterns of violence and drug trafficking among some gangs. The chapter by Skolnick, Bluthenthal, and Correl also clarifies the underlying economic forces promoting the sale of drugs as an entrepreneurial activity. And the analysis of wilding behavior by Cummings reveals the economic motivations fueling random violence. In my own city, Louisville, striking parallels to those events reported by Hagedorn in Milwaukee have emerged.[19] While initially denying that the city had a "gang problem," public officials now acknowledge that gangs, violence, and drug traffic appear to be emerging in Louisville's minority communities. Drive-by shootings of car windows in middle-class neighborhoods have also occurred.

Consistent with Wilson's prognoses, a permanent class of poor people is emerging in Louisville. This urban underclass is comprised largely of minorities who are increasingly marginal to the city's economy. The neighborhoods populated by the underclass are characterized by high rates of crime, institutional instability, and impoverished households headed by females. Some middle-class blacks have abandoned their old neighborhoods, thus creating a crisis of leadership in the inner city. This growing underclass was not necessarily created by traditional forms of racial discrimination. Rather, Louisville's new urban poverty is exacerbated by severe dislocations in the manufacturing and industrial sectors of its regional economy. Urban minorities have suffered disproportionately as a result of these larger economic changes.

A comparison of Louisville with other middle-sized cities reveals the magnitude of its growing urban underclass. In comparison to nine similar cities (Buffalo, Cincinnati, Columbus, Indianapolis, Kansas City, Milwaukee, Pittsburgh, Providence, and Rochester), Louisville consistently reveals higher levels of black poverty and unemployment and lower levels of educational attainment.[20] Evidence also shows that Louisville has a higher level of mismatch between the educational qualifications of its minority work force and the type of jobs that are currently available. The size of Louisville's urban underclass is proportionately larger than that found in many other cities. While the underclass in Louisville is largely black, evidence also reveals a larger proportion of whites living in poverty than in comparable cities. Cross burnings and racial violence have risen during the past five years.

In 1988, the National Interreligious Commission on Civil Rights held public hearings on the status of civil rights in Louisville. The title of their final report was aptly selected: *A Tale of Two Cities*.[21] The commission found massive socioeconomic discrepancies between black and white residents and considerable evidence suggesting the existence of a growing urban underclass. Consistent with Wilson's thesis and the author from whom the title was borrowed, the 1980s appeared to be the best of times and the worst of times for Louisville's black residents.

Between 1983 and 1986, the number of homeless in Kentucky increased 21 percent to more than thirty-five thousand people. In Louisville, more than one-third of the homeless are minority families.[22] Unemployment rates among blacks in Louisville have continued to escalate during the 1980s, moving from a recent low of 6.9 percent in 1970, to 15.7 percent in 1980, to more than 20 percent in the late 1980s. In 1988, approximately 70 percent of births to black mothers were out of wedlock.[23] This figure has increased steadily from 1970 when 45 percent of black births were out of wedlock. These trends suggest increasing strains on black families in the city, and a shrinking base of employment opportunities for black males in particular. Like the patterns observed by Wilson, unemployment reported by minority youth is extremely high.

These structural strains are fully revealed through closer examination of the city's black neighborhoods. Despite pockets of middle-class enclaves in Louisville's black communities, examination of specific neighborhoods shows they are more consistent with the negative profiles developed by Wilson in his national analysis. In 1980, Louisville had twelve neighborhoods that ranged from 70 percent to 97 percent black. The vast majority of the city's black population resides in these communities. Some neighborhoods report more than 50 percent of its residents living in poverty. While selected neighborhoods show isolated pockets of socioeconomic stability, the general pattern sustains Wilson's concerns over a growing class of poor blacks, comprised largely of women and children.

Louisville, not without violent struggle, has made major strides to distance itself from a segregationist and racist past. During the decades of the 1960s and 1970s, major policy changes occurred in the city leading to reduction in overt discrimination and substantial improvements in relations between blacks and whites. During this same time period, however, the city was also devastated by sweeping changes in its industrial and manufacturing base. These larger economic forces appear to have severely eroded the ability of the city's minority population to avail itself of opportunities created through reduction of discrimination. Ironically, the city's opportunity structure was radically altered at the very time when civil rights gains were accelerating.

Cities like Louisville are clearly creating the conditions under which the appeal of gangs and illegal enterprise will be hard to resist. Consistent with Hagedorn's observations about Milwaukee, the deindustrialization and segmentation of Louisville's urban economy ". . . snatched away the ladder of mobility."[24] We also agree with his observation that "Gangs today in small cities are a red flag telling us the underclass is not just a problem for the New Yorks and Chicagos."[25] Clearly, public policy directed toward gangs will have to contend with the underlying economic forces that seem integral to their growth and perpetuation. Effective public policy will also have to acknowledge that the problem is national in scope, and not just limited to the ills and social pathologies traditionally found in the nation's largest urban areas.

Summary Observations

In this concluding chapter we have argued, perhaps pessimistically, that social science research has exerted minimal influence on the course of contemporary urban policy. Certainly, concern over the nation's cities and their inhabitants will slide further from public consciousness if the crises in the Middle East continues and the recession deepens. Despite the current international malaise and the shifting nature of public policy, social scientists have an important political role to play in shaping the intellectual debate over the urban underclass, the specific problems they encounter, and the types of public policies most likely to be effective.

Our relationship with those who make policy, and our responsibilities to those who are the victims of social ills, however, are not easily balanced. A social science which enhances the interests of the urban poor and the business community, and is appealing to those currently in positions of political power, is very difficult to develop. Unfortunately, the self-interest of the poor and liberal intellectuals is not easily reconciled. And when self-interest is not mutual, a political relationship is fair-weather at best. Conversely, it is much easier to create a social science which enhances and glorifies those groups and constituencies who are in a position to assert their interests. While many social scientists have modified their research and intellectual interests to fit current policy and funding priorities, few made serious efforts to lobby in behalf of saving or restoring social programs supporting the poor, minorities, and the unemployed. Despite the fact that many social scientists have made a career of studying the poor and the dispossessed, we offered little political assistance to them when the Reagan-Bush budget axe swung in their direction.

It seems clear that sociology and other branches of the social sciences do have in common long-range interests with the urban underclass, the poor, women, and minorities. Those intellectuals who are employed at urban universities have special responsibilities to these constituencies. Common interests include support of public policies leading to a more equitable distribution of wealth and income in the society, and the establishment of a research agenda capable of promoting this objective. In order to achieve these goals, however, we would do well to keep in mind the advice of C. Wright Mills when he discussed the unequal relationship between social scientists and policy makers:

To *appeal* to the powerful on the basis of any knowledge we now have is utopian in the foolish sense of that term. Our relations with them are more likely to be only such relations as they find useful, which is to say that we become technicians accepting their problems and aims, or ideologists promoting their prestige and authority.[26]

It has been our intention in this volume to provide a wide array of perspectives, theories, and facts about contemporary youth gangs. In order to facilitate additional research, we have provided the reader with an extensive bibliography. It identifies both popular and scholarly analyses of gangs. In order to maximize the influence of social science knowledge in he policy-formation process, it will obviously be necessary to create accurate data bases dealing with gangs. While we have been critical about the role of social science research in the policy process, it is apparent that effective social programs must be based upon verifiable theories and concepts. Like any research endeavor, however, our volume raises as many questions as it answers.

Based upon the findings appearing in the numerous case studies and comparative analyses, there appear to be three general areas of research requiring further investigation. First, it is clear we need to understand more clearly the psychological factors that contribute to selected aspects of gang behavior. Drawing from the chapter examining wilding behavior, future researchers will need to identify and isolate the psychological variables differentiating youth who are and are not drawn into wilding behavior. We also need greater understanding of the individual and collective psychology associated with the wilding attact itself.

In the chapter by Pinderhughes, we are left with a desire to know more about the role of violence in creating group solidarity among gang members. We also need to know more about the role of violence in creating a sense of community within ethnic neighborhoods experiencing racial transition. While certain forms of intergroup violence among youth may assume ritualistic qualities in ethnic settlements, it remains unclear whether the larger adult community endorses the behavior as part of an effort to maintain neighborhood cohesion and reinforce territoriality.

The analysis of gang graffiti by Hutchison also reveals the importance of psychological variables to future research efforts. Symbols form a basis for group solidarity and cohesion. While we know that graffiti are part of the larger array of "colors" differentiating group membership, we know very little about the relationship between individual psychology and gang symbols. Wilding gangs apparently have no symbols associated with their behavior. Nor do the type of "near gangs" described by Pinderhughes. Symbolism and its psychological manifestations, however, seem clearly related to recruitment, cohesion, and group maintenance among established gangs. The dynamics of these relationships, however, remain unclear.

Second, the need to know more about the relationship between community structure and gangs is emphasized by several of our authors. In the opening chapter, Monti reviewed some of the early theories about gang structure and community organization. Later he examined this relationship in greater detail through comparative analysis of gangs in St. Louis. It seems apparent that we need to establish comparative data bases between cities detailing gang activity, behavior, organization, and structure. These data bases might make it possible to analyze gang activity according to city-wide and neighborhood characteristics.

The chapter by Skolnick, Bluthenthal, and Correl revealed the importance of gang structure to various forms of illegal enterprise. Given the increasing presence of drugs in inner-city neighborhoods, it is obviously important to know more about how gangs interface with the underground economy. It is also important to know more about how other community institutions interface with both the underground economy and the social organization of gangs. The research by Skolnick et al. underscores the central importance of community and neighborhood variables in the study of contemporary gangs and their activities, especially those related to deviant entrepreneurship.

Likewise, the analysis of Chicago schools by Hutchison and Kyle shows that community and neighborhood institutions are strongly influenced by gangs and their daily activities. It was clear that gangs exercised a seriously negative effect on the educational activities of students, teachers, and administrators. In fact, it appeared that the daily operations of the school itself were seriously undermined by the presence of gangs. We need to know more about how gangs affect other community institutions, and are related to the cluster of positive or negative forces eroding or enhancing the quality of life in many urban neighborhoods.

The chapter by Vigil shows that some gangs are based in established cultural and institutional traditions. His research shows that gangs differ between communities, and that cultural variables often exert a strong influence on how they are operated and organized. His research also reinforces the need to establish comparative data bases between cities and communities. We have accumulated enough case studies to entertain the possibility of creating a computerized information system that will help us better understand the relationship between community organization, gang structure, and gang activities.

Third, the central importance of underclass theory is revealed in many of our chapters. Moore maintains that any new research on gang violence and drugs must take into account variations in the development of the local underclass, especially its relationship to the larger urban economy. While not directly referencing underclass theory, Hutchison and Kyle show its importance to contemporary gangs. The problems studied by them appear to be part of the larger pattern of "social dislocations" identified by Wilson in his description of underclass community institutions. We need to know more about these larger patterns of "dislocations," and how gang activity contributes to them.

The chapter by Padilla also reinforces the centrality of underclass theory. Working gangs have surely adapted to the absence of economic opportunities found in many urban communities. Contrary to popular stereotypes, however, gang members engaging in illegal enterprises do not earn much money and remain marginal to the economic mainstream. Similar to the findings and observations of Moore, and Skolnick et al., the Padilla study shows we need to know more about how gangs adapt to the absence of opportunities created by downturns in a city's regional economy.

Our case studies and comparative analyses also have important ramifications for the policy options examined in our volume. Destro identifies the civil rights issues associated with the development of gang control strategies. While membership in a gang is clearly not illegal, popular conceptions about their activities sometimes compel public officials to risk violation of civil liberties during the enforcement process. On the other hand, some gangs do pose a serious threat to life and property in many urban neighborhoods, thereby justifying aggressive law enforcement. Accurate research dealing with gangs, therefore, is a critically important objective not only for the law enforcement community, but also for residents of inner-city neighborhoods, as well as those young people who are members of gangs.

Jackson's analysis of gang control legislation in California reinforces Monti's earlier observations that social policy dealing with gangs is largely based upon removal from the community and other forms of punitive intervention. Some California statutes reflect public hysteria about gangs, and appear to be influenced by the type of "moral panic" described by Moore. It is clear from Jackson's chapter that many states with serious gang problems opt for social control policies implemented through the criminal justice system. To the extent that gang activities are illegal, the problem is accurately and necessarily defined as a law enforcement issue. Public policies based solely upon social control premises, however, overlook the economic arguments stressed in our concluding chapter.

California is not alone in its unidimensional approach to gang control. Spergel and Curry recently compared public policy toward gangs in forty-five American cities. They report that: ". . . suppression and social intervention were the most prevalent strategies used by agencies and cities in addressing the problem."[27] Despite the popularity of the social control approach, however, their data showed that ". . . strategies of community organization and opportunities were associated clearly and strongly with perceptions of agency effectiveness in addressing the problem."[28] While the research conducted by Spergel and Curry examined only perceptions of program success or failure, the significance of the economic and other opportunity variables only reinforces many of the policy arguments made in this concluding chapter.

As Mills contends, theoretical knowledge, facts, and data bases often have little to do with the creation of effective public policy. The evidence and arguments appearing in this volume support the conclusion that without a fundamental alteration in the distribution of economic opportunities in urban America, we are not likely to see a decrease in the magnitude of the gang problem. In this regard, we are inclined to agree with William Wilson when he observes that contemporary urban problems are not necessarily sustained by the same patterns of inequality found in the past. Public policies designed to eliminate discrimination and guarantee civil rights for all citizens do not necessarily assure material improvements in the quality of urban life or the creation of jobs and tangible opportunities.

As America's cities gradually move toward a postindustrial urban economy, we are inclined to argue that policies designed to stimulate economic development, employment, and training will probably have more impact on the future of the underclass than other policy initiatives. The gang problem is no exception. National economic development strategies must deliberately enfranchise the diverse groups and constituencies living without hope in many inner-city neighborhoods. Securing a more stable future for those born into the nation's urban underclass will require a national development policy capable of competing with the financial and psychological rewards that lure many young Americans into urban gangs.

NOTES

1. E. S. Savas, *Privatizing the Public Sector* (Chatham, N.J.: Chatham House Publishers, Inc., 1982).

2. C. Ronald Huff, "Two Generations of Gang Research," in *Gangs in America*, ed. C. Ronald Huff (Newburry Park, Calif.: Sage Publishers, 1990), pp. 24-34.

3. Leslie Inniss and Joe R. Feagin, "The Black Underclass Ideology in Race Relations Analysis," *Social Justice* 16 (4): 13-34.

4. Ibid.; Huff, *Gangs in America*.

5. William Wilson, *The Truly Disadvantaged* (Chicago: University of Chicago Press, 1987), pp. 5-8.

6. Fritz Malchup, *Knowledge: Its Creation, Distribution, and Economic Significance* (Princeton, N.J.: Princeton University Press, 1980), p. 9.

7. Daryl Chubin and James L. McCartney, "Financing Sociological Research: A Future Only Dimly Perceived," the *American Sociologist* 17 (November 1982): pp. 226-35.

8. Malchup, *Knowledge: Its Creation*.

9. Chubin and McCartney, "Financing Sociological Research," p. 233.

10. Sar Levitan and Robert Taggart, *The Promise of Greatness* (Cambridge, Mass.: Harvard University Press, 1976).

11. Walter B. Miller, "Why the United States Has Failed to Solve Its Youth Gang Problem," in *Gangs in America*, ed. Huff, p. 274.

12. Ibid., p. 276.

13. Ibid., p. 283.

14. Huff, "Two Generations of Gang Research."

15. Barry Bluestone and Bennett Harrison, *The Deindustrialization of America* (New York: Basic Books, 1982).

16. James O'Connor, *The Fiscal Crisis of the State* (New York: St. Martin's Press, 1973).

17. Wilson, *The Truly Disadvantaged*, p. 11.

18. John M. Hagedorn, *People and Folks* (Chicago: Lake View Press, 1988), p. 111.

19. Scott Cummings and Michael Price, "Race Relations in Louisville: Southern Racial Traditions and Northern Class Dynamics." Policy Paper Series, No. 1 (Louisville, Ky.: Urban Research Institute, 1990), pp. 1-38.

20. John Kararda, "Jobs and the Underclass in Large and Mid-size Metropolitan Areas" (Paper presented at the conference New Perspectives on Racial Issues, Robert LaFollette Institute of Public Affairs, University of Wisconsin, Madison, June 1-3, 1990).

21. National Interreligious Commission on Civil Rights, *A Tale of Two Cities: The Status of Civil Rights in Louisville* (Louisville, Ky.: The Kentuckiana Interfaith Community, 1988).

22. Ibid.

23. Department of Health Services, Kentucky, *Annual Vital Statistics Report* (Frankfort, Ky.: Cabinet for Human Resources, 1988).

24. Hagedorn, *People and Folks*, p. 128.

25. Ibid.

26. C. Wright Mills, *The Sociological Imagination* (New York: Oxford University Press, 1959), p. 193.

27. Irving A. Spergel and G. David Curry, "Strategies and Perceived Agency Effectiveness in Dealing with the Youth Gang Problem," in *Gangs in America*, ed. Huff, p. 308.

28. Ibid.

Contributors

RICKY BLUTHENTHAL is a graduate student in the Department of Sociology, University of California, Berkeley.

THEODORE CORREL is working toward two degrees: a J.D. from Boalt Hall, and a Ph.D. from the Jurisprudence and Social Policy Program, University of California, Berkeley.

SCOTT CUMMINGS is Professor of Urban Policy at the University of Louisville. He has written several books dealing with urban development politics, intergroup relations, and minority business enterprise. Author of numerous articles and book chapters, Dr. Cummings also serves as the Editor of the Journal of Urban Affairs.

ROBERT A. DESTRO is an Associate Professor of Law at the Catholic University of America. He is also the Director of the University's interdisciplinary Program in Law and Religion. Mr. Destro served as a Commissioner on the U.S. Commission on Civil Rights from 1983-89. Prior to joining the faculty at Catholic University in 1982, Mr. Destro was General Counsel for the Catholic League for Religious and Civil Rights from 1977 to 1982. He has authored publications and manuscripts that have appeared in major law journals and other publications dealing with constitutional law, religious freedom and the rights of those with disabilities.

RAY HUTCHISON is chair of the sociology program and Associate Professor of Urban and Public Affairs at the University of Wisconsin-Green Bay. His research interests are in the areas of race and ethnic relation and urban sociology, with a particular emphasis on the Asian American and Hispanic American population in the midwest. In 1989 he was the recipient of the UW-System Faculty Research Scholar Award from the Institute on Race and Ethnicity for his research on the Hmong community in Green Bay and northeast Wisconsin. He also is series editor of *Research in Urban Sociology (JAI Press)*.

PATRICK G. JACKSON is an Associate Professor of Criminal Justice Administration at Sonoma State University. He has published a book on parole supervision *The Paradox of Control: Parole Supervision of Youthful Offenders* and numerous articles and book chapters on theories about gangs, the role of defense counsel in the disposition of felony cases, the uses of jails, pretrial preventive detention, arson and other issues in such journals as *Criminology*, the *British Journal of Criminology*, *Rutgers Law Review* and others. He is presently conducting a study of inmate and staff responses to a new generation jail in northern California.

CHARLES KYLE has a Ph.D. in Sociology from Northwestern University and is presently Assistant to the President of Triton College in River Grove, Illinois. He is finishing a study of the educational histories of incarcerated juveniles and has done numerous studies on the Chicago Public Schools which were sponsored by governmental agencies and are available from ERIC. His research interest include Hispanics, urban education, youth at risk, and migrant workers. He has co-authored with Edward Kantowicz a forth coming book titled: *Kids First—Primero Los Ninos: Chicago Public School Reform in the 1980's*. His most recent publications are "The Magnitude of and Reasons for Chicago's Hispanic Drop-out Problem: A Case Study of two Chicago Public Schools" in the *Renato Rosaldo Lecture Monograph Series* of the Mexican American Studies and Research Center of the University of Arizona, Vol. 6, Series 19881989 and co-authored with Edward Kantowicz an article titled "Bogus Statistics: Chicago's Latino Community Exposes the Dropout Problem" in *Latino Studies Journal* of DePaul University in Chicago, Illinois, Vol. 2, No.2, May, 1991.

DANIEL J. MONTI is Associate Professor of Sociology and Urban Studies at Boston University. He is the author of *A Semblance of Justice* which deals with school desegregation and *Race, Redevelopment and the New Company Town* which deals with public-private partnerships and the rebuilding of inner-city neighborhoods. He also has written several dozen articles on subjects that include public housing, civil unrest, and educational reform.

JOAN MOORE is a professor of Sociology at the University of Wisconsin Milwaukee. She has worked for a number of years on a series of studies of East Los Angeles gangs. *Homeboys* (1978) and *Going Down to the Barrio* (1991) reflect those experiences. In addition, she has been concerned with the relevance of theories of poverty to Latino communities, co-editing a volume of studies of poverty communities tentatively titled *Beyond the Underclass Debate*.

FELIX M. PADILLA is Associate Professor of Sociology, Director of the Center for Latino Research, and Editor of the Latino Studies Journal, DePaul University in Chicago, Illinois. He has written extensively on the relationship involving various Latino group which leads to the creation of wide-scale bond referred to as Latino Ethnic Consciousness. He also has done work on the topic of the Sociology of Salsa Music. And more recently, the emphasis of his work has been the youth gang. His major publications include: *Latino Ethnic Consciousness* (Notre Dame University Press, 1985); *Puerto Rican Chicago* (Notre Dame University Press, 1987); *The Youth Gang as an American Enterprise* (Rutgers University Press, 1992); and *Outside the Wall: The Life of a Prisoner's Wife* (Forthcoming).

HOWARD PINDERHUGHES is a President's Fellow at the University of California where he is engaged in research on the relationship between racial attitudes among youth and the rise in racial conflict. He is also a Research Associate at the Institute for the Study of Social Change. He received his Ph.D. in 1991 from the University of California at Berkeley.

CARY J. RUDMAN is a Principal Consultant for the California Assembly Office of Research, where he specializes in criminal and juvenile justice issues with particular attention to gang and drug problems. He has authored a number of reports through the Assembly Office of Research and published articles in *Crime and Delinquency*, *Journal of Criminal Law and Criminology* and others. He is interested in constitutional law issues in juvenile, criminal and civil justice and has played a significant role in the drafting of legislation in juvenile justice. His present work involves the creation of an Omnibus California Civil Rights Restoration Act.

JEROME H. SKOLNICK is a sociologist and Claire Clements Dean's Professor of Law (Jurisprudence and Social Policy Program), University of California, Berkeley.

JAMES DIEGO VIGIL is Professor of Anthropology and Director of the Center for Research on Urban Policy and Ethnicity at the University of Southern California in Los Angeles. Starting his career as a public school teacher he later pursued graduate study at UCLA and earned his M.A. and Ph.D. Following this interest in children and youth, especially adolescents, he began to examine some of the problems those groups encountered. These investigations have focused on schooling, street gangs and crime, ethno-history, and ethnic identity. Expanding this data base, he has recently honed a comparative perspective to include other ethnic minority youth's experiences. *Barrio Gangs* (University of Texas Press, 1988), *From Indians to Chicanos: The Dynamics of Mexican American Culture* (Waveland Press, 1984), and articles in such journals as *Social Problems, Human Organization, Aztlan, Ethos,* and *Places* are among some of his publications.

Selected Bibliography

BOOKS, BOOK CHAPTERS, DISSERTATIONS

Anderson, Elijah. (1990). *Streetwise: Race, Class, and Change in an Urban Community*. Chicago: University of Chicago Press.

Anti-Defamation League. (1988). *Young and Violent: The Gang Menace of America's Neo-Nazi Skinheads*. New York: Anti-Defamation League of B'nai B'rith/Civil Rights Division, October.

Asbury, Herbert. (1927). *Gangs of New York*. New York: Garden City Publishing Company.

Barker, George Carpenter. (1982) *Pachuco: An American-Spanish Argot and Its Social Functions in Tucson, Arizona*. Tucson: University of Arizona.

Bernstein, Saul. (1964). *Youth on the Streets Work with Alienated Youth Groups*. New York: Association Press.

Berntsen, Karen. (1979). "A Copenhagen Youth Gang: A Descriptive Analysis." In *New Paths in Criminology*, edited by Sarnoff A. Mednick, S. Giora Sloham, and Barbara Phillips. Lexington, Mass.: Lexington Books.

Bloch, Herbert Aaron and Arthur Niederhoffer. (1958). *The Gang: A Study in Adolescent Behavior*. New York: Philosophical Library.

Bordua, David J. (1962). "A Critique of Sociological Interpretations of Gang Delinquency." In *The Sociology of Crime and Delinquency*, Marvin E. Wolgang, Leonard Savitz, and Norman Johnston (eds.). New York: Wiley.

Bresler, Fenton. (1980). *The Chinese Mafia*. Briarcliff Manor, N.Y.: Stein and Day.

Brown, Walan Karl. (1976). *Gangways: An Expressive Culture Approach to Understanding Gang Delinquency*. Philadelphia: University of Pennsylvania.

Campbell, Anne. (1984). *The Girls in the Gang: A Report from New York City*. New York: Basil Blackwell.

Cartwright, D. S., B. Tomson, and H. Schwartz. (1975). *Gang Delinquency*. Calif.: Brooks/Cole Publishing Co.

Cloward, Richard A. and Lloyd Ohlin. (1960). *Delinquency and Opportunity: A Theory of Delinquent Gangs*. Glencoe, Ill.: Free Press.

Cohen, Albert K. (1955). *Delinquent Boys: The Culture of the Gang*. Glencoe, Ill.: Free Press.

Cohen, Bernard. (1969). "The Delinquency of Gangs and Spontaneous Groups." In *Delinquency: Selected Studies*, edited by Thorsten Sellin and Marvin E. Wolfgang. New York: Wiley.

Cohen, Stanley. (1972). *Folk Devils and Moral Panics: The Creation of the Mods and Rockers*. London: McGibbon and Kee.

Dolan, Edward F. and Shan Finney. (1984). *Youth Gangs*. New York: Julian Messner.

Downes, David M. (1966). *The Delinquent Solution: A Study in Subcultural Theory*. New York: Free Press.

Fong, Robert S. (1987). *A Comparative Study of the Organizational Aspects of Two Texas Prison Gangs: Texas Syndicate and Mexican Mafia*. Dissertation Abstracts International.

Galea, John. (1982). *Youth Gangs of New York*. New York: St. Martin's Press.

Gardner, Sandra. (1983). *Street Gangs*. New York: Franklin Watts.

Gonzalez, Alfred Guerra. (1981). "Mexicano/Chicano Gangs in Los Angeles: A Sociohistorical Case Study." Unpublished D.S.W. thesis, University of California Berkeley.

Hagedorn, John and Perry Macon. (1989). *People and Folks: Gangs, Crime, and the Underclass in a Rustbelt City*. Chicago: Lake View Press.

Harris, Mary Ginzel. (1983). "Mexican-American Girls and Gangs: A Social Psychological View. Dissertation, University of Southern California.

Hirschi, Travis. (1969). *Causes of Delinquency*. Berkeley: University of California Press.

Horowitz, Ruth. (1983). *Honor and the American Dream: Culture and Identity in a Chicano Community.* New Brunswick, N.J.: Rutgers University Press.

Huff, C. Ronald, ed. (1990). *Gangs in America.* Newbury Park: Sage Publications.

Ianni, Francis A. J. (1974). *Black Mafia: Ethnic Succession in Organized Crime.* New York: Simon and Schuster.

Kantor, David and William Ira Bennett. (1968). "Orientation of Street-Corner Workers and Their Effect on Gangs," in *Controlling Delinquents,* edited by Stanton Wheeler. New York: Wiley.

Keiser, R. Lincoln. (1979). *The Vice Lords: Warriors of the Streets.* New York: Holt, Rinehart and Winston.

Klein, Malcolm W. (1971). *Street Gangs and Street Workers.* Englewood Cliffs, N.J.: Prentice Hall.

Klein, Malcolm W. and Cheryl L. Maxson. (1987). "Street Gang Violence." In *Violent Crime, Violent Criminals,* edited by M. E. Wolfgang and N. Weiner. Beverly Hills, Calif.: Sage Publications.

Klein, Malcolm and Barbara G. Myerhoff. (1967). *Juvenile Gangs in Context: Theory, Research and Action.* Englewood Cliffs, N.J.: Prentice Hall, 1967.

Krisberg, Barry. (1975). *The Gang and the Community.* San Francisco: R and E Research Associates.

Kyle, Charles. (1984). "Los Preciosos: The Magnitude of and Reasons for the Hispanic Dropout Problem in Chicago: A Case Study of Two Chicago Public High Schools." Unpublished Ph.D. dissertation, Evanston, Ill., Northwestern University.

Ley, David. (1975). "The Street Gang in Its Milieu." In *The Social Economy of Cities,* edited by Gary Gappert and Harold M. Rose, pp. 247-73. Beverly Hills, Calif.: Sage Publications.

Liebow, Elliott. (1967). *Tally's Corner: A Study of Negro Streetcorner Men.* Boston: Little, Brown.

McGuire, Hilary. (1979). *Hopie and the Los Homes Gang: A Gangland Primary.* Phoenix: Alba Books.

MacLeod, Jay. (1987). *Ain't No Making It.* Boulder, Colo.: Westview Press.

Maxson, Cheryl L. (1983). "'Gangs' Why We Couldn't Stay Away." In *Evaluating Contemporary Juvenile Justice,* edited by James R. Kluegel. Beverly Hills: Sage Publications.

Maxson, Cheryl L. and Malcolm W. Klein. (1983). *Agency Versus Agency: Disputes in the Gang Deterrence Model.* In *Evaluating Contemporary Juvenile Justice,* edited by J. R. Kluegel. Beverly Hills: Sage Publications.

Maxson, Cheryl L. and Malcolm W. Klein. (1986). *Street Gangs Selling Cocaine: The Confluence of Two Social Problems*. Los Angeles: Social Science Research Institute, University of Southern California.

Merry, Sally. (1981). *Urban Danger*. Philadelphia, Pa.: Temple University Press.

Miller, W. B. (1969). "Lower Class Culture as a Generating Milieu of Gang Delinquency." In *Delinquency, Crime and Social Progress*, edited by D. Cressey and D. Ward, pp. 332-48. New York: Harper and Row.

——. (1974). "American Youth Gangs: Past and Present." In *Current Perspectives on Criminal Behavior*, by A. Blumberg. New York: Alfred A. Knopf.

——. (1976). "Youth Gangs in the Urban Crises Era." In *Delinquency, Crime and Society*, edited by James F. Short, Jr., pp. 91-128. Chicago: University of Chicago Press.

——. (1980). "Gangs, Groups, and Serious Youth Crime." In *Critical Issues in Juvenile Delinquency*, edited by D. Shichor and D. Kelly. Lexington: Lexington Books.

——. (1983). "Youth Gangs and Groups." In *Encyclopedia of Crime and Justice*, edited by Sanford H. Kadish. New York: Free Press.

Moore, Joan W., Robert Garcia, Carlos Garcia, Luis Cerda, Frank Valencia. (1978). *Homeboys: Gangs, Drugs, and Prison in the Barrios of Los Angeles*. Philadelphia: Temple University Press.

Morales, Armando. (1972). *Ando Sangrando: A Study of Mexican American-Police Conflict*. La Puente: Perspectiva Publications.

Muehlbauer, Gene. (1983). *The Losers: Gang Delinquency in an American Suburb*. New York: Praeger.

Patrick, James. (1973). *A Glasgow Gang Observed*. London: Eyre Methuen.

Perkins, Useni Eugene. (1987). *Explosion of Chicago's Black Street Gangs, 1900-Present*. Chicago: Third World Press.

Phelps, Roy David. (1988). *The History of the Eastside Dudes, a Black Social Club in Central Harlem, New York City, 1933-1985: An Exploration of Background Factors Related to Adult Criminality*. New York: Fordham University Press.

Poston, Richard W. (1971). *The Gang and the Establishment*. New York: Harper and Row.

Puffer, J. Adams. (1912). *The Boy and His Gang*. Boston: Houghton Mifflin Company.

Quicker, John C. (1983). *Homegirls*. San Pedro, Calif.: International Universities Press.

Ranker, Jess. (1957). *A Study of Juvenile Gangs in the Hollenbeck Area of Los Angeles*. (Unpublished Master's thesis, University of Southern California).

Robin, Gerald D. (1967). "Gang Member Delinquency in Philadelphia." In *Juvenile Gangs in Context: Theory, Research and Action*, edited by M. W. Klein and B. G. Myerhoff. Englewood Cliffs, N.J.: Prentice Hall.

Romo, Ricardo. (1983). *East Los Angeles: History of a Barrio, 1900-1930*. Austin: University of Texas Press.

Salisbury, Harrison Evans. (1958). *The Shook-Up Generation*. New York: Harper.

Shaw, C. R. (1930). *The Jack-Roller*. Chicago: University of Chicago Press.

Short, James F. (1975). "Gangs, Violence and Politics." In *Violence and Criminal Justice*, edited by Duncan Chappell and John Monahan. Lexington, Mass.: Lexington Books.

———. (1968). *Gang Delinquency and Delinquency Subcultures*. New York: Harper and Row.

———, ed. (1976). *Delinquency, Crime, and Society*. Chicago: University of Chicago Press.

———. (1976). "Gangs, Politics and the Social Order." In *Delinquency, Crime and Society*, edited by James F. Short, Jr. Chicago: University of Chicago Press.

Short, James F. and Fred Strodtbeck. (1965). *Group Processing and Gang Delinquency*. Chicago: University of Chicago Press.

Spergel, Irving. (1964). *Slumtown, Racketville, Haulburg*. Chicago: University of Chicago Press.

———. (1966). *Street Gang Work*. New York: Doubleday-Anchor Press.

———. (1966). *Street Gang Work: Theory and Practice*. Reading, Mass.: Addison-Wesley.

———. (1985). *Youth Gang Activity and the Chicago Public Schools*. Chicago: University of Chicago Press, School of Social Service Administration.

Spergel, Irving A. and G. David Curry. (1987). *Gangs, Schools and Communities*. Chicago: University of Chicago, School of Social Service Administration.

Stafford, Mark. (1984). "Gang Delinquency." In *Major Focus of Crime*, edited by Robert F. Meier. Beverly Hills: Sage Publications.

Suttles, Gerald. (1971). *The Social Order of the Slum*. Chicago: University of Chicago Press.

Taylor, Carl S. (1990). *Dangerous Society*. East Lansing: Michigan State University Press.

Tennyson, May A. (1967). "Family Structure and Delinquent Behavior." In *Juvenile Gangs in Context*, edited by M. W. Klein and B. G. Meyerhoff. Englewood Cliffs, N.J.: Prentice Hall.

Thrasher, F. (1927). *The Gang*. Chicago: University of Chicago Press.

Tilly, Charles. (1979). "Collective Violence in European Perspective." In *Violence in America*, edited by Hugh Graham and Ted R. Gurr. Beverly Hills: Sage Publications.

Tracy, Paul E. (1988). "Subcultural Delinquency: A Comparison of the Incidence of Gang and Nongang Member Offenses." In *From Boy to Man, From Delinquency to Crime*, edited by Marvin E. Wolfgang, Terrance P. Thornberry, and Robert M. Figlio. Chicago: University of Chicago Press.

Trostle, Lawrence Charles. (1987). *The Stoners: Drugs, Demons and Delinquency: A Descriptive and Empirical Analysis of Delinquent Behavior*. Dissertation Abstracts International, Ann Arbor, MI: The Humanities and Social Sciences.

Vigil, James Diego. (1988). *Barrio Gangs: Street Life and Identity in Southern California*. Austin: University of Texas Press.

―――. (1988). "Street Socialization, Locura Behavior, and Violence Among Chicano Gang Members." In *Violence and Homicide in Hispanic Communities*, edited by Jess Kraus and Armando Morales. Washington, D.C.: National Institute of Mental Health.

Weisheit, Ralph, ed. (1990). *Drugs, Crime and the Criminal Justice System*. Cincinnati: Anderson Publishing Company.

Werthman, Carl and Irving Piliavin. (1967). "Gang Members and the Police." In *The Police: Six Sociological Essays*, edited by David Bordua. New York: Wiley.

Whyte, William Foote. (1943). *Street Corner Society: The Social Structure of an Italian Slum*. Chicago: University of Chicago Press.

Williams, John, Eric Dunning, and Patrick Murphy. (1984). *Holligans Abroad*. London: Routledge and Kegan Paul.

Wolfgang, M. and F. Ferracuti. (1967). *The Subculture of Violence*. London: Tavistock.

Yablonsky, L. (1962). "The Delinquent Gang as a Near-Group." In *The Sociology of Crime and Delinquency*, edited by M. Wolfgang. New York: Wiley and Sons.

―――. (1963). *The Violent Gang*. New York: Macmillan.

MAGAZINES AND NEWSPAPERS

Allen, D. M. (1959, September). "Gangs of New York; Teen Gangs Elsewhere," *Newsweek* 54: 53-55.

Anderluh, Richard B. (1988, April 12). "Goldberg's Anti-Gang Proposal: A Task Force for Jobs and Recreation," *Los Angeles Herald Examiner*.

Associated Press. (1988), July 11). "Gangs Spark Fears," *Salem, Oregon Statesman-Journal*.

Baker, Bob. (1988, April 14). "Gang Murder Rates Get Worse," *Los Angeles Times*.

———. (1988, April 23). "Tough Boss Shows Gang Members New Way of Life," *Los Angeles Times*.

———. (1988, June 8). "Homeboys: Players in a Deadly Drama," *Los Angeles Times*.

Baker, Susan and Tipper Gore. (1989, May 29). "Some Reasons for Wilding," *Newsweek*, pp. 6-7.

Banks, K. (1985). "A Wave of Gang Violence (Vietnamese in Vancouver)," *Maclean's* 98: 50-51.

Barich, Bill. (1986, November). "The Crazy Life (Los Angeles County Youth Gangs)," *The New Yorker* 62: 97-98+.

Barko, N. (1960, September). "LENA and the Forty-Five Gangs," *Reporter* 23: 26-28.

Bernstein, Dan. (1980, June). "East L.A.'s Gang Project," *Corrections Magazine*, 36-42.

Bernstein, S. "No More Rumbles; Summary of Youth on the Streets," *Sr. Schol*, 83.

Berton, P. (1985). "A Crackdown on the Bikers (Motorcycle Gangs)," *Maclean's*, 98: 13.

Bing, Leon. (1988, August). "Reflections of a Gangbanger (Interview with Member of L.A. Gang)," *Harper's* 277: 26.

Bird, Brian. (1990, January). "Reclaiming the Urban War Zones," *Christianity Today* 34: 16-20.

Bolitho, W. (1930, February 1). "Psychosis of the Gang," *Survey* 63: 500-6.

———. (1930, March 1). "Gangster Traumatism," *Survey* 63: 661-65.

Bosc, Michael. (1984, July). "Street Gangs No Longer Just a Big City Problem (suburbs)," *U.S. News and World Reports* 97: 108-9.

Bowman, W. R. (1937, May). "Games or Gangs," *Review of Reviews* 95: 36-37.

Briseno, Olga. (1988, March). "Two 'Bloods' Say Jobs Would Put End to Gangs." *San Diego Union*.

Brower, Montgomery. (1988, May). "Gang Violence: Color It Real (Los Angeles)," *People Weekly* 29: 42-47.

Bruman, C. (1983). "Boat People in a New Land (Vietnamese Gangs)," *Maclean's* 96: 19.

Carney, Jay. (1986, August). "Sunbelt Import (Youth Gangs)," *Time* 128: 17.

Chambers, B. (1944, December 4). "Boy Gangs of New York: 500 Fighting Units," *New York Times Magazine*, 16+.

Chambers, B. (1946, April). "Juvenile Gangs of New York," *American Mercury* 62: 480-86.

Chambers, B. (1948, August). "Boy Gangs of Mousetown," *Reader's Digest* 53: 143-58.

Chason, W. (1954). "Teenage Gang from the Inside," *New York Times Magazine*, 17+.

Chaze, W. L. (1981). "Youth Gangs Are Back—On Old Turf and New," *U.S. News* 90: 46-47.

Daly, Michael. (1985, June). "Hunting the Wolf Packs (Transit Police Decoy Unit)," *New York* 18: 28-40.

DeMott, John S. (1985, December). "Have Gang, Will Travel," *Time* 126: 34.

Doyle, Brian. (1984, October). "The Streets According to Chief Crazy Lady (Sister A. Chunka's Work with Youth Gangs)," *U.S. Catholic* 49: 25-31.

Garland, P. (1967, August). "Gang Phenomenon: Big City Headache; Negro Youth Gangs," *Ebony* 22: 96+.

Gibbons, Sandi. (1988, April 12). "Half of Gang Cases Are Rejected," *Daily News*, Van Nuys, California.

Goldberg, Danny. (1988, March 15). "Curbing Liberties No Way to Fight the Gang Problem," *Los Angeles Herald Examiner*.

Gonzalez, D. L. (1988, October 24). "Drug Gangs: The Big Sweep," *Newsweek* 112: 26.

Gregor, Anne. (1989, May). "Death Among the Innocent (Gang Related Murders in Los Angeles)," *Maclean's* 102: 38.

Gunst, L. (1989). "Johnny-too-bad and the Sufferers (Jamaican Drug Posses)," *The Nation* 249: 549+.

Gwynne, S. C. (1990, April). "Up from the Streets (Gangs)," *Time* 135: 34.

Hackett, George and Michael A. Lerner. (1987, April). "L.A. Law," *Newsweek* 109: 35-36.

Haslanger, Phil. (1986, October). "A Rival to the Gangs (Milwaukee's centro de la comunidad unida)," *The Progressive* 50: 15.

Hedges, Stephen J. (1989, June). "When Drug Gangs Move to Nice Places," *U.S. News and World Report* 106: 42.

Hicks, Jerry. (1988, April 25). "D.A.'s New Special Prosecution Team Plans to Fight Gangs on Its Own Turf," *Los Angeles Times*.

Hoyt, F. C. (1920). "Gang in Embryo," *Scribners Magazine* 68: 146-54.

Hull, Jon D. (1987, August). "Life and Death with the Gangs (Los Angeles)," *Time* 130: 21-22.

Jones, S. V. (1954). "Cougars: Life with a Brooklyn Gang," *Harpers* 209: 35-43.

King, P. (1989). "A Snitch's Tale: The Killer Gang," *Newsweek* 114: 45.

Knap, Chris. (1988, March 18). "Proposed Prosecution Team Would Target County Gangs," *Orange County Register*. California.

Knapp, Elaine S. (1988). "Kids, Gangs and Drugs," *Embattled Youth*. Lexington, Ky.: The Council of State Governments, pp. 10-15.

Kunen, James S. (1989, May 22). "Madness in the Heart of the City," *People*, 107-11.

Lamar, Jacob V. (1988, April). "A Bloody West Coast Story (Crackdown on Street Gangs in Los Angeles)," *Time* 131: 32.

Leo, John. (1985, July). "Parasites on Their Own People (Immigrants)," *Time* 126: 76.

Lewis, Gregg. (1987, November). "The Insane Dragons Meet the Unknown Vice Lords (Youth for Christ's Work with Gangs in Chicago)," *Christianity Today* 31: 10+.

Lubow, A. "In a Deadly Explosion of Teenage Unhappiness, One Life is Cut Short, Another Blighted by Murder," *People Weekly* 23: 155-56.

McCarthy, T. J. (1943, June). "Report from Los Angeles: Zoot Suit Incident," *Commonwealth* 38: 243-44.

McClellan, H. (1929, March). "Boys, Gangs and Crime," *Review of Reviews* 79: 54-59.

McGarry, T. W. (1988, April 16). "Police Plan New Tactic to Curb Gangs," *Los Angeles Times*.

McGarry, T. W. and Steve Padilla. (1988, April 24). "Experts Warn Gang Sweeps May Have a Negative Effect," *Los Angeles Times*.

MacIver, R. M. (1962, June). "West Side Story: Moscow to Cairo," *Saturday Review* 45: 17-18.

McWilliams, C. (1943, June). "Zoot-Suit Riots," *New Republic* 108: 818-20.

McWilliams, C. (1950, June 10). "Nervous Los Angeles: Wolf-Pack Crusade; Juvenile Mexican American Delinquents," *Nation* 170: 570.

Mantz, H. J. (1950). "Audubon County Troublesome Gang," *Annals of Iowa* 30: 269.

Marsh, Peter and Anne Campbell. (1978, October 12). "The Youth Gangs of New York and Chicago Go into Business," *New Society*, 836, pp. 67-69.

Martin, J. B. (1943, September). "Polka-Dot Gang: Natural History of some Chicago Juvenile Criminals," *Harpers* 187: 356-64.

Mattick, Hans W., Frank Carney, and John Callaway. (1968). "Street Workers and Gangs," *Chicago Today* 5 (2): 34-38.

Maxwell, Joe. (1990, February). "YFC Worker Claims Police Harass Street Youth (G. McLean of Metro Chicago Youth for Christ)," *Christianity Today* 34: 42-43+.

Merina, Victor. (1988, April 27). "Anti-Gang Plan Would Put Officers in the Park," *Los Angeles Times*.

Miller, A. (1962, November). "Bored and the Violent; Adolescent Gangs, New York, Liningrad, Tokyo," *Harpers* 225: 50-52.

Miller, W. (1977, May). "Rumble This Time," *Psychology Today* 10 (12): 52.

———. (1982). "Youth Gangs: A Look at the Numbers," *Child Today* 11: 10-11.

Miller, Walter B. (1973, November/December). "Race, Sex and Gangs: The Molls," *Trans-Action* 11, (1): 32-35.

Monroe, S. (1981, January 1). "Gangs of Chicago," *Newsweek* 97: 88.

———. (1990, July 16). "Complaints About a Crackdown," *Time* 136: 20+.

Moore, Joan W. (1978, April 17). "Cooking Gang Statistics," *Los Angeles Herald Examiner*.

Morganthau, T. (1982). "Vietnamese Gangs in California," *Newsweek* 100: 22.

Moses, K. and K. Willenson. (1981). "Japanese Graffiti," *Newsweek* 98: 58.

Murphy, S. (1978). "Year with the Gangs of East Los Angeles: Interviews with Female Members," *Ms* 7: 56-64.

Murr, Andrew. (1990, May). "When Gangs Meet the Handicapped (Social Work Program in Bellflower, California)," *Newsweek* 115: 70.

Neill, S. B. (1978, January). "Violence and Vandalism: Dimensions and Correctives," *Phi Delta Kappan* 59: 302-7.

Noah, T. (1981). "Jimmy's Big Brothers (J. Griffin's Erroneous Account of Blood Brothers Black Gang in the *New York Times*)," *New Republic* 184: 14-16.

Oliver, Gordon. (1988, June 24). "Police Chief Works on Anti-Gang Strategy," *The Oregonian*, Portland, Oregon.

O'Reilly, J. and B. W. Cate. (1981, August). "Combat at Hollywood and Vine," *Time* 118: 27.

Overend, William. (1988, October 20). "New LAPD Tally May Cut Gang Killing Score," *Los Angeles Times*.

Pearl, Janet A. (1988). "Former Gang Members Earn Cash, Self-Respect," *Columbus Dispatch*, Columbus, Ohio.

Pinkerton, J. P. (1990, August). "East Side Story," *The American Spectator* 23: 24-25.

Rebelo, Kristina. (1990, May). "You See a Red Rag, Shoot (Interview with M. B. Green)," *Sports Illustrated* 72: 46.

Recktenwald, William and Nathaniel Sheppard. (1984). "Gangs: Chicago," *Chicago Tribune* (collection of five articles in special publication), January 8-12.

Redl, F. (1943, October). "Zoot Suits: An Interpretation," *Survey* 79: 259-62.

Reinhold, Robert. (1988, May 22). "In the Middle of L.A.'s Gang Warfare," *New York Times Magazine*, 30-33, 66-74.

Robbins, William. (1988, November 25). "Armed, Sophisticated and Violent, Two Drug Gangs Blanket Nation," *New York Times*.

Sager, Mike. (1988, September). "Death in Venice (Effect of Crack on Gangs in Venice, California)," *Rolling Stone*, 64-68+.

Salmans, S. and J. Dotson. (1975, July). "Return of the Youth Gangs," *Newsweek* 86 (3): 20.

Sample, Herbert A. (1988, April 20). "Brown Urges State Assault on Gangs," *Bee Capitol Bureau*, Sacramento, Calif.

Samuels, G. (1960, July). "Tangled Problem of the Gang Girl," *New York Times Magazine*, 13+.

Sandoval, Frances and S. Kanfer. (1989). "Mothers Against Gangs Organization," *People Weekly*, 32 (Fall): 126.

Schwartz, Bob. (1988, March 8). "Santa Ana OKs School Anti-Gang Pilot Project," *Los Angeles Times*.

Shapiro, W. (1985). "Kids Who Kill," *Newsweek* 106: 55.

Shorris, Earl. (1989, December). "The Priest Who Loves Gangsters (Mission for Gang Members Run by G. J. Boyle)," *The Nation* 249: 737.

Shumach, M. (1956, September). "Teenage Gang, Who and Why?," *New York Times Magazine*, pp. 7+ (Sept. 2), discussion on pp. 6+ (Sept. 16), pp. 6+ (Sept. 23).

Smith, A. Wilson. (1989). "Gang Warfare, Soviet-style," *Maclean's* 102: 44.

Smith, H. J. (1925, June 6). "Two Little Barons of the Valley," *Colliers* 75: 8-9.

Smith, S. J. (1976, June). "Ex-street Gang Hood, Now on the Bench, Urges a Better Deal for Juvenile Offenders," *People* 5 (25): 62.

Stanley, A. (1990, June 18). "All Ganged Up," *Time* 135: 50-52.

Starr, Mark. (1985, January). "Chicago's Gang Warfare," *Newsweek* 105: 32.

Starr, Mark and S. McGuire. (1981). "Do the Bandidos Fit Their Name?" *Newsweek* 98: 49.

Stitt, T. (1946, June). "Juvenile Gangs of New York: Reply," *American Mercury* 62: 762.

Stover, Del. (1987, February). "Dealing with Youth Gangs in the Schools," *The Education Digest* 52: 30-33.

Strassman, Nell. (1988, June 17). "Parents Battle Gangs on Westside," *Long Beach Press Telegram*, Long Beach, California.

Sudo, Philip. (1989, November). "Turf Wars (Drug Gangs)," *Scholastic Update* (Teachers' edition) 122: 6.

Sullivan, Randall. (1986, August). "Leader of the Pack (Murder of L.A. Youth Gang Member M. Miller)," *Rolling Stone*, 50-52+.

Thomas, Mary. (1990, May). "Isaiah Thomas' Mother Tells . . . How to Save Inner-City Children from Gangs," *Ebony* 45: 29-30.

Thrasher, F. M. (1926, October 15). "Gang," *Survey* 57: 71-74.

———. (1939, July). "Juvenile Gangs and Crime," *Current History* 50: 43-44.

Traub, J. (1987, April 5). "The Lords of Hell's Kitchen," *New York Times Magazine*, 38+.

Tuck, R. D. (1943, August). "Behind the Zoot Suit Riots: Los Angeles and Its Mexicans," *Survey G* 32: 313-16.

Waldron, W. (1940, March). "Gang Goes Uphill: Story of Hill City Municipality of Negro Youth in Pittsburgh's Harlem," *Survey Graphic* 29: 182-85.

Walker, L. A. (1982). "Vanilla Fires," *People Weekly* 18: 24-29.

Wallace, Bill. (1988, April 20). "Explosion of Street Gangs," *San Francisco Chronicle*.

Watson, G. (1990, January). "Gangs Put $5,000 Bounty on Drug Activist's Life," *Jet* 77: 38.

Weinstein, B. (1980, March). "Portrait of Street Gang (Brooklyn Youth Gangs)," *Sr. Scholar* 112: 14-16.

Wiessler, D. A. (1982). "Motorcycle Gangs Go Gray Flannel," *U.S. News and World Report* 93: 65.

Will, George F. (1988, March). "A West Coast Story (Urban Gangs)," *Newsweek* 111: 76.

———. (1990, July 30). "America's Slide into the Sewers," *Newsweek*, p. 64.

Willis, Paul. (1973, March 29). "The Triple-X Boys," *New Society* 23, 693-95.

Willwerth, James. (1990, February). "Fighting the Code of Silence (R. Rodriguez Battles Gangs in Santa Ana, California)," *Time* 135: 59.

Yablonsky, L. (1960, August). "Violent Gang," *Commentary* 30: 125-30.

———. (1966, January 22). "Watch Out Whitey; Negro Youth Gangs and Violence," *New Republic* 154: 29-30, 37-38.

Zing, D. (1955, August 23). "Teenage Gang from the Inside," *Look* 19: 32-37.

(1928, April 21). "Curing Bad Gangs with Better Ones," *Literary Digest* 97: 30.

(1933, April 8). "Gangs without Gangsters," *Literary Digest* 115: 14.

(1937, May). "Busting Gangs as They Blossom," *Literary Digest* 123: 19-20.

(1943, June). "Zoot-Suit Riots; 125 Hurt in Los Angeles Fights," *Life* 14: 30-31.

(1943, June). "Zoot Suits and Service Stripes: Race Tension behind the Riots," *Newsweek* 21: 35-36.

(1943, June). "Zoot Suit War," *Time* 41: 18.

(1943, June 19). "Zoot Suit Epidemic Movement Widely Scattered Over the United States without an Official Organization," *Science News Letter* 43: 388.

(1943, June 23). "Portent of Storm: Los Angeles Zoot Suit Riots," *Christian Cent.* 60: 735-36.

(1948, November 1). "Harlem Gang Leader," *Life* 25: 96-104.

(1952, November 24). "Gentlemen Hoodlums: Nazi Storm Trooper's Club," *Newsweek* 40: 27.

(1953, September). "Gangs Ruled this Neighborhood Until a College Stepped In," *Ladies Home Journal* 70: 28+.

(1955, May 16). "Problem Grows Worse; What to Do When Kids Shoot Down Kids?" *Newsweek* 45: 32-34.

(1955, November 19). "Boys Join Gangs Because Love from Father Is Lacking," *Science News Letter* 68: 326.

(1959, September). "Sportsmen vs. Forsyths: The Frightful Aftermath," *Life* 47: 36-38.

(1961, January). "Gangs Poorly Organized," *Science Newsletter*, 79: 4.

(1964). "It's Better than Beating Up Old Ladies with Bicycle Chains; Merseyside Gangs in Liverpool Turn to Rock n' Roll," *Time* 83: 73.

(1964, May). "Report of a Harlem Gang that Preys on Whites," *U.S. News* 56: 10.

(1967, October). "James Gang Rides Again; Mission Rebels of San Francisco," *Time* 90: 31.

(1973, April). "Los Angeles: Street Crime and Youth Gangs," *Black Enterprise*, 21.

(1973, July). "Return of the Gang," *Time* 102 (4): 31B.

(1973, September). "With Youth-Gang Violence on the Rise," *U.S. News* (12): 61.

(1975, June). "Portrait of a Gang Leader," *Time* 105 (27): 12.

(1975, July). "Street Gangs Turn from "Rumbles" to Wanton Crime," *U.S. News* 79 (1): 15.

(1978, September 9). "City Will Use Computer in War on Teen Gangs," *Arizona Republic*, B1-2.

(1979, August). "Chicano Response: The Youth Gang Controversy," *Phoenix Magazine*, 152-57.

(1979, August). "Youth Gangs: They're Back, Growing Worse," *U.S. News* 87: 46.

(1979, November 28). "Gangs Proliferate," *Tucson Citizen*.

(1980, June 18). "Teen-age Gangs: Will Phoenix Surrender or Battle Punks?" *Arizona Republic*, A6.

(1981, October 17). "Police Chief Calls for Greater Efort to Thwart Gangs," *Arizona Republic*, D5.

(1983, January 19). "Mi barrio," *Phoenix Gazette*, MB1-24.

(1983, October). "You Can Only Take So Much (J. Hawkins Fights Back Against Criminals in Watts)," *Time* 122: 32.

(1984, April). "Priest Threatens to Expel Pupils Involved in Gangs (G. Clements of Holy Angels School, Chicago)," *Jet* 66: 30.

(1984, September). "Member of L.A. Family Embroiled in Gang Feud to Stand Trial for Murder (Case of J. Hawkins, Jr.)," *Jet* 66: 27.

(1984, November). "L.A. Moves to Halt Gang Killing Spree in City," *Jet* 67: 30.

(1986, February). "Gangs That Rival the Mob," *U.S. News and World Report* 100: 29.

(1986, November). "Chicago to Kaddafi: Let's Get Together (El Rukin Gang Members Charged with Conspiring to Commit Terrorist Acts in the U.S. on Behalf of Libya)," *Newsweek* 108: 31.

(1988, January). "Ethnic Gangs and Organized Crime," *U.S. News and World Report* 104: 29-31+.

(1988, March). "The Drug Gangs," *Newsweek* 111: 20-25+.

(1988, April). "Street Sweepers (Police Raids on Los Angeles Gangs)," *U.S. News and World Report* 104: 14.

(1988, April 25). "Gangs: Will Life Imitate a Movie (*Colors*)," *Newsweek* 111: 25.

(1988, May). "We Tip Holds Carwash Proceeds to Benefit Gang Violence Fund," *Los Angeles Times*, January 15.

(1989, March). "When You're a Crip (or a Blood) (discussion with L.A. Gang Members)," *Harper's* 278: 51-59.

(1989, May). "Gang Terror," *Maclean's* 102: 2, 36-42+.

(1990, May). "Gangs and Supergangs," *New Dimensions* 4 (special issue): 20-45.

JOURNALS

Adams, Stuart. (1967). "A Cost Approach to the Assessment of Gang Rehabilitation Techniques," *Journal of Research in Crime and Delinquency* 4 (1) January: 166-82.

Adler, Peter, Carlos Ovando, and Dennis Hocevar. (1984). "Familiar Correlates of Gang Membership: An Exploratory Study of Mexican American Youth," *Journal of Behavioral Sciences*, 6: 65-76.

Amandes, Richard B. (1979). "Hire a Gang Leader: A Delinquency Prevention Program That Works," *Juvenile and Family Court Journal* 30: 37-40.

Bensinger, G. J. (1984). "Chicago Youth Gangs: A New Old Problem," *Journal of Crime and Justice* 7: 1-16.

Bloch, H. A. (1963, May). "Juvenile Gang; A Cultural Reflex," *Ann Am Acad* 347: 20-29.

Bogardus, Emory S. (1943). "Gangs of Mexican American Youth," *Sociology and Social Research* 28: 55-56.

Bookin-Weiner, Hedy, and Ruth Horowitz. (1983). "The End of the Youth Gang: Fad or Fact?," *Criminology* 21: 585-602.

Bowker, Lee H., Helen Shimota Gross, and Malcolm W. Klein. (1980). "Female Participation in Delinquent Gang Activity," *Adolescence* 15 (Fall): 509-19.

Bowker, Lee H. and Malcolm W. Klein. (1983). "The Etiology of Female Juvenile Delinquency and Gang Membership: A Test of Psychological and Social Structural Explanations," *Adolescence*, 72, winter, pp. 739-51.

Breen, Lawrence and Martin M. Allen. (1983). "Gang Behavior: Psychological and Law Enforcement Implications," *FBI Law Enforcement Bulletin* 52: 19-24.

Brown, Walan K. (1977). "Black Female Gangs in Philadelphia," *International Journal of Offender Therapy and Comparative Criminology* 21 (3): 221-28.

——. (1978). "Black Gangs as Family Extensions," *International Journal of Offender Therapy and Comparative Criminology* 22 (1): 39-45.

————. (1978). "Graffiti, Identity and the Delinquent Gang," *International Journal of Offender Therapy and Comparative Criminology* 22 (1): 46-48.

Burns, Edward and Thomas J. Deakin. (1989). "A New Investigative Approach to Youth Gangs," *FBI Law Enforcement Bulletin* 58: 20-24.

Campbell, Anne. (1984). "Girls' Talk: The Social Representation of Aggression by Female Gang Members," *Criminal Justice and Behavior* 11: 139-56.

————. (1987). "Self Definition by Rejection: The History of Gang Girls," *Social Problems* 34: 451-66.

Campbell, Anne, Steven Munce, and John Galea. (1982). "American Gangs and British Subcultures," *International Journal of Offender Therapy and Comparative Criminology* 26: 76-89.

Cartwright, Desmond S. (1966). "Multivariate Analysis of Gang Delinquency: I. Ecological Influence," *Multivariate Behavioral Research* 1 (3): 321-37.

Cartwright, Desmond S., Kenneth I. Howard, and Nicholas A. Reuterman. (1970). "Multivariate Analysis of Gang Delinquency: II. Structural and Dynamic Properties of Gangs," *Multivariate Behavioral Research* 5 (3): 303-23.

————. (1980). "Multivariate Analysis of Gang Delinquency: IV. Personality Factors in Gangs and Clubs," *Multivariate Behavioral Research* 15 (1): 3-22.

Cattalini, Gina. (1988). "Youth Gangs: Breaking the Cycle of Failure," *Youth Policy* (April/May): 25-26.

Chambliss, William J. (1973). "The Saints and the Roughnecks," *Society* 11: 24-31.

Cohen, A. K. (1955). "Research in Delinquent Subcultures," *Journal of Social Issues* 14: 20-37.

Curry, G. David and Irving A. Spergel. (1988). "Gang Homicide, Delinquency, and Community," *Criminology* 26: 381-405.

Daniels, S. (1987). "Prison Gangs: Confronting the Threat," *Corrections Today* 49: 66.

Dapson, L. A. (1938). "Loomis Gang," *New York History* 19: 269.

Davis, Mike and Sue Ruddick. (1988). "War in the Streets (Black Gangs)," *New Statesman and Society* 1: 27-30.

Derico, Major Julius. (1988, March 9). "The Emergence of Youth Gangs in the Metropolitan Atlanta Area, Paper presented to U.S. House Select Committee on Children," *Youth and Family*.

Engel, S. W. (1973). "Psychotherapy with German Gang-boys," *International Journal of Offender Therapy and Comparative Criminology* 17 (3): 250-60.

Erlanger, Howard S. (1979). "Estrangement, Machismo and Gang Violence," *Social Science Quarterly* 60: 235-48.

Fagan, Jeffrey. (1989). "The Social Organization of Drug Use and Drug Dealing Among Urban Gangs," *Criminology* 27: 633-69.

Fattah, David. (1987). "The House of Umoja as a Case Study for Social Change," *The Annals of the American Academy of Political and Social Science* 494: 37-41.

Fields, Allen. (1984). "Weedslingers: A Study of Young Black Marijuana Dealers," *Urban Life* 13: 247-70.

Finestone, H. (1957). "Cats, Kicks and Colour," *Social Problems* 5: 3-13.

Fox, Jerry R. (1985). "Mission Impossible? Social Work Practice with Black Urban Youth Gangs," *Social Work* 30: 25-31.

Friedman, C. J., Frederika Mann, and Albert S. Friedman. (1973). "A Profile of Juvenile Street Gang Members," *Adolescence* 11: 527-33.

Friedman, Jack C., Fredrica Mann, and Howard Adelman. (1976). "Juvenile Street Gangs: The Victimization of Youth," *Adolescence* 11, 44, Winter 527-533.

Gandy, John M. (1959). "Preventive Work with Street Corner Groups: The Hyde Park Youth Project, Chicago," *Annals of the American Academy of Political and Social Sciences*, p. 322.

Gannon, Thomas M. (1967). "Dimensions of Current Gang Delinquency," *Journal of Research in Crime and Delinquency* 4: 119-31.

Gerrard, Nathan L. (1964). "The Core Member of the Gang," *British Journal of Criminology* 4: 361-71.

Giordano, Peggy C. (1978). "Girls, Guys and Gangs: The Changing Nature of Female Delinquency," *The Journal of Criminal Law and Criminology* 69: 126-32.

Gordon, Robert A. (1967). "Social Level, Disability and Gang Interaction," *American Journal of Sociology* 73: 42-62.

Gorn, Elliot J. (1987). "Good-Bye Boys, I Die a True American": Homicide, Nativism, and Working-Class Culture in Antebellum New York City," *The Journal of American History* 74: 388-410.

Greeley, Andrew and James Casey. (1963). "An Upper Middle Class Deviant Gang," *The American Catholic Sociological Review* 24: 33-41.

Gross, Helen S. and Malcolm W. Klein. (1980). "Female Participation in Delinquent Gang Activities," *Adolescence* 15: 509-19.

Hardman, Dale G. (1967). "Historical Perspectives of Gang Research," *Journal of Research in Crime and Delinquency* 4 (1) (January): 5-27.

———. (1969). "Small Town Gangs," *Journal of Criminal Law* 60 (2) (June): 173-81.

Harrison, Faye V. (1988). "The Politics of the Social Outlaw in Urban Jamaica," *Urban Anthropology and Studies of Cultural Systems and World Economic Development* 17: 259-77.

Helmreich, William B. (1973). "Black Crusaders: The Rise and Fall of Political Gangs," *Society* 11 (1): 44-50.

———. (1973). "Race, Sex and Gangs: Black Crusaders: The Rise and Fall of Political Gangs," *Trans-Action* 11 (1): 44-50.

Hindelang, Michael J. (1976). "With a Little Help from Their Friends: Group Participation in Reported Delinquent Behavior," *The British Journal of Criminology* 16: 109-25.

Hoben, J. B. (1941). "Loomis Gang," *New York History* 22: 437.

Hopper, Columbus B. and Johnny Moore. (1983). "Hell on Wheels: The Outlaw Motorcycle Gangs," *Journal of American Culture* 6 (2) (summer): 58-64.

Horowitz, Ruth. (1982). "Adult Delinquent Gangs in a Chicano Community: Masked Intimacy and Marginality," *Urban Life* 3-26.

———. (1986). "Remaining an Outsider: Membership as a Threat to Research Rapport," *Urban Life*, January, pp. 409-30.

———. (1987). "Community Tolerance of Gang Violence," *Social Problems* 34: 437-50.

Horowitz, Ruth and Gary Schwartz. (1974). "Honor, Normative Ambiguity and Gang Violence," *American Sociological Review* 39: 238-51.

Huff, C. Ronald. (1989). "Youth Gangs and Public Policy (Cleveland and Columbus, Ohio)," *Crime and Delinquency* 35: 524-37.

Jacobs, James B. (1974). "Street Gangs Behind Bars," *Social Problems* 21 (3): 395-4090.

Joe, D. and N. Robinson. (1980). "Chinatown's Immigrant Gangs: The New Young Warrior Class," *Criminology* 18: 337-45.

Johnstone, John W. C. (1981). "Youth Gangs and Black Suburbs," *Pacific Sociological Review* 24 (3): 355-75.

———. (1983). "Recruitment to a Youth Gang," *Youth and Society*, 281-300.

Karacki, Larry and Jackson Toby. (1962). "The Uncommitted Adolescent: Candidate for Gang Socialization," *Sociological Inquiry* 32: 203-15.

Katz, Jack. (1989). "Youth Violence—A Special Kind of Addiction," *Human Rights* 16: 20-23+.

Klein, Julius and Derek L. Phillips. (1968). "From Hard to Soft Drugs: Temporal and Substantive Changes in Drug Usage Among Gangs in a Working-Class Community," *Journal of Health and Social Behavior* 9 (2) (June): 139-45.

Klein, Malcolm W. (1965). "Juvenile Gangs, Police, and Detached Workers: Controversies About Intervention," *Social Service Review* 39 (2) (June): 183-90.

———. (1966). "Factors Related to Juvenile Gang Membership Patterns," *Sociology and Social Research* 51: 49-62.

———. (1968). "Impressions of Juvenile Gang Members," *Adolescence* 3 (9) (spring): 53-78.

Klein, Malcolm W., Margaret A. Gordon, Cheryl L. Maxon. (1986). "The Impact of Police Investigations on Police-Repoted Rates of Gang and Non-Gang Homicides," *Criminology* 24: 489-512.

Klein, Malcolm and Lois Y. Crawford. (1967). "Groups, Gangs and Cohesiveness," *Journal of Research in Crime and Delinquency*, 4: 63-75.

Krisberg, Barry. (1974). "Gang Youth and Hustling: The Psychology fo Survival," *Issues in Criminology* 9 (1): 115-31.

Labov, Teresa. (1982). "Social Structure and Peer Terminology in a Black Adolescent Gang," *Language in Society* 11 (3) (December): 391-411.

Langer, John. (1977). "Drug Entrepreneurs and Dealing Culture," *Social Problems* 24: 377-85.

Lowney, Jeremiah. (1984). "The Wall Street Gang: A Study of Interpersonal Process and Deviance among Twenty-Three Middle-Class Youths," *Adolescence* 527-38.

McBride, Wesley D. and Robert K. Jackson (1989). "In L.A. County, A High-Tech Assist in the War on Gangs," *The Police Chief* 56: 28.

Maxon, Cheryl L., Margaret A. Gordon and Malcolm W. Klein. (1985). "Differences Between Gang and Non-Gang Homicides," *Criminology* 23: 209-22.

Meier, Robert F. (1988). "Discovering Delinquency: Special Essay," *Sociological Inquiry* 58: 231-39.

Miller, Walter B. (1958). "Lower Class Culture as a Generating Milieu of Gang Delinquency," *Journal of Social Issues* 14: 5-9.

———. (1966). "Violent Crimes in City Gangs," *Annals of the American Academy of Political and Social Science* 364: 96-112.

Moland, John and James F. Short. (1976). "Politics and Youth Gangs: A Follow-up Study," *The Sociological Quarterly* 17: 162-79.

Moore, Joan W. (1985). "Isolation and Stigmatization in the Development of an Underclass: The Case of Chicano Gangs in East Los Angeles," *Social Problems* 33: 1-12.

Moore, Joan W., James Diego Vigil, and Robert Garcia. (1983). "Residence and Territoriality in Chicano Gangs," *Social Problems* 31: 182-94.

Moore, Joan W., and James Diego Vigil. (1987). "Chicano Gangs: Group Norms and Individual Factors Related to Adult Criminality," *Aztlan* 18 (2): 27-44.

Morash, Merry. (1983). "Gangs, Groups, and Delinquency," *The British Journal of Criminology* 23: 309-335.

Myerhoff, Howard L. and Barbara G. (1964). "Field Observations of Middle Class Gangs," *Social Forces* 42: 328-36.

Nutch, Frank J. and Milton Bloombaum. (1968). "A Smallest Space Analysis of Gang Boy's Behaviors," *Pacific Sociological Review* 11 (2) (fall): 116-22.

O'Connell, Richard J. (1988). "L.A. Gangs: Setting Up Shop All Over the U.S.," *Crime Control Digest* 22 (48): 1, 7-9.

Oetting, E. R. and Fred Beauvais. (1987). "Common Elements in Youth Drug Abuse: Peer Clusters and Other Psychosocial Factors," *Journal of Drug Issues* 17: (winter/spring): 133-51.

Olesky, Walter. (1981). "The Inner City Battle Zone," *Police Product News* 5 (7): 26-29, 32-33.

Pfautz, Harold W. (1961). "Near-group Theory and Collective Behavior: A Critical Reformulation," *Social Problems* 9: 167-74.

Savitz, Leonard, Lawrence Rosen, and Michael Lalli. (1980). "Delinquency and Gang Membership as Related to Victimization," *Victimology* 5: 152-60.

Scott, Peter. (1956). "Gangs and Delinquent Groups in London," *British Journal of Delinquency* 7 (1): 4-24.

Short, James. (1964). "Aleatory Risks Versus Short-run Hedonism in Explanation of Gang Action," *Social Problems* 12: 127-40.

———. (1974). "Youth, Gangs, and Society: Micro- and Macrosociological Processes," *The Sociological Quarterly* 15: 3-19.

———. (1976). "Politics and Youth Gangs: A Follow-up Study," *The Sociological Quarterly* 17 (2): 162-79.

Sobchack, Thomas. (1982). "New York Street Gangs or The Warriors of My Mind," *Journal of Popular Film and Television* 10 (2): 77-85.

Soref, Michael J. (1981). "The Structure of Illicit Drug Markets," *Urban Life* 10: 329-52.

Spergel, Irving A. (1984). "Violent Gangs in Chicago: In Search of Social Policy," *Social Service Review* 58: 199-225.

———. (1986). "The Violent Gang Problem in Chicago: A Local Community Approach," *Social Service Review* 60: 94-131.

Spergel, Irving and David Curry. (1988). "Gang Homicide, Delinquency, and Community Criminology," *Criminology* 58: 381-405.

Stanfield, Robert Everett. (1966). "The Interaction of Family Variables and Gang Variables in the Aetiology of Delinquency," *Social Problems* 13: 411-17.

Stover, Del. (1986). "A New Breed of Youth Gang is on the Prowl and a Bigger Threat than Ever," *The American School Board Journal* 173 (8): 19-24, 35.

Sudo, P. (1989). "Turf Wars (Drug Gangs)," *Scholastic Update* (Teacher's edition) 122: 6.

Takata, Susan R. and Richard G. Zevitz. (1987). "Youth Gangs in Racine: An Examination of Community Perceptions," *The Wisconsin Sociologist* 24 (4) (fall) : 132-41.

———— . (1990). "Divergent Perceptions of Group Delinquency in a Midwestern Community: Racine's Gang Problem," *Youth and Society* 21: 282-305.

Taylor, Carl S. (1988). "Youth Gangs Organize for Power, Money," *School Safety* (spring): 26-27.

Thompson, David W. and Leonard A. Jason. (1988). "Street Gangs and Preventive Interventions," *Criminal Justice and Behavior* 15: 323-33.

Thompson, Mark. (1989). "The Untouchables: Vietnamese Robbery Gangs Are a Headache for U.S. Cops," *Far Eastern Economic Review* 145: 31-32.

Thrasher, F. M. (1925). "Chicago Gangs 1920-1930," *Social Science Quarterly* 1: 847.

Vigil, James Diego. (1983). "Chicano Gangs: One Response to Mexican Urban Adaption in the Los Angeles Area," *Urban Anthropology* 12 (1) (spring): 45-75.

———— . (1988). "Group Processes and Street Identity: Adolescent Chicano Gang Members," *Ethos* 16 (4): 421-45.

Washburn, Philo C. (1976). "Student Protesters and Gang Delinquents: Toward a Theory of Collective Deviance," *Sociological Focus* 9 (1) (January): 27-46.

Weisfeld, Glenn E. and Roger Feldman. (1982). "A Former Street Gang Leader Reinterviewed Eight Years Later," *Crime and Delinquency* 28: 567-81.

Wilkins, M. (1986). "Jail Birds (Girls-in-Gangs Films)," *Film Comment* 22: 62-65.

Williams, Mark T. and John R. Snortum. (1982). "A Police Program for Employment of Youth Gang Members," *International Journal of Offender Therapy and Comparative Criminology* 26 (3) (December): 207-14.

Yablonsky, Lewis. (1959). "The Delinquent Gang as a Near-Group. *Social Problems* 7: 108-17.

———— . (1960). "The Violent Gang," *Commentary*, 30 (2): 125-30.

Zatz, Marjorie S. (1985). "Los Cholos: Legal Processing of Chicano Gang Members," *Social Problems* 33: 13-30.

———— . (1987). "Chicano Youth Gangs and Crime: The Creation of a Moral Panic," *Contemporary Crises* 11: 129-58.

Zimring, Franklin E. (1981). "Kids, Groups, and Crime. Some Implications of a Well-Known Secret," *Journal of Criminal Law, Criminology and Police Science* 72: 867-85.

Zucker, M. (1978). "Walls of Barrio Are Brought to Life by Street Gang Art: East Los Angeles," *Smithsonian* 9: 105-11.

GOVERNMENT DOCUMENTS AND INSTITUTE PUBLICATIONS

Attorney General's Youth Gang Task Force. (1981). *Report on Youth Gang Violence in California*, Sacramento, CA.

Beavers, Gerald. (1988, September). *National Youth Gang Suppression and Intervention Project*. Chicago: School of Social Service Administration, University of Chicago.

Bobrowski, Lawrence J. (1988). *Collecting, Organizing and Reporting Street Gang Crime*. Chicago: Chicago Police Department, Special Functions Group. Mimeo.

Boca, Chris. (1988, June). *Juvenile Gangs in Albuquerque*. Albuquerque Police Department at the Coordinating Council Meeting, Office of Juvenile Justice and Delinquency Prevention.

Bryant, Dan. (1989). *Communitywide Responses Crucial for Dealing with Youth Gangs*. Washington, D.C.: U.S. Dept. of Justice, Office of Justice Programs, Office of Juvenile Justice and Delinquency Prevention.

Caltabriano, Michael L. (1981). *National Prison Gang Study*. Unpublished report to the Federal Bureau of Prisons. Quoted in *Prison Gangs: Their Extent, Nature and Impact on Prisons*, edited by G. M. Camp and C. G. Camp. Washington, D.C.: U.S. Government Printing Office, July 1985.

Camp, George M. and Samuel Graham Camp. (1985, July). *Prison Gangs: Their Extent, Nature and Impact on Prisons*. Washington, D.C.: U.S. Government Printing Office.

Camp, Samuel Graham and George M. Camp. (1988, September). *Management Strategies for Combatting Prison Gang Violence*. South Salem, New York: Criminal Justice Institute.

Chicago Crime Commission. (1983, July). *Gang Crimes Coordinating Council Conference*. Chicago: Chicago Crime Commission.

Chicano Pinto Research Project. (1979). "A Model for Chicano Drug Use and for Effective Utilization of Employment and Training Resources by Barrio Addicts and Ex-offenders. Final report for the Department of Labor and National Institute of Drug Abuse. Los Angeles, CA.

Chin, Ko-Lin. (1986). *Chinese Triad Societies, Tongs, Organized Crime, and Street Gangs in Asia and the United States*. Dissertation Abstracts International, The Humanities and Social Sciences, Ann Arbor, MI.

Clayton, Wayne. (1983, March 1). *The El Monte Plan—Hire a Gang Leader*. El Monte Police Department, Los Angeles County, California. Mimeo.

Collins, H. Craig. (1979). *Street Gangs*, Profiles for Police. New York: New York City Police Department, pp. 14-55.

Commission de Police du Quebec. (1980). *Motorcycle Gangs in Quebec*. Quebec: Ministere des Communications.

Coplen, Bruce R. (1988). *National Youth Gang Suppression and Intervention Project*. Interview. Chicago: University of Chicago School of Social Service Administration and the U.S. Office of Juvenile Justice and Delinquency Prevention.

Creamer, Robert. (1988, November). *National Youth Gang Suppression and Intervention Project*. Survey. Chicago: School of Social Service Administration, University of Chicago.

Daley, Richard M. (1985). *Gang Preventions Unit*. Report. Chicago: Cook County State's Attorney's Office.

Davidson, John L. (1987, September). *Juvenile Gang Drug Problem*. Grant proposal to Office of Criminal Justice Planning, Sacramento, California.

Deukmajian, George. (1981, June). *Report on Youth Gang Violence in California*. Sacramento, California: Department of Justice, State of California.

DeWitt, Charles B. (1983). *Gang Crimes Investigation/Supervision Unit*. A project proposal submitted to the Office of California Justice Planning by the Santa Clara County Justice Division and Department of the Youth Authority.

Donovan, John. (1988, August). *An Introduction to Street Gangs*. Sacramento, California.

Duran, M. (1978). "Youth Gang Warfare" (in Briarkahn, *Prison Gangs in the Community*). Sacramento, Calif.: California Board of Corrections.

Geis, Gilbert. (1965, June). *Juvenile Gangs*. President's Committee on Juvenile Delinquency and Youth Crime.

Guccione, Jean. (1987, December 30). *Computer on Gang Members Being Readied*. California Office of Criminal Justice Planning News File.

Hahn, James K. (1987, November 5). *Hahn Launches Legal Offensive Against Street Gangs*. Los Angeles City Attorney's Offices, News Release.

Hinshaw, Dwayne. (1988, September). *National Youth Gang Suppression and Intervention Project*. Survey. Chicago: School of Social Service Administration, University of Chicago.

Illinois Department of Law Enforcement. (1983). *Gang Prosecutions Unit*. Report. Chicago: Cook County State's Attorney's Office, p. 2.

Joe, Delbert and Norman Robinson. (1978, March). *Chinese Youth Gangs: An Investigation of their Origins and Activities in Vancouver Schools*. Toronto, Ontario. Department of Corrections.

Kahn, Brian. (1978). *Prison Gangs in the Community—A Briefing Document for the Board of Corrections*. Sacramento, Calif.: California Board of Corrections.

Klein, Malcolm W. (1968). *From Association to Guilt: The Group Guidance Project in Juvenile Gang Intervention*. Los Angeles, Calif.: Youth Studies Center, University of Southern California and the Los Angeles County Probation Department.

———. (1969). *Violence in American Juvenile Gangs*. In Mulvihill and Tumin, *Crimes of Violence*, National Commission on the Causes and Prevention of Violence, vol. 13.

Klein, Malcolm W., Cheryl L. Maxson, and Margaret A. Gordon. (1987). *Police Response to Street Gang Violence: Improving the Investigative Process*. Los Angeles: Center for Research on Crime and Social Control, Social Science Research Institute, University of Southern California.

Klein, Malcolm W., Cheryl L. Maxson, and Lea C. Cunningham. (1988, May). *Gang Involvement in Cocaine "Rock" Trafficking*. Project Summary/Final Report. Los Angeles: Center for Research on Crime and Social Control, Social Science Research Institute, University of Southern California.

Kraus, Jess F., Susan B. Sorenson, and Paul D. Juarez, eds. (1988). *Research Conference on Violence and Homicide in Hispanic Communities: Proceedings*. UCLA Publication Services, Los Angeles, CA.

Long Beach Unified School District. (1987). *Alternatives to Gang Membership*. Long Beach, Calif.: The Board of Education.

Los Angeles County Sheriff's Department. (1985). *Testimony*. California State Task Force on Youth Gang Violence, Los Angeles, CA, February 16-18.

———. (1986, August 1). *Field Operations Directive 86-39*. Gang Activity Reporting.

Love, Ruth. (1981). *Gang Activity Task Force: A Report with Recommendations for Dealing with Gang Activity in the Chicago Public Schools*. Chicago: City of Chicago, Board of Education, pp. 1-2.

Miller, Walter B. (1975). *Violence by Youth Gangs and Youth Groups as a Crime Problem in Major American Cities*. Dept. of Justice and Law Enforcement Assistance Administration, Office of Juvenile Justice and Delinquency Prevention, National Institute for Juvenile Justice and Delinquency Prevention. Washington, D.C.: U.S. Government Printing Office.

———. (1976). *Violence by Youth Gangs and Youth Groups in Major American Cities.* Washington, D.C.: National Institute for Juvenile Justice and Delinquency Prevention, CPO.

———. (1977, September). *Conceptions, Definitions and Image of Youth Gangs.* Center for Criminal Justice. Harvard Law School.

———. (1982, February). *Crime by Youth Gangs and Groups in the United States.* A Report Prepared for the National Institute of Juvenile Justice and Delinquency Prevention of the U.S. Department of Justice, CPO.

———. (1982). *Crime by Youth Gangs and Groups in the United States.* Washington, D.C.: National Institute for Juvenile Justice and Delinquency Prevention.

Moore, Joan W. and John Long (1981). *Barrio Impact of High Incarceration Rates.* Los Angeles: Chicano Pinto Research Project.

National Institute for Juvenile Justice and Delinquency Prevention. (1976). *Violence by Youth Gangs and Youth Groups in Major American Cities: Summary Report.* Washington, D.C.: U.S. Dept. of Justice, Law Enforcement Assistance Administration, Office of Juvenile Justice and Delinquency Prevention.

Needle, Jerome and W. Stapleton. (1983). *Police Handling of Youth Gangs.* (NCJ-88927). Washington, D.C.: U.S. Dept. of Justice, Office of Juvenile Justice and Delinquency Prevention, National Institute for Juvenile Justice and Delinquency Prevention.

New York City Youth Board. (1960). *Reaching the Fighting Gang.* (p. 305, illus. 24 cm). New York.

New York State Assembly, Subcommittee on the Family. (1974). *The Resurgence of Youth Gangs in New York City.* Study Report No. 1, July. New York.

———. (1974, October). *Armies of the Streets. A Report on the Structure, Membership and Activities of Youth Gangs in the City of New York.* Study Report No. 2. New York.

Nidorf, Barry J. *Gang Member Supervision Program.* Los Angeles: Los Angeles County Probation Department.

Office of Criminal Justice Planning. (1987, July). *California Gang Violence Suppression Program.* Program Guidelines. Sacramento, Calif.: Office of Criminal Justice Planning, pp. 3-4.

Pennell, Susan. (1983, December). *San Diego Street Youth Program. Final Evaluation.* San Diego: Association of Governments.

Pennell, S. and C. Curtis. (1982). *Juvenile Violence and Gang Related Crime.* San Diego: Association of Governments.

Philibosian, Robert H. (1983). Testimony before U.S. Senate Subcommittee on Juvenile Justice. *Gang Violence and Control.* Committee on the Judiciary, 98th Congress, 1st Session. Hearings, February 7, 9, California, p. 4.

Phoenix Police Department. (1981). *Latin Gang Member Recognition for the Field Police Officer*. Phoenix: Community Services Division, Juvenile Gang Reduction Unit.

Pineda, C. (1978). *Chicano Gang Barrios in East Los Angeles*. Sacramento: California Board of Corrections.

————. (1978). "Chicago Gang-Barrios in East Los Angeles," *Maravilla, California— Genesis of Gang-Barrios, Observations and Using Community Organization Techniques to Mitigate Gang-Barrio Violence*. Sacramento, Calif.: California Board of Corrections.

Pitchess, Peter J. (1979, May). *Street Gangs*. Los Angeles County Sheriff's Department, Los Angeles County, Youth Services Bureau, Street Gang Detail.

Portland Office of the Superintendent. (1988). *Variety of Collaborative and Coordinated Efforts Relating to Gang Activities and Potentially Dangerous Situations*. Administrative Letter. April 20, No. 863-98. Portland: Oregon Public Schools, Education Service Center.

Potts, Randall. (1988). "Gang Violence: Narratives of Marginal Meaning," UC School of Social Service Administration.

Prophet, Matthew. (1988, February 4). *Youth Gangs*. News Conference. Superintendent, Portland Public Schools, Portland, Oregon.

Quicker, John C. (1982). *Seven Decades of Gangs*. Prepared for the California Commission on Crime Control and Violence Prevention.

Reddick, Alonzo J. (1987, October). *Issue Paper: Youth Gangs in Florida*. Committee on Youth, Florida House of Representatives.

Rosenbaum, Dennis P. and Jane A. Grant. (1983, July 22). *Gangs and Youth Problems in Evanston: Research Findings and Policy Options*. Center for Urban Affairs and Policy Research, Northwestern University.

San Diego Association of Government. (1982, June). *Juvenile Violence and Gang-Related Crime*. San Diego, Calif.: Association of State Governments.

Schubert, J. G. and L. O. Richardson. (1976). *Youth Gangs: A Current Perspective*. Washington, D.C.: Law Enforcement Assistance Administration.

Sherman, Lawrence William. (1970, November). *Youth Workers, Police and the Gangs: Chicago, 1956-1970*. Master's thesis in the Division of Social Sciences, University of Chicago.

Silbert, Jeffrey M., Leon Cristiano, and Gina Nunez-Cuenca. (1988, April). Proposal. *Juvenile Gang Information and Coordination Project*. A draft of a proposal prepared for the Dade-Miami Criminal Justice Council, Juvenile Justice Committee by the Department of Justice Assistance.

Simandl, Robert J. (1983). *Identification of Chicago Street Gangs*. Chicago Police Department.

Smaka, Frank, Gary Nicol, and Tom Keller. (1983). *The Cuban Freedom Flotilla: From Mariel Harbor to Las Vegas*. Las Vegas: Las Vegas Metropolitan Police Department.

Spergel, Irving. (1983). *Violent Gangs in Chicago: Segmentation and Integration*. Chicago: University of Chicago, School of Social Service Administration.

Spergel, Irving A., G. David Curry, Ron Chance, Ruth E. Ross, Amy Chak, Alba Alexander, Dawn Isis, Phyllis Garth, and Roberto Caldero. (1989). *National Youth Gang Suppression and Intervention Project*. Field Survey. U.S. Department of Justice, Office of Juvenile Justice and Delinquency Prevention and the School of Social Service Administration at the University of Chicago.

Stokes, William. (1988, March 8). *"Gang Intervention Project Legislative,"* by Chairman Dade-Miami Council, Criminal Justice Council.

Takata, Susan R. (1987). *Community Networking: Racine's Response to the Problems of Youth Gangs*. Kenosha: Dept. of Sociology, University of Wisconsin.

Tompkins, Dorothy Louise Campbell. (1966). *Juvenile Gangs and Street Groups—A Bibliography*. Berkeley: Institute of Governmental Studies, University of California.

Torres, Dorothy M. (1980). *Gang Violence Reduction Project Evaluation Report*. Sacramento: California Youth Authority.

———. (1985, June). *Gang Violence Reduction Project Update*. Sacramento: California Department of the Youth Authority Program Research and Review Division. Mimeo.

Tracy, Paul E. (1982). *Gang Membership and Violent Offending: Preliminary Results from 1968 Cohort Study*. Draft. Philadelphia, Pa.: Center for Studies in Criminology and Criminal Law, University of Pennsylvania.

United States Attorney General. (1981). *Attorney General's Task Force on Violent Crime—Public Hearing*. Chicago, Ill.

United States Congress, Crime in America, Youth Gang Warfare, hearings, 91st Congress, 2d session pursuant to H. Res. 17, July 16 and 17, 1970. (Hearings held in Philadelphia, Pa.).

United States Congress House Committee on the Judiciary, Subcommittee on Criminal Justice. (1989). *Organized Criminal Activity by Youth Gangs: Hearings Before the Subcommittee on Criminal Justice of the Committee on the Judiciary, House of Representatives, One Hundredth Congress, Second Session, June 6 and August 8, 1988*. (Serial No. 146 U.S. Congress House Committee on the Judiciary). Washington, D.C.: U.S. G.P.O. (For sale by the Supt. of Docs., Congressional Sales Office, U.S. Government Printing Office.)

United States Congress Senate Committee on the Judiciary, Subcommittees on Juvenile Justice. (1983). *Gang Violence and Control in the Los Angeles and San*

Francisco Areas with a View to What Might Be Done by the Federal Government. (Serial No. J-98-7). Washington, D.C.: U.S. Government Printing Office.

———. (1983). *Gang Violence and Control: Hearings Before the Subcommittee on Juvenile Justice of the Committee on the Judiciary, United States Senate, Ninety-eighth Congress, First Session, on Gang Violence and Control in the Los Angeles Area.* (Serial J-98-7 U.S. Congress Senate Committee on the Judiciary). Washington, D.C.: U.S. Government Printing Office.

Valdivia, Steve E. (1988, June). *Community Youth Gang Services—Report.* Prepared for the Coordinating Council Meeting. Office of Juvenile Justice and Delinquency Prevention, U.S. Department of Justice, Washington, D.C. by the Community Youth Gang Service Project, Los Angeles, Calif.

Vigil, James Diego. (1987). *An Ethnograph, Enumeration of a Barrio in Greater East Los Angeles.* Washington, D.C.: U.S. Bureau of the Census.

———. (1987). *Street Socialization, Locura Behavior and Violence Among Chicano Gang Members.* In "Violence and Homicide in Hispanic Communities," J. Kraus et al., eds., pp. 231-41. Washington, D.C.: Office of Minority Health, National Institute of Mental Health.

———. (1989). *An Emerging Barrio Underclass: Irregular Lifestyles Among Former Chicano Gang Members.* New Directions for Latino Research and the Social Science Research Council, Public Policy Research on Contemporary Hispanic Issues. Austin: University of Texas, pp. 1-13.

Index

QC-138A
80-3

4261-26
5-08

ROOSEVELT UNIVERSITY LIBRARY

KF3467.M3   C001

MACKINNON, CATHARINE A.

SEXUAL HARASSMENT OF WORKING WOMEN$ NEW

3 3311 00069 372 3

WITHDRAWN

KF3467 .M3

MacKinnon, Catharine A.

Sexual harassment of working women :

/KF3467.M3>C1/